Praise for *Metasemantics and Intersectionality in the Misinformation Age*

"I am extremely excited to see this book. Debates about language—words like 'woman' and 'racism'—have been absolutely central to vital political issues for some time. They have also been weaponised, used to argue that important issues are "just about language." This book takes these debates seriously—both politically and linguistically. It is wonderfully wide-ranging, deeply grounded in both intersectional theory and analytic philosophy of language. We've been needing a book like this for a long time!"
—Jennifer Saul, *University of Waterloo, Canada*

"This timely work draws together various themes—knowledge and oppression, truth and misinformation, language and power—and grounds them in a discussion of practical issues that should concern us all. Bridging conversations in linguistics and politics, this book is a long overdue and necessary complement to debates that examine the intersection of the political with other philosophical sub-disciplines, like epistemology and ethics. To come across a work that reveals something you have understood but have been unable to express, that examines how language can empower and disempower, is both exciting and will speak to many who have felt themselves silenced without fully understanding why."
—Briana Toole, *Claremont McKenna College, USA*

"A truly impressive melding of hard-core analytic philosophy and serious politics."
—Naomi Scheman, *University of Minnesota, USA*

"This book presents a novel and sophisticated metasemantic theory of how words acquire their meanings, and applies the theory to highly politically controversial terms. Anderson's account provides a radically new and illuminating perspective on disputes that inhabit the borderlands between the straightforwardly factual and merely verbal differences. The book will be of great interest to those working on metasemantics as well as political philosophers."
—Cory Juhl, *University of Texas at Austin, USA*

"A unique and important attempt at combining (or perhaps more aptly juxtaposing) analytical philosophy with critical theory and post-structural elements. It is timely given the current political arena and addresses important political and linguistic questions. The work makes a convincing case for the metasemantic view and provides an answer to what truth means in a "post-truth" world in which the very idea of "post-truth" has been usurped in the same ways as the work outlines racism and the category of woman has been."

—Laci Hubbard-Mattix, *Washington State University, USA*

Derek Egan Anderson

Metasemantics and Intersectionality in the Misinformation Age

Truth in Political Struggle

Derek Egan Anderson
Boston University
Boston, MA, USA

ISBN 978-3-030-73341-4   ISBN 978-3-030-73339-1 (eBook)
https://doi.org/10.1007/978-3-030-73339-1

© The Editor(s) (if applicable) and The Author(s), under exclusive licence to Springer Nature Switzerland AG 2021
This work is subject to copyright. All rights are solely and exclusively licensed by the Publisher, whether the whole or part of the material is concerned, specifically the rights of translation, reprinting, reuse of illustrations, recitation, broadcasting, reproduction on microfilms or in any other physical way, and transmission or information storage and retrieval, electronic adaptation, computer software, or by similar or dissimilar methodology now known or hereafter developed.
The use of general descriptive names, registered names, trademarks, service marks, etc. in this publication does not imply, even in the absence of a specific statement, that such names are exempt from the relevant protective laws and regulations and therefore free for general use.
The publisher, the authors and the editors are safe to assume that the advice and information in this book are believed to be true and accurate at the date of publication. Neither the publisher nor the authors or the editors give a warranty, expressed or implied, with respect to the material contained herein or for any errors or omissions that may have been made. The publisher remains neutral with regard to jurisdictional claims in published maps and institutional affiliations.

Cover illustration: © Maram_shutterstock.com

This Palgrave Macmillan imprint is published by the registered company Springer Nature Switzerland AG.
The registered company address is: Gewerbestrasse 11, 6330 Cham, Switzerland

To Melissa and Egan, the center of my world

Acknowledgments

This book is based on research I conducted in graduate school and in the years immediately following. Thank you to all the professors and graduate students who helped shape my understanding of philosophy and intersectionality. Special thanks to Cory Juhl for many, many conversations about the nature of truth and semantics.

Deep thanks to all the intersectional feminists in my life who helped me understand the realities behind social justice movements, especially my partner Melissa Kibbe without whom I could not possibly have written this book. Thank you also to my parents James and Deborah who have always encouraged me to be a philosopher of meaning.

Contents

1 **Truth in Political Struggle** 1
 References 5

2 **Politically Contested Terminology** 7
 2.1 Hijacking the Word "Racism" 7
 2.2 Linguistic Hijacking and Gender Terminology 13
 2.3 Misinformation and Truth in a Language 19
 References 23

3 **On the Possibility of Semantic Corruption** 25
 3.1 One Word, Two Meanings? 25
 3.2 Semantic Corruption and Metasemantic Struggle 28
  3.2.1 The Role of Deference and Authority 30
  3.2.2 Different Possible Meanings of "Racist" 32
  3.2.3 From Different Possible Meanings to Different Actual Meanings 34
  3.2.4 The Semantic Corruption Model 35
 3.3 Looking Ahead 37
 References 38

4 **Toward a Conception of Misinformation as Epistemic Violence** 41
 4.1 The Semantic Data Objection 42
  4.1.1 Metalinguistic Negotiation? 44

		4.2	The Actual Practice Objection	45
		4.3	The Role of Truth Objection	48
			4.3.1 Turning from Truth to Ontology?	51
		4.4	The Democracy as a Space of Reasons Objection	53
		4.5	The Epistemic Violence Model	57
		References		65
	5	Model-Theoretic Semantics for Politically Contested Terminology		67
		5.1	Overview	67
		5.2	A Brief History of Model Theory	69
			5.2.1 Frege: Mathematicising Semantics	69
			5.2.2 Tarski: Creating Model Theory	80
			5.2.3 Montague: Treating English as a Formal Language	90
		5.3	Situated Evidence for Semantic Theories of English	94
		References		99
	6	Toward an Intersectional Metasemantics		103
		6.1	What Is a Metasemantic Theory?	104
		6.2	Questioning Naturalistic Reductionism in Metasemantics	107
		6.3	A Brief History of Metasemantics	110
			6.3.1 Linguistic Meaning from Mental Contents	110
			6.3.2 Internalism Versus Externalism About Mental Contents	115
			6.3.3 Famous Arguments for Externalism	120
		6.4	Externalist Metasemantics Without Reductive Naturalism	124
		6.5	Ideal Language Metasemantics	127
		References		131
	7	Power and Regimes of Truth		133
		7.1	Situated Skepticism About the Concept of Power	133
		7.2	Foucault on Power	137
		7.3	Two Objections to a Foucauldian Theory of Power	149
			7.3.1 The Naturalistic Objection	149
			7.3.2 The Overly-Reductive Objection	153

7.4	Regimes of Truth		155
	7.4.1	The Battle for Truth	155
	7.4.2	What Is a Discourse?	160
	7.4.3	What Is a Regime of Truth?	162
	7.4.4	Political Struggles for Truth and Justice	168
	7.4.5	Syntacticism About the Regime of Truth	170
	7.4.6	Truth, Science, and Democracy	173
7.5	Epistemic Violence and Intersectionality in the Misinformation Age		178
References			181

8 An Analytic Philosopher's Unified Theory of Intersectionality — 183

8.1	A Methodological Worry		184
8.2	A Brief History of Intersectionality		188
8.3	Intersectionality as Structural Oppression		194
	8.3.1	Single-Axis Frameworks	196
	8.3.2	What Is a Matrix of Domination?	202
8.4	Political Intersectionality		212
8.5	Intersectional Social Identities		216
	8.5.1	Anti-essentialism About Social Identities	220
8.6	Intersectionality as Critical Theory		224
8.7	Intersectionality as Political Praxis		228
8.8	Toward an Intersectional Theory of Truth		230
References			231

9 Intersectional Metasemantic Adequacy — 235

9.1	Taking Stock		235
9.2	General Metasemantic Adequacy		237
9.3	Objections to GMA		242
	9.3.1	Objection 1: The Argument for GMA Confuses Sentences with Propositions	243
	9.3.2	Objection 2: The Revisionist's Objection	248
9.4	Intersectional Metasemantic Adequacy		252
9.5	Objections to IMA		254
9.6	Satisfying IMA		257
References			257

10 A Metasemantics for Intersectionality — 259
10.1 The Plan — 259
10.2 Constructing an Intersectional Metasemantics — 260
    10.2.1 Preliminaries — 261
    10.2.2 Externalism — 262
    10.2.3 Deference-Based Metasemantics — 264
    10.2.4 Deferring to Ideal Linguistic Communities — 267
    10.2.5 Languages as Historically Rooted — 272
    10.2.6 Semantics Guided by Communal Goals — 277
    10.2.7 Ambiguity and Multiple Definitions — 280
    10.2.8 Meaning Change — 281
    10.2.9 Intersectional Reference Magnetism — 284
    10.2.10 Intersectional Metasemantics in Action — 286
10.3 Objections — 288
10.4 Truth, Democracy, and Epistemic Violence — 294
References — 296

11 Situated Knowledge and the Regime of Truth — 299
11.1 Overview — 299
11.2 Truth, Knowledge, and Objectivity in Intersectional Epistemology — 301
11.3 Situated Knowledge, Situated Ignorance, and Epistemic Oppression — 306
    11.3.1 Situated Linguistic Understanding — 307
    11.3.2 Situated Evidence and Situated Information — 312
    11.3.3 Situated Testimony — 318
    11.3.4 Ideology — 319
    11.3.5 Science and Situated Experience — 322
11.4 Truth in Political Struggle — 326
References — 327

Index — 329

Abbreviations

GMA   General Metasemantic Adequacy
IMA   Intersectional Metasemantic Adequacy

CHAPTER 1

Truth in Political Struggle

Kwame Ture said, "You know the truth from constant struggle against lies. That's how you know the truth. Constant struggle against lies."[1] This is not a transcendent metaphysical theory of truth. It is a practical view of truth grounded in political struggle. It is not the nature of truth that it should be covered up with lies. Rather, it is the nature of structural oppression that it seeks to cover up the truth. Lies and misinformation are crucial for creating and sustaining oppressive power structures. Transforming an oppressive system into something that more closely resembles a just society requires overcoming the lies and misinformation that sustain that system. Hence, the struggle for truth and the struggle for justice are intertwined.

What is truth and how is it related to political struggle? These are big philosophical questions, but as anyone following politics lately has probably noticed, they are highly relevant today. We see groups of people constructing narratives and worldviews that are dramatically at odds with one another. We find people sinking deeply into these narratives. The deeper we go, the more cut off from one another we become. Attention to history shows that this is not really new. Which worldview you inhabit is predictable on the basis of your politics. The narratives we live by are created and spread by political forces in service of political ends. Our

[1] Ture (2013).

© The Author(s), under exclusive license to Springer Nature Switzerland AG 2021
D. E. Anderson, *Metasemantics and Intersectionality in the Misinformation Age*,
https://doi.org/10.1007/978-3-030-73339-1_1

fragmented understanding of reality almost appears to give rise to some kind of radical political subjectivism in which the opposing factions literally inhabit different realities. But in truth there is only one reality we are all part of. Political struggle is about coming to terms with this reality as a collective.

Our present political situation is characterized both by complex forms of social inequality and by pervasive misinformation, ignorance, and ideological barriers that prevent the truth of that social inequality from being widely understood and accepted. We seem to be enmeshed in different meanings and different epistemological communities with little chance of reaching any consensus view of reality. Objectivity seems very far off—if by objectivity we mean getting everyone to agree about what is going on and what needs to be done in order to promote justice, freedom, equality, safety, and well-being. Yet, I will argue, we must use a concept of objective truth to see ourselves through this difficulty and engage in the democratic process of figuring out what we should do given how reality really is.

This book develops a framework for understanding the role of objective truth in political struggle by merging the perspectives of two disparate camps of philosophical thought. The first perspective comes out of twentieth-century analytic philosophy. The second emerges from Black feminist thought, intersectionality studies, trans feminism, critical race theory, and other critical theories. The result of the synthesis will be a theory of truth based in formal semantics on which truth is objective and transcends political divisions, but which is centrally concerned with social power and the ways that systems of domination exist and evolve through the strategic use of misinformation to shape people's conceptions of reality.

For the traditional analytic philosopher, truth is apolitical. True and false things are asserted in political discourse, but truth *itself* is just an abstract relation between language and reality. The analytic philosopher's case studies are mathematical discourses, scientific theories, and odd sentences like "It is raining and it might not be raining"[2] and "Every farmer who owns a donkey beats it."[3] These are data for model-theoretic semantics, the construction of quasi-mathematical theories linking natural language expressions to domains of real-world entities using functions, sets, variables, and morphisms. In this abstract realm, truth and other

---
[2] Yalcin (2007).
[3] Kamp and Reyle (1993).

semantic properties have nothing essential to do with social identity or political struggle.

For the critical theorist, the queer theorist, the poststructural feminist, the student of Indigenous studies, language and thought are so steeped in politics, history, and social inequality that it makes no sense to talk about truth without talking about power. On the most extreme version of this approach, sometimes attributed to Michel Foucault, truth just *is* power. There is no distinction between saying what is true and having the power to convince or compel a significant population to accept what you say. Moreover, all meanings are seen as socially situated, and nothing can be interpreted across the horizons of political or social identity (Haraway, 1988). Each group has its own proprietary language that tracks with its own conception of reality, in which it defines its own meanings. Consequently, a statement can only be true relative to some social group or other. From the critical poststructuralist perspective, a notion of truth that transcends social situation is itself a tool of power and a source of manipulation and control.

My synthesis of these perspectives is focused on clarifying and facilitating difficult conversations around racism and gender-based oppression. Specifically, I am concerned to address issues that seem to be disputes about *semantics*, issues such as: what does the word "racism" mean? Does it refer to patterns of historically rooted oppression and domination, such that white people cannot properly be called victims of racism? Or does it refer to mere differential treatment on the basis of race, such that promoting the welfare of one racialized group over the other counts as "racist" even when the one racialized group has historically been marginalized and oppressed for the benefit of the other? What does "woman" mean and who counts as a woman? Do trans women fall under the extension of "woman?" Is the sentence "Trans women are women" literally true when spoken in ordinary, mainstream contexts—those contexts informed by a culture that is historically trans-exclusionary, in which conversational participants typically do not understand or accept the existence of non-traditional gender identities—or is the sentence only true when spoken in contexts that provide the social scaffolding for trans identities to be respected (Bettcher, 2013)?

Disagreements about gender and racism are often conceived as disagreements over semantics. Each side uses the crucial words of the discourse, "racist" and "woman," in distinctive ways with distinctive meanings. These differences in meaning then imply differences in the truth-conditions of sentences. The result is that each political faction can speak truly in its own language even when the factions appear to contradict one another. When one group says, "Trans women are women," and the other says, "Trans women are not women; they're men," both speak truly, albeit with different meanings of the word "women." When one asserts, "Affirmative action is racist," and the other asserts, "Affirmative action is not racist," both statements can be true, if the word "racist" has different meanings in the two sentences.

I want to argue against this picture for a view that many people intuitively realize, that arguing about word meanings is trifling and insignificant in a way that undermines the relevance of these conversations for the democratic process. If these politically heated arguments about gender and racism turn out to be merely arguments about semantics, then they are not nearly as interesting or important as they might seem to be.

Political disputes about gender and racism are important in a way that semantical disputes are not. That is because we are really arguing about racism itself, not about the meaning of "racism." We are arguing about whether trans women are women, not about what "woman" means.

Rendering a substantive political dispute as a semantic issue tends to divest the dispute of its political significance. I think this effect is often produced strategically. Framing a substantive dispute as a semantic debate deflects and derails the line of thought that threatens to upend the status quo. Rendering arguments about gender and racism as semantic rather than as substantive first-order debates is a tool of the oppressor. It is therefore strategically imperative that advocates for social justice find a way to talk about contentious political issues without falling into the trap of semantic assent.

I am working to understand political discourse as aimed at first-order truths, not at semantics. My approach depends on a certain view of metasemantics. Metasemantics is the theory of where meanings come from. On the view I will develop and argue for, the meanings of words are shared across political camps. Even though people vehemently disagree with one another about the nature of racism and gender, they in fact mean the same thing by "racist" and "woman." How can people mean the same thing by "woman" if they disagree about what women are? Stay tuned.

On my view, political struggle in the misinformation age is not a struggle for control over the meanings of words. It is rather a struggle for control over our epistemic norms and practices, over our social institutions that we rely on for information, and over the character of our social epistemic networks of trusted friends and family members. The solutions to our epistemological problems cannot be pursued in the abstract. Simply clinging to the concept of objective truth cannot alleviate the socially situated, politically motivated skepticism we are seeing in post-truth politics. Instead, we must focus on confronting, as a society, the ways in which power shapes our disparate understandings of reality. This is precisely the point at which our political perspectives are dissociated and contradict one another—who is oppressed? Who is dominating whom? But nothing less ambitious than the work of talking across the political divide about structures of power and their effects on truth has a chance of succeeding.

The central political reality that informs this book is the existence of intersectionality, the system of interlocking forms of oppression made up of racism, patriarchy, cis-hetero supremacy, neoliberal capitalist domination, ablism, and others (Collins, 2002; Crenshaw, 1990). Intersectional critical theory is aimed at exposing the ways in which systems of domination rely on misinformation and ideological confusion in order to maintain themselves. On the perspective to be defended, a theory of truth for natural languages must proceed by taking the reality of intersectionality as its starting point. Only by attending to the ways that misinformation functions to sustain intersecting systems of oppression can we accurately represent the semantics of the languages we speak.

An objective theory of truth is necessary for us to understand that some politically situated perspectives are objectively more accurate than others. There are facts—and there are no alternative facts—about things like the nature of racism and the nature of gender. Social and political forces produce widespread ignorance and misinformation about these facts. Widespread ignorance and misinformation are part of the oppressive system itself. They function to reproduce its structure in new iterations and protect it from critical inquiry and activism. Only through confronting the systems of power that spread misinformation can social justice initiatives make progress, and that confrontation must be carried out using a concept of objective truth. But how should we understand objective truth such that it may play this crucial role in political struggle? That is the central question this book aims to answer.

References

Bettcher, T. M. (2013). *Trans Women and the Meaning of 'Woman'*. In The Philosophy of Sex: Contemporary Readings Sixth Addition. Eds. Power, Nicholas, Raja Halwani, and Alan Soble. 2012. pp. 233–250.

Collins, P. H. (2002). *Black Feminist Thought: Knowledge, Consciousness, and the Politics of Empowerment.* Routledge.
Crenshaw, K. (1990). Mapping the Margins: Intersectionality, Identity Politics, and Violence Against Women of Color. *Stanford Law Review, 43,* 1241.
Haraway, D. (1988). Situated Knowledges: The Science Question in Feminism and the Privilege of Partial Perspective. *Feminist Studies, 14*(3), 575–599.
Kamp, H., & Reyle, U. (1993). *From Discourse to Logic.* Kluwer Academic Publishers.
Ture, K. (2013). Dr. Kwame Ture Converting the Unconscious to Conscious. [Video]. Youtube. Retrieved November 15, 2013, from https://www.youtube.com/watch?v=9qjnr-iOrfU
Yalcin, S. (2007). Epistemic Modals. *Mind, 116*(464), 983–1026.

CHAPTER 2

Politically Contested Terminology

2.1 Hijacking the Word "Racism"

In the summer of 2019 President Trump tweeted that four junior congresswomen, all women of color, should "go back and fix the totally broken and crime infested places from which they came."[1] The next day one of the four women targeted by this remark, Alexandria Ocasio-Cortez, responded via Tweet:

> It's important to note that the President's words [yesterday], telling four American Congresswomen of color "go back to your own country," is hallmark language of white supremacists.
>
> Trump feels comfortable leading the GOP into outright *racism*, and that should concern all Americans.[2]

Ocasio-Cortez uses the word "racism" in accord with a theoretical understanding of racism developed in critical race theory and intersectionality studies. On this understanding, racism involves the systematic oppression of groups of people on the basis of racial categorization.[3] According

---

[1] Trump (2019a).
[2] Ocasio-Cortez (2019).
[3] This conception has been developed by many scholars. See, for example, Crenshaw (1988), Gotanda (1991), Bonilla-Silva (1997), Collins (2002), Charles Mills (2014), Kendi (2019).

© The Author(s), under exclusive license to Springer Nature Switzerland AG 2021
D. E. Anderson, *Metasemantics and Intersectionality in the Misinformation Age*,
https://doi.org/10.1007/978-3-030-73339-1_2

to this perspective, racism in the US in the twenty-first century takes the form of white supremacy. It essentially involves the disempowerment and disenfranchisement of people of color, those who already have less social, economic, and political power within a society that has always overwhelmingly promoted the power and interests of white citizens and continues to do so.

The refrain "go back where you came from" functions as a white supremacist weapon, consistently deployed against people of color and implying that the target is both not authentically American on account of their race—implying that the generic American is white—and also implying the targeted persons are not welcome to stay. Many people of color in many contexts will encounter variations of this refrain, always with the effect of attacking their right to exist within the US. It is also a constant refrain within white nationalist conversations, fostering solidarity among racist white folks who see the US as a country created by and for white people. For these reasons, it is widely known that what Ocasio-Cortez says is true. "Go back where you came from" is hallmark language of white supremacists. The use of this language is part of the wide and multifaceted pattern of racial oppression in the US. Therefore, Trump's tweet was racist.

Trump defended himself. His response had two components. First, he aimed to discredit Ocasio-Cortez's use of the word "racist" directed at him, writing, "Whenever confronted, they call their adversaries, including Nancy Pelosi [Democratic Speaker of the House], 'RACIST.' Their disgusting language … and the many terrible things they say about the United States must not be allowed to go unchallenged."[4] Here Trump is attacking Ocasio-Cortez's use of the word "racist" by suggesting it is being deployed purely for political gain and also claiming that such uses of "racist" to highlight and criticize white supremacy in the US must be challenged. Calling her language 'disgusting,' Trump accuses Ocasio-Cortez and likeminded critics of misapplying the term "racist" against him. According to Trump, Ocasio-Cortez called his tweet "racist" not because it is true that his use of "go back where you came from" was racist, but rather because she wished to defame and demonize him on the social-political stage.

Many white people have voiced similar misgivings about uses of the term "racist," maintaining that the word functions primarily to attack and

[4] Trump (2019b).

demonize anyone who disagrees with anti-racism advocates. Crucially this line of criticism presupposes that, in the majority of cases, applications of "racist" are not veridical, are not true. If "racist" is being used primarily to attack and demonize, then those cases to which the word is being commonly applied are not true examples of racism.

Thus, there appears to be substantive disagreement about what racism is. Advocates of the critical race theory understanding of racism (including Ocasio-Cortez) believe that Trump's tweets were racist, while Trump and his supporters—many of whom fear that "racist" is being deployed indiscriminately for political gain—believe his tweets were not racist. There is genuine disagreement here about what racism *is*. This is not a semantic disagreement merely about what the word "racism" means.

Trump and Ocasio-Cortez have different theories of racism. They do not agree about what makes something count as racist. But this does not automatically entail that they use the word "racism" with different meanings. A disagreement about what racism *is* does not necessarily entail a disagreement about what the word "racism" means.

Consider an analogy: Isaac Newton argued that light was a stream of particles, while opponents such as Christian Huygens argued that it was a wave phenomenon. It does not follow that Newton and Huygens *meant* different things by the word "light." Indeed, they both referred to the same phenomenon. They merely disagreed about its nature. Insofar as it is possible to refer to a singular phenomenon and disagree about its nature, it is possible that Trump and Ocasio-Cortez can both refer to the same phenomenon—racism—yet disagree about its nature. I maintain that such disputes happen very often in politics. We disagree about the nature of politically significant phenomenon while speaking a shared language with shared meanings. It is important to see political discourse in this light, as aimed at first-order truth and not semantics, even when fundamental disagreements arise.

Trump's second line of defense is, somewhat ironically, to redeploy the word "racist" against his adversaries in order to defame and demonize them. He tweets: "The 'Squad' is a very Racist group of troublemakers who are young, inexperienced, and not very smart."[5] In another tweet about a month later, Trump wrote, "The Amazon Washington Post did a story that I brought racist attacks against the 'Squad.' No, they brought

---

[5] Trump (2019c).

racist attacks against our Nation."[6] What is Trump claiming? It seems very unlikely that Trump is intending to assert that 'the Squad'—Alexandria Ocasio-Cortez, Ilhan Omar, Ayanna Pressley, and Rashida Tlaib—are contributing to the systematic oppression of people of color. Rather, Trump's claim is that these women are racist in virtue of putting race and racism at the center of the political conversation in the US.[7]

Why would it be racist to put race and racism at the center of the political conversation? There is a familiar, alternative pattern of usage invoking the terms "racist" and "racism" to which Trump is presumably subscribing here, which accompanies an opposing view of racism. On this way of thinking, it is racist to recognize the race of a person or group, or to cite someone's race as a cause for action or concern. Neil Gotanda (1991) calls this the "colorblind" conception of racism.

When Iowa State Senator Steve King claimed that it would be racist and sexist to put Harriet Tubman's image on the twenty-dollar bill, he presumably had the colorblind conception of racism in mind.[8] King's thought process was presumably something like: people want to put Harriet Tubman on the twenty because she is Black and a woman. But to act for those reasons—because she is Black and because she is a woman—is racist and sexist, because acting on the basis of race and gender are sufficient for racism and sexism.

Is it true that putting race and racism at the center of US politics is racist? Is it true that putting Harriet Tubman on the twenty-dollar bill is racist? Someone might say, well, that depends on what you mean by "racist."

---

[6] Trump (2019d).
[7] Here it may be worth considering the possibility that Trump has no coherent idea what he means when he says something is "racist." This possibility was suggested by a reviewer who noted that Trump has often said contradictory things and, when confronted with such facts, he has sometimes seemed confused and/or failed to acknowledge any contradiction in his speech. If Trump does not understand what he himself means, then we might say that while his words have a semantic meaning, his speech acts lack a speaker meaning. His intentions perhaps do not fix a content for his speech act due to his lack of care, precision, understanding, or whatever. This form of speech—making assertions without having any clear understanding of what one takes those assertions mean—may even be typical of political speech in the misinformation age. However, throughout this book I assume that a person can speaker-mean to assert a content even if they are very confused about what it is they are saying. Hence, even if Trump has no coherent view of what he means when he says something is "racist," he may still speaker-mean to assert propositions about racism—even propositions he does not himself understand.
[8] Owen (2016) reports this story.

If by "racist" you mean what Donald Trump and Steve King have in mind when they use the word, then it is true that such things count as "racist." When you use it as Ocasio-Cortez does, then putting Harriet Tubman on the twenty is not "racist." On this kind of view, the dispute over the nature of racism is really a semantic dispute over the meaning of "racist."

Whether it is possible for Trump and King to actually mean something different from Ocasio-Cortez is one of the central questions of this book. I think the answer is no. Our words do not automatically mean whatever we say or think they mean. They don't mean whatever our political allies say or think they mean. Public language expressions have a shared meaning across political factions. Trump, whether he likes it or not, refers to racism every time he uses the word "racism," and racism is not what he thinks it is. On the view I am defending, Trump and King speak falsely in a common language, the same language Ocasio-Cortez speaks, the same language all English speakers use.

From the perspective of critical race theory and intersectionality studies, it is neither sexist nor racist to put Harriet Tubman's image on the twenty-dollar bill. Tubman is a symbol of the strength of women of color to fight both patriarchy and racism. She freed her family from slavery after escaping herself. She helped free dozens of other slaves through the Underground Railroad. Later she joined with the Union Army and guided the raid at Combahee Ferry, liberating over 700 slaves. Meanwhile Andrew Jackson, whose face has featured on the twenty-dollar bill since 1928, owned hundreds of slaves during his lifetime. He began his military and political career organizing militia to kill off the Chickasaw tribe and steal their land in order to redistribute it among poor whites. He fought a genocidal war against the Muskogee nation and later commanded US forces during the Seminole Wars. He was responsible for the Trail of Tears.[9] Jackson's image on the twenty-dollar bill is a testament to the brutal, racist history of the US.

The foregoing considerations prove beyond reasonable doubt that Steve King's assertion that it would be racist to put Harriet Tubman's image on the twenty-dollar bill is *false*. King's conception of racism is likewise mistaken. Steve King has false beliefs about racism. His assertions spread these false beliefs. Likewise, Trump's beliefs about racism and his assertion that Ocasio-Cortez is racist on account of her criticisms of white

---

[9] For an extensive critical discussion of Jackson's career as a "famed Indian Killer" and his role in the systematic genocide of Indigenous groups, see Dunbar-Ortiz (2014), Chap. 3.

supremacy are false. In general, a white supremacist understanding of reality is largely coextensive with misunderstanding and ignorance about racism (Mills, 2007, 2014). These are central claims in this book. They highlight the importance of a notion of objective truth and falsehood in political disputes.

Moreover, I argue that semantic facts about the falsehoods expressed by people who are misinformed about the nature of racism, or misinformed about the nature of gender, or misinformed on any politically contentious topic, are fundamental data for understanding truth and meaning. A metasemantic theory for English—one that tells us what our words mean and why, which entails what the truth conditions of our statements are—must crucially be sensitive to the function of misinformation and false representation of politically contested matters of fact. The function of misinformation, I will argue, is closely tied to the reproduction and perpetuation of interlocking systems of social domination, including racism and sexism.

The misuses of terminology perpetrated by Trump and King are attempts to use politically significant terminology that is crucial to social justice movements against the people for whom those social justice movements are carried out. My name for this phenomenon is *linguistic hijacking* (Anderson, 2020). They are hijacking the word "racist," using it against people of color. Patterns of linguistic hijacking perpetrated by dominant agents spread misinformation and false belief about systems of oppression and function to preserve the status quo against movements that seek to create a more just society.

The notion of 'hijacking' raises the question of proprietorship. In what sense does the word "racism" belong to people of color, such that it can be "hijacked" by elite white men such as Trump and King? On the view developed in this book, linguistic proprietorship is closely bound up with politically contested claims about reality. It is because racism really is a form of systemic oppression that afflicts people of color and not white people in the US, and because "racism" refers to racism, that the term functions as a crucial epistemic resource for anti-racist activity. The word's ideal function given our historically situated linguistic practice is to communicate information about racism. It becomes hijacked when it is used to spread misinformation and false belief about racism.

Accordingly, whether one takes a given use of "racism" to be an instance of linguistic hijacking depends on one's theory of racism. Such theories are contested along political lines, but some people are objectively correct in their understanding and others not so much.

If Trump's theory of racism is true, then he is not hijacking the word "racism" but using it correctly. If Ocasio-Cortez's theory of racism is true, Trump's usage does constitute hijacking. So, whether a misuse of "racism" counts as an example of linguistic hijacking depends on what the true theory of racism is. Proprietorship of the word "racism" is determined by first-order truths about racism. Issues of proprietorship will be politically contentious. We should expect nothing else. But the fact that something is politically contentious does not mean there is no objective truth about the matter. That is another of the central themes of this book.

2.2 Linguistic Hijacking and Gender Terminology

As with the word "racism," there are bitter political struggles surrounding gender terminology. I will use "gender terminology" to refer to the open-ended set of expressions that are crucially bound up in discussions about gender. Gender terminology includes most obviously words like "man" and "woman," "boy" and "girl," as well as pronouns "he," "she," and "they," among many others; it includes gendered social role terms like "mother" and "father," "brother" and "sister"; it also includes some terms referring to sexuality, including "heterosexual," "homosexual," "lesbian," "gay," "bi-sexual," "pan-sexual" since these terms carry implications about gender; also included are "trans," "cis," "agender," "non-binary," "genderqueer," and so on, through the wide array of gender identities that have been introduced or identified.

I propose to include 'sex' terminology such as "male" and "female" as gender terminology as well. While a distinction is often drawn between gender and sex—gender is often construed as socially constructed and/or performed, while sex is construed as grounded in biology—this distinction is contested along political lines. For example, calling a trans woman "biologically male" is often used by transphobes to delegitimate her identity as a woman. Terms like "male" and "female" irrevocably carry implications about gender, such that calling someone "male" connotes that they are a man, while calling someone "female" connotes that they are a woman. Moreover, as Rachel McKinnon points out, governments and sports leagues typically do not distinguish between sex and gender (McKinnon, 2019). The language used to craft rules and laws typically mixes sex and gender terminology indiscriminately. This provides a further reason to count sex terminology as gender terminology. Lastly, the majority of transphobic political agitators in both real and virtual spaces refuse to grant a distinction between sex and gender, maintaining the view that a person is male if and only if he is a man and female if and only if she is a woman. Hence, sex terms are clearly part of the politics of gender.

Just as misuses of the word "racist" function to spread misinformation and false belief about racism, misuses of gender terminology function to spread false belief and misinformation about gender. And as with disputes around the word "racism," one's view about whether a given use of gender terminology counts as a misuse will be closely tied to one's political perspective. One cannot be politically neutral with regard to questions about which uses of gender terminology are misuses. Throughout this book, I defend a trans inclusive perspective. I presuppose the truth of trans people's beliefs and assertions about their own genders. Accordingly, I understand statements like "Trans women are really men" to constitute misinformation. They spread ignorance about gender. I will argue that these facts are crucial to understanding the metasemantics of English.[10]

That trans women are women and that contrary statements constitute misinformation are politically contentious claims. But just because something is politically contentious does not mean it's false, nor that both sides have an equal claim to be justified in their beliefs. The justification for believing that trans women are women depends on accepting trans people's experiences of gender as crucial evidence for the nature of gender. This itself is a politically contentious epistemological assumption—the fact that trans people's experiences provide crucial evidence for understanding gender will not be accepted by transphobes. But this is to be explained by the fact that transphobes do not understand what evidence is relevant for understanding gender. Accepting a trans inclusive starting point is part of doing trans philosophy (Bettcher, 2019), and it is a common practice to assume the legitimacy of trans identities within the philosophy of gender.[11]

Ben Shapiro writes, "If you are a biological man and you believe you are a woman, you suffer from a mental disorder."[12] Ostensibly a 'biological

---

[10] Throughout this book I do not assume any view of the metaphysics of gender, other than that trans women are women. This view is compatible with the denial that there is any substantive metaphysical explanation of why trans women are women, or why anyone is a woman. It is also compatible with any substantive theory of gender on which trans women are women.

[11] See, for example, Jenkins (2016).

[12] Shapiro (2018).

man' is someone who was assigned 'male' at birth, who was born with sex traits associated with being a man, although using the term "biological man" is obviously contentious and aggressive when Shapiro uses it. Shapiro's statement is a straightforward denial that a so-called 'biological man' could have a true belief that she is a woman. In claiming that such beliefs are caused by mental illness, Shapiro implies that such beliefs are delusional and hence false.

According to trans feminists, trans women's beliefs about their gender are true. So are the expressions of these beliefs in language, as when a trans woman asserts, "I am a woman." This raises the metasemantic issue again. Is Ben Shapiro speaking truly in his own language when he asserts, "Trans women are men with mental disorders?" using gender terminology with his own preferred meanings?

The dispute over whether trans people suffer from mental disorders is best understood as a factual dispute about the nature of gender and the nature of mental disorders. It should not be conceived as a matter of semantics. The American Medical Association and the American Psychiatric Association both deny that being transgender is a mental disorder. As of 2022, the World Health Organization will no longer classify being transgender as a mental disorder. These are not merely semantic stipulations. Rather, these classificatory decisions are based on empirical evidence about gender and also about mental disorder.

The Shapiro example highlights the relevance of metasemantic theorizing for understanding empirical knowledge. If Shapiro's claims were *analytic*—if they were true by definition of the words "woman" and "mental disorder" as Shapiro uses them—then empirical evidence would have no bearing on their truth. Anything that is true by definition cannot be refuted by empirical evidence, if we presuppose the traditional distinction between analytic sentences and synthetic sentences. On my view, a metasemantic account of the meanings of politically contested terms must capture the way in which empirical data is relevant for settling political disputes. An acceptable metasemantics must allow for the possibility that Shapiro's view—that being trans is a mental illness—can be refuted on the basis of empirical evidence.

These issues harken back to famous disputes between Quine and Carnap about the analytic/synthetic distinction. Carnap (1950) theorized that conceptual disputes could always be traced to differences in meaning and that everyone always speaks truly when expressing what they take to be an analytic sentence. Quine (1951, 1960) contested the intelligibility of distinguishing analytic sentences from synthetic sentences. According to Quine, we should reject the idea that some sentences are true in virtue of meaning alone, and along with it the idea that conceptual disagreements are always disputes about meanings. According to Quine, there is no way to tell ahead of time what kinds of empirical evidence may be relevant to settling a conceptual dispute, and it's always wrong-headed to claim that a dispute is merely linguistic and thus rule out the applicability of evidence or experience for settling the matter at hand.

My view is aligned with the Quinean perspective on this issue. We cannot know and should not stipulate ahead of time that any statement or belief is immune to rational revision in light of future empirical evidence, not even statements that represent conceptual disputes about gender or racism. It is empirically false that trans women, in virtue of being trans, have mental disorders. Treating Shapiro's statement as analytic misrepresents the evidential relations that are relevant for disproving his claim. Moreover, a view on which Shapiro speaks truly misrepresents the way in which his rhetoric functions to spread false beliefs and misinformation about gender, which is part of gender-based oppression. All these facts are important data that an adequate metasemantic theory must capture.

Characters like Ben Shapiro are best understood as ideological misinformation brokers that spread false beliefs and enable transphobic agitators to reject, avoid, and otherwise refuse to uptake relevant empirical evidence. This kind of refusal to countenance empirical evidence is endemic to what has been called the post-truth era (McIntyre, 2018). Most of the concern raised about post-truth politics has been aimed at critiquing the flagrant rejection of empirically ascertainable truths. How many people were at Donald Trump's inauguration? How many people have died of COVID-19? How many legitimate votes were cast for Joe Biden in 2020? These are empirically decidable in principle, although the relevant empirical evidence has been contested in the political sphere.

By contrast, relatively little concern has been directed at the ways in which language is used to spread conceptual misinformation. This has something to do with unspoken but widely held convictions about what is a factual dispute versus what is a verbal or semantic disagreement. Very often conceptual debates are written off as merely semantic and dismissed on those grounds, or at least their importance has been diminished when compared to the flagrant disavowal of empirical evidence. Metasemantic theorizing is needed to defend the claim that disputes about racism and gender are more than merely verbal disagreements, while still capturing the sense in which political power struggles can affect our ability to think and talk about these things effectively and accurately.

For another example of a politically charged conceptual dispute, consider the following diatribe against the possibility of trans women lesbians delivered by Magdalene Berns:

> Lesbians don't have penises. If you're born with a penis and balls, you're male. You don't get assigned reproductive organs. Males are defined by their biological sex organs. Likewise, a homosexual is someone who's attracted to members of the same biological sex. Males can't be lesbians.[13]

Berns's sentiments are emblematic of a position that is often described as 'trans exclusionary radical feminist,' or TERF. Trans-exclusionary radical feminists (TERFs) prototypically maintain that trans women are really men. Consequently, initiatives aimed at promoting trans women's rights and well-being are seen as anti-feminist, as drawing on and reinforcing male privilege, and as eroding the spaces and protections put in place for women and girls. Some TERFs do not deny that trans women are women but insist that trans women are biologically male and because they are biologically male they should be excluded from protections, spaces, and institutions that are provided for women. In her diatribe, Berns grants that trans women are women, but she maintains that trans women should be excluded from the lesbian community on the grounds that they are male. Among other consequences, this view entails that spaces and events that are reserved for lesbians should be closed off to trans women.

Berns, like Shapiro, is a misinformation broker. She is spreading false beliefs about gender and sexuality. Specifically, she is spreading the false belief that trans women can't be lesbians. Part of the correct explanation of her activities is that her utterance "Lesbians don't have penises" is empirically false. Likewise, the purported definitional claims are not guaranteed to be true: "males are defined by their biological sex organs" and "a homosexual is someone who's attracted to members of the same biological sex" are both highly questionable. If a trans inclusive perspective on gender is accurate, then those definitions are inaccurate. The reality of trans gender is empirically determinable, but not by purely biological data, not by theories that refuse to incorporate sociological, psychological, and phenomenological data about gender experience. It also cannot be

---

[13] Quote transcribed from a Magdalene Berns speech in Genderfree (2019).

determined by what passes for commonsense, because commonsense is deeply affected by cultural biases, propaganda, and controlling images (Collins, 2002).

Whether a biological definition of gender is part of commonsense and whether it is widely felt to be scientific are sociological facts. They are determined by power dynamics that enshrine certain perspectives as commonsense and denigrate certain pieces of information as scientifically irrelevant. Similar considerations apply to theories of racism. What feels like commonsense is a matter of how the people in your community feel, and what feelings they validate in you. Your impression of whether there can be a science of racism is also conditioned by your social sphere. If everyone around you convinces you to believe that anti-white racism is possible by definition, then the thought of doing science about racism seems nonsensical. It's like doing science to figure out whether bachelors are unmarried.

I think there is a strong inclination among analytically trained philosophers to see a contrast between the case involving Magdalene Berns and the case involving Ben Shapiro. Where Shapiro's assertion that trans people all have mental disorders seems more straightforwardly susceptible to empirical refutation, Berns's assertion that males cannot be lesbians seems more like it might be an analytic truth. "Lesbians are not male" might seem to be in the ballpark of "Bachelors are not married." Its truth seems to consist in the relationship between the semantic features of "lesbian" and "male," for example, the meaning of "lesbian" excludes anything from its extension that could possibly be in the extension of "male" given what that word means.[14] Likewise, the sentence "trans women are male" seems to fall into the category of analytic truth (although there are, I believe, strong trans feminist reasons to deny this). It follows from (i) trans women are male and (ii) lesbians are not male that (iii) trans women are not lesbians. So (iii) also has the status of analytic truth on this understanding, since any sentence derivable from analytic sentences is itself analytic (Carnap, 1936, 1956). Similar analytic arguments can be given against the fundamental assertions of trans reality. For example, (iv) "Women are not male" sounds analytic to many people, true in virtue of the meanings of "women" and "male."[15] Then from (i) and (iv) it follows that trans women are not women.

[14] For the concept of extension see Chap. 5.
[15] See, for example, Byrne (2020).

Trans feminists who support the full-fledged womanhood of trans women must deny these lines of reasoning. If trans women really are full-fledged women, then there is no reason to deny they can be lesbians. Being a lesbian, on this trans-inclusive understanding, only requires that one be a woman and that one be sexually oriented exclusively toward women. Logically, this requires either denying (i) that trans women are male or (ii) that lesbians are not male. But where (i) and (ii) are seen to express analytic truths, this denial is impossible. It is therefore imperative, from a trans feminist perspective, to deny the truth and the analyticity of (i) or (ii). Likewise, trans feminists are committed to denying the truth and analyticity of (i) or (iv) in order to maintain the central trans feminist proposition that trans women really are women.[16]

2.3 Misinformation and Truth in a Language

Denying that "Trans women are male" is analytic requires a metasemantics on which the meanings of "woman" and "male" are not up to Magdalene Berns. To represent her as speaking falsely, we need a metasemantics on which the meanings of her words accord with a trans inclusive theory of gender and sexuality, even though she herself does not subscribe to that theory. Likewise to represent Trump as speaking falsely when he uses the word "racist," we need a metasemantics on which the meaning of his word accords with a critical race theory of racism, even though he denies the truth of such a theory (and perhaps does not even understand it). On the metasemantics I will introduce in Chap. 10, the function of "woman" in English is to refer to women (including trans women); the function of "lesbian" is to refer to lesbians (including trans lesbians); the function of "racism" is to refer to racism (which is a form of systemic

---

[16] I personally think the right way to go here is to deny that trans women are male and accept that trans women are female, by denying that maleness and femaleness are biological properties. I think all women are female. Given this view, both (iii) and (iv) are true: lesbians are not male and women are not male. This view requires denying the sex/gender distinction in its traditional form, that is, resisting the claim that trans women are biologically male. Then obviously Berns's view that being a lesbian necessarily entails having certain biological features is false. On my view, the concepts of maleness and femaleness were inappropriately and inaccurately exported from the social sphere into the biological domain, applied to plant and animal kinds by virtue of the perceived analogy between biological reproductive roles and gendered social roles. It was and is inappropriate and inaccurate to use gender terminology "male" and "female" as if they were austere scientific concepts without gender connotations.

oppression). On the metasemantics to be proposed, linguistic hijackings are always misrepresentations of objective reality that function to reinforce intersecting systems of domination.

When someone misuses the word "racist," they tend to spread misinformation about racism. This presupposes that there is a real fact of the matter, a truth about racism, that is independent of the way the misinforming speech characterizes things. Racism must really be a certain way, independently of how we talk about it, in order for some speech about it to count as misinformation. Likewise, when someone misuses the word "woman" they spread misinformation about women, or about gender more broadly. There must be a way that gender *is* in order for it to be misrepresented or obscured. Characterizing the way things actually are is part of the function of language, so presumably it is possible to state truths about racism and gender using the language we speak. The possibility of using language to misinform is parasitic on the possibility of using language to speak truly. Misinformation represents the world inaccurately, while good information represents the world as it is. Accurately describing misinformation is just as important for a metasemantic theory as is accurately representing true sentences.

One of my overarching goals is to defend this perspective about the relationship between politically contentious realities and the language we use to describe them, in which some of us speak truly and others speak falsely about one shared reality. We speak a shared language and refer to the same things regardless of political orientation. Those who speak falsely are spreading misinformation and false belief by using the shared language. In order to develop this perspective, we must attend to the meanings of words and where they come from.

As I hope the examples introduced above make clear, disagreements about what counts as "racism" or who counts as a "woman" are not merely disagreements about how to use words. Rather, we must see them as disagreements about the reality of racism and gender.[17] To achieve this point of view, we must have a theory of truth in a language that ties the shared language to that objective reality, even when some members of the

---

[17] The reality of gender and the reality of racism are not wholly independent of the way we talk and act, of course. Racism includes racist speech, as well as racist institutions that are built up, maintained, and facilitated by speech. Much of what gender *is* may have to do with the ways we talk and think about gender. But however the metaphysical facts about gender and racism are created and maintained, they are part of the one objective reality.

community misuse language in order to misdirect, confuse, ignore, misrepresent, and misinform about politically important and controversial topics.

A theory of truth for a public language is closely connected with a semantic theory for that language. A semantic theory assigns semantic properties to expressions of a language. The truth or falsity of a sentence depends in part on what the words in that sentence mean. Take the sentence "Affirmative action is racist." Part of the explanation for this sentence's being false involves the semantic meanings of the words "racist" and "affirmative action." The correct semantic theory for English tells us what "racist" and "affirmative action" mean and tells us what the truth conditions are for sentences they appear in. Chapter 5 will go into some detail about how such a semantic theory works.

The truth conditions of a sentence are closely connected with the semantic properties of the words of that sentence. "Racist" refers to something that is implicated in perpetuating or benefiting from racial oppression. This is why "Affirmative action is racist" is true if and only if affirmative action is implicated in perpetuating or benefiting from racial oppression; it isn't, so the sentence is false. If "racist" had had a different meaning—if its semantic properties had been different—it might have referred to any process that makes a distinction on the basis of race. In that case, the sentence "Affirmative action is racist" would have been true if and only if affirmative action involves making distinctions on the basis of race. In that case, the sentence would have had different truth conditions and it would have been true.

This counterfactual difference in truth-value would *not* be the result of a change in racism itself, nor would it suffice to bring about such a change. Merely using the word "racist" differently would not in itself suffice to alter the vast material inequality and oppression that the racial order imposes. The difference in truth-value would be merely a semantic difference. Hence, a sentence's truth-value depends in part on the semantic features of its component words and in part on the reality of the things to which those words refer. So if Trump speaks falsely when he says Ocasio-Cortez is "racist," if Shapiro speaks falsely when he says "trans women are really men," then this implies something about the meanings of their words as well as the realities of which they are speaking falsely.

Analytic philosophers of language have developed tools for representing the semantic properties of linguistic expressions as objective features of the world. The semantic properties of expressions are objective in the sense that if the semantic theory for those properties is correct, then it is correct for all people regardless of how those people understand, use, or choose to interpret those words. In Chap. 5, I will consider whether we should think any such semantic theory is true, or whether we should think of semantic interpretation as inherently subjective. I will argue that although each of us endeavors to interpret the language as best we can, there is an objectively true semantic theory for our shared natural language.

Assuming there is an objectively true semantic theory for the shared language we speak, what makes it the case that this semantic theory is true? This is not quite the same as asking: how do we know what the meanings of our words are? Rather, I am asking: how did the words get the meanings they currently have? What makes it the case that one semantic theory is true rather than another? Why does "racism" refer to racism rather than something slightly different, or something completely different? Can the meaning of "racist" be changed, and if so how? Is it possible for my word "racist" and your word "racist" to have different meanings? If so, how did they come to have different meanings? These are questions in the domain of *meta*semantics. As we will see, thinking about metasemantics is central to adjudicating the issue of whether and how linguistic hijacking and other misuses of language can be seen as spreading misinformation about things like racism and gender.

This is only a preliminary overview of the relevance of semantics and metasemantics for political struggle. The next chapter introduces two competing metasemantic models for the words "racist" and "woman." On one model, the semantic corruption model, political struggles over issues like racism and gender are largely a matter of wresting control of the semantics of politically contested terminology.[18] On this model, linguistic hijackings of "racist" and "woman" function to alter the meanings of words to serve the interests of dominant groups. On the other model, the epistemic violence model, hijacking misuses function to manipulate our epistemic capabilities—our ability to know reality—without changing the meanings of words. The contrast between these two views helps to motivate the perspective to be defended in later chapters that our belief in a metasemantic theory for our own language should be very sensitive to our most deeply held political convictions.

---

[18] This model is developed in detail in Anderson (2020).

References

Anderson, D. (2020). Linguistic Hijacking. *Feminist Philosophy Quarterly*, 6(3). https://doi.org/10.5206/fpq/2020.3.8162
Bettcher, T. M. (2019). What Is Trans Philosophy? *Hypatia*, 34(4), 644–667.
Bonilla-Silva, E. (1997). Rethinking Racism: Toward a Structural Interpretation. *American Sociological Review*, 62, 465–480.
Byrne, A. (2020). Are Women Adult Human Females? *Philosophical Studies*, 177, 1–21.
Carnap, R. (1936). Testability and Meaning. *Philosophy of Science*, 3(4), 419–471.
Carnap, R. (1950). Empiricism, Semantics, and Ontology. *Revue internationale de philosophie*, 20–40.
Carnap, R. (1956). *The Methodological Character of Theoretical Concepts*. Bobbs-Merrill.
Collins, P. H. (2002). *Black Feminist Thought: Knowledge, Consciousness, and the Politics of Empowerment*. Routledge.
Crenshaw, K. W. (1988). Race, Reform, and Retrenchment: Transformation and Legitimation in Antidiscrimination Law. *Harvard Law Review*, 101, 1331–1387.
Dunbar-Ortiz, R. (2014). *An Indigenous Peoples' History of the United States* (Vol. 3). Beacon Press.
Genderfree, P. (2019). Tribute to Magdalene Berns RIP. YouTube. Retrieved August 27, 2019, from https://www.youtube.com/watch?v=G5KLj7z55Uk
Gotanda, N. (1991). A Critique of "Our Constitution is Color-Blind". *Stanford Law Review*, 44, 1–68.
Jenkins, K. (2016). Amelioration and Inclusion: Gender Identity and the Concept of Woman. *Ethics*, 126(2), 394–421.
Kendi, I. X. (2019). *How to Be an Antiracist*. One World.
McIntyre, L. (2018). *Post-truth*. MIT Press.
McKinnon, R. (2019). Participation in Sports Is a Human Right, Even for Trans Women. *APA Newsletter*, 19(1, Fall).
Mills, C. (2007). White Ignorance. *Race and Epistemologies of Ignorance*, 247, 26–31.
Mills, C. W. (2014). *The Racial Contract*. Cornell University Press.
Ocasio-Cortez, A. (2019). Twitter. (@AOC). *It's Important to Note That the President's Words Yday, Telling Four American Congresswomen of Color "go back to your own country."* 15 July 2019, 8:40am. https://twitter.com/AOC/status/1150746839790039040
Owen, T. (2016). Congressman Says Putting Harriet Tubman on the $20 Bill is 'racist' and 'sexist'. Vice News. https://www.vice.com/en/article/8x37dg/iowa-congressman-steve-king-harriet-tubman-andrew-jackson-20-bill-racist-sexist

Quine, W. V. (1960). Carnap and Logical Truth. *Synthese*, *12*(4), 350–374.
Quine, W. V. O. (1951). Two Dogmas of Empiricism. *The Philosophical Review*, *60*(1), 20–43. https://doi.org/10.2307/2181906. JSTOR 2181906. Reprinted in His 1953 *From a Logical Point of View*. Harvard University Press
Shapiro, B. (2018). So, Here's a Giant List of All The Dumb Stuff I've Ever Done (Don't Worry, I'll Keep Updating It). *The Daily Wire*. https://www.dailywire.com/news/so-heres-giant-list-all-dumb-stuff-ive-ever-done-ben-shapiro
Trump, D. (2019a). Twitter. (@realdonaldtrump). *Why Don't They Go Back and Help Fix the Totally Broken and Crime Infested Places from Which They Came* 14 July 2019, 5:27am. [Account Suspended].
Trump, D. (2019b). Twitter. (@realdonaldtrump). *Whenever Confronted, They Call Their Adversaries, Including Nancy Pelosi, 'RACIST.'* 14 July 2019, 5:02pm. Tweet. [Account Suspended].
Trump, D. (2019c). Twitter. (@realdonaldtrump). *The 'Squad' Is a Very Racist Group of Troublemakers Who Are Young, Inexperienced, and Not Very Smart.* 22 July 2019, 7:48am. Tweet. [Account Suspended].
Trump, D. (2019d). Twitter (@realdonaldtrump). *The Amazon Washington Post Did a Story That I Brought Racist Attacks Against the 'Squad.' No, They Brought Racist Attacks Against Our Nation.* 2 September 2019, 5:09am. Tweet. [Account Suspended].

CHAPTER 3

On the Possibility of Semantic Corruption

This chapter frames a fundamental question about whether political struggles around racism and gender should be seen as primarily struggles for control over the meanings of words. In the next chapter I will argue against this approach, but it is helpful to first set out what I take to be the wrong view so that we can see more clearly what is wrong with it and what a better view would look like.

3.1 One Word, Two Meanings?

Consider the following exchange from the movie *Die Hard: With a Vengeance*, in which Bruce Willis's character John McClane, a white police officer, confronts Samuel L. Jackson's character Zeus Carver, a black man from Harlem.

John McClane: I'll tell you what your problem is, you don't like me cause you're a racist!
Zeus Carver: What?
John McClane: You're a racist! You don't like me 'cause I'm white!
Zeus Carver: I don't like you because you're gonna get me *killed*!

McClane's usage reflects what we might call the Die-Hard view of racism, which emphasizes anti-whiteness as a central case of racism. The

Die-Hard view is also reflected in Ben Shapiro's (2010) claim that "The Obama administration is racist," on the grounds that it was concerned explicitly with the problematic behaviors of white police officers and with addressing wealth gaps between whites and people of color. The Die-Hard view is also reflected in Trump's claim that 'the Squad'—US representatives Ocasio-Cortez, Omar, Pressley, and Tlaib, all of whom are women of color—are "racist" for framing white supremacy as a cause for political concern. It is also the view of those who oppose the Black Lives Matter movement on the grounds that it is "racist" against white people.

On what I take to be the correct view of racism, anti-white racism is impossible given the current economic and socio-political conditions of the US.[1] On this view, racism is a form of systemic oppression. It is a sociopolitical order enforcing the dominant position of one racialized group (white people) and subordinating another group (people of color) in order for the social, cultural, political, psychological, and economic gain of the dominant group. Let's call this the structural oppression view of racism. This is the view that Ocasio-Cortez was drawing on when she responded to Trump's "go back to your own country" tweet by calling it racist.

If the structural oppression view is true, then the Die-Hard view is false. Anti-white sentiments are not racist, for they do not contribute to the oppression of white people. McClane's accusation that Zeus Carver is a racist is false. Shapiro's sentence "The Obama administration is racist" is also false on the structural oppression view of racism. Actions taken to check the racist behaviors of white police officers as such are not racist efforts—they are anti-racist efforts. Efforts that aim to redistribute white wealth to people of color are not racist efforts; they are anti-racist. Black Lives Matter is not racist either. It opposes structural oppression in its critique of police power as an enforcer of white domination.[2]

It's crucial to note here that if statements such as "The Obama administration is racist" and "BLM is racist" are *false*, then "racist" as it occurs in these sentences must refer to racism understood as racialized structural oppression. Hence, if they are false, then Ben Shapiro and the anti-BLM

---
[1] See Collins (2002) for one canonical statement of this concept of racism as structural oppression.
[2] See Kendi (2019) for an explanation of this distinction between racism and anti-racism. Crenshaw (1988) notes that "Neoconservative doctrine singles out race-specific civil rights policies as one of the most significant threats to the democratic political system," and argues that this kind of ideological resistance to anti-racist policies in fact embodies a strategy for preserving white domination.

agitator use the word "racist" with the same meaning as their political opponents, those of us who believe racism is a form of structural oppression. Shapiro and the anti-BLM agitator clearly do not believe this about racism. Hence, even though we believe different things about racism, we use the word "racism" to refer to the same thing.

But when people disagree about what counts as "racist," are they really using the word "racist" with the same meaning? Or are they using it with different meanings? There is a widely accepted, usually implicit view that Trump and Ocasio-Cortez could be using the word "racist" with different meanings, so they could both be speaking truly even though they apparently disagree with one another. This symmetry gives rise to a sense that their dispute, while politically charged, is actually trivial. They are merely arguing over semantics.

The question of whether Trump and Ocasio-Cortez are using the word "racist" with different meanings is partly a question about the correct semantic theory for the language. What are the meanings of the words "racist" (as spoken by Trump) and "racist" (as spoken by Ocasio-Cortez)? Are they the same or different? It is also a *metasemantic* question. If Trump and Ocasio-Cortez are using "racist" with different meanings, then there must be some kind of metasemantic explanation for how they manage to do this. What is required for two people to use the same word with two different meanings, as opposed to using it with the same meaning? If Trump and Ocasio-Cortez are not sharing a language, why not?

This chapter explores one possible metasemantic view that would ground the claim that Trump and Ocasio-Cortez are not using "racist" with the same meaning. I call this view the *semantic corruption model*, because on this model linguistic hijacking misuses of "racist" function to corrupt the meaning of the word, changing it to serve the interests of white people. As we will see, if the semantic corruption model provides the right metasemantic theory for "racist," then Trump and Ocasio-Cortez really do mean different things by that word.

My purpose here is to present the semantic corruption model in its best light. Indeed, I have found it compelling myself.[3] But I think there are important reasons to reject this picture. I will present my arguments against semantic corruption in Chap. 4 once we have the semantic corruption model more clearly in view.

---

[3] See Anderson (2020) for a more complete exposition and defense of the semantic corruption model.

3.2 Semantic Corruption and Metasemantic Struggle

In order for people to share a language, they must engage in coordination around how the symbols—the sounds, the gestures, and the ink marks—are supposed to be used. What is the correct way to use a word? Words have many uses, but one central use is in the service of speaking truly, of saying what is the case. I will call these *veridical uses* of words, uses in which the word is incorporated in a true sentence. One of the major coordination tasks for establishing the meaning of a word in a community is settling which applications of that word count as veridical uses.

Coordination requires each person to engage in a practice of giving corrections to and accepting corrections from others in their language-sharing community. You are not free to simply mean whatever you wish to mean with your words through sheer force of will; you must interface with other users of the language, coordinate with them. One central way to coordinate is to accept correction from other users where your word usage deviates from what is taken to be veridical usage. Another central way for you to participate in the coordination project is for you to correct the way others use their word, to bring their usage in line with what you take to be the correct meaning. Most often this type of correction appeals to the ways in which others use the words in question. Rarely, a person could introduce a brand new meaning and try to convince people to adjust their usage to accord with this new meaning. But even in such cases, success requires getting the community to coordinate on that new meaning.

When we accept a view like this, it is natural to see the semantic properties of particular uses of expressions as a function of how those expressions are used in the community the user belongs to. What I mean when I use the word "racist" depends on what other people in my community mean when they use that word. This is a *social externalist view of semantic properties* (Burge, 1979). *Externalism* means the semantics (also called *the contents*) of a person's words are determined in part by what those words are used to mean in the community the person belongs to, which is external to what goes on inside that person's mind or brain. My internal understanding of the veridical usage of the word, the set of rules stored in my brain for applying "racist," does not determine what that word means as I use it. My internal rule may or may not accord with the communal rule for applying it veridically. Hence, my understanding of the meaning of a word can be mistaken. I can apply a word in cases where it does not apply, given what the word really means in my community.

Social externalism allows for a person to use a word with its communally accepted meaning while they themselves have imperfect knowledge about what the word means or what it veridically applies to. This typically goes hand in hand with having incomplete knowledge (or even total ignorance) about the subject matter to which the word refers. A person who is ignorant of what exactly a fermion is may still use the word "fermion" to refer to fermions. For example, they could ask, "What is a fermion?" In asking such a question, a person refers to fermions even if they have no idea what a fermion is.

By the same power of reference, President Trump can use the word "racist" to refer to racism, even if he does not know what racism is. When he says the Squad is "racist," he does not know what he is talking about. He is manifesting his ignorance about racism itself, as well as asserting something false. It is commonplace that people are able to use words to make false statements. Making false statements paradigmatically occurs when one does not know what one is talking about (unless it's a case of lying). In Trump's case, the word "racist" still refers to racism, even though he himself does not know what racism is. Somehow or other, the meaning of "racist" as Trump uses it is determined by factors beyond his own understanding of racism. On the social externalist view, these factors have to do with the community of speakers to which Trump belongs.

What does it mean to be a part of a community of speakers? Are Trump and Ocasio-Cortez really part of the same community? If there are two different communities, one that uses the word "racist" as Trump does and one that uses it as Ocasio-Cortez does, then perhaps each speaks with a different meaning. Moreover, perhaps it is possible to choose which community you wish to be a part of. If you choose to be part of Trump's community, your word "racist" will mean whatever Trump's community means. This might be a different meaning from what I mean "racist" if my community uses "racist" to refer to something else. If this kind of metasemantics is correct (but, as I will argue later, it is incorrect) then the issue becomes, which community do you choose to belong to?

Assuming for now that multiple communities of English speakers exist and can use words with different meanings, we are led to ask such questions as: which community, Trump's or Ocasio-Cortez's, is the most influential in the public sphere? Whose meaning of "racist" is historically the most widespread? Whose is spreading fastest now? Whose will achieve widest coverage in the long run? These questions represent the basic thought behind the semantic corruption model, that semantics are a function of networks of coordination. The semantic corruption model frames the struggle around competing conceptions of racism as a metasemantic struggle for control of the meaning of the word "racism." If Trump's meaning spreads and Ocasio-Cortez's meaning diminishes, then Trump's statements about what he calls "racism" become true as asserted by a greater and greater number of people.

3.2.1   *The Role of Deference and Authority*

In his original investigation of social externalism for semantic contents, Burge (1979) noticed that deference can play an important role in determining communal membership and consequently in determining the semantic properties of one's thoughts and expressions. Part of what makes it the case that a person uses a word in accord with her community—and with the same meaning as others in that community—is that she is willing to defer to others whom she takes to speak the same language. Deference means willingness to accept correction, to defer to the instruction or usage of another, to conform one's usage to another's.

First-language learning surely involves a lot of deference in this sense, as the child defers to the parents and others in the linguistic community about the proper way to apply words. This does not require explicit correction on the part of parents, only that the child takes the parents and other speakers in the community to be reliable guides to correct usage. In a sense we are always still learning our first language. Sometimes we learn in subtle ways, gaining new knowledge of subtle inflections and nuances of meaning. Sometimes we learn in very noticeable ways, as when we realize we've been misusing a word or when we come across a new word we've never heard. We are always open at least in principle to learning new facts about how any given word is applied, even words we take ourselves to know very well.

I took myself to know the meaning of the word "intermittent." I thought it meant occurring non-continuously at regular intervals. But then I found out that being "intermittent" requires occurring at *ir*regular intervals. I used to be willing to say that the steady dripping of a faucet was intermittent, but now I realize that is not true.

When I realized that I was using "intermittent" inaccurately, I didn't respond by saying: Oh, I've been speaking a different language from other users of English! Rather, I took myself to have been misapplying the word, using it with the same meaning as everyone else but still using it inaccurately. It is false in English to say that the steady dripping of the faucet is intermittent. It was not true in 'my language' that "intermittent" applied veridically to steadily dripping faucets. 'My language' is the language I speak with others in my community, which is English.

Even for a word you are fully confident about, there are possible scenarios in which you would take yourself to learn something new about how that word is properly used. One of Burge's examples is the word "contract." You may think a contract must be written down in order to be valid, in which case you might be surprised to learn that a verbal contract is still legally binding. Someone who learns this learns something new about how the word "contract" is veridically applied, how it is used to form a true sentence. But they are not learning to use the word "contract" with a new meaning. Rather, they always used "contract" with this meaning, the meaning it has in our community. They were just ignorant of a certain correct application of "contract," viz. to verbally declared binding agreements.

One could explain this error in usage by saying the person did not know exactly what a contract was. The fact that they didn't know what a contract was explains the fact that they were disposed to misapply the word "contract." They may even have misunderstood the meaning of the word "contract," in the sense that they didn't know exactly what it applies to. But all of these facts are consistent with saying that they used the word "contract" with its ordinary English meaning and said things that were false.

The same goes for "racist." If someone misapplies "racist" according to its public meaning, they speak falsely in the shared language, not truly in their own private language. Often white people do this because they do not know exactly what racism is. By the same token, they may be said to misunderstand what "racism" means, in the sense that they do not quite understand how the word is veridically applied. But these are consistent with saying that a person used "racist" with its ordinary English meaning and said things that were false.

Burge suggested that the ability to misapply a word and speak falsely in accord with communal meaning often relies on deference. His example was a person who misapplied the word "arthritis" to an ailment in his thigh. This person believed "arthritis" applied veridically to the ailment in his thigh, but he was mistaken. The fact that he used the word in accord with his community is revealed through the fact that, in telling his doctor, "I think I have arthritis in my thigh," and being told, "No, arthritis only occurs in joints," the person deferred to the doctor's usage. Because the person is willing to adjust his usage to accord with his community's pattern of usage, via deferring to the doctor, he counts as using the word with the veridicality conditions sanctioned by the community. This attitude of deference is part of what it takes to belong to a linguistic community.

You can also count as using a word as part of a communal practice if, instead of deferring, you assume a position of authority and try to correct the usage of the other person. Imagine Burge's character had tried to convince the doctor that the doctor was wrong about the correct use of "arthritis." He tries to convince the doctor that "arthritis" *does* apply to the ailment in his thigh. Obviously, the man would not be in a great position to succeed; we would surely take the doctor's word over his. But insofar as the man is trying to correct the doctor's usage, he is still participating in their shared communal activity of coordinating on the meaning of "arthritis" and so still speaking the same language. Even though he does not defer to the doctor, he still uses "arthritis" with the same meaning as when the doctor uses it because he is participating in the same communal effort as the doctor of coordinating on the meaning of "arthritis." This is necessary in order for us to understand the man who tries to correct the doctor as *being wrong* about how to apply the word "arthritis" in their shared language. When the man tries to correct the doctor's usage, he speaks falsely. Just because the patient does not defer to the doctor does not mean he is speaking his own language. Two people can use a word with the same meaning even when they disagree about how to apply that word, so long as they are engaged in coordinating.

3.2.2 *Different Possible Meanings of "Racist"*

The point of Burge's "arthritis" thought experiment is to show that social externalism is true, that what our words mean and what concepts we use are not fixed by what goes on inside our brains but depend in part on how our community thinks and speaks. Burge invites us to consider what the confused patient *would have meant* by "arthritis" had his community used that word differently. Suppose the doctor and everyone else had applied "arthritis" to a wider variety of ailments than the word is currently applied to, including the very ailment the man had in his thigh. In that case, when he said, "I have arthritis in my thigh," the doctor would say: "Yes, you're right."

Burge points out, first, that we should see the man's statement "I have arthritis in my thigh" as true in this scenario. By the standards of his counterfactual community, including the doctors, he is judged to be speaking truly. We shouldn't assess his statement by *our* standards of veridicality. We should judge it by his community's standards.

Second, we should note that he still does not have (what we call) arthritis in his thigh, since arthritis only occurs in joints. He does not have arthritis in his thigh, yet his sentence "I have arthritis in my thigh" is true. We must conclude "arthritis" does not refer to arthritis in this scenario. It refers to something else. More generally, we conclude that what a person means by a word depends in part on what others in their community use that word to refer to.

The same would seem to hold for the word "racist." We can imagine a counterfactual world in which the word "racist" is not used to express the property that it actually expresses. In this imaginary world "racism" does not refer to racism. Instead, it refers to anything that makes explicit mention of race. In this alternate possible world, the word "racist" is veridically applied to racially discriminatory affirmative action, to Black Lives Matter, and to cases of anti-white prejudice. So in this alternate universe, when John McClane says, "You're a racist! You don't like me 'cause I'm white!" he speaks truly. When counterfactual Ben Shapiro says, "The Obama administration is racist," his sentence is true, given the counterfactual meaning of "racist." And when Trump calls Ocasio-Cortez "racist," he speaks truly in this other possible world.

Note that in this counterfactual scenario, by stipulation, all the facts about structural oppression are exactly as they are in the actual world. All the truths about racism in this counterfactual world are therefore just the same as they are here, given that racism is a kind of structural oppression. So it is not true even in this counterfactual world that Zeus Carver is racist for despising John McClane on account of his whiteness, even though McClane's sentence "You're a racist!" is true in the language he speaks.[4]

---

[4] Note this example may be confusing for any reader who believes that prejudice against white people counts as racist. The example is itself situated against the background theory that racism is race-based oppression, and since the Black man from Harlem's prejudicial attitude of mistrust and dislike of the white cop does not contribute to the racial oppression of the white cop, his prejudice does not count as racist.

The difference in the truth-value of his sentence is entirely due to the fact that "racist" has a different meaning in that world. Likewise, the Obama administration was not racist in the counterfactual world, even though Shapiro's statement "The Obama administration is racist" was true. All the facts about racism are exactly the same, even though the truth-conditions of sentences employing "racist" are different.

I haven't explained why the words "racist" and "racism" have different meanings in this counterfactual scenario. I've simply stipulated that the counterfactual community does use those words with different meanings. Burge does not fill in the details about how and why the word "arthritis" acquired a different meaning in the counterfactual scenario either. I've left those details out of the counterfactual about an alternate meaning of "racist." But note that such a difference in meaning seems to be possible. There's no intrinsic feature of the physical syntactic item "racist"—nothing about the printed shape made of ink or about the sound we make when we say the word—that entails it should be used to refer to racism. It might have referred to something completely different, like the property of being a person who races cars. It could have even referred to kittens, or anything else.

Since there is no obvious reason why the word "racist" couldn't have had a different meaning, it seems possible that it could have referred to the things Trump and Shapiro apply the word to. It seems "racist" could have been veridically (truthfully) applied in a way that accords with the Die-Hard view of racism, if the linguistic community had used the word differently. Then many statements about racism that are actually false would have been true, given the alternative meaning of "racist," even though facts about racism would have been unchanged.

3.2.3 *From Different Possible Meanings to Different Actual Meanings*

This counterfactual possibility raises the question: couldn't there be a multitude of linguistic communities existing in the actual world? Couldn't there be two communities of people who speak different idiolects of English, one that uses "racist" in accord with the Die-Hard view and one that uses it in accord with the structural oppression view? Suppose that Trump and Shapiro are in one community and Alexandria Ocasio-Cortez is in the other. Then when Trump says, "The Squad is racist," he speaks truly in his language. When Alexandria Ocasio-Cortez says, "Trump's tweet was racist," *she also speaks truly*, given what her word "racist" means. Indeed, many people suppose that the actual world really is like this, that there are many linguistic communities using a common stock of words (sounds, shapes, gestures) with different meanings, and disagreements about "racism" are just semantic disputes between different linguistic communities.

Again, I have not explained how two such communities living in the same reality in close proximity could use the word "racist" differently in these two particular ways. Ultimately, on the view I defend in Chap. 10, they cannot mean different things by "racist" given the social and political realities we actually live in and given the function of language to represent those realities. But it at least *seems* possible that two such communities could exist side by side, one using "racism" in accord with the Die-Hard view and another using it in accord with the structural oppression view. On the semantic corruption model, these groups form distinctive subcommunities of people who don't speak exactly the same language.

When the Die-Hard community uses "racist," the word has in its extension[5] such things as the Obama administration, affirmative action that privileges people of color over whites, and antipathy toward white people qua white people. If Ben Shapiro is part of this Die-Hard community, then when he says, "The Obama administration was racist," he speaks truly, given what "racist" means in his community. Meanwhile, supposing Alexandria Ocasio-Cortez is part of the anti-racist community, when she says, "The Obama administration was not racist," she also speaks truly, given what the word "racist" means in her linguistic community.

3.2.4 The Semantic Corruption Model

The semantic corruption model is a tool for modeling this kind of picture. It describes an ever-changing network of deference relations between all the individuals in a linguistic community, where these deference relations indicate the degree of willingness of each person to conform their verbal behavior to the behavior of others. The networks are dynamic in the sense that the strength of these deference relationships can change over time. A person may begin deferring to one group, but then over time they could shift their allegiance. The meanings of their words change as their

---

[5] The extension of a word is the set of things to which the word may be veridically applied. The concept of extension is part of model-theoretic semantics, which will be presented in more detail in Chap. 5.

deferential attitudes shift to favor one group over another. If we think of this on a large scale, we can represent linguistic subcommunities as networks of individuals who defer to one another and not to members of outgroups. Then the meanings attached to words by linguistic subcommunities can change, too, if and when the whole subcommunity changes its deferential attitudes. The semantic corruption model thus presents a dynamic metasemantics, a theory of how the meanings of words change over time, possibly in different ways for different subcommunities.

On the semantic corruption model, the political debate about racism takes the form of a metasemantic struggle. Each side attempts to spread its own preferred meaning of "racist" by convincing people to join their deference network and by weakening the resolve of those who defer to the group that uses the word differently. As one side becomes victorious over the other, their preferred usage gains total coverage over the whole network. Since they use "racist" to refer to something other than systemic oppression, and since racism is a form of systemic oppression, the Die-Hard group does not use "racist" to refer to racism.

In the possible outcome where Trump and Shapiro's preferred usage of "racist" overtakes the entire network, the word "racist" ceases to refer to racism. This would be a dire outcome, since "racist" functions as an epistemic resource for spreading knowledge about racism and facilitating anti-racist initiatives only insofar as it refers to racism. If those who are opposed to anti-racist initiatives manage to coopt the term "racist" and put it to their own uses, corrupting the semantics of the term so that it no longer refers to racism, that would be a severe blow to anti-racist movements.

Some people command more deference than others. Those who wield a lot of metasemantic influence will appear within the network as nodes that attract strong deference arrows. Call these people *deference magnets*. They play a bigger role in determining the semantics of the language than those who attract less deference from others. Sometimes people act as deference magnets in virtue of being seen as experts in a given domain of discourse. But often deference magnets are just popular figures who command deference through popularity and exposure rather than by virtue of some special claim to knowledge. They may just be eloquent speakers, or they may be speakers who are good at playing upon fears and biases. For example, when Ben Shapiro asserts that trans women are men with a mental illness, he is acting as a strong deference magnet even though he is not an expert on gender. He's a deference magnet even though in fact he does not know what he's talking about. Sometimes deference magnetism is facilitated by argumentation and evidence, but perhaps more commonly it is simply a matter of having a public presence, a loud voice, playing to people's fears, biases, and misconceptions, and making assertions over and over again within the public sphere.

On the semantic corruption model, the struggle for control over the meaning of a word is largely a contest of strength between opposing deference magnets. As individuals use words in opposing ways, they affect the ways in which others within the community use their words. When Shapiro talks or writes about how the Obama administration was "racist," his actions reinforce the strength of the Die-Hard network of deference relations. He can draw people into the Die-Hard network. He can also weaken the resolve of less strongly committed members of the anti-racism network, by convincing them directly or by altering the usage of others throughout the total deference network. As the total usage pattern shifts toward the Die-Hard usage, "racist" and "racism" come to express concepts chosen by the dominant white population that has a vested interest in ignoring, obscuring, and delegitimating concerns about racism conceived as structural oppression against people of color.

On the semantic corruption, we find that the meanings of words and the truth conditions of sentences differ with respect to who is asserting those sentences, what their political affiliations are, and what their political agendas are aimed at. Thus, the semantic corruption model entails a kind of poststructuralism about truth and meaning. Public debates over the nature of racism and gender are largely a matter of group stipulation, backed by social power and situated by politics. Truth is relativized to different political factions. Everyone speaks truly even when they appear to disagree with one another because everyone is speaking their own language. And there is no way for empirical evidence to bear on the propositions being debated because everyone's beliefs are analytic, true in virtue of the meanings of the words used to express them, in accord with the beliefs of the political faction to which the speaker belongs.

3.3 Looking Ahead

In the next chapter, I introduce a number of objections to the semantic corruption model. These objections then motivate a different approach to the metasemantics of politically contested terminology, on which the semantics of English expressions are closely tied to what an ideal version of the actual linguistic community would use the words to mean. On the view I will propose, we defer not to any actual community, but to the best possible version of our historically located linguistic community, where the best possible version of our community is characterized both epistemically and politically. The linguistic usage of the ideal linguistic community tracks what is actually the case; its members are well-informed about the domains they talk about; active ignorance and misinformation have been eliminated; and their usage patterns reflect these facts. It is because we all defer to such an idealized community—because we aim at it in our linguistic practices and correct one another and accept corrections with the aim of bringing it about—that our actual community is in fact unified in using a single semantically interpreted language. On this view words already mean what they should mean, because what they actually mean is a function of how they should be used.

Of course, different political factions will disagree about what an ideal version of our linguistic community looks like. They disagree about how words should be used. They disagree about the reality we live in and about what needs representing. They disagree about what constitutes information and misinformation. They disagree about what social and political institutions are based on misinformation and ignorance. Because different factions disagree about how an ideal linguistic community would use their words, they will disagree about the actual meanings of words in the shared language. But this disagreement does not entail that there is no single unified community, nor does it rule out our speaking a single language with shared meanings.

Even where we have intractable political disagreements over these things, someone can be objectively correct in their understanding of reality and someone can be objectively misled. Disagreement only guarantees that both cannot be right. Even though there may be irresolvable disputes, there is a truth that transcends the embattled perspectives locked in disagreement. This truth includes the true semantic theory for the language and the true metasemantic theory that determines its characteristics.

References

Anderson, D. (2020). Linguistic Hijacking. *Feminist Philosophy Quarterly*, 6(3) https://doi.org/10.5206/fpq/2020.3.8162

Burge, T. (1979). Individualism and the Mental. *Midwest Studies in Philosophy*, 4, 73–121.

Collins, P. H. (2002). *Black Feminist Thought: Knowledge, Consciousness, and the Politics of Empowerment.* Routledge.

Crenshaw, K. W. (1988). Race, Reform, and Retrenchment: Transformation and Legitimation in Antidiscrimination Law. *Harvard Law Review, 101,* 1331–1387.

Kendi, I. X. (2019). *How To be an Antiracist.* One World.

Shapiro, B. (2010). Obama's Race War. *Creators.* Retrieved January 30, 2021, from https://www.creators.com/read/ben-shapiro/07/10/obamas-race-war

CHAPTER 4

Toward a Conception of Misinformation as Epistemic Violence

This chapter presents four objections to the semantic corruption model. The focus of these objections is that, on the semantic corruption model, hijacking misuses are represented as veridical. If the semantic corruption model is correct, then Trump's statements about what is "racist" count as true. Consequently, the semantic corruption model supports a kind of poststructuralism where differences in politics reliably produce differences in meanings of words and truth of statements.

The objections point toward a different model, what I call the *epistemic violence model*, on which misuses of "racist" such as Trump's are false, and the debate over racism is primarily an epistemic struggle—a struggle between knowledge and ignorance—rather than a metasemantic struggle over the meanings of words. The last section of this chapter briefly outlines what an epistemic violence model looks like. I then go on to develop this view in later chapters.

While the objections of this chapter are framed in terms of the semantic corruption model, they can be deployed against any metasemantic theory that renders true the false statements (what I will later call controlling propositions) that constitute ideological support for interlocking systems of oppression that include white supremacy, patriarchy, neoliberal capitalist domination, and cis-heterosexual supremacy. For example, the view advocated by Carnap (1936, 1950) that each of us is free to stipulate our own linguistic frameworks is also indicted by these objections.[1]

4.1 The Semantic Data Objection

We don't come up with a metasemantic theory apropos of nothing. Our theorizing must be based on data. The data for metasemantic theorizing is our judgments about the semantic properties of sentences and expressions. Chapter 9 presents a thorough defense of this principle. An acceptable metasemantic theory must comport with our most confident judgments about which statements are true and which are false. It must render as true those statements we're most certain are true, and it must render as false those we're most certain are false.

We must therefore be concerned with the question: what are the crucial semantic data upon which to base our metasemantic beliefs? Arguably one such crucial datum is the following fact. When Ben Shapiro said, "The Obama administration is racist," he spoke falsely. Further semantic data include the fact that Shapiro believed falsely that the Obama administration was racist and that he spread that false belief to a number of people or affirmed and reinforced it among his followers. A metasemantic theory that tells us he spoke and believed truly would misrepresent these semantic facts. But this is just what the semantic corruption model does.

Likewise, it is a semantic datum that Ocasio-Cortez spoke truly when she tweeted that Trump's "telling four American Congresswomen of color 'go back to your own country,' is hallmark language of white supremacists," and asserts that this behavior is an instance of "outright racism." In Chap. 2, I argued that these claims are straightforwardly true. Therefore, the correct metasemantics should entail that her statements are true. The semantic corruption model gets this part right.

But another datum is the falsity of Trump's charge that Ocasio-Cortez and the other members of 'The Squad' are racist. The semantic corruption model gets this one wrong. It delivers the verdict that Trump spoke truly when he called Ocasio-Cortez racist. But he didn't. The falsity of Trump's misuse of the word "racist" is a fundamentally important semantic datum.

---

[1] For an in-depth criticism of Carnap's principle of tolerance along these lines, see my article "Restricting Logical Tolerance" Anderson, forthcoming in *Minnesota Studies in Philosophy of Science*.

It is an example of the kind of misrepresentation of racism that undergirds the continuity and perpetual re-establishment of white supremacist power within the social fabric.

Yet another datum is the fact that Trump willfully misunderstands the concept of racism and hijacks the word to spread false beliefs and misinformation about who is being racist, partly in order to deflect blame from himself. The semantic corruption model gets this datum wrong, too. It represents Trump as spreading true beliefs—although these beliefs are not about who is being racist since his word "racist" does not denote racists. An acceptable metasemantic model should represent Trump as speaking falsely because hijacking misuses are inaccurate. They constitute misinformation, and misinformation should not be conflated with truth.

Taking these points to be crucial data, they stack up against the semantic corruption model. Further data can be collected across the spectrum of political discourse. Every false statement made by bigots, transphobes, racists, misogynists, and xenophobes counts as data against the semantic corruption model insofar as that model renders those people as speaking truly. For example, the statement "women don't have penises" is false if a trans inclusive theory of gender is true. If trans women really are women, then some women have penises. The fact that the sentence "women don't have penises" is false but circulates widely and is made to function as if it were true by the socially embedded institutions that adjudicate which sentences are true (see Chap. 7 for extended discussion) is part of the explanation for the prevalence of trans exclusionary ideology. These kinds of trans exclusionary statements are sources of misinformation and as such should be represented as false within an accurate semantics for English. That means any metasemantics that delivers a semantics on which they are true—such as the semantic corruption model—fails to capture the semantic facts.

These considerations suggest a general epistemic constraint on metasemantic theorizing. An acceptable metasemantics must respect first-order moral and political commitments that are sufficiently firm. Our judgments about moral and political truths, as we actually make them with respect to moral and political discourse, are already interpreted. They already have semantic features. These interpretations serve as evidence in assessing metasemantic theories. A metasemantic theory is only justified insofar as it adequately captures our most firmly held first-order commitments to truth in the language under consideration, for these are the data that drive the theory. I call this the *general metasemantic adequacy* constraint. I will argue for it in detail in Chap. 9.

From this general constraint it follows that whoever has strong moral and political commitments about correct applications of "racist" and "racism" also has strong epistemic reasons to reject any metasemantic theory that conflicts with those commitments. The semantic corruption model entails that certain contentious statements, for example, certain tokens of "Affirmative action is racist," come out true. So, this can constitute an epistemic reason to reject that model.

4.1.1   Metalinguistic Negotiation?

Let us consider a reply to this objection, which I raised in Anderson (2020). The reply appeals to widespread tacit metalinguistic negotiation (Plunkett & Sundell, 2013) to defuse the semantic data objection. Metalinguistic negotiation occurs when two or more parties to a dispute use a crucial word with different meanings and attempt to convince the other side to adopt their own usage—more or less just what the semantic corruption model entails. *Tacit* metalinguistic negotiation occurs when the disputants act as if, and perhaps believe, that they are conducting a first-order debate. They think and act as if they are debating, for example, what racism *is*, when really the debate is a negotiation about what "racism" should be used to mean. A tacit negotiation has the appearance of being conducted in a shared language, when actually the participants are using words with different meanings.

If most political debates are tacit metalinguistic negotiations, then the semantic data are not what they appear to be. The data appear to go against the semantic corruption model, but they don't. The judgment that Trump speaks falsely when he calls Alexandria Ocasio-Cortez racist is in error if Trump and Ocasio-Cortez are engaged in tacit metalinguistic negotiation. Likewise, the judgment that Ben Shapiro speaks falsely when he says that trans women are men fails to be data if he is really engaged in tacit metalinguistic negotiation. Generalizing, naïve judgments about truth and falsity in political speech are mostly mistaken if everyone is tacitly engaged in metalinguistic negotiation. If tacit metalinguistic negotiation is widespread, then the semantic data are not what they seem. They are actually in support of the semantic corruption model. The presupposition that there is widespread tacit metalinguistic negotiation thus provides the semantic corruption model with some defense against the semantic data objection.

This was the reply to the semantic data objection I defended in Anderson (2020). Now I am going to counter my own defense of the semantic corruption model.

Merely claiming that the data are an illusion is not convincing absent a strong reason to believe that appearances are not what they seem. The metalinguistic negotiation presupposition entails massive widespread error in semantic judgment. Why should we automatically assume that our most natural and most politically invested semantic judgments are in error? Absent a compelling *error theory*—a theory which explains why our ordinary judgments are massively incorrect—the tacit metalinguistic negotiation thesis has no legs to stand on. Why would we expect that everyone's naïve semantic judgments are systematically and fundamentally in error? Without some independent reason for believing that tacit negotiation is the norm, we should take semantic judgments at face value. This means treating those judgments as data.

Further, as I will argue in Chap. 5, we should be committed to a principle which I call the *informed speaker constraint*, which says that semantic judgments only count as data if they are coming from people we take to know what they are talking about with respect to the subject under discussion. Anyone committed to intersectionality theory has strong reason to treat false speech about things such as racism and gender as important semantic data, because they have strong reason to see such statements as sources of false belief and misinformation.

I believe there are other strong reasons to reject the metalinguistic negotiation hypothesis. These reasons are connected with the remaining three objections to the semantic corruption model, the actual practice objection (Sect. 4.2), the role of truth objection (Sect. 4.3), and the democracy as a space of reasons objection (Sect. 4.4), which each gives reasons to reject the semantic corruption model. These additional objections to the semantic corruption model serve to bolster the case made by the semantic data objection by providing further reasons to reject the metalinguistic negotiation defense of the semantic corruption model.

4.2 The Actual Practice Objection

In the course of politically heated disagreement, we do not act as if we speak a different language than our opponents speak. We don't act as if we merely disagree about semantics. When a debate over racism or gender arises, the two sides will rarely conduct their argument in terms of semantics. We almost always take ourselves to be arguing for the truth of what we believe and the falsity of what our opponent believes in terms of non-semantic facts. We act as if we disagree about what racism *is*. Our actual practice presupposes that the truth of our view entails the falsity of our opponent's view. This is closely tied to the point of engaging in debate at all. The truth has a bearing on what we should do and arguing about what is true is relevant to our personal and political decision-making. Our actual practices of political argumentation reflect our commitment to this principle.

A defender of the Die-Hard view of racism—the view that says racism includes any and all race-based oppression—will ask for an explanation: how can discrimination against white people not be racist? This is not a request for a semantic theory of the word "racist" but a request for a rebuttal of the Die-Hard view of racism itself. They think race-based discrimination really is racist, and anti-racism advocates deny the truth of their theory of racism. The defender of the Die-Hard view typically cites features of what they perceive to be anti-white racism with the intention of showing that it is racist in accord with the public meaning of the word "racist." They are not interested in arguing for their own distinct meaning of "racist." They do sometimes claim that anti-racism advocates are trying to change the meaning of "racist," but even this rhetorical move presupposes that, in the first instance, we are speaking a shared language with a shared meaning, and the appropriate response for anti-racism advocates is to deny that any meaning change is under discussion.

Skeptics of trans gender identities will typically make assertions about what men and women *are*. They will argue that men and women have certain biological features by their very essence. They are not ready and willing to adopt a postmodernist view on which their preferred use of "woman" as a biological kind is merely one option, a stipulation undertaken by their community. They think trans equality advocates have false beliefs about gender and speak falsely when they talk about gender. They see conversations as occurring in the common language of both cis and trans people. They presuppose that "woman" means one and only one thing in English, viz. a person with certain biological features.[2]

---

[2] See Bettcher (2013) on what she calls single-meaning positions. Bettcher argues that multiple meaning positions—views on which there are more than one meaning for gender terms, some trans exclusionary and some trans inclusive—are inherently liberatory precisely because multiple meaning positions deny that "woman," for example, has only one meaning.

There is a reason our discourse tends to focus on first-order facts rather than semantics. We care about the metaphysical reality much more than we care about semantics. The only real relevance of semantics is its function of getting us coordinated in our investigation of reality. As long as we can be relatively sure we are 'onto' the same phenomenon, our primary concern is the discussion of the reality that our linguistic representations function to represent. Semantic debates are very rare outside philosophical discourse. If an argument appears to devolve into semantics, it is usually abandoned in frustration.

This is also why opponents of social justice movements will often try to turn substantive debates into semantic ones by claiming that our dispute is merely about the meanings of words. Such a move disrupts the force of the argument in a way that protects the status quo.

Sometimes politics does turn explicitly to semantics, but even then it is not usually understood as a case of metalinguistic negotiation. When an anti-trans agitator claims that trans people use the word "woman" incorrectly, they do not see themselves as trying to get trans women to change what they mean by "woman." Rather, they are claiming that trans women speak falsely and apply the word "woman" inaccurately by the shared standards of English. Their 'semantic assent' is aimed at claiming that the trans identity advocate is misusing the word "woman." They are attempting to correct that misusage, in something like the way the doctor tries to correct the confused man's usage of "arthritis." The trans exclusionary enforcers take themselves to stand with the full community of adept English users in rejecting the trans woman's use of "woman." Likewise, if a defender of the Die-Hard view of racism turns his attention to semantics, it is much more likely he will take himself to be correcting the anti-racist's usage of "racist," as opposed to introducing a new and different meaning of "racist" for his opponent to consider adopting.

When arguing over the interpretation of words, we appeal to common practices, to historical precedents, to unambiguous cases, and to pragmatic considerations, in much the same way as interpretations of law are

I agree that multiple meaning positions have some strategic value, but my approach here is guided more by the strategic value in labeling transphobic speech as false, as misinformation, as ideological distortions that facilitate active ignorance about gender. My single-meaning position does not grant that mainstream transphobic enforcers speak truly. My single-meaning position also entails that trans women are paradigm cases of women, given the meaning of "woman," even though their status as such is regularly denied due to active ignorance.

conducted. When interpreting a law, we do not usually take ourselves to be establishing by fiat what the words mean; rather, we typically treat interpretation of the law as a rational process of sousing out what the language of the law *already* means. What the law already means has something to do with how it should be applied in present and future cases. I take it that political disputes around word meanings typically proceed in a similar fashion. We argue about what words now mean by appealing in part to how they should be used. We implicitly aim at pushing our community to act linguistically as a better possible version of itself, but this is part and parcel with taking our words to presently already mean what they would mean when deployed by this more ideal community. Chapter 10 goes into much more detail about this conception of metasemantics, which is a version of what I call ideal language metasemantics. I will argue that ideal language metasemantics is appropriate for an intersectional theory of objective truth. I will argue that our actual practice already works this way.

The semantic corruption model is *revisionary* with respect to our ordinary conception of political argumentation. It attempts to revise the way we ordinarily conceive of political discourse. It goes against common practice in that it represents the goals and activities of common practice as something other than what they are normally taken to be. A revisionary account should not be accepted without strong reason.

This also provides additional force for the semantic data objection. A defender of the semantic corruption model can't simply point to the *mere possibility* of widespread tacit metalinguistic negotiation to diffuse the semantic data objection. They have to give us some good, substantive reasons to believe that such tacit negotiations really are widespread, because such a presupposition contradicts our actual practices.

4.3 The Role of Truth Objection

There is a venerable tradition dating back to Socrates that sees truth as deeply important to politics in a way the semantic corruption model seemingly eschews. From the Socratic perspective, both the knowledgeable and the benighted have the same thing in mind when they enter into philosophical debate, even if one or both parties are hopelessly confused.

When Socrates confuses Euthyphro about his conception of piety and thereby calls into question Euthyphro's decision to prosecute his own father, Socrates is pointing out that Euthyphro lacks an understanding of piety itself. He convinces him that this fact should make him doubt the justification he thinks he has for his action. For Socrates, having false beliefs is often of great moral and political importance. A critic in the spirit of Socrates would refuse to abandon the presupposition that there is a truth about racism that is under discussion when people engage in conceptual debates using the word "racism" and that knowledge of racism as well as false beliefs about it have moral and political significance. Knowing truths about racism is important for deciding what to do about racism, and confronting ignorance about racism is crucial for dismantling racist institutions.[3]

A Socratic philosopher should want a model of political discourse that gives discussion of racism the kind of significance it would have in a Platonic dialogue. We should be concerned with the nature of racism, not the meaning of the word "racism." The semantic corruption model is incompatible with this kind of significance because it represents disagreements over racism (or "racism") as disagreements not about the nature of racism itself but only as a battle over semantics.

The Socratic view of truth suggests a certain view of semantics, where ascertaining the meaning of a word is part and parcel with ascertaining the highest knowledge of the subject matter at hand. In Euthyphro, Socrates ultimately argues that neither he nor Euthyphro adequately knows what piety is. This must be compatible with the word "piety" referring to piety, even when no one knows quite what piety is. We can reach a state of aporia while still talking about the same thing. Our language must therefore be capable of representing things no one quite understands, and moreover, we must be capable of talking about the very same thing which neither of us quite understands.

It's not that Socrates and Euthyphro have no clue at all what piety is. They both understand it to a limited extent, enough to be able to identify some cases of piety as uncontentious. Relatedly, both Socrates and Euthyphro take themselves to have enough knowledge to ascertain that they do not quite know what piety is. This requires that they know at least that there is something, namely piety, about which they are confused.

In like fashion, disagreements over the nature of racism or gender are crucially guided by presuppositions about at least some cases. Parties to

---

[3] To be sure, truths about racism are truths about socially constructed realities, but these truths are not constructed purely by usage patterns of the word "racism" or the concept it expresses. Racism has its own existence, independent of linguistic behavior.

the dispute take themselves and their opponents to be 'onto' the same topic and establish this fact by agreeing on some fundamental points, usually some particular cases that are not in dispute. While most debates over racism or gender do not end up in a state of aporia (instead, both parties typically leave the conversation thinking they are right and the other side is hopelessly confused and misinformed), there is always the sense that one side is mistaken or lacking knowledge of the objective truth of the matter under discussion.

There is a crucial duality, which we can call *accuracy duality*. The search for the answer to the question 'what is piety' would also lead to a clearer understanding of the meaning of the word "piety" and a firmer grasp of what it takes to deploy that word veridically. We learn how to apply a word more accurately by learning more about that to which the word refers. Likewise, if one wants to understand more clearly what the word "racism" means, or if one wants to ascertain more clearly who is in the extension of "woman," the best ways to go about gaining that clearer understanding are to learn more about racism and gender, respectively.

Knowledge of reality is not completely disconnected from knowledge of semantics. Knowledge of reality informs our knowledge of semantics. The confusion comes when we put the cart before the horse and start talking about understanding the meanings of words without centering the question of how we understand that to which the words refer.

Truth matters because knowledge of reality matters. Knowledge of reality facilitates true thought and speech, which in turn enables accurate transmission and reproduction of knowledge. This connection between increasing knowledge of reality and increasing accuracy of linguistic usage is crucial to the Socratic conception of political discourse. If all of politics is merely the construction of semantic truths with no connection to an extra-linguistic reality, then political dispute is *merely* semantic. If a dispute is merely semantic, it ceases to participate in accuracy duality. There is no way for knowledge of reality to facilitate true thought and speech, since the truth of thought and speech is in some sense merely stipulated truth.

It is part of our deep political commitment to truth that we take our political initiatives and governmental objectives to be guided and constrained by truth. In a society that is organized so that truth governs, the debate over what the society should do is informed by what it takes to be the case—what in its best judgment it thinks is true.

Plato most clearly articulated this goal for political organization in *The Republic*. He argued that society should be run by philosopher kings, but not because philosophers should get to tell people what to do, but rather because the truth should tell people what to do. And not just the truth about contingent physical reality but also the truth about what is good and right. Philosophers are, on Plato's understanding, the people who are most centrally interested in and capable of ascertaining the truths that are relevant to running the society and so should be in charge for that reason. In today's modern democracies, we do not govern by the assumption that philosophers are the best channel for determining the truth about the world and what we should do (and for good reason). But the fundamental principle is the same. We attempt to organize our institutions so that our political decisions are based on what is true.

The semantic corruption model violates accuracy duality. There is no sense in which knowledge of the reality of racism is a proper guide to use of the word "racist," since anyone may use that word however they wish so long as they are able to find a community that supports their preferred usage. Accuracy is merely a matter of conforming one's usage to one's community. There is no standard of accuracy generated by reality itself. The fact of what racism is has no bearing on how one should use the word "racist." Insofar as accuracy duality is an important desideratum for a metasemantic theory, the semantic corruption model is unacceptable.

By the same token, the semantic corruption model misrepresents the way in which our social institutions are designed to be truth responsive. Our arguments about the nature of racism and gender are part of the political process because we aim to organize our society to be responsive to what racism and gender really are. Of course, there are deep disagreements about what racism and gender are, and these are part and parcel with deep disagreements over how to organize the society. But on the semantic corruption model, the disagreements we are having are not about the reality of racism or gender or how we should organize our society in response to these realities. Instead, they are merely power struggles over the meanings of words.

4.3.1 *Turning from Truth to Ontology?*

A proponent of the semantic corruption model can attempt to reply to this objection by shifting the focus from truth onto ontology.[4] Truth is a property of representations—viz. those representations that correspond

---

[4] I developed this defense in Anderson (2020).

with reality. Ontology is the tabulation of things and properties that exist in reality, without any special concern for representation.

The defender of the semantic corruption model can say: the focus of Socratic dialogue is really all about ontology. Truth is only derivatively important. We care primarily about what racism *is*. After we determine the reality of racism, we should not really care if someone speaks truly by using "racism" to refer to something other than racism. Perhaps the word "racism" is ambiguous: Trump uses it with one meaning and Ocasio-Cortez with another. This does not undermine the value of having true beliefs *about racism* (as Ocasio-Cortez does), nor does it diminish the badness of Trump's active ignorance *about racism*, not knowing truths about racism, even as he speaks truly about what he calls "racism."

On the semantic corruption model, the semantic features of the word "racism" change, but those changes do not alter the ontology of racism. Linguistic hijackings of "racist" do not change the facts about what is racist. They only change what people mean by "racist." This is bad precisely because it undermines peoples' ability to think and speak truly *about racism*. Thus, the defender of the semantic corruption model can try to make the case that while the semantic corruption model does not support accuracy duality, it does provide a way of thinking about the importance of reality in political thought. The struggle is not merely about who gets to stipulate the popular meaning of "racist." It is more centrally about what aspects of the real ontology are represented in thought and speech.

But this reply actually highlights the sense in which disputes over veridical uses of "racism" and "woman" really are first-order disputes, for those disputes are straightforwardly concerned with ontology. When Trump and Ocasio-Cortez disagree, their disagreement is centered on what racism *really is*. Ocasio-Cortez is making a claim that draws on her view of what racism really is, while Trump denies that he is racist and really thinks she is.[5] They are not primarily concerned with the meaning of the word, nor is there any sign that they are using the word with different meanings. Given that they are focused on debating ontology, it seems they must be engaging in a coordinated conversation about a certain ontological question: the nature of racism. Their disagreement is aimed at racism, so it

---

[5] Someone might argue that Trump actually knows what racism is but is playing ignorant anyway for rhetorical effect. This may be true. The debate is still concerned with first-order truths.

clearly makes sense to ascribe racism as the content of the word "racism" as each uses it.

On the other hand, if they are not jointly talking about racism but engaging in metalinguistic negotiation, then how can the ontologist's reply to the objection be sustained? If we ascribe different meanings to their respective uses of "racism," then how can we understand them as debating about ontology? But if we understand them as debating about ontology, as the reply suggests we should, then we cannot see them as engaging in a purely metalinguistic negotiation as the semantic corruption model would require. The turn from truth to ontology reply thus does not help the semantic corruption model.

4.4 THE DEMOCRACY AS A SPACE OF REASONS OBJECTION

Socratic dialogue aimed at truth is not only knowledge for the sake of knowledge. Dialogue is also social and political activity. It is aimed at determining the course of action for the society via the exchange of reasons.

Democratic social organization requires coordination on goals and actions through dialogue. At least part of this process involves rational discourse, along with political bargaining and compromising (and surely many other less scrupulous things like lying, misinforming, and obfuscating in order to promote the interests of the dominant group). In the rational discourse, each participant endeavors to explain why their preferred course of action should be taken. Even where rational discourse is only nominally guiding the democratic will, the central activity is the giving of reasons for and against various courses of action.

Lynch (2012) defends this view that democracy is a *space of reasons*, a term he attributes to Wilfred Sellars et al. (1997). Lynch writes,

> To say that democracy is a space of reasons is to say that the practice of democratic politics requires the practice of giving and acting for reasons. That is, in the democratic state, disagreements between citizens ought to be handled in the arena of reason alone, and arguments legitimizing uses of state power must be backed by reasons. And crucially, the "reasons" spoke of are reasons for believing what is *true*, as opposed to reasons for believing what will win us the election, make us rich or damn our enemies.

I don't mean to take on the full scope of Lynch's thesis here. Specifically, I don't think it is crucial to defend the idea that reason *alone* is the proper way to resolve disagreements or that truth must be the *only* proper guide for democratic political action. For one thing, there is a question about which truths the society ought to represent and respond to. This is a pragmatic issue about which truths we decide are important to us, which truths we care to act on. There are many truths that are irrelevant to our society, like how many grains of sand are on Mars. We have to decide which truths are relevant, and there may be an element of pragmatism there. There is a related pragmatic question about which properties we should use our words to refer to; as I will argue later, our word meanings depend on how an ideal version of our linguistic community would apply its terms, and this is partially a pragmatic question concerning which properties are most pragmatically important for the society to represent using its language. But even more generally, there may be pragmatic reasons for doing things that are left undecided by knowing all the truths.

Later, Lynch presents a less stringent role for truth in the democratic process: "Our political reasons … must be given against a common background of standards against which we measure what counts as true and false." Presupposing a common background of standards for ascertaining truth is consistent with allowing other factors to help guide democratic action. Presupposing standards entails only that the participants in a democracy have a significant level of agreement about what reality is like and about how to assess the truth and falsity of various claims.

Even this may be going too far as a criterion of a functioning democracy, as there could be massive disagreement about what the proper standards of evaluation are. This can happen especially when different political factions have massively different background theories; for example, when a large chunk of the population is in the grip of an expansive and false conspiracy theory. But even under such conditions, an objective concept of truth is relevant for directing democratic action. After all, conspiracy theorists believe their conspiracy theory is *true* and want to take action on that basis.

In its most relaxed form, we can take Lynch's thesis to be: there is an important role for truth in democracy insofar as the application of the concept of truth is treated as of great importance for directing democratic action, and in order for the concept of truth to play this role, we must also engage in a collective epistemological project of ascertaining which guides to truth are to be trusted. We recognize that disagreements about the proper standards of evaluation are important precisely because truth matters so centrally in democratic politics.

It is because truth is a guiding ideal that recent attacks on our traditional socially and politically supported standards of truth and justification are perceived as so corrosive to the political process.[6] The architects of post-truth politics are deeply aware of the importance of truth and perceive the willingness of their political constituency to adopt standards of evaluation that more closely align with their political goals. Surely this can be a cause for cynicism about the role of truth in democracy, but I think the central takeaway is that control over the standards of truth and justification is crucial to political struggle due to the central role that truth plays as a guiding ideal for democratic action. It's because truth is so important to democracy that post-truth politics within a democracy is so dangerous.

We make claims about what is the case and these claims are seen as a legitimate guide to action only insofar as they are taken to be true. In concerns over racism, this manifests as attempts to show what is true and what is false about the nature and extent of racism in order to guide political action. The truth or falsity of the claim that affirmative action is racist matters as to whether affirmative action should be practiced. In concerns about gender, the truth of the claim that trans women really are women underlies every initiative to include trans women in women's spaces. Convincing people of the truth or falsity of a proposition underlying a political initiative is a crucial part of the process of enacting that initiative. This is, on my view, what it is to conceive of democracy as a space of reasons.

The other side of this coin, which is of equal if not greater significance, is that ideological misinformation, propaganda, racist and sexist controlling images (Collins, 2002), and other forms of active ignorance are potent engines of injustice and oppression precisely because they present falsities as if they were true. In Chap. 8, I will argue that misinformation and active ignorance are the lifeblood of interlocking systems of oppression. The primary role of intersectional critical theory is to challenge the misinformation, misconceptions, and oppressive false definitions that are circulated and supported through the institutions that we as a society rely on to ascertain truth in the service of politics. We can infer from the falsity of such ideological misrepresentations, which are made to function as true,

---

[6] See, for example, McIntyre (2018).

that any metasemantics assigning truth to such misrepresentations is out of accord with an intersectional theory of reality.

Now if the semantic corruption model is accepted, the debate about racism is transformed into a struggle over semantics. But insofar as the debate is construed as merely a battle over the meaning of "racism," conversations about "racism" lose their political force. That is because arguing for a semantic interpretation of a word does not provide the kind of motivating reason necessary for successful engagement in the democratic space of reasons. The fact that "racism" means x rather than y is not in itself a strong reason to enact a policy or pursue a certain course of action. Only facts about racism itself—including what aspects of the society are racist, which action types are racist, what institutions are racist, and so on—can provide the proper kind of reason to motivate addressing those issues. Insofar as anti-racism activists are seen as merely pushing their own preferred semantics of "racism," the debate is divested of most of its political force. Likewise, perhaps, for gender terminology.[7] If trans activists are seen as merely pushing a new, subversive meaning of "woman," their actions may not have the kind of political force needed to motivate democratic action.

Transforming an issue into a merely semantic debate divests it of its political significance. Semantics—that "racism" means x rather than y—are not reasons for political action. When the dialectic around racism reaches the point where it is seen as merely a semantic debate, this is a win for the powers that aim to preserve the status quo. Insofar as the dominant group wishes to resist reforms that would divest them of their power, it is an excellent strategy for them to turn every debate about a political issue into a debate about semantics. The semantic corruption model plays into their hands in this regard.

This objection goes beyond the pragmatics of winning the debate in the public sphere, however. Debates about racism *do* have political significance. They are not merely a matter of maintaining or altering semantic

---

[7] Here I say only *perhaps* the cases are equivalent because there may be important differences. For example, Bettcher (2013) presents the struggle over gender terminology as partly a struggle over the culture surrounding gender ideology. The culture surrounding gender involves the ways gender words are used, and this may be part of what constructs gender itself. So on Bettcher's view the struggle over linguistic usage is partly constitutive of a *metaphysical* struggle over factors that ground the existence and nature of gender. I think this is plausibly very different from struggles over veridical uses of "racism" which have no constitutive bearing on racism itself.

properties. They are a matter of giving substantive first-order reasons for making political changes. The semantic corruption model fails to capture this fact. On that model, none of the participants in a political debate gives each other any first-order reasons for taking democratic action in response to racism. If tacit metalinguistic negotiation is widespread, then even those who appear to be giving each other substantive first-order reasons for political action are actually only contesting for various alternate usage patterns of the term.

4.5 The Epistemic Violence Model

Rather than thinking of the battle over misinformation surrounding gender and racism as a struggle for control over the meanings of words, we should think about misinformation as a means of affecting our shared epistemic lifeways (Dotson, 2014) or what Foucault (1980) calls the *regime of truth* of the society: the collection of ways in which social power operates within a given society and within individuals and groups comprising that society to legitimate certain statements as true and others as false and determines what counts as justification for those statements. To describe misinformation as a source of epistemic violence is to describe it as contributing to an oppressive regime of truth which perpetuates systemic physical violence, exploitation, epistemic oppression, and social, legal, and material inequality.[8]

My account of epistemic violence is an explication of that notion as it arises in post-colonialist studies in the work of Spivak (2003) and developed within analytic philosophy by Dotson (2011, 2014). Spivak cites Foucault as a conceptual starting place. She writes, "Foucault locates epistemic violence, a complete overhaul of the episteme, in the redefinition of sanity at the end of the European eighteenth century." My analysis of linguistic misinformation in terms of epistemic violence does work to unpack and clarify the Foucauldian notion Spivak is working with, the notion of epistemic violence as influence over the episteme.[9]

---

[8] The relationship between epistemic violence and epistemic oppression mirrors the relationship between violence and oppression *simpliciter*, viz. violence is a tool of oppression and oppression involves systematically inflicting violence. Analogously, epistemic violence is a tool of epistemic oppression, and epistemic oppression systematically inflicts epistemic violence.

[9] The epistemic violence model is derived from my readings of Dotson and Foucault, but I do not mean to attribute it to those authors. Specifically, I do not claim that either Dotson

What Foucault (1970, 1980) calls the *episteme* is the collection of apparatuses that determines which knowledge claims count as legitimate within a society at a time. One specific aspect of the *episteme* is the regime of truth, which is concerned specifically with the operation of the concept of truth within a society (Foucault, 1980). The term 'apparatus' is a crucial technical term in Foucault's understanding of social power (Agamben, 2009), which will be unpacked and discussed in detail in Chap. 7. "Apparatus" refers to systems of interconnections between various elements present in the social sphere and that impact and organize our lives. An apparatus is an abstract organization of social power relations that tends to be very heterogeneous in its composition. Our practices of judging truth and falsehood constitute a collection of apparatuses that are manifested and maintained within a social fabric that includes our scientific institutions, our courts, our intelligence communities, our marketing research firms, our schools, our families, our friend groups, our cohorts, and much more.

Take, for example, the apparatus that determines the educational standards and core curricula for grade school children in the US. This apparatus includes academic discourses around education, state laws concerning education standards, review boards and hearings, election campaigns for local and state politicians, academic discourses around content (e.g., the theory of evolution), arguments on social media platforms, journalism, religious organizations aiming to change the standards of education, guiding ideals about the separation of church and state, and indefinitely many other things. To describe an apparatus is to describe how these many heterogeneous elements operate in concert—and not necessarily in harmony—to produce an effect within the social fabric.

The episteme is a very large and abstract apparatus that determines, within a society at a given time, what counts as knowledge and what counts as ignorance according to the society at large. It includes procedures for judging what is true and what is false, procedures for adjudicating which beliefs are justified and which are not, standards for identifying whether a study counts as scientific or pseudoscientific. It coordinates us

---

or Foucault would necessarily accept the metasemantic background assumptions I introduce for this model. Both Foucault and Dotson advocate forms of theoretical disunity, which would allow for the possibility of adopting both the epistemic violence model and the semantic corruption model simultaneously, even though they are in a certain sense incompatible with each other.

about what counts as commonsense and what is not, what propositions can be assumed and what must be argued for, who is an expert, and who is an ignoramus or a charlatan.

The elements of the social epistemic fabric are organized by culture and power. Which channels of information are empowered, and which are diminished, is partly a function of whose perspectives are centered within socially supported epistemic frameworks. The power to control these frameworks is continuous with, and in some sense identical with, the power that is imposed on marginalized groups for the benefit of dominant groups.[10]

Patricia Hill Collins (2002) describes the situation as follows:

> [H]istorically, the differential treatment of U.S. Blacks, women, the working class, and other subordinated groups meant that the United States operated as a nation-state that disproportionately benefited affluent White men. Because this group controls schools, the news media, and other social institutions that legitimate what counts as truth, it possesses the authority to obscure its own power and to redefine its own special interests as being national interests.[11]

This passage both expresses the sense in which misinformation is the lifeblood of oppression and the way in which dominant social power reinforces itself by influencing what counts as true. White power seeks to control social institutions that legitimate what counts as truth in order to obscure the nature of racism, to protect racist ideology from critical inquiry. Dominant power also seeks to possess the authority to obscure its own power to affect what counts as truth. Part of the goal of misinformation is to mask its own effects. Misinformation is only effective insofar as it manages to pass for truth, and this cannot be effectively accomplished when the spread of misinformation is recognized as such as a strategy of power seeking to protect itself.

For all this, Collins is careful not to say that the power of our epistemic institutions actually legislates truth itself. She says that these social

---

[10] For an extensive discussion of closely related themes, see Berenstain et al. (2021), who argue that dominant epistemologies have the power to control, suppress, and even destroy the epistemic life worlds of marginalized groups and cultures in order to support white supremacist colonial heteropatriarchy; they argue that dominant epistemologies function as a means of those systems of domination to exert systemic governmental control.

[11] Collins (2002), pp. 248.

institutions have the power to "legitimate what counts as truth." But legitimating a sentence as true is not the same as making it true. Foucault also is also careful about this. The episteme does not determine what *is* true or false (Foucault, 1980), as I will argue in detail in Chap. 7. It does not, for example, make the theory of evolution true. Evolution is part of reality that exists beyond the effects of our social organization or our socially embedded epistemology. The episteme rather determines whether a society takes the theory of evolution to be true, whether it takes it to be justified on the basis of credible scientific reasoning, whether it is deemed commonsensical or counterintuitive, and whether these things are supported by or run counter to the overall organization of the social sphere, viz. the laws, educational institutions, academic discourses, television programs, standards of commonsense, and so on.

Just as the episteme does not make the theory of evolution true, it also does not *make* it scientifically justified. Rather, it embodies the way in which the society sees the theory as in good or bad scientific standing. Whether a scientific theory really is justified is separate from whether a society takes it to be justified, or whether the socially empowered institutions within the society operate as if the theory were scientifically justified. The episteme influences social coordination about judgments concerning what is scientific, what is rational, what is intuitive, what is commonsensical, including social coordination in the form of political or governmental action. Scientific theories regarding human-caused climate change may be objectively accurate, and belief in climate change may be objectively justified, even within societies where those beliefs are not socially sanctioned, are widely regarded with suspicion, and in which the truth of climate change fails to inform any political or governmental action.

Is the theory of racism as structural oppression taken to be a scientific theory or as a semantic stipulation? Is it viewed as commonsensical or as counterintuitive? Is the belief that racism is a form of structural oppression widely assumed to be rational within the discourse of our present society? These are sociological questions. They are concerned with how the society on the whole responds to the ideas of critical race theory. Answers to these questions do not entail anything about whether the anti-racist understanding of racism really is true, or scientific, or rational, and so on. Struggle over the sociologically embedded episteme is not struggle for control over truth itself, but rather over the sociological factors that lend legitimacy to some views of racism over others.

Is the nature of gender settled by the biological sciences? Is it counterintuitive to think that women can have penises? Is it irrational for someone who lived the first fifteen years of life as a man to suddenly perceive herself as a woman? The regime of truth determines the socially accepted answers to these questions. It coordinates the masses in their epistemic deliberations. It does not, however, determine whether gender *really is* biological or social or something else. It only determines how the various answers to these questions are supported or opposed by the organization of social power relations.

The episteme and the regime of truth—the part of the episteme concerned with the way the concept of truth interacts with social power throughout the society—exist on an ontologically vast scale. They permeate psychology, culture, law, economics, scholarship, journalism, entertainment, media, education, politics, and more. They include rules of accreditation for institutions of learning, procedures for conferring titles of knowledge on individuals (such as PhDs or MDs), procedures for granting tenure, learning objectives in lower and higher education as well as the political pressures that determine those objectives, prevailing opinions of genius, unconscious criteria of evaluations of credibility among speakers, and much more. The regime of truth exists on an order of ontological magnitude comparable to capitalism or patriarchy. An exhaustive list of its components and aspects would be all but impossible.

Linda Tuhiwai Smith describes the regime of truth as implicated in the colonization of Indigenous land and the subjugation of Indigenous peoples through the weaponization of science and philosophy in ways that enable and justify imperialism and colonization (Smith, 2013). The natural world and the natural social order are made to appear as if Indigenous colonized populations are epistemically less advanced, more primitive than European settlers, which in turn justifies treating Indigenous groups as objects of study, as artifacts of the natural history of Europeans qua 'more advanced' humans. These practices are tied to white supremacy and patriarchy, which draw power from the social epistemic apparatus and work to maintain its configuration. By undermining Indigenous knowledge that threatens to upend the status quo, the regime of truth supports what Tuck and Yang (2012) call *settler moves to innocence*, the epistemic practices that justify the continuation in perpetuity of white settler appropriation of Indigenous land.

Misuses of language perpetuate linguistic hijacking, spread and reinforce stereotypes and controlling images (Collins, 2002), and draw on epistemic power (Dotson, 2018) to disseminate misinformation and enable active ignorance. These are ways of influencing the episteme and the regime of truth, of pushing it into a configuration that promotes the interests of dominant groups and drawing on that configuration to reinforce and justify the status quo. Misuses of the words "racist" and "woman" are not true, but they are made to function within the social cognitive economy as if they were true. By affecting the social epistemic fabric, they create more epistemic power for those who benefit from the spread of misinformation about oppression.

When, for example, someone tries to challenge 'our' usual way of understanding gender—that is, the cis-normative way that prevails among dominant and mainstream perceptions of reality—one must confront what are widely taken to be scientific reasons for believing gender is biological. But in so doing, in challenging those ways of understanding gender, one appears to be unscientific. One appears to disregard the scientific evidence. It seems as if one is willfully disregarding the facts in order to achieve a political end. Trans inclusive feminists get painted as opponents of 'the scientific view of gender.' They are seen as failing to accept the conclusions supported by 'our best scientific theories of biology.' They are made to appear irrational. The prevailing epistemological system represents them as lacking epistemic virtue.

When the epistemological system of a society has been preconfigured by dominant identities in a way that functions to help them ignore and suppress knowledge of the ways in which the prevailing system privileges those dominant identities and reinforces interlocking systems of oppression, the epistemological resilience (Dotson, 2014) of the system helps to preserve those systems.

We can think of linguistic hijacking as contributing to the epistemological resilience of an episteme that empowers and enforces oppressive ideologies by making oppressive ideological claims, arguments, and ideas function as true, appear intuitive, rational, scientific, commonsensical, and so on. A white supremacist regime of truth makes the false claim that affirmative action is racist appear to be true and intuitive. A cis-normative regime of truth makes the false claim that trans women are really men appear to be a scientific truth. A colonialist episteme renders Indigenous epistemologies irrational. A patriarchal episteme makes it commonsense that women are bad at being mechanics, soldiers, politicians, and philosophy professors. Linguistic hijacking reinforces such systems, as does misinformation about racism and gender, as do controlling images and propositions.

These are crucial features of the epistemic violence model. On this model, when a political agent says, "Affirmative action is racist," that agent refers to racism and communicates false beliefs about racism. They do not speak truly in their own language; however, they do reinforce patterns of acceptance concerning the proposition that affirmative action is racist. When such claims become accepted across large and powerful swaths of the community, this does not alter the semantics of "racism." Instead, it influences public opinion of what counts as an accurate and intuitive usage of that term. It influences judgments about what counts as a veridical usage, but it does not change what a veridical usage of "racist" really is. The dominant elite and the mainstream public alike can thus be utterly incorrect in their opinions. From this perspective, the insular white communities that refuse to defer to people of color with regard to "racism" have not created their own meaning of "racism." They do not think and speak truly; rather, they firmly hold onto false beliefs about racism and espouse those beliefs in language that is semantically equivalent to the language of their opponents.

Typically, people who hijack "racism" justify their usage by appeal to features of the regime of truth itself. When someone insists that any clear-thinking individual will recognize that "racism" refers to intentional race-based discrimination or when they cite the fact that 'most people' or 'everyone they know' agree with their understanding, they rely on prevailing judgments that their use of "racism" meets standards of clarity and precision that are widely shared and commonsensical. Prevailing standards of clarity and precision often do support this usage precisely because those standards reflect the interests of the dominant group that has exerted its influence on the regime of truth. Thus, inaccurate definitions of "racism" are widely seen within the white community as clear and precise. This is part of what makes it easy for white folks to use and disseminate inaccurate definitions. Quintessentially, on the epistemic violence model, these definitions are false.[12]

---

[12] Some philosophers baulk at the idea of a false definition. They think definitions are necessarily true (by definition, I suppose). On my picture a 'false definition' is a false statement about the meaning of a word in a natural language, presented as if it were an accurate definition of that word in that language, where the falsity of the definition is grounded in the semantics of the natural language in which it is stated. According to this usage, "A square is

Note that, unlike the semantic corruption model, the epistemic violence model is not itself a metasemantic theory. It is a theory of epistemic violence designed to explain the epistemic harms of linguistic hijacking and other forms of misinformation in conjunction with some metasemantic theory or other that gets the semantic facts right. Getting the semantic facts right means rendering statements like "Trans women are men" false and "Anti-white racism is on the rise in the US" as false. The epistemic violence model does not tell us where the meanings of the words "racism" or "women" come from, or why both Trump and Ocasio-Cortez mean the same thing when they say "racist." It presupposes some other theory, an adequate metasemantic theory for justifying the presupposition that our first-order commitments are true. In Chap. 9 I argue that we should presuppose that some such adequate metasemantic theory is true. In Chap. 10, I develop one such metasemantic theory, a theory that explains how we could all mean the same thing by "racist" and "woman," even those who are speaking falsely and spreading misinformation about racism and gender. The intersectional metasemantics I develop explains how we could all mean what the intersectional feminist and critical race theorist means by "racist" and "woman," even those who disagree whole heartedly with intersectional theories of racism and gender.

The epistemic violence model together with the intersectional metasemantics I introduce in Chap. 10 supports a view of political struggle which includes: (1) a view of truth and knowledge as aspects of an objective reality that transcends political disagreements; (2) a view of situated perspectives in which one or more groups may be systematically misinformed about the objective truth about things such as racism and gender; (3) the view that misuses of words such as "racist" and "woman" are a crucial source of misinformation about such objective realities as those involving racism and gender; (4) the view that such misinformation is strategically crucial for the reproduction of systems of oppression including racism and gender-based oppression; (5) an explanation of the importance of viewing political discourse through an intersectional lens, one that presupposes the existence of interlocking systems of oppression, where (6) dominant groups are less likely due to their political and social situatedness to recognize the reality and extent of interlocking systems of oppression; (7) an explanation of the role that social power plays in maintaining ignorance

---

a polygon with three equal sides" is a false definition for the English word "square." I think this comports with normal usage of the word "definition."

(especially within dominant groups) about the reality and extent of interlocking systems of oppression, and the function this ignorance plays in preserving and reproducing those systems of oppression; (8) an explanation of the role of political struggle in bringing the objective truth to light. The next chapter introduces concepts for giving a theory of objective truth drawn from model theory. This way of thinking about truth is intended to provide an abstract concept of semantics that can be merged with the perspective outlined here concerning the relationship between power and truth. Power does not determine which model-theoretic semantics is true of English, but it strongly influences what is believed to be true, what is seen as justified, and what so-called truths hold power within the sociopolitical order.

References

Agamben, G. (2009). *"What Is an Apparatus?" and Other Essays*. Stanford University Press.
Anderson, D. (2020). Linguistic Hijacking. *Feminist Philosophy Quarterly*, 6(3).
Anderson, D. (forthcoming). Restricting Logical Tolerance. *Minnesota Studies in Philosophy of Science*.
Berenstain, N., Dotson, K., Paredes, J., Ruíz, E., & Silva, N. (2021). Epistemic Oppression, Resistance, and Resurgence. *Contemporary Political Theory*.
Bettcher, T. M. (2013). Trans Women and the Meaning of 'Woman'. In The Philosophy of Sex: Contemporary Readings Sixth Addition. Eds. Power, Nicholas, Raja Halwani, and Alan Soble. 2012. pp. 233–250
Carnap, R. (1936/2002). *The Logical Syntax of Language*. Open Court Publishing.
Carnap, R. (1950). Empiricism, Semantics, and Ontology. *Revue internationale de philosophie*, 20–40.
Collins, P. H. (2002). *Black Feminist Thought: Knowledge, Consciousness, and the Politics of Empowerment*. Routledge.
Dotson, K. (2011). Tracking Epistemic Violence, Tracking Practices of Silencing. *Hypatia*, 26(2), 236–257.
Dotson, K. (2014). Conceptualizing Epistemic Oppression. *Social Epistemology*, 28(2), 115–138.
Dotson, K. (2018). Accumulating Epistemic Power: A Problem with Epistemology. *Philosophical Topics*, 46(1), 129–154.
Foucault, M. (1970). *The Order of Things*. Tavistock.
Foucault, M. (1980). *Power/Knowledge: Selected Interviews and Other Writings, 1972–1977*. Vintage.
Lynch, M. P. (2012). Democracy as a Space of Reasons. *Truth and Democracy*, 114–129.

McIntyre, L. (2018). *Post-Truth*. MIT Press.
Plunkett, D., & Sundell, T. (2013). Disagreement and the Semantics of Normative and Evaluative Terms. *Philosophers' Imprint, 13*(23).
Sellars, W., Rorty, R., & Brandom, R. (1997). *Empiricism and the Philosophy of Mind* (Vol. 1). Harvard University Press.
Smith, L. T. (2013). *Decolonizing Methodologies: Research and Indigenous Peoples*. Zed Books Ltd.
Spivak, G. C. (2003). Can the Subaltern Speak? *Die Philosophin, 14*(27), 42–58.
Tuck, E., & Yang, K. W. (2012). Decolonization Is Not a Metaphor. *Decolonization: Indigeneity, Education & Society, 1*(1).

CHAPTER 5

Model-Theoretic Semantics for Politically Contested Terminology

5.1 Overview

There has been a tendency within critical theory to move from the observation that all knowledge is situated[1]—produced and distributed under the influence of social power dynamics shaped by interlocking systems of oppression, which generate distinctive life experiences and distinctive perspectives on reality for distinctive social identities—to the conclusion that objective truth does not exist.[2] Or if there is an objective truth, it cannot be objectively knowable, since each distinctive situated perspective will have its own view of what counts as knowledge and there will be no way to adjudicate which of these views is correct.

The first of these worries is about truth itself. How can there *be* an objective truth where there are irresolvable disagreements rooted in situated perspectives? The second worry is about the possibility of knowledge. How can we *know* the objective truth, when we cannot transcend our limited perspectives? This chapter begins to address the first worry, which

---

[1] See Haraway (1988) for a canonical statement of the view; see Pohlhaus Jr (2012) for an excellent contemporary discussion of epistemic situatedness focused on the situatedness of conceptual resources.

[2] Code (1993), for example, reaches this conclusion, although she notes it is not perfectly satisfactory. Haraway (1988) also notes that this conclusion threatens to follow from her understanding of situated knowledge.

© The Author(s), under exclusive license to Springer Nature Switzerland AG 2021
D. E. Anderson, *Metasemantics and Intersectionality in the Misinformation Age*,
https://doi.org/10.1007/978-3-030-73339-1_5

will take us through Chap. 10. Chapter 11 deals with the epistemic worry about how to obtain objective knowledge from within a politically fragmented social fabric.

The kind of objective truth we are concerned with is truth in a shared language. In this case, the shared language is English. Sentences of English can be objectively true or false. Objective truth does not depend on how distinctive groups choose to interpret sentences. The sentences of English such as "Racism is a form of structural oppression" and "Trans women are women" are univocally true given the objective semantic features of the language that obtain for all speakers. This is the kind of theory of truth we need for understanding political discourse within a discursive field that is beset with oppressive social power dynamics.

A sophisticated approach to modeling objective truth has been developed within the field of formal semantics over the past sixty-plus years across a range of disciplines including psychology, linguistics, philosophy, cognitive science, mathematics, and computer science. Formal semantics uses model theory, a branch of mathematics which is part of set theory. Model-theoretic semantics provides a tool for thinking about the kind of objective truth that transcends political divisions. We can use model-theoretic semantics to theorize the semantics of politically contentious speech in order to assign objective truth conditions for sentences like "Trans women are men," which is objectively false in English, and "Racism against white people is impossible," which is objectively true.

This chapter aims to do at least three things at once: (a) provide a broad overview of the historical development of model-theoretic semantics as part of the science of linguistics, (b) provide a crash course in applying model-theoretic semantics, so the reader will know how to apply it to derive objective truth conditions for statements such as "Trump is not racist" or "I am a woman," and (c) argue that this approach to thinking about semantics is justified from a critical perspective that is suspicious of using mathematical logic for analyzing natural language semantics. In the course of presenting these ideas, I will raise the question of whether we should believe that any objective semantic theory for English is true, or if the multiplicity of situated perspectives undermines this possibility. The final section of this chapter concludes with some considerations about what the proper evidence for the correct semantic theory of English might be. Here I argue that the data for semantic theorizing about words such as "racist" and "woman" cannot be treated as politically neutral.

5.2 A Brief History of Model Theory

Critically analyzing a concept depends in part on knowing the historical origins of the concept, including who created it and why. Let us investigate the historical origins of model-theoretic semantics, both as a helpful guide to grasping its core concepts and also to ascertain whether its promise of objective truth is suspicious in some way in light of its origin story.

Model-theoretic semantics is rooted in the history of logic. Partee (2011) traces this root back at least as far as Aristotle's studies of logic, but she claims that the modern forefather of formal semantics is Gottlob Frege, a nineteenth-century mathematician and logician who was concerned with developing a logical foundation for mathematics.[3] Frege (1879, 1884) initiated a new research program in which logic became a branch of mathematics, concerned centrally with studying mathematical reasoning itself as a formal system (Pedriali, 2017). As I will show, this historical connection with mathematical reasoning helps to explain the apolitical, ahistorical character of formal semantics.

5.2.1 Frege: Mathematicising Semantics

According to Partee (2011), Frege made three major contributions to the study of natural language semantics. Here we will only be concerned with two of them.[4] The first was to conceive of meanings as mathematical functions. A mathematical function maps entities in one domain to entities in another. The meaning of the symbol "+" is a function that takes pairs of numbers as inputs and returns single numbers as outputs. Input 2 and 3 and the plus function returns 5.

---

[3] Locating Frege as the most important source of modern logic is contentious. Another major contender for this role, who I will not discuss in any detail, is Charles Sanders Peirce, who independently arrived at some of the crucial insights of Frege at roughly the same time. Both Frege and Peirce strongly influenced logicians of the next generation. Ramsey, Russell, Whitehead, and more or less every logician at the turn of the twentieth century was acquainted with both Frege's and Peirce's theorizing about logic. Sousing out the lines and degrees of influence is beyond the scope of this chapter. I will proceed without further argument with Partee's narrative that Frege was the foremost founder. Many thanks to David Yaden for bringing this issue to my attention.

[4] The third important contribution, which I am leaving out of the discussion here, is Frege's (1879) theory of quantification. My aim in this chapter is to articulate and defend the possibility of giving an objectively true semantics *at all*, and for this purpose it would only complicate the argument to worry about the details of quantification.

According to Frege, the meanings of predicates are functions like this. They are mappings from inputs to outputs. Take, for example, the word "loves." We can think of the meaning of "loves" as a function that accepts ordered pairs of inputs <x,y> and returns an output from the set {True, False}. It outputs True if x loves y and false otherwise. We specify the inputs to this function in a sentence when we fill in the ellipses around the predicate "…loves…" using noun phrases. For example, you could use the noun phrases "Derek" and "his mother" to construct the sentence "Derek loves his mother." The output of this function will be True if and only if Derek loves his mother and False if and only if Derek does not love his mother. Since I do love my mother, the *loves* function maps this ordered pair to the value True. Therefore, the sentence "Derek loves his mother" is true. If you input the ordered pair Trump and Ocasio-Cortez to the same function, you get the output False. This is because, while Derek loves his mother, Trump does not love Ocasio-Cortez.

Generalizing this approach, we arrive at the idea that every meaningful expression of English semantically contributes either a function or an input to a function to the complex expressions it composes. When you carry out all the functions that form the composite meaning of the sentence, the output will be one of two truth-values: True or False.

The function-argument approach can be applied to a wide swath of language. The function associated with the one-place predicate "is a woman" takes a singular input and maps it to True if and only if that input is a woman and outputs False otherwise. To articulate the meaning of "woman," we simply specify the function that maps the set of women to True. Then "I am a woman" is true just in case the thing referred to by the first-person pronoun "I" (i.e., the speaker) is a woman. "I am not a racist" is true just in case the speaker is not a racist (not in the set of things that are racist). "Trump is not a racist" is true just in case Trump is not a racist.

If this semantic theory for "I am a woman" is true, then that sentence is *objectively true* whenever the speaker who asserts it really is a woman. The truth condition does not depend on what anyone thinks about the concept of womanhood or gender. It does not even really matter what anyone believes the meaning of the word "woman" is. The semantic theory gives the truth condition of "I am a woman" purely in terms of whether the speaker is a woman. Moreover, the fact that the sentence has this truth condition depends only on the contribution that each expression makes to the semantic structure of the sentence.

But what function does "is a woman" contribute? This is closely related to asking *who are the women?* The semantic value of "is a woman" is the function that maps all and only women to True. Deciding who is a woman and who is not is, of course, a politically loaded issue. Trans inclusionary groups will have a different answer than trans exclusionary groups.

Frege's approach to semantic theorizing does not in itself help us decide which group is right. Rather, it lets us state the view that "is a woman" has an objective meaning for all speakers, regardless of how they use or interpret the expression. We can also state that "woman" has a particular semantic feature objectively. We can say that it objectively has, as its meaning, the function that maps women to True. It may be contentious but objectively true that the semantic function of "woman" objectively applies to both cis and trans woman. Then "I am a woman" is objectively true in English when asserted by a trans woman, regardless of whether those who hear such assertions believe that trans women are women and regardless of how trans exclusionary populations would typically use the word "woman."

Frege (1879, 1884) was not primarily interested in applying his semantic treatment to expressions of ordinary language like "loves" and "is a woman." He was originally concerned with formulating a perspicuous and precise language for describing mathematical proofs. According to Pedriali (2017), Frege's aim "was to define a formal system where the meaning of every term would be precisely specified and kept constant in all its occurrences and where every form of inference required for arithmetical proofs would be codified." The purpose of Frege's precise language is to explicitly demonstrate every single step in an arithmetical proof.[5] According to Frege, proofs are meant to track the objective logical relationships between mathematical propositions.

If we presuppose as Frege did that the mathematical realm exists objectively, then the attempt to formulate a precise language for expressing mathematical entailments could be seen as a science. The 'scientists' are studying an objective realm of abstract objects and trying to coordinate on a language that describes that realm precisely. Any actual, current disagreements about the semantics for this language will be worked out in

---

[5] This was not the only purpose with which Frege was concerned. Much of what he says in defense of his semantic framework draws on our knowledge of natural language, and he also clearly intended his framework to be applicable to languages in general and so to natural languages as well as mathematical ones. Thanks to Josh Dever for emphasizing this point and also for contributing several other insights to this chapter.

the course of investigation, just as in physics or chemistry we work to construct a precise, unambiguous, true description of reality.

On Frege's view, in articulating a theory of the ideal language for mathematical reasoning, we are licensed to ignore any contemporary differences of usage and differences in interpretation. Frege (1892) points out that "[n]obody can be forbidden to use any arbitrarily producible event or object as a sign for something." Frege also notes that different individuals may associate different senses with the same public language term, that such differences in interpretation can be 'tolerated,' so long as all parties recognize that the referent is the same. But he goes on to say in a footnote that such variations "are to be avoided in the theoretical structure of a demonstrative science and ought not to occur in a perfect language." In other words, insofar as we are constructing an ideal formal language for doing logic or mathematics, our aim should be to eliminate differences of use and interpretation. A "perfect language" would be free of ambiguity and would also discourage a plurality of interpretations through its perspicuous design, being built to coordinate everyone's interpretation. We do not need to worry about differences in our actual use or interpretation, since these differences would disappear once we coordinate on the ideal mathematical language. We can just focus on describing the ideal language.

This methodology aimed at constructing a more ideal language for reasoning has implications for how disputes are settled. Where disagreements arise, they are not to be settled by looking at linguistic usage patterns. We do not examine how mathematicians have used the words "prime number" or survey the general population to ascertain the proper definition of that expression. Rather, disputes are to be settled by discussing the target domain itself—in this case the mathematical realm that is being described. In proceeding this way, we interpret our words as we use them *now* by reference to the ways in which those words would be deployed in a more complete and precise mathematical theory. In effect, we allow the hypothetical objective reality of the mathematical world—that which we are trying to ascertain and understand—to coordinate our interpretations of the formal language.

In Chap. 10, I will argue that this practice is very much part of ordinary language interpretation as well: we interpret expressions in our current language, including those expressions as they are used by others in our linguistic community, in light of our assessment of objective reality and the roles we think those expressions would play in a more complete and precise statement of that reality, within a community that has eliminated misinformation and ignorance from its discourse.[6]

The presupposition that there is an objective reality to be discovered and to which our natural language expressions objectively refer is deeply influential in the contemporary research field of natural language semantics. The guiding idea is that we can formulate a theory that captures the real truth conditions and logical relations between statements of English and other natural languages (Dowty et al., 1981; Kamp & Reyle, 1993; Heim & Kratzer, 1998). Doing formal semantics for natural language involves describing the logical relations between the semantic values of sentences and expressions of a natural language, where those semantic values are understood as a certain class of mathematical objects. In effect, one provides a formalized version of the natural language one is studying—English, or a fragment of English—that precisely specifies the meanings of every expression and makes explicit what the logical entailments of sentences are.

Developing a formal language for everyday logical inferences, standard methodology licenses us to ignore actual or historical differences of usage and interpretation of the natural language in question. This is why in logic courses you don't learn much about sociolinguistics. The aim of the formalization process that we teach to students is to use a fully perspicuous and precise language for stating logically valid arguments and to coordinate on a shared interpretation of this perspicuous and precise language for natural language sentences. The project is analogous to formulating a more precise language to express the logic of mathematics. The aim is to disambiguate and precisify the natural language. The fact that real people use natural language expressions in conflicting ways and disagree about interpretations does not have any bearing on this project of constructing an ideal, precise formal language for constructing logically valid arguments.

Frege's second great contribution to the study of natural languages is known as the principle of compositionality.

---

[6] It's unclear whether Frege himself held this view of natural language. Conservatively, we might suppose that Frege himself was neutral about whether natural languages should be interpreted in accord with a more perfect ideal version of that language, although the footnote in "Sense and Reference" suggests he may have been sympathetic to the ideal-language view I will defend in Chap. 10.

The Principle of Compositionality: The meaning of a complex expression is a function of the meanings of its parts and of the way they are syntactically combined (Partee, 2011).

The principle of compositionality tells us that the meaning of every complex expression is built up from component parts. The working assumption is that sentences are complex expressions, as are some of their parts. "Derek runs" is made of two component expressions, "Derek" and "runs." "Derek is probably going to eat pasta for dinner" contains a complex predicate. The truth-value of that sentence depends on the meaning of "eat pasta for dinner," and that meaning in turn depends on the meaning of "pasta." Compositionality for the kind of truth-functional language we are considering tells us that every sentence's semantic value, True or False, is determined by the semantic values (objects and functions) of the component parts of the sentence.[7]

In understanding a sentence, you grasp more than its truth-value. Each sentence is composed of a structure of semantic values that underpin the sentence's truth-value. When you understand a sentence, you know the semantic functions of each of the component expressions and you understand the way these functions work together to determine the conditions under which the sentence is true. If you understand the sentence "John is happy," you understand that the sentence is true if and only if the person named "John" taken as input to the function denoted by the predicate "is happy" outputs the value True. If you know who "John" refers to and you know what function "is happy" denotes, then you know that "John is happy" is true if and only if John is happy.

The meaning of a sentence, the thing which you understand when you understand the sentence, thus provides a truth condition. Understanding a sentence requires at least knowing the condition under which the sentence is true (or false). If, for example, you didn't know the condition under which "John is happy" is true—if you did not know that John's

---

[7] Note: it is not necessary that every compositional semantic theory assign {true, false} as the compositional value of every sentence. Other kinds of compositional semantics are possible that are not centered on the concept of truth. And even in contemporary truth-functional formal semantics, it is an oversimplification to suppose that every sentence will have true or false as its compositional semantic value, and this supposition is not entailed by compositionality itself. Nevertheless, it is a helpful oversimplification for understanding the basic concepts of a truth-functional compositional semantics.

being happy would make that sentence true and his being sad would make it false—then you could not be said to understand that sentence.[8]

The truth condition for "John is happy" can be specified independently of whether any given speaker or group of speakers understands the truth condition for that sentence. The truth of this sentence doesn't depend on how you or I interpret the phrase "is happy," so long as John really is happy and "is happy" really denotes the function that delivers True if and only if the input to the function is happy. The truth of the sentence also does not depend on whether we know what it is to be happy or whether we know if John is truly happy.

Are you truly happy? Am I? Who knows! But if you are, then your assertion of the sentence "I am happy" is true. If you are unhappy, then "I am happy" is false when you say it. This is the case even for people who do not know what happiness is.

I can wonder whether I am truly happy. I can also wonder what happiness is. In contemplating these things, I am also contemplating in a certain sense what it takes for "I am happy" to be true. In a way I am thinking about semantics, because I am thinking about what the truth condition for that sentence is. But I am not *merely* thinking about semantics or word meanings. I'm primarily thinking about happiness itself. What is it? Do I have it? If I don't know what happiness is, then I am not quite in a position to state perspicuously what the meaning of "I am happy" is. But my uncertainty or my ignorance of this truth condition does not mean I can't talk or think about happiness or that there is no objective reality about what happiness is. Nor does my uncertainty or ignorance about the nature of happiness mean I am unhappy. Maybe I am happy, despite not knowing exactly what that means, in which case "I am happy" is true when I say it.

Many people, I suppose, might be unhappy because they lack an understanding about what being happy requires. But this ignorance has no effect on the semantics of the word "happy" as they use it. In particular, it does not affect the truth conditions of their assertion, "I am happy." A person who is ignorant of what happiness is, and whose ignorance causes them to be unhappy, still speaks falsely when they assert, "I am happy." The fact that they don't know what happiness is does not change what they mean by "happy." The fact that "I am happy" is false when uttered

---

[8] This insight is often attributed to Davidson (1967) who identified the task of a theory of meaning for a language with the task of giving a finite recursive theory for the truth conditions of the sentences of that language.

by an unhappy person depends on the word "happy" having the same meaning for both happy and unhappy people.

Likewise, for "racist." On the Fregean picture, the semantic value of "racist" is a function that maps inputs to True if and only if that input is racist and False if and only if not racist. If I say, "I am not racist," that sentence is False if I am racist. Often racist people say, "I am not racist," but they speak falsely. The fact that they do not think they are racist may be explained in part by the fact that they have been misinformed or systematically misled about what racism is. But this misinformation and confusion does not affect the truth condition of their statement. When someone falsely asserts, "I am not racist," the word "racist" has the very same meaning for them as it does for those who can truly assert that they are not racist. "I am not racist" does not become true when the speaker is an ignorant racist person. We should therefore not accept any metasemantic theory on which a person's ignorance causes the meaning of "racist" to shift for them and produce a true sentence in their own language.

A person may or may not be aware of the semantic value attached to an expression. For all that Frege's theory tells us, the true semantics of a language might be widely unknown to its speakers. There is no essential connection postulated between how a word is currently used and what its semantic value is. Nor are the semantics of expressions seen as a product of the history or the culture in which they were created. Rather the semantic interpretation of the ideal language is guided by the reality that the language aims to represent. There are objective concepts, for example, being happy or being racist, that the ideal language expresses. When we theorize about the semantics of this ideal formal language, it does not matter whether anyone has ever spoken or understood this language.

The subject matter of mathematics is not concerned with history or politics, social interaction or communication. The addition function does not exist in virtue of its uses in communication. For Frege, meanings are exactly the same kinds of entities—mathematical functions. The ways in which they combine to produce truth-values are akin to formal, mathematical properties. They are not essentially connected with human speech at all. The semantics Frege theorizes for the ideal mathematical language would have existed even if humans did not, because the truth-conditions and logical relations among mathematical propositions do not depend on human activity. In much the same spirit, the semantics for natural language would have existed even if humans did not. Even though the spoken language itself would not have existed if people had not been here to speak it, the functions that are contingently expressed by the spoken language would still have existed.

Frege's work on semantics seems to be utterly removed from human experience and interaction (or it is at least neutral about the relationship between semantics and historical usage patterns). Logic in the Fregean tradition thus appears to most analytic logicians to be completely apolitical. However, we must interrogate that assumption in the context of the present study. We are looking for a theory of objective truth that can serve as a touchstone for theorizing across political divides. If that is our project, then any claim to objectivity and value neutrality becomes suspicious, for such a claim might stealthily privilege a certain vantage point, might serve an agenda, and might reflect a socially situated way of seeing things (Code, 1993). If we begin our inquiry mired in post-truth politics, where any claim to objectivity is suspicious, where the claim to have attained an objective truth binding on one's political opponents is seen to be a potential power move in the field of strategic political conflict, we must establish the legitimacy of any claim to objectivity by situating it within this field of power relations.

How could Frege's logic be seen as engaged in the field of socialpolitical power relations? The idea of a function that maps some inputs to True and some to False is merely a mathematical concept. It does not operate in concert with any particular political agenda. A theory of formal logic seems as remote from political interest as pure mathematics, and exactly as innocuous. Yet I think there are two legitimate concerns that could be raised.

The first is that Frege's brand of objective truth, while politically innocuous when applied to purely formal languages, becomes politically contentious when applied to natural languages. A certain kind of postmodernist opponent might claim that the act of postulating objective truth conditions is a form of political power insofar as a population is compelled to take the postulation seriously (Haraway, 1988; Nye, 1990). Frege's logical machinery outfits us for a certain kind of political engagement.

I think this is true. For example, when investigating Ben Shapiro's claim that "The Obama administration is racist," Frege's theory enables us to argue that Shapiro's statement was objectively false. Without a clear and defensible concept of objective truth and falsehood, such a defense becomes mired in confusion. Hence, it is not just theoretically important to have a clear conception of objective truth, it is politically powerful. But then the point must be conceded that there *is* political power in applying even such an abstract framework as Frege's truth-conditional semantics. Therefore, the concern (Nye, 1990) that Frege's mathematical semantics might function to fortify dominant power structures is not absurd, despite what most contemporary logicians would probably think.

The second related concern is that Frege's theory *as a piece of writing* is a human creation, an artifact produced at a particular point in history, created by a person with a particular view of reality conditioned by a particular culture and set of life experiences. As an artifact, the theory enters into the field of cause and effect within a social world. It was formulated in a historical socially situated context and can be used for political purposes; indeed, that is my aim within this book, to use this type of mathematical approach to linguistic semantics as a basis for objectivity within political discourse. Put to such a use, surely the theory can be legitimately interrogated for its causes and effects within the political landscape. To point to its abstract content and role in pure mathematical discourse does not immediately rebut the possibility that, given its material causes and effects within a political discourse, Frege's theory could be criticized or even rejected on political grounds. The question is empirical. Has Frege's logic contributed to structural oppression? Does it continue to do so in a systematic way?

Andrea Nye's (1990) book *Words of Power* interrogates Frege's logic along these lines. The very idea of mathematizing language, according to Nye, misrepresents the real nature of language (according to her), which is always open to interpretation. Any attempt to regulate or govern the proper interpretation of language is politically loaded, a way of forcing others to accept one's own interpretation as the only rational one and to remove the inherent subjectivity involved in all interpretation, of reality as well as language. To theorize formal truth conditions C for a sentence S and to insist that these are the correct truth conditions for S, on the basis of whatever evidence ("all the people I surveyed agree that, intuitively, C gives the correct truth conditions for S!"), is then a means of asserting political dominance. Nye claims that Frege's theory has in fact caused material harms and contributed to oppression and so should be criticized on political grounds as a human artifact that has reinforced dominant epistemic power.

I know this criticism probably sounds absurd or even nonsensical to the traditional logician. But I think a logician who finds this absurd or nonsensical (or even insulting) should recognize the possibility that *that very reaction* is conditioned by one's social positioning in a way that has been influenced by social power. It is at least possible that the logician's scandalized reaction to Nye's political criticism of Frege is an example of the kind of conditioned response supported by an oppressive regime of truth that seeks to marginalize and ridicule challenges to its own way of conceiving things. To question the possible political influences on one's intuitions and judgments about seemingly incontrovertible a priori truths is, I believe, a healthy form of skepticism, even when (perhaps especially when) one cannot even make sense of how one could possibly be wrong.

Nevertheless, I mean to defend Frege here. My defense is not apodictic or abstract, however. I take Nye's criticism seriously and want to meet it on its own ground. Regardless of whatever harm may have been done using the concept of an objective truth that transcends subjective interpretation, I think we have strong political reasons to appeal to such a notion of truth. This book presents an extended argument for that position. In order to recognize the existence of ignorance and misinformation that perpetuates interlocking systems of oppression, we must have a way of affirming and defending objective truths about those interlocking systems stated in a common language shared by political adversaries and identifying misinformation as objectively false. We must be able to contrast ignorance with knowledge in terms of access to an objective reality.

Thus, Frege's approach to a linguistic semantics, that of specifying an objective truth function that does not depend on one's perspective, understanding, or personal interpretation of the language, is a crucial political tool. I think this is the case even if, as Nye suspects, the notion of objective truth is also part of the oppressor's epistemic power base and has contributed to oppression in the past. We will return to this theme in Chap. 7 when we investigate Foucault's (1980) concept of a regime of truth, which is the set of power relations into which the word "true" enters within a society.

For Frege truth is an abstract object, The True. But what is this abstract object? Is it a big T floating in abstract space just to the left of the number line? Does it really exist, or is it a metaphysical fiction? How is Truth qua abstract object related to the physical world we observe around us? Frege gives us tools for thinking about how a sentence could objectively have a truth condition and a truth-value, determined by the semantic features of its component expressions. But he has not given a substantive theory of what truth itself is.[9]

---

[9] In the Grundgesetze (Frege, 1893), Frege stipulates that The True is the 'course of values' of the identity function, in other words, the sequence of everything which is identical

For the first decades of the twentieth century, there were no prospects for defining truth in a precise and illuminating way. Among empirically minded philosophers, there was a rough consensus that such a project was more or less hopeless.[10] The concept of truth was suspect. It was not until Alfred Tarski (1933) proposed his concept of truth for formalized languages that the concept of truth received widespread acceptance (Mancosu, 2008; Simmons, 2009).

5.2.2 Tarski: Creating Model Theory

Tarski was like Frege, another mathematician working on logic. His work is aimed at understanding the concepts of truth, definability, and logical consequence. Logical consequence is the relation that one sentence A stands in to another sentence B when A's being true logically entails B's being true. Tarski's techniques for investigating these concepts would eventually be seen as techniques of model theory, a field he helped to create.

Model theory is a branch of mathematics. Quintessentially it studies abstract formal languages as its object, a project Frege introduced. Model theory adds to Frege's project by postulating formal structures called models, which are collections of objects—including sets and functions, but also other things like tables and chairs and people, as well as their relationships with each other—that are postulated alongside the sentences and expressions of the language under investigation. A model is used to interpret the expressions of the language under investigation, which is referred to as the object language (here *object* means the object of study).[11]

---

with itself, or in other words, everything; and The False is its compliment, which is the set of things which are not self-identical, which is nothing at all. While this is a definition of sorts, it is not a substantive theory of truth. It's a stipulation identifying The True and The False with everything and nothing, respectively. While this may present a certain degree of metaphysical satisfaction, depending on your aesthetic preferences, it's not really any different than stipulating that The True is the number 42 and The False is the number 45. There's nothing substantive or illuminating about such stipulations. They can't be used for any further reasoning or justifications. Later Frege (1918) endorses a redundancy theory of truth, asserting that "P" and "P is true" express the same thought, writing that "nothing is added to the thought by my ascribing to it the property of truth." Thanks again to Josh Dever for encouraging me to get these details down.

[10] Carnap (1934); Neurath (1983); Reichenbach (1938); see also Anderson (2019).

[11] Frege was opposed to the tradition from which model theory is descended. As we will see, model theory is all about stipulating the domain of discourse, the model under consid-

Models can include anything at all. One model might include all and only natural numbers together with their ordering relations; another might be made up of edges and vertices constructing a graph of a city's subway system; another might include the subway system itself, including the metal of the rails and the cement of the ceilings; another model might include everything in the physical universe.

The name "model" can be confusing, since most people imagine models to be small-scale three-dimensional representations of other three-dimensional objects, for example, model cars, model solar systems, and so on, or perhaps large-scale models representing tiny things, like plastic models of atoms. Another sense of model that could be confusing is model as a kind of simulation, as when we model a hurricane using computer software.

The models in model theory are not three-dimensional objects and they are not simulations. Rather, they are abstract objects. Traditionally, they are thought of in terms of set theory. A model is a set, in the mathematical sense of that word, which includes the domain of discourse that a language represents. An interpretation of a language in a model specifies functions that link expressions in the language to things in the model.

For example, an interpretation assigns a set of things in the domain to every predicate. This is called the extension of that predicate. An interpretation for the English word "dog" might assign the set of all dogs as its extension, and it might assign a particular dog as the extension of the name "Max." Then "Max is a dog" will be true in virtue of the fact that the dog named by "Max" is in the extension of the predicate "is a dog." This requires a truth definition, a way of specifying what each model-theoretic interpretation contributes to the truth conditions for the sentences it occurs in. Tarski came up with the first truth definition of this kind. More on this soon.

A model provides mathematical building blocks for formally describing language. By giving a domain or collection of entities to be used in defining the semantic values of words and sentences, it lets a semantic theory go beyond theorizing about just words themselves. A model provides a way for us to talk about relationships between words and things in the environment. The use of models has proven to be very fruitful within

eration. For Frege, logic is not concerned primarily with models; it is concerned with the entire universe. For discussion, see Heijenoort (1967) and Pedriali (2017).

mathematics and logic and has become a cornerstone of linguistic semantics in the formal tradition (Dowty et al., 1981; Partee, 2011).

Model theory can be helpfully illustrated as a development of certain investigations conducted in geometry during the nineteenth century. Back in the day, geometers were engrossed in finding out whether Euclid's fifth axiom—the parallel postulate, which says that parallel lines never intersect—was logically independent of the other four axioms of Euclid's system, also known as Euclidean geometry. Being logically independent would mean it was not entailed by the other axioms. If the fifth axiom is *not* logically independent, then we don't really need it. It is redundant. We could do all our proofs using Euclid's first four axioms. People had been operating with five axioms for over two thousand years without anyone ever figuring out whether or not the fifth axiom was redundant, so figuring this out would be a grand accomplishment.

As a way of testing whether the parallel postulate was logically independent of the other axioms, geometers such as Lobachevsky, Gauss, and Reimann began trying to construct or imagine geometrical spaces in which the first four axioms were true, but in which the fifth axiom was false. Such a space would show that the fifth axiom is independent, since if the fifth axiom were logically entailed by the other four then the fifth could not be false while the other four were true. Eventually such 'non-Euclidean geometries' were discovered, spaces where parallel lines intersected or diverged but in which the other four axioms still held. The discovery of non-Euclidean spaces proved that the first four axioms did not logically entail Euclid's parallel postulate.

This is a model-theoretic investigation. It proceeds by testing the properties of sentences in a language—in this case, the language of geometry, which includes expressions like "point," "line," and "intersect"—by investigating different models to which the language could be applied, in this case different kinds of geometric spaces. In model-theoretic terms, we say that a non-Euclidean geometry is a model that *satisfies* the first four axioms but does not *satisfy* the fifth. We find that different models satisfy different axioms, that is, make different axioms true. The idea of satisfaction of an expression by a model is crucial for understanding contemporary formal logic and its child, formal semantics.[12]

---

[12] For an extremely thorough and excellent overview of the development of non-Euclidean geometry and its impact on formal logic, see Nagel (1939). The fact that Tarski himself was

In applying the language of geometry to non-Euclidean spaces, it was quickly realized that the words "point," "line," and so on could potentially take on different meanings. Insofar as different things appeared in Euclidean versus non-Euclidean spaces, the interpretation of the geometrical axioms might shift. When we have a domain and a language, which things in the domain are the referents of the expressions of the language? Different models (or different interpretations of a language in the same model) give different answers. This is a general feature of model theory. The relationship between the words in the language and the things in the domain of the model must be specified. Different models of a language fragment can have different domains, or they can have the same domain but be given different interpretations, or they can have both different domains and different interpretation functions.

The old-timey geometers did not have the mathematical tools of model theory. They formulated their various interpretations of geometric language intuitively, without any formalized rules for how to interpret a language in a model. This was possible because the geometers had a shared sense of what the words referred to in relation to the various spaces they considered. Presumably this shared sense was based on a shared history and a shared knowledge of their subject matter, about points and lines and what "point" and "line" would mean in the new spaces they were imagining.

This intuitive approach was controversial as a mathematical practice because of its lack of formalization and precision. Those who demanded a more rigorous approach tried to exclude any appeal to models or 'extra-linguistic reality' from the officially sanctioned reasoning process, focusing instead on logical syntax, that is, focusing on the expressions of the language without any reference to a domain of discourse.

The foremost proponent of focusing on syntax over semantics in geometry was David Hilbert, who introduced what he called the axiomatic method (Hilbert, 1899). The axiomatic method involves conducting investigations purely in terms of syntactic items (words and sentences) and the syntactic derivation rules (rules for deriving one sentence from others) that can be specified without regard to how words might be interpreted or what they might refer to. The syntactic approach to linguistic analysis continued to be dominant for the first decades of the twentieth

---

following the example of non-Euclidean geometers is evident in his earliest application of his model-theoretic approach (Tarski, 1931). See also Simmons (2009).

century. This meant ignoring properties such as truth and reference, since these were semantic features and semantics was conceived as not properly part of logic (see Carnap, 1934).

Tarski's contribution initiated a major shift in logic by providing an exact, algorithmic specification of how to interpret formal languages using models. Tarski (1933) showed that this could be done without contradiction. Although this early work was not itself focused on exploring the full scope of model theory, the techniques he introduced allowed for semantics to be treated as part of logic, including a conception of truth as a kind of correspondence between language and extra-linguistic reality.[13]

Tarski's work on truth was extremely influential in the development of modern logic because it allowed for the definition of a logical truth as a sentence that is true in all models. *True in all models* means that for every (admissible) interpretation of the sentence in every model, it will come out true. Tarski also gave a semantic view of logical consequence. A set of sentences G entails a sentence S just in case every model that makes true all the sentences in G also makes S true. These are the views of logical truth and entailment you typically learn in a second-level logic course in any accredited university. They have been extremely influential in shaping contemporary logic and formal semantics.[14]

Tarski's (1933) process of constructing an interpretation of an object language involves selecting an appropriate metalanguage in which to construct the theory of the object language. A metalanguage is simply the language used to talk about the object language. Distinguishing the metalanguage from the object language is crucial, as it lets you talk about a language without talking about the language you are using to talk (among

---

[13] Although whether this is Tarski's own preferred way of understanding his theory is a matter of debate—see Mancosu, 2008. Specifically, it is not clear that Tarski thought of himself as theorizing about a correspondence relation between language and reality beyond the words. But it does seem that even if this was not his preferred interpretation, Tarski was happy enough to let others interpret his work on semantics this way.

[14] In the context of this book it may be important to note that while Frege is known to have endorsed anti-Semitic views in his private diaries, including speculating that Jews should be deprived of their political rights and expelled from Germany, Tarski on the other hand was Jewish and lost many relatives and colleagues to the holocaust, surviving the war by haphazardly finding himself in the US at its outbreak (Eastaugh, 2017). Insofar as Frege's anti-Semitism might be seen as relevant for assessing the logical tradition he initiated (Nye, 1990), it must be equally important to note that the logical tradition was transformed into its modern guise by a displaced Jewish logician who personally sustained dreadful losses due to racism and anti-Semitism.

other things, this allows a theory of truth to avoid the liar paradox; see Tarski, 1933). The metalanguage, like the object language, is something that we specify or stipulate. The theorist is an authority when saying what their metalanguage is.

Tarski gives instructions about what the metalanguage must contain in order to give a definition of truth for a given object language. The metalanguage must have sufficient vocabulary to describe the semantic features of the object language, that is, to name each expression in the object language and describe its semantic properties. How do we make sure the metalanguage has the appropriate resources for this task? Tarski's solution is to simply copy the object language into the metalanguage, so that the metalanguage can say everything the object language can say. He also adds to the metalanguage a name for every expression in the object language. Here it is important to keep clear about the difference between the predicate itself and the name for that predicate. For example, the predicate *is happy* is added to the metalanguage along with a name for that predicate, which is standardly written as the expression in quotes: "is happy" is the name of the predicate *is happy*. To make it look even more like a name, instead of using quotes let's call it The Happy Predicate.

Tarski's idea is, we can specify the conditions under which The Happy Predicate is satisfied by using The Happy Predicate itself, in the following way. The Happy Predicate (i.e., "x is happy") is satisfied when applied to x just in case x is happy. Here we use The Happy Predicate itself in the metalanguage to specify the condition under which it is satisfied in the object language: x satisfies "is happy" if and only if x is happy.

The definition can sound redundant, but it's actually a major breakthrough insofar as it provides a systematic way to associate expressions of the object language with elements of the model that are used to interpret those expressions.[15] The variable x ranges over things in the model. The predicate "is happy" is a piece of the object language. This linguistic

---

[15] Note that in Tarski (1933) where he first develops this technique of copying the object language into the metalanguage, he did not explicitly describe the metalanguage construction technique in model-theoretic terms; he defines a truth predicate in the metalanguage for the object language without mentioning models or providing tools for interpreting names and predicates differently using different models and interpretation functions. Nevertheless, we can see his procedure as a model-construction technique, one that paved the way for a fuller and more expansive model theory by providing one systematic way of describing a relationship between an object language and a domain of entities and properties, that is, those referred to by expressions of the object language.

expression is distinct from the property of being happy. Intuitively, the idea is that the predicate "is happy" applies to x if and only if x is happy. This was Frege's intuitive approach to interpreting the language, that is, to interpret the predicate "is happy" as mapping x to The True if and only if x is happy. Tarski improves on the intuitive approach by giving an exact method for defining the satisfaction condition for the predicate, one that extends to every predicate in the object language. You can give a recursive definition of truth using Tarski's method. Moreover, by using the predicate of the object language inside the metalanguage in a systematic way, Tarski's method guarantees that the statement of the satisfaction condition in the metalanguage will match up with the way the expression is used inside the object language.[16]

Unlike the intuitive approach, Tarski's method can be expanded to apply algorithmically to every expression in the object language. If our object language includes the predicate "is racist," then we copy that predicate into the metalanguage and use it to define the satisfaction condition for "x is racist." "x is racist" is satisfied if and only if x is racist. We also get "x is a woman" is satisfied if and only if x is a woman. Seeing the pattern, we can state a more general condition. For every one-place predicate "x is F" we can define the semantic value using the schema: "x is F" is satisfied if and only if x is F. This schematic approach supplies a definition of truth for every sentence constructed using any one-place predicate in the language.[17]

---

[16] Frege (1879) does give a recursive definition of truth for sentences constructed using the logical operators (*and*, *not*, *if...then*..., etc.), which is part of what makes him arguably a stronger candidate than Peirce to hold the title of foremost founder of modern logic. But Tarski goes further by providing the basis for defining truth more generally for sentences, not just those constructed using logical operators.

[17] Tarski generalizes the definition further to include all predicates of any arbitrary length: n-place predicates. An n-place predicate has n arguments and so can require up to n distinct objects in the model to satisfy it. Since the predicates of a formal language can have n-place predicates for any number n, a full definition requires defining satisfaction relations involving indefinitely many objects in the model. For this reason, Tarski defines satisfaction using infinitely long sequences of objects. By defining satisfaction in terms of infinite sequences, he guaranteed that the definition would cover every case; it would cover any predicate having any arbitrary number of argument places. Of course, the natural languages we speak don't use predicates with more than four or five places, so infinite sequences are a bit overkill.

Tarski reasoned that an adequate definition of truth must satisfy what he called condition T. Here's how condition T works. For every sentence S in the object language, take the name for sentence S—which we write using quotes: "S"—and then use the sentence to specify its own truth condition. So we get a list of truth-condition sentences (T-sentences), one for

Notice the truth definition just adduced for "Trump's tweets were racist" does not depend on how anyone uses the word "racist" or whether people typically think of Trump's tweets as racist or use the word "racist" to express this belief. For all the semantic theory says, the truth of the sentence depends only on whether Trump's tweets were in fact racist. As with Frege's logic, the semantic theory is not concerned with things such as history, politics, or the role of symbols in communication. It is solely concerned with identifying truth conditions and entailment relations between sentences.

Tarski's (1933) approach is only one way to generate a model-theoretic interpretation of an object language. Many, many other models and other interpretations are possible for any fragment of language. Tarski's original construction technique does not yet take full advantage of the flexibility of the model-theoretic framework. Just as you could introduce a model for Euclid's axioms that interprets "point" to refer to politicians and "line" to refer to allegiances, you could also introduce a model for talk of "racism" and "structural oppression" that includes only geometrical objects. You can stipulate weird or absurd models that have nothing to do with the language as we use it.

In order to conceive of a natural language as having objective truth conditions, we must believe that some models are accurate representations of its semantics and other models are inaccurate. We have not yet reached the point in the history of formal semantics where the question of giving an accurate model-theoretic semantics for a natural language has occurred. But we have reached the point where we have all the formal tools necessary for constructing such a semantic theory.

---

every sentence S in the language. Then for every sentence S in the language, we have: "S" is true if and only if S. This set includes "John is happy" is true if and only if John is happy. It also includes "Trump's tweets were racist" is true if and only if Trump's tweets were racist. This list of T-sentences specifies the goal of a definition of truth, a condition of adequacy. Any adequate definition of truth must entail, for every sentence in the object language, the corresponding T-sentence. Tarski (1933) shows that his method for defining truth in terms of satisfaction by infinite sequences meets condition T for certain regimented formal languages, such as the calculus of classes introduced by Whitehead and Russell (1910). He thinks it can be extended to some fragments of natural language as well, writing "if we translate into colloquial language any definition of a true sentence which has been constructed for some formalized language, we obtain a fragmentary definition of truth" for that colloquial, that is, natural, language (Tarski, 1933, pp. 165, footnote 2), although he believes truth cannot be defined in general for the whole of any natural language (ibid., section 1).

Let us consider how different people might model the truth condition for "Trump is racist." Within the domain of a model—the set of all things that are taken to exist in relation to the language in question—we can partition things into subsets. The predicate "x is racist" is interpretated as corresponding to a subset of the total set of things in the universe, namely the set of racist things. This is the extension of the predicate—the set of things that satisfy the predicate. But what set is the extension of "x is racist"? On one interpretation of "racist" the set will include Trump. On this interpretation, the sentence "Trump is racist" will be true. On another interpretation the set corresponding to "racist" will not include Trump and "Trump is racist" will be false. Your judgment about which is the correct interpretation for the English word "racist" will be strongly influenced by your understanding of what racism is. When people disagree about how the world actually is, they will also tend to disagree about how to model the semantic features of the language they speak. What model a person constructs for interpreting their public language—a language which they share with their political opponents—typically depends on their own situated perspective, especially where political factors are relevant.

This political dimension of semantic interpretation was not noticed, at least not often, in the history of logic. Tarski's original application of his truth definition was for the formal language of the calculus of classes created by Whitehead and Russell (1910). Russell and Whitehead's work was an extremely influential piece of mathematical logic. It unified many logicians in a shared logical notation and a shared set-theoretic understanding of mathematics. Being a treatise on pure mathematics, it held no obvious political implications. Political differences among logicians had little or no impact on the uptake or interpretation of the text, at least among the elite white men who were included as participants in the discourse at that time. Hence, Tarski's model construction technique was naturally seen as a completely apolitical piece of pure mathematics. There continues to be little suspicion that Tarski's model construction technique might have political implications or political presuppositions built into it, since the prototypical application of this technique interprets merely mathematical language, and its later applications to natural language semantics are typically regarded as part of a value-neutral science of meaning.

In applying Tarski's method to politically contentious discourses, the politically and socially embedded aspects of the object language become relevant. When two parties who disagree politically interpret a shared fragment of the public language using Tarski's method, they are liable to implicitly invoke different domains—because they see reality differently—and they are likely to invoke different interpretation functions because they disagree about the extension of words like "racist" and "woman." These semantic modeling disagreements reflect politically situated disagreements about reality.

At this point you might think, since people can interpret an object language using different models and different interpretations, this means model-theoretic semantics will be useless for giving a univocal theory of truth for a politically charged public language such as English. When I interpret the sentence "BLM is racist," I use a model on which the sentence is false, while Donald Trump (if he understood model theory) would presumably accept a model on which the sentence is interpreted as true. My model and Trump's do not match. Is this a case in which we speak different languages, or perhaps even inhabit different realities? Indeed, model theory could be used to articulate this kind of radical subjectivism about truth, reality, and linguistic interpretation. So how is the model-theoretic approach to linguistic semantics getting us any closer to a theory of univocal truth that can be used to characterize objective reality and objective misinformation?

The fact that we *could* use model theory to articulate a radical semantic subjectivism only shows that model theory is flexible enough to give a theory of relative truth. While model theory has the mathematical resources to portray truth as relative, it can also be used to give a model for a shared language, an exact specification of a univocal truth definition for sentences such as "BLM is racist" that treats the shared public language as having an objective semantics, with truth conditions that are what they are regardless of how folks in different political camps might interpret them. If "racist" in English denotes the set of things that benefit from or contribute to racism-qua-structural-oppression, then it has this meaning for all users of English. This is what contemporary formal semantics sees itself as doing: trying to formulate objectively true semantic theories for English and other natural languages that attribute objective semantic features to public language expressions.

Tarski was not constructing models for natural languages. The project of doing formal semantics for natural languages began in earnest with a student of Tarski's, Richard Montague.

5.2.3 Montague: Treating English as a Formal Language

Partee (2011) writes, "the most important figure in [the history of formal semantics] was undoubtedly Richard Montague, whose seminal works in this area date from the late 1960s and the beginning of the 1970s." Montague's great contribution was to blaze a trail by applying model-theoretic techniques directly to natural language (Montague, 1970a, 1970b, 1970c, 1973).

Tarski (1933) had argued that his technique for defining model-theoretic truth could not be applied to 'colloquial' language without resulting in paradox. Many other logicians believed that formal languages were simply different in kind from natural languages such that the mathematical techniques appropriate to formal languages could not be applied to natural languages.

Montague broke with this tradition. Applying model theory to natural language, Montague made several advances in areas that had not been attempted simply because they were not relevant to formal mathematical language. For example, he created semantic theories for indexical words such as *I*, *now*, and *here*, expressions that are central to colloquial language but have no use in purely mathematical discourses. Although the details of Montague's semantics have been superseded in many ways by newer and more sophisticated theories, these later successes were made possible by Montague's work insofar as he showed that progress could be made in these areas and many others. Many contemporary semanticists see themselves as doing Montagovian Semantics, working in the tradition Montague initiated.

Where did this break with tradition come from? How was Montague convinced that we could apply model theory to natural language semantics?

Montague was skeptical that there could really be a deep divide between natural and formal languages. How, for example, are we able to use formal logic to reason about premises and conclusions that we state in English? When we teach students of logic to reason according to formal principles, we teach them to translate arguments from their natural language into a formal, precise language. How could this possibly be relevant to their thoughts and beliefs if natural language itself did not have its own logical structure and its own semantics that could be formalized using the language of formal logic?[18]

Here we find at least two reasons to believe that English has semantic properties akin to those of a formal logical language. The first is epistemological. We take logical reasoning in a formal language to justify beliefs stated in natural language. There must therefore be a logical relationship of entailment between sentences of the formal language and sentences of the natural language. If this entailment is understood model-theoretically, as Tarski proposed—and this is our best and most widely accepted theory of logical consequence[19]—then the semantics of natural language sentences must be understood model-theoretically as well. A sentence of the formal language S_F entails a sentence of the natural language S_{NL} if and only if all the models of S_F are models of S_{NL}. This only makes sense if we understand truth for natural language sentences in terms of truth in a model.

The second reason is empirical, an observable cognitive psychological feature of humans. Human students have the ability to perform translations of natural language sentences into formal language sentences and back again. Moreover, speakers tend to agree with one another about how to do these translations. They agree about which translations of natural language sentences into formal language are correct and which are not. Their judgments are based on whether the formal translations preserve logical inferences involving natural language sentences. These facts suggest that natural language speakers have a kind of competence in understanding the semantics of natural language that is closely tied to their implicit understanding of formal language semantics. Accordingly, we might even be able to study the psychological competence involved in language comprehension by modeling the relevant psychological processes using model theory (Kamp, 1981). This creates an interdisciplinary bridge between formal semantics and cognitive science. Insofar as these psychological processes are treated computationally—as if the mind were a computer implementing a program—computer science also becomes involved in the study of natural language semantics.

---

[18] See the email excerpt from Hans Kamp, Montague's student, presented in Partee (2011, pp. 23-24) which gives this account of Montague's impetus for deploying model theory to the task of characterizing the semantics of natural language.

[19] Although see Etchemendy (1994) for an extensive discussion of Tarski's concept of logical consequence and reasons to be skeptical that it really is the ultimate theory of real logical consequence.

This range of fruitful interdisciplinary connections is part of why model-theoretic semantics has come to be viewed as a science. It is no longer merely about modeling formal relationships between propositions or formal abstract structures. Now formal semantics is part of an empirical theory of the psychological processes involved in language production and comprehension. That science has been flourishing and expanding for decades.

But what is this science a science of? What is the scientific evidence it uses to adduce its conclusions? From the perspective of critical theory we must always be wary of the use of the term 'science,' for as Foucault (1988, 2012) argues and as feminist epistemologists have pointed out (Code, 1993; Scheman, 1995), to call something "science" is to claim a kind of legitimacy and objectivity for a domain of discourse. Insofar as the domain of formal semantics becomes embroiled in political discourse—through the analysis of politically charged language—its claims to objectivity and scientificity may be seen to waiver.

Natural language semantics studies the semantic properties of natural language expressions, modeling them using the model-theoretic conceptual apparatus Tarski developed. If there is an objective science to be had in this area, it must be that natural language expressions have objective semantic properties, such as objective truth conditions, and that we can determine what these semantic features are on the basis of empirical evidence. Both of these presuppositions may be called into question. But let us first examine the reasons for thinking there are such objective semantic properties and empirical evidence to support their existence.

Consider the sentence "Everyone loves someone." Logic teachers love to put this sentence on the chalkboard and invite students to explain the two possible interpretations of this sentence: (a) there is one person who is loved by every other person; (b) each person loves another person, but there's no one person such that everyone loves them. Every single time we give this sentence in class, 99–100% of the students will recognize and understand this semantic ambiguity. This is empirical evidence for a kind of psychological regularity. What explains this regularity of judgment? Hypothesis: our brains are wired in such a way (through nature or nurture, who knows) to ascertain semantic features of our spoken language. Moreover, we can use formal language to disambiguate the two semantic readings of this sentence. We can write $\exists x \forall y$ (y LOVES x). This expresses (a) that there exists some x such that for all y, y loves x. And we can write $\forall y \exists x$ (y LOVES x), which expresses (b), for every y there is some x such that y loves x. The fact that students can learn these translations and agree that they do in fact disambiguate what was ambiguous in the natural language sentence seems to be evidence for the empirical claim that our linguistic competence with natural language semantics is expressed in our ability to use formal language as a guide to reasoning.

Likewise, we can observe patterns of reasoning in natural language, such as (i) *Ellen is a pediatrician*, therefore (ii) *Ellen is a doctor*. We can treat judgments about this entailment from (i) to (ii) as empirical evidence for the claim that competent language users of English judge (ii) to be semantically entailed by (i). This is empirical evidence for the claim that people interpret English sentences as standing in certain semantic entailment relationships. We can leverage this fact to study, empirically, which sentences entail which other sentences. We can also test whether people agree about the truth conditions of particular sentences and thereby find empirical evidence in support of or against a particular model-theoretic interpretation of that sentence. These procedures for gathering empirical evidence involve simply asking people to make judgments about semantic features of language. The presupposition, which is crucial for Montague's program of having an empirical science of formal semantics for natural language, is that speakers' judgments carry empirical information about the semantics of the language they speak.

Unlike a pure model theorist, the natural language semanticist does not construct the language she studies using formal rules. She discovers its structure and properties by studying how it is used and understood by the people who speak it. She does not pick an arbitrary interpretation to assign meanings to the language she studies. Rather, she uses the framework of model theory to represent the semantic features that are (supposedly) already there to begin with. Empirical natural language semantics describes semantic properties such as truth, reference, and entailment as objective features of the language fragment it studies, as a thing discovered in nature.

Natural language semantics postulates models for the interpretation of natural language expressions, but the correct models for interpreting English and other natural languages are taken to be identical with (or sometimes described as *embeddable in*) the objective reality we inhabit (Kamp, 1981). So in postulating a semantic interpretation of "racist" or "woman," we presuppose a model that includes the real properties instantiated in the real objective world—racism and womanhood in this case—and attempt to describe the truth conditions of sentences of English by reference to those features of the world, as we understand it to be.

But what is the evidence for deciding what the correct semantics of English is? Consider again judgments concerning the truth conditions of "Trump is racist" or the entailment from "Affirmative action discriminates on the basis of race" to the sentence "Affirmative action is racist." If we simply record people's judgments about the semantic features of these sentences, the theory we arrive at would seem to depend on whom we ask. If we ask defenders of the Die-Hard view of racism, we will get one set of evidence. If we ask defenders of the structural racism view, we will get another set of evidence conflicting with the first. We seem forced to conclude that either "racist" has multiple meanings in English or else we must presuppose that one group and not the other is a privileged source of information concerning the semantics of "racist." I believe this shows that natural language semantics as an empirical discipline is inherently bound up with politics.

5.3 Situated Evidence for Semantic Theories of English

It has seemed to some that natural language semantics can maintain its status as an objective science by simply postulating an ambiguity in the meaning of "racist" corresponding to the multiple politically situated perspectives that inform the use of that term. Two observations are in order.

First, insofar as political pressures shape this theoretical decision, it is odd to claim that natural language semantics is an apolitical science. Ambiguity seems to be forced in the case of "racist" precisely because the domain of discourse is politically contested. Hence, politics are shaping the semantic theory.

Second, postulating an ambiguity is not politically neutral. It favors the discourse around "racist" and "racism" that insists the debate is merely semantic. By attempting to relegate debates about racism to the status of debates about word meanings rather than substantive first-order political issues, this kind of semantic interpretation facilitates active ignorance about racism and hence supports the continued existence of white supremacy. It also gives semantic authority to those who are ignorant of the nature of racism as a form of structural oppression, allowing the ignorant to define their own meaning of "racist." Therefore, a semantic theory that postulates an ambiguity for "racist" is not politically neutral.

Moreover, to legitimate a theory on which "racist" is ambiguous by calling it 'scientific' lends further political force by supporting those who would claim that debates over racism are merely semantic. This is an operation of the regime of truth, to be discussed in Chap. 7, which renders white reactionary positions as if they are aligned with our best science of meaning.

The empirical investigation of semantics cannot avoid becoming embroiled in politics. Does this entail that such an investigation cannot be scientific? I would say the answer is no. Semantics can be scientific even though it is also inherently political. This is a consequence of the view, which I accept and will defend to some extent later, that all scientific inquiry is politically entangled (Harding, 1992; Scheman, 1995). Attempts to extricate scientific practice from the field of politics are always fraught, at least when those scientific fields are engaged in studying humans. Perhaps we can forge apolitical sciences of particle physics and chemistry. In any case, I strongly doubt that a science of semantics can remain apolitical. It can only do so insofar as it refrains from analyzing politically significant language.

For the most part, empirical semantics has been carried out with regard to domains that are politically uncontroversial. This is because linguists seek data (that is, semantic judgments) that will be seen as uncontroversial. Once we extend the project to politically controversial terrain, the methodology becomes uncomfortable. When begin soliciting semantic intuitions about hotly contested language, the claim of formal semantics to be a natural science with the implication of political neutrality starts to seem questionable. But I propose to do semantics for politically controversial language in more or less exactly the same way as it is carried out for natural language fragments that are relatively uncontroversial. Doing so requires that in categorizing good versus bad evidence for a semantic model we cannot remain politically neutral.

Consider a fragment of English including the predicate "is racist" as our object language. On an intersectional model, reality contains systemic racism and things are racist insofar as they contribute to or benefit from that phenomenon. The model interprets "racist" as applying veridically to the set of things that are racist in this sense. If this is the correct model of semantics for English, that interpretation unambiguously applies to all assertions about what is "racist" made by any speaker of English, regardless of what they think about the meaning of "racist" or the reality of racism. Thus, formal semantics has supplied us with the power to *state an objective theory of truth* for sentences such as "BLM is racist" on which that statement is objectively false no matter who asserts it or what their personal politics are, and on which that truth condition does not depend on how the speaker understands the meaning of "racist" or what they understand about racism.

But now we must ask, what is the evidence that this model is correct for English? A proponent of the Die-Hard view of racism will want to argue for a different model of English semantics. What empirical evidence can be used to decide between competing models for the semantics of English? My view is that empirical support for the correct model of English semantics for "racist" is crucially circumscribed by the question: which speakers are knowledgeable about racism itself?

A semantic theory that gets the wrong extension for "dog" or "superconductor" would be less accurate, all other things equal, than a theory that gets those extensions right. A semantics that assigns true to the sentence "Robert Shaw is a superconductor" is defective. When ascertaining the semantic value of the word "superconductor," we had better avoid asking people who don't know what a superconductor is. Judgments about the meaning of the word "evolution" are likewise not necessarily trustworthy when the sources are young earth creationists.

The same goes for politically contested terminology such as "racist" and "woman." Judgments about the meaning of "woman" made by members of transphobic communities are not good data for the actual semantics of "woman." It may be that a majority of people in the US would judge "Affirmative action is racist against white people" to be true, yet there is good reason to believe it is false. Hence, the judgments of a majority of people about the meaning of "racist" are suspect. Semantic judgments can only be trusted insofar as we take the speaker to be informed about the subject matter of which they are speaking.

Accuracy in a semantic theory is not primarily a matter of capturing speaker judgments. It is a matter of capturing semantic facts. Speaker judgments are a guide to semantic facts only insofar as those speakers are a reliable source of semantic information. Whether a speaker is a reliable source of semantic information depends in part on their knowledge of reality. A person who doesn't know what superconductors are is a bad guide to the semantics of the word "superconductor." A person who doesn't know what icaros are is not a good guide to the meaning of "icaro." People who don't know what racism is are a bad guide to the meaning of "racism."

A speaker is only a good source of semantic information with regard to an expression if they are knowledgeable about the domain the expression functions to semantically represent. Let us record this important point about sources of semantic information in the following principle.

Informed Speaker Constraint. A speaker who is misinformed or ignorant about D cannot be counted as a source of semantic information concerning representations of D. Only a speaker who is informed about D can be treated as a reliable source of information concerning the semantics of expressions that function to semantically represent aspects of D.

This constraint is not widely recognized or practiced in contemporary linguistics, but it is of great importance. Semanticists must take care to assess the knowledge of those who count as providing empirical evidence for theorizing about semantics in order to judge whether they are a reliable source of information. This principle ties semantic data to other background theories of reality insofar as we need background theories to assess who is knowledgeable and who is not. Semantics is thus properly seen to be confirmationally connected to other scientific disciplines in this way via the informed speaker constraint.

This principle is foregrounded when political discourse is being analyzed. The attempt to remain politically neutral and ascribe ambiguities to politically contested terminology flaunts this principle, for it disregards the question of whether both sides count as sufficiently knowledgeable about the domain in question. Remaining politically neutral requires the semanticist to treat both sides as equally good sources of information about semantics. Yet in the case of "racist" there are strong empirical reasons to regard many English speakers as ignorant about the target domain. A responsible science of semantics must be responsive to this politically contentious reality, and this cannot be done in a politically neutral way.

Semantics can proceed as science only insofar as it works to verify its evidential sources. In cases of politically contentious speech, this cannot be done without taking a stand on politically controversial matters such as the nature of racism and the nature of gender. Whose judgments are trustworthy sources of evidence for semantic theorizing will depend on background theory about what is the case in these domains. This does not mean that semantics can't be treated as science, only that we must accept that good science can be enmeshed with politics.

A model for the semantics of the word "whale" in English must distinguish between whales and non-whales in its domain of discourse. If it does not incorporate the distinction between whales and fish, then it will deliver the wrong truth conditions for many sentences, such as "That is a fish!"

The distinction between whales and fish is not semantic; it's biological. The semantics for the phrase "Higgs boson" in English must likewise take into account the fact that it refers to Higgs bosons and not other elementary particles, and so the domain for an accurate semantic model for English must distinguish between Higgs bosons and other particles. This is not a semantic distinction but a distinction from physics. In exactly the same way, natural language semantics is responsible for getting the domain right about politically contested phenomena such as the nature of racism and gender. This means an adequate semantics must reflect the best theories of gender and racism, just as it must reflect knowledge of physics and biology.

This means that whether a particular semantic theory appears to be in good scientific standing will also depend on background views about such things as gender and racism. Perspectives on what counts as scientific and about what reality really contains are politically situated. But there is an objective fact of the matter, and the correct semantics for English must be responsive to this objective fact, which transcends political disagreements. Intractable disagreement between trans inclusive and trans exclusive political factions over the nature of gender does not mean that both sides speak truly in their own language, and it does not mean there is no reality of gender.

Political controversy over the semantics of gender terminology stems from political controversy over gender itself, not the other way around. Likewise, controversy over the semantics of "racism" stems from the argument over whether racism is necessarily a form of structural oppression. These are not really arguments about semantics. Our semantic beliefs are epiphenomenal. They track our first-order commitments about reality itself.

Moreover, we can predict that there will be intractable disagreement over the nature of racism, and thus also over the semantics of "racism," given that ignorance of racism is a necessary precondition on its continued existence (Baldwin, 1963; Mills, 2014). Wherever racism continues to exist, there will be disagreement about its nature and also disagreement over the semantics of words for describing it. We can also expect disagreement over the semantics of "woman" to continue as long as there is a strong political interest in delegitimating trans identities. But wherever we find these kinds of predictable disagreements where dominant groups refuse to uptake the knowledge of marginalized groups in order to preserve the status quo, we can also reliably predict that the dominant groups are fueling their side of the disagreement through practices of active ignorance and misinformation. We have strong reason to conclude that both sides in such political disputes are not equally knowledgeable. The socially marginalized side is knowledgeable, while the dominant side is systematically ignorant. It is thus empirically responsible to base our semantic models for such contested terminology on the semantic judgments of members of marginalized groups.

The usual method in empirical semantics is to appeal to semantic intuitions. This process is typically conducted using the least politically controversial sentences we can find, which helps give formal semantics the credentials of scientific authority, since science is preconceived to be inherently politically neutral. But for any judgments to count as semantic data, the speaker must be knowledgeable. We cannot use the semantic intuitions of speakers who do not have knowledge of the domain of speech under investigation. When we investigate the semantics of politically contentious language, we must ascertain who is knowledgeable and who is ignorant. It is politically contentious to determine who is knowledgeable about racism and gender and who is subjected to systematic ignorance. So empirical semantic theorizing must also be politically contentious. Semantics must align with our politically situated judgment as to who has knowledge of the subject about which they speak.

References

Anderson, D. (2019). Rejecting Semantic Truth: On the Significance of Neurath's Syntacticism. In *Neurath Reconsidered* (pp. 363–382). Springer.
Baldwin, J. (1963/2013). *The Fire Next Time*. Vintage.
Carnap, R. (1934/2002). *The Logical Syntax of Language*. Open Court Publishing.
Code, L. (1993). Taking Subjectivity into Account. In L. Alcoff & E. Potter (Eds.), *Feminist Epistemologies*. Routledge.
Davidson, D. (1967). Truth and Meaning. In *Philosophy, Language, and Artificial Intelligence* (pp. 93–111). Springer.
Dowty, D. R., Wall, R. E., & Peters, S. (1981). *Introduction to Montague Semantics*. Springer.
Eastaugh, B. (2017). Tarski. In A. Malpass & M. A. Marfori (Eds.), *The History of Philosophical and Formal Logic: From Aristotle to Tarski*. Bloomsbury Publishing.
Etchemendy, J. (1994). The Concept of Logical Consequence.
Foucault, M. (1988). *Madness and Civilization: A History of Insanity in the Age of Reason*. Vintage.
Foucault, M. (2012). *The Birth of the Clinic*. Routledge.

Frege, G. (1879). Begriffsschrift, a Formula Language, Modeled upon that of Arithmetic, for Pure Thought [1879].
Frege, Gottlob (1884/1953). *The Foundations of Arithmetic*. Evanston: Ill., Northwestern University Press.
Frege, G. (1918). 'Thoughts', in *His Logical Investigations* (p. 1977). Blackwell.
Frege, G. (1892/1948). Sense and Reference. *The Philosophical Review*, *57*(3), 209-230.
Frege, G. (1893/1903). *Grundgesetze der Arithmetik*, Jena: Verlag Hermann Pohle, Band I/II. Complete translation by P. Ebert and M. Rossberg (with C. Wright) as *Basic Laws of Arithmetic: Derived using concept-script*, Oxford: Oxford University Press, 2013. Partial translation of Volume I, *The Basic Laws of Arithmetic*, by M. Furth, Berkeley: University of California Press, 1964.
Haraway, D. (1988). Situated Knowledges: The Science Question in Feminism and the Privilege of Partial Perspective. *Feminist Studies*, *14*(3), 575–599.
Harding, S. (1992). Rethinking Standpoint Epistemology: What is "strong objectivity?". *The Centennial Review*, *36*(3), 437–470.
Heijenoort, J. (1967). Logic as Calculus and Logic as Language. *Synthese*, *17*(1), 324–330.
Heim, I., & Kratzer, A. (1998). *Semantics in Generative Grammar*. Blackwell.
Hilbert, D. (1899/1902). *The Foundations of Geometry*. Open court publishing Company.
Kamp, H. (1981). A Theory of Truth and Semantic Representation. *Formal Semantics-the Essential Readings*, *1*, 189–222.
Kamp, H., & Reyle, U. (1993). *From Discourse to Logic*. Kluwer Academic Publishers.
Mancosu, P. (2008). Tarski, Neurath, and Kokoszynska on the Semantic Conception of Truth. In D. Patterson (Ed.), *New Essays on Tarski and Philosophy* (p. 192). Oxford University Press.
Mills, C. W. (2014). *The racial contract*. Cornell University Press.
Montague, R. (1970a). English as a Formal Language.
Montague, R. (1970b). Pragmatics and Intensional Logic. *Synthese*, *22*(1), 68–94.
Montague, R. (1970c). Universal Grammar. *1974*, 222-46.
Montague, R. (1973). The Proper Treatment of Quantification in Ordinary English. In *Approaches to Natural Language* (pp. 221–242). Springer.
Nagel, E. (1939). The Formation of Modern Conceptions of Formal Logic in the Development of Geometry. *Osiris*, *7*, 142–223.
Neurath, O. (1983). Physicalism: The Philosophy of the Viennese Circle. In *Philosophical Papers 1913–1946* (pp. 48–51). Springer.
Nye, A. (1990). *Words of Power: A Feminist Reading of the History of Logic*. Routledge.
Partee, B. H. (2011). Formal Semantics: Origins, Issues, Early Impact. *The Baltic International Yearbook of Cognition, Logic and Communication*, *6*(1), 13.

Pedriali, W. (2017). Frege. In A. Malpass & M. A. Marfori (Eds.), *The History of Philosophical and Formal Logic: From Aristotle to Tarski*. Bloomsbury Publishing.

Pohlhaus, G., Jr. (2012). Relational Knowing and Epistemic Injustice: Toward a Theory of Willful Hermeneutical Ignorance. *Hypatia, 27*(4), 715–735.

Reichenbach, H. (1938). Experience and Prediction.

Scheman, N. (1995). Feminist Epistemology. *Metaphilosophy, 26*(3), 177–190.

Simmons, K. (2009). Tarski's Logic. In D. Gabbay (Ed.), *The Handbook of the History of Logic* (pp. 5–511). Elsevier.

Tarski, A. (1931/1956). On Definable Sets of Real Numbers. *Logic, Semantics, Metamathematics*, 110-142.

Tarski, A. (1933/1956). The Concept of Truth in Formalized Languages. *Logic, Semantics, Metamathematics, 2*(152-278), 7.

Whitehead, Alfred North, & Russell, Bertrand. (1910/1963). *Principia Mathematica by Alfred North Whitehead and Bertrand Russell*. University Press.

CHAPTER 6

Toward an Intersectional Metasemantics

In the previous chapter, I presented the rationale for employing a model-theoretic semantic theory for natural language. I traced the development of this approach from earlier logical concepts into the multi-disciplinary field of formal semantics and showed how formal semantics can assign objective truth conditions for politically contested public language.

I also argued that judgments of speaker competence are highly political when the object of study is a politically contentious fragment of language. Whether a person counts as competent in the use of "woman," for example, depends crucially on whether we presuppose that trans women really are women, in which case transphobic agitators would count as poor candidates for competence with "woman." Thus, empirically ascertaining the correct semantics for English is not a politically neutral exercise.

In this chapter, I argue that metasemantics is also socially situated and explain how this is relevant to how we should understand linguistic hijacking and other modes of misinformation. I also argue that a metasemantics for intersectionality should have a number of features. I argue that it should be externalist, that semantics should be conceived (as Frege conceived it) as determined by the character of an ideal language, and that it should not be constrained by the reductive naturalistic tradition that characterizes most of the history of analytic metasemantics.

6.1 What Is a Metasemantic Theory?

In *Moby Dick*, Herman Melville (1851) writes,

> The uncertain, unsettled condition of this science of Cetology is in the very vestibule attested by the fact, that in some quarters it still remains a moot point whether a whale be a fish. In his System of Nature, A.D. 1776, Linnaeus declares, "I hereby separate the whales from the fish." But of my own knowledge, I know that down to the year 1850, sharks and shad, alewives and herring, against Linnaeus's express edict, were still found dividing the possession of the same seas with the Leviathan.[1]

Melville (or is it only his protagonist Ishmael?) suggests that whales are fish because they live in the sea as fish do. Whales are not fish. They breathe air, give birth to live young, are descended from land mammals, and so on. But Melville is not disputing these facts. He is arguing that whales should count as "fish" because they live and swim in the ocean. We can read this as a semantic claim. Melville is claiming that "fish" refers to anything that lives and swims in the ocean. Then since whales live and swim in the ocean, they would count as "fish."

What made it the case that "fish" only referred to the scaly, egg-laying water-breathers? It seems possible that "fish" could have meant something other than it in fact does, such that "Whales are fish" would have been true and Melville would have been right. Perhaps Melville *was* right in 1851, given how people used the word "fish" back then.

The true semantic theory for English tells us that "fish" does not include whales in its extension. The true *meta*semantic theory for English tells us under what circumstances Melville's alternative semantics would have been realized. It also tells us whether in fact "fish" referred to whales in 1851. Metasemantics doesn't just tell us which semantic theory is correct; it also explains why that semantic theory is correct rather than some other semantic theory. It explains why the semantic features of our language are what they are. It also explains why different semantic theories would have been true under different circumstances.

Metasemantic theories have traditionally been aimed at explaining the semantics of language in virtue of the social, historical, psychological, biological, or physical facts that undergird the existence and distribution of semantic features—the metaphysical facts that determine which semantic

---

[1] *Moby Dick*, Chapter 32.

theory is true. We might refer to the contingent, actual metaphysical basis of the semantics of our current language as the *metasemantic apparatus*, in connection with Foucault's concept of an apparatus. Then we would think of metasemantics as historically located and contingent. We could also think of metasemantic theorizing as a more fundamental endeavor, as trying to give something like the laws of nature for how the semantic features of any language whatsoever are determined.

Burgess and Sherman (2014) characterize metasemantics as "in the business of providing metaphysical explanations of semantic facts" and as specifying "how or why these symbols [i.e. expressions of a natural language] come to have meanings—perhaps unearthing more basic or fundamental facts in virtue of which such semantic states of affairs obtain." They go on to affirm that basic metasemantics is to be conceived as explaining semantic facts in terms of more fundamental, non-semantic facts, and suggest that these facts should comport with natural sciences. In other words, metasemantics should be aimed at giving reductive naturalistic explanations for semantic theories.

This has been perhaps *the* driving interest in the philosophical pursuit of metasemantics within the analytic tradition: explaining where semantic properties come from in reductive naturalistic terms, in terms of more fundamental sciences such as physics, chemistry, and biology. This would mean, for example, explaining why "whale" refers to whales and "fish" refers to fish by talking about things like causal processes, biological processes, perhaps the evolution of the human brain, but not mentioning the contents of thoughts or intentions or political motivations (at least not at the 'fundamental' level), because these must themselves be understood in semantic terms and so be explained in reductive naturalistic terms.

The traditional reductionist aim for metasemantics has largely been motivated by a kind of physicalism about the universe. In the beginning there were no words or sentences; there were no languages or thoughts or brains, just a Big Bang and a hot energy soup. In the beginning nothing was represented by anything else. Things existed, but nothing had truth-conditions or referred to anything because there were not yet any complex systems to create representations. After billions of years of cosmic and then biological evolution, creatures with brains and language arrived on the scene. Semantic features appeared around the same time and must have somehow arisen from the biological and physical events that came before. This parable has been understood to entail that the existence of semantic features must be explicable in terms of the kinds of physical processes that gave rise to them, or upon which they supervene.[2] This has also widely been understood to entail that whatever semantic features exist now must be explicable in terms of more fundamental physical and biological features of human existence.

The reductive naturalist tradition is worried about making semantics fit into the rest of scientific discourse. It maintains that (a) everything that really exists is physical or reducible to physical phenomena and (b) that semantic properties are not obviously physical in this sense; therefore, (c) semantic theories are in need of some kind of theoretical unification with the physical sciences in order to legitimate semantic properties as scientific. Yalcin (2014) identifies this project of finding a naturalistic explanation for semantic features as the sole or essential aim of metasemantic theorizing, writing "Metasemantics ... inquires into the nature of certain properties investigated by natural language semantics ... It asks whether and how these semantic properties might admit of some illuminating reduction to, or unification with, nonsemantic properties."

For the Melville case, this program would have us settle the question of what "fish" meant in 1851 by looking at things like what causal relations does the word "fish" enter into, including causal chains that stretched back deep into the history of the word's usage. But in explaining this, you cannot appeal to what the word meant or what it referred to or what true sentences it was part of, since that kind of explanation would make use of semantic concepts and so would fail to be reductive in the relevant sense. A reductive explanation cannot appeal to properties at the same 'level of reality' as those it is trying to explain.

Why must semantic properties be reduced to non-semantic properties? The reason commonly offered is that all properties must somehow be grounded in the physical, since all things are physical, and the fundamental physical properties do not include semantic properties. As Fodor (1987) put it, "I suppose that sooner or later the physicists will complete the catalogue they've been compiling of the ultimate and irreducible properties of things. When they do, the likes of spin, charm, and charge will perhaps appear upon their list. But *aboutness* surely won't."

Semantic properties are not postulated by quantum physics or chemistry or biology, but then if these non-semantic physical entities are all that

---

[2] A set of facts A supervenes on another set of facts B if and only if the A facts could not be different without the B facts being different. Lewis (1983) defines minimal physicalism as the thesis that all facts supervene on the physical facts.

exist in some fundamental sense, then semantics must ultimately arise from their properties and activities. If semantic properties cannot be explained in terms of non-semantic physical properties or processes, then semantics must somehow be nonphysical and therefore metaphysically suspect. Putnam (1981) puts it this way: "If only physicalist properties and relations exist, then reference, to exist, must be a physicalist relation." Fodor (1987) said: "If the semantic and the intentional are real properties of things, it must be in virtue of their identity with (or maybe their supervenience on?) properties that are themselves neither intentional nor semantic." Metasemantics in the analytic tradition has been largely pursued through wrestling with this riddle. How can semantic features exist in a physical world which is fundamentally not representational?

6.2 QUESTIONING NATURALISTIC REDUCTIONISM IN METASEMANTICS

Characterizing metasemantics as essentially or necessarily concerned with naturalistic reduction[3] relies on a few questionable assumptions about science and metaphysics. First, it presupposes what has been called the *unity of science* (Neurath, 1937), the idea that all adequate scientific theories should be combinable into one monolithic theory, which uses a single vocabulary and allows for explanations of all phenomena in that single vocabulary. Must the science of semantics be unified with the science of physics? While we have made some helpful inter-theoretic connections between certain sciences such as physics and chemistry and biology, the ideal of unity is hardly a standard of acceptability within scientific discourse. We don't require that working epidemiologists provide reductive theories connecting their work to quantum physics. We don't ask economists to reductively reconstruct their theories in non-economic, purely biological terms. It is a philosophical assumption, and a contentious one, that every theory must be reducible to more basic sciences in order to be acceptable.

The second assumption is the metaphysical principle underlying the philosopher's requirement for unified science, that anything that really exists must be explicably grounded in fundamental physical properties. This presupposition requires that the universe is hierarchically ordered

---

[3] This review of reductionism glosses over some distinctions that could be drawn between different kinds of reduction. For more detail, see Sarkar (1992).

into a number of metaphysical levels such that each level is constituted by or explained in an intelligible way in virtue of the underlying level, with physics at the bottom, chemistry above that, neurobiology toward the upper-middle echelon, and semantics somewhere above that. But there is no scientific reason to suppose that such an explanatory hierarchy exists. Scientific theorizing does not presently give us a unified theory of everything, not even within physics to say nothing of a grand unified theory that unifies physics with economics, psychology, and semantics. Therefore, we do not at present have a strong scientific reason to think that semantics is reducible to physics.

Is there a philosophical reason to believe in reductionism? If the universe is entirely physical, how could there be true scientific theories that do not reduce to physics? I think Jerry Fodor gives the best answer to this when he writes, "I expect to figure out why there is anything except physics the day before I figure out why there is anything at all[.]"[4] It is a great mystery why anything exists, and likewise a mystery why there are many different kinds of things with distinctive natures. I claim, with Fodor, we do not need to worry about such grand metaphysical questions in order to do metasemantics. We can postulate semantic and metasemantic theories for English without worrying about how those theories are unified with physics, biology, or any other natural science.

Another presupposition of reductive naturalistic metasemantics is semantic scientific realism, the idea that semantic properties are part of a scientific theory that limns the causal structure of the universe. I reject this presupposition. We do not need to theorize semantic properties as part of the causal order. I am not suggesting that semantic properties are *unreal*. I don't know what it means to say that truth is not real, or that there is no such thing as reference. But I think it is a questionable assumption that the truth condition of a sentence must in every case be some kind of physical property that enters into cause-and-effect explanations of physical event types (Field, 1972), or that semantic properties must supervene on such events. We do not have to explain semantic properties or justify our semantic interpretations by appealing to causal factors. By the same reasoning, we should not require that every admissible metasemantic theory must only postulate semantic properties that are causally implicated in the order of physical events.

---

[4] Fodor (1997) pp. 161. It is a paradox in the history of twentieth-century analytic philosophy that Fodor is the archetypal voice both for the disunity of science (Fodor, 1974, 1997) and for the reductionist criterion for semantics and intentionality (Fodor, 1987).

Note that *some* semantic properties may be causally efficacious on the view of metasemantics I'm proposing. I'm only arguing that 'x is causally efficacious' should not be considered a necessary condition on postulating that 'x is a semantic property.' Metasemantics should not be a priori restricted such that semantic properties can only be postulated if they are somehow related to causality between physical event types.

This is relevant because, among other things, it frees up metasemantic theorizing from the requirement that semantic properties must be explained in terms of physical processes or even causally implicated in our applications of words. It allows us to postulate explanations of semantic properties that have something to do with ideal ways of representing things, where these ideal ways may never have actually been implemented by any causal process. It also frees us from thinking that semantic properties came into existence as a result of past causal processes, as opposed to postulating that word meanings have something to do with the kind of language we *should* be speaking in order to represent reality accurately. On the view of metasemantics I will defend, semantic properties are determined by such an ideal version of our language.

We should also not demand that metasemantic explanations must be devoid of all reference to semantic properties. We can admit that semantic properties can be invoked as parts of explanations concerning other semantic properties, and we don't have to insist that there be some set of semantic properties that are reducible to purely non-semantic ones. We might postulate that "racism" and "woman" have the meanings they do in virtue of what people think and say, where those thoughts and assertions are characterized in terms of their semantic content, without presupposing that those contents or some others down the line must ultimately be explained in terms of non-semantic features. We could even go so far as to speculate that certain metasemantic relationships might be reciprocal. For example, we might postulate that what the group means by a word is shaped by what individuals mean by it, *and* that what individuals mean by that same word is influenced by what the group uses it to mean, or by what people have meant in the past, or by what people in a more epistemically virtuous community would mean by those same words. Once we have jettisoned the naturalistic reductionist requirement, semantic facts can function as parts of explanations for other semantic facts. I will describe these ideas in more detail in Sect. 6.4.

6.3 A Brief History of Metasemantics

The development of metasemantics within analytic philosophy has been strikingly narrow, focused on a limited set of questions and implicitly imposing conditions on what kinds of projects are viable, namely those that fit into a reductive naturalistic methodology. I want to investigate the trajectory this programmatic metasemantics by making explicit some of the assumptions that have guided its development, while also giving the reader some background in the field. I also want to explore the sociological dimension of the development of this research field and the way in which sociological pressures steered the discourse away from confronting the kind of politically contentious language with which this book is centrally concerned.

6.3.1 Linguistic Meaning from Mental Contents

Analytic metasemantics is overwhelmingly focused on mental content as opposed to the semantics of spoken natural languages. This is because it has been widely presupposed that representation first exists as a property of minds and then becomes infused into language by some further process. The idea of explaining linguistic meaning by reference to mental contents is part of the cognitive science revolution—the rejection of behaviorism within psychology and philosophy.

In the early part of the twentieth century the received view among scientists and analytic philosophers (or so they say) was that truth and representation were not proper objects of scientific study. This received view manifested as support for behaviorism among psychologists—the view that scientific psychology must be restricted to explaining observable behavior by reference to reinforcement patterns associated with observable stimuli without postulating complex mental states that intervene between the two. In psychology, the most famous defense of behaviorism in the domain of linguistic meaning was P.F. Skinner's *Verbal Behavior*, where Skinner proposed to interpret all linguistic events in terms of proximal stimulations that caused observable linguistic events (Skinner, 1957).

Among empirically minded philosophers, the received behaviorist view in psychology delegitimated the existence of mental content. Postulating or theorizing about mental contents came to be seen as metaphysical speculation, ungrounded in any possible empirical evidence, maybe even meaningless (Hempel, 1949). The only things that could be studied scientifically were thought to be observable behaviors, so all meaningful forms of psychological talk were thought to be reducible to talk about observable behaviors. Even in his famous rebuttal of this kind of logical empiricism, W.V.O. Quine (1951, 1960) maintained that psychological states could play no role in a scientific theory of word meanings.

The consensus around behaviorism began to collapse with the publication of Noam Chomsky's influential attack on Skinner's behaviorism about language (Chomsky, 1959), which is widely cited as ushering in the cognitive revolution—the sociological legitimation and proliferation of empirical science concerning mental representation. Chomsky argued that verbal behavior cannot be understood by reference to external stimulus and behavior alone but must instead be explained by postulating computational processes occurring within the mind of the speaker. The cognitive revolution opened the door to theorizing about psychological states and processes as a ground for explaining the meanings of linguistic expressions.

Jerry Fodor's (1975) influential book *The Language of Thought* also contributed to this cognitive science research program grounding natural language semantics in mental representation. Fodor argued that in order to explain our ability to learn and use a natural language, we must postulate that humans have an inner mental language that has many of the same features as natural language, including sentential structure, a compositional syntax, and a semantics that mirrors the semantics of the spoken language. The inner language, sometimes called *Mentalese*, was postulated to have its own words, also called *concepts*, and its own sentences 'written' in the internal language using these Mentalese words. The inner language could be thought of as a kind of computer code that the brain uses to organize information about all kinds of things, including the meanings of linguistic expressions.

Postulating an inner mental language enables cognitive scientists to describe states including beliefs, desires, fears, thoughts, and so on, as consisting in computational relations between mental sentences encoded in people's brains. For example, if I believe that President Trump is racist, then according to the language of thought hypothesis I must have a sentence written in the language of thought, encoded in my brain somehow or other, which has the same truth-conditional content of the natural language sentence, "Trump is racist." This would be a Mentalese sentence that is true if and only if President Trump is racist. I then express my belief by using a sentence of the natural language with the same content.[5]

Mentalese sentences can occupy a number of distinct computational roles that affect how I behave. One of these roles is *believing* a mentalese sentence. For me to *believe* that Trump is racist involves having a Mentalese sentence that is true if and only if Trump is a racist, which also modulates my mental and physical activities in the way a belief does: that piece of mental code causes me to become upset if he's elected president, to not trust what Trump says about racism, to vote against him, and so on. For me to *doubt* that Trump is a racist, on the other hand, would involve having the same Mentalese sentence incorporated differently into my mental machinery, such that it causes me to be antagonized by claims that Trump is racist, causes me to perceive his Tweets and immigration policies in ways that are consistent with him being non-racist, causes me to speak out against those who accuse him of being racist, and so on. For me to believe that I am a woman would be for me to have a certain Mentalese sentence that is true if and only if I am a woman, situated inside my cognitive economy such that it influences my emotions, reasoning, and behavior in ways that constitute my having that belief. More generallhy, to believe that P is to have x. x describes a property, i.e. having a piece of mental code which is causally influencing certain things, influencing them in ways that are consistent with holding the belief that P.

The concepts and beliefs encoded in my language of thought are available for explaining why my spoken words and sentences mean what they do. For example, the word "woman" may refer to women in part because it expresses the concept WOMAN, a word in the language of thought. Then explaining the semantics of "woman" and other natural language expressions is partly a matter of explaining the semantics of the mental code the language is used to communicate. This perspective was very influential in the naturalized semantics program, which focused almost entirely on explaining the semantic features of mental representations.

In the same year that Skinner published *Verbal Behavior*, Paul Grice published an influential article, "Meaning," arguing for the view that linguistic meanings should be understood in terms of the role that linguistic expressions play in communicating thought contents (Grice 1957). Grice argued that linguistic meanings are the result of our intentions to express our thoughts using a common bank of symbols. On Grice's view, "Whales

---

[5] For criticism of this view, see Schiffer (1987) who argues that it is problematically circular.

are fish" expresses the proposition that whales are fish if and only if, in uttering that sentence, I intend for my audience to recognize that I mean for them to form the belief that whales are fish on the basis of hearing what I said.

Linguistic expressions on Grice's view are tools for communicating thoughts. Their effectiveness is grounded in convention. It's because we all coordinate in using certain symbols to express certain thoughts that we can expect people to infer our thoughts when we make utterances. Expanding Grice's idea into a full metasemantic theory for all the expressions of a language is very complicated and difficult (see Schiffer, 1972 for the canonical attempt). No fully satisfactory approach was ever developed. Yet the idea that somehow or other the contents of linguistic expressions could be explained by reference to mental states was (and continues to be) very influential. It provided a perspective in philosophy of language to compliment the popular view in philosophy of mind that mental contents are the source of linguistic meanings.

Suppose our linguistic expressions inherit their meanings from the contents of our mental states, and the contents of our mental states are a function of the semantic properties of mental representations. Then for the reductive naturalist the question becomes: in virtue of what naturalistic, reductive properties and events do mental representations come to have the semantic properties *they* have?[6]

I pause to emphasize that all the presuppositions built into this program—physicalism, reducing semantics to the physical, even the idea that the semantics of natural language expressions can be ascertained scientifically—are partially the product of social factors. The program that was built upon these presuppositions was *cool and popular*. It was considered an important program among the philosophers who were legitimated as leaders of the field. It was also exciting to those philosophers. It was

---

[6] Note there was never a consensus about the language of thought hypothesis and many philosophers were antagonistic to Fodor's program (Loar, 1981; Stich, 1983; Dennett, 1987; Schiffer, 1987). But alternative approaches were still largely responsive to many of the same issues that the language of thought program confronted in its attempt to naturalize mental content and explain linguistic semantics in terms of mental representation. Competing theories often answered the same kinds of questions in different ways, in accord with the same basic principles of reductive naturalism, or else were skeptical of semantics altogether in virtue of a perceived failure of reductive naturalism. My choice to focus on the language of thought hypothesis in presenting the historical development of naturalistic metasemantics is more exegetically than theoretically motivated.

supported by grant money. You could write many dissertations on these topics and people would say: that's cutting-edge work. Working on these questions, with these presuppositions, landed people jobs at prestigious institutions. In short, there was social support for this program. There was power behind it.

This sociological fact does not entail that there was no epistemically good rationale for pursuing a reductionist naturalistic metasemantics. The fact that social power backs a research program is logically independent of the question of whether that research program was on the right track in terms of discovering the truth. It may be that a research program should have been pursued, that it was epistemically justified, even though it was also backed by social power.

But the social dimension helps to explain at least the following feature: the project of naturalizing semantics is liable to seem idiosyncratic and narrow to someone coming to this material from outside the discipline in which these questions were formulated. This phenomenon highlights a way in which power influences what is perceived as true within a community. To be sure, no one was forcing anyone at gunpoint to believe that reductive naturalistic metasemantics was an important program. But if you wanted to participate in the zeitgeist in analytic philosophy of mind and language in the 1980s, you had to get onboard with the presuppositions of this program. To entertain your doubts about it or to voice them would have alienated you from that zeitgeist and all the opportunities it presented, at least to some extent.

These observations help to highlight the sense in which the naturalistic metasemantic project is socially and historically situated. It is partly a product of the historical moment in which it was produced and of the prevailing norms and opinions among those who developed it. The discourse was shaped by the interests of the people who were in power at that time—the professors who determined who got into graduate programs, who got jobs, who got invited to exclusive conferences, and who got prestigious awards—including the epistemic norms they found appropriate for good philosophical work. Being invited to share in that power meant not rocking the boat. You could rock it a little, especially if you could convince the big shots that you were a budding philosophical superstar with big new ideas, but if you tried to go in a totally different direction from what the mainstream thought was interesting or cogent, then your work would not be seen as interesting by those who controlled the field and consequently you and your ideas would be marginalized.

The socially enshrined aspirations of the metasemantic project were not entirely free from politics—specifically the aspiration that semantic features of the language should be grounded in or explained in terms of natural phenomena that were themselves thought to be purely apolitical. Metasemantics was conceived as part of a value-neutral, objective scientific investigation. But one of the central contentions of this book is that metasemantics is deeply political. Attempting to extricate metasemantics from political context ends up marginalizing the theoretical significance of politically contested language. So, conceiving of metasemantics as apolitical and focusing on uncontested language is therefore not politically neutral. Treating metasemantics as a form of value-neutral science is itself a value-laden political action. This value-laden political action was enforced through the sociological power of analytic philosophy departments who were uninterested in and unwilling to make politically contentious discourse of central importance to the metasemantic program.

6.3.2 *Internalism Versus Externalism About Mental Contents*

We have seen the naturalization program was strongly influenced by the cognitive science revolution. It presupposed that linguistic expressions inherited their semantics from the semantic properties of mental representations. From this perspective the most important question becomes: where do the semantic properties of mental representations come from?

Internalism in this domain is the view that mental contents are determined by features that are intrinsic to the speaker, such as the physical states of their brain, as well as the thoughts and ideas they entertain within their own subjective consciousness. In the naturalistic program, these subjective states are assumed to be identical with or fully determined by states of the brain. Internally defined mental states do not make reference to anything outside the boundaries of the physical organism.

Linguistic content internalism follows from mental content internalism if we suppose the semantic features of public language expressions are affixed by the semantic features of mental states. If linguistic internalism is true, then what a person means when they say "Whales are fish" depends on their internal brain state, by their subjective mental states, what they believe, or what intentions or decisions they have made about the way they use the word "fish." On this kind of metasemantics, one could in principle tell what a person meant by saying "Whales are fish" by looking very closely at all the information contained within that person's brain, or perhaps by looking *per impossible* into their inner mental world.

Internalism entails that if Trump and Ocasio-Cortez use the word "racist" with different meanings, this must be due to some internal difference between them, some kind of mental or physical difference that would explain why they meant different things. Likewise, if they use "racist" with the same meaning, this must be in virtue of some crucial similarity in their internal features. This is a fairly commonsensical view. If they mean the same thing, then this must be in virtue of some similarity in the ways they think or act concerning the meaning of "racism," and this similarity must have something to do with the way they are internally organized neurobiologically or within their subjective consciousness.

Which internal features account for sameness or difference of meaning? There are many different kinds of internalism with different answers to this question. On some versions, meaning depends on which inferences a person is liable to make. This is sometimes called "conceptual role semantics." The meaning of a mental symbol is its role in the cognitive economy of the individual's mental life. According to this kind of view, if Ocasio-Cortez is willing to infer that something counts as "racist" if it negatively impacts life chances for people of color, while Trump is unwilling to infer the same conclusion on the same basis, then they employ different concepts and use the word with different meanings.[7] If Melville sincerely infers from "x is a whale" to "x is a fish," then his word "fish" applies to what he calls "whales."

The cognitive roles that determine the meanings of mental symbols might not be limited to deductive inferences but may be thought to encompass the whole range of uses or processes in which that symbol participates in the mental life of the individual. In this way, conceptual role semantics is the mental embodiment of Wittgenstein's (1953) famous

---

[7] This is only a rough sketch, but see Loar (1981) for an elaboration of one such position. Some but not all versions of conceptual role semantics characterize meanings this way as well; see Field (1977) for a statement of meaning as inferential role, and see Greenberg and Harman (2005) for the view that the meaning of a concept consists in its entire spectrum of use within the cognitive economy (i.e., not just the inferences it enters into, but every cognitive activity it participates in). Note that in conceptual role semantics, the metaphysics of meaning (what are meanings?) and the metasemantics of meaning (what makes it the case that an expression has the semantic value it does) are very tightly bound together. The meaning of the expression *is* the role it plays in inference, *and* it having this role in inference is what makes it the case that the expression has the meaning it does.

slogan that "the meaning of a word is its use in the language," a use theory of meaning for the words of Mentalese. But to be an internalist theory, the use of an inner word must be specified in purely internal ways without any reference to things and properties in the external world outside the mind/brain of the speaker.

According to a different kind of internalism, you simply decide by fiat what your words mean. According to Carnap (1936, 1950), each person is free to stipulate the semantic features of their words. As long as you are clear and coherent in setting up your linguistic framework, there is no ground for criticizing any of your choices. On this view, the word "fish" when you use it means whatever you decide it means. If Melville says that "fish" applies to whales, then it does (in his language). Likewise, if Trump says "racist" does not apply to him, then it doesn't apply to him as he uses the word, although it might apply to him when someone else uses it. Assuming that our decisions about word meanings can be understood purely in terms of what is going on inside our minds/brains at the point in time where we specify our linguistic framework, Carnap's view is a form of internalism.

There are many other kinds of internalism that can be imagined, but they are similar in the following way. On internalist views, sameness of meaning is due to sameness of internal factors and difference in meaning is due to differences in those same internal factors. It is therefore typical among internalist metasemantics that the person who says, "Trump is racist," and the person who says, "Trump is not racist," would assert *different* propositions, that is, mean different things by "racist," insofar as their different opinions reflect different metasemantically relevant internal factors. In order to mean the same thing by the word "racist," two individuals would have to be similar with regard to how their brains/minds are organized with respect to their conception of racism. Hence, two people who disagree politically about issues connected with racism will tend to mean different things by "racism" on an internalist picture. Internalism makes it very plausible that your words share meanings with the words of others only when you and the other agree by-and-large on the right way to apply that word.

Externalism on the other hand is the view that semantic features of words depend on factors beyond the intrinsic physical or mental features of the individual. Meanings are determined in part by external factors. What you mean by your words is not fixed by your inner subjective consciousness or by the physical properties of your brain. Instead, the meanings of your words can depend on your relationship to the physical, social, abstract, and virtual environments you inhabit. You do not have to be aware of these external relationships. You might not even know what your words mean because their meanings can be fixed by relationships you are unaware of. The famous slogan for this family of views is Putnam's (1975): "Meaning just ain't in the head."

On an externalist view, what Melville means by "fish" is not a matter of what he believes fish are, for example. It's not a matter of what he would classify as a fish or even what he would say the definition of "fish" is. What he means depends instead on some relationship he stands in to fish themselves, the creatures swimming around out there beyond his mind/brain—for example, having seen them, touched them, eaten them—and it might also depend on his relationship with other speakers in his community who use the word "fish" in connection with those physical creatures swimming in the oceans, lakes, and streams.

A person can talk about fish in virtue of belonging to a community of people, some of whom have seen them, touched them, and eaten them. Some people saw the creatures swimming, they caught them and ate them, and they called them "fish." Then they passed on the word to others in their community. The people who heard the word perhaps had no idea what they were talking about, yet these people could ask, "What are fish?" and in using the word "fish" they referred to fish in formulating their question. In the beginning, even the people who had seen and caught fish did not know exactly what fish were or what made them different from, say, whales; yet they coordinated with one another to facilitate using "fish" as a word for fish.

On the standard externalist metasemantics, the meaning of "fish" depends on both a social element and on the physical nature of fish. If people had decided to use "fish" to refer to any animal they caught and ate, then "fish" would refer to deer as well as salmon. That is the social aspect: the socially facilitated group decision about what the word stands for. But the meaning of "fish" is not just a matter of coordinating in this way. If the physical environment were different such that there were no fish in the water but only aquatic mammals, then the things people saw swimming in the water, caught and ate, and called "fish" would be mammals. In that case, "Whales are fish" would have been true, though "fish" would not have referred to fish. The meaning of "fish" thus depends in part on what is out there in the world.

6 TOWARD AN INTERSECTIONAL METASEMANTICS 119

Externalism helps to explain how Melville could have been wrong when he said whales were "fish." The meaning of "fish" does not depend solely on what Melville thinks it means, or even what his fellow humans think it means. Instead, it depends on an open-ended list of interconnected factors about the interactions between people, their uses of the word "fish," and the creatures to which they apply the term. When we look to the relationship between people and the environment, we find that "fish" was being used to refer to a kind of aquatic creature with properties that set it apart from mammals. Whales are mammals, not aquatic creatures of the kind "fish" denoted, so "Whales are fish" was false when Melville said it, even if he disagreed with the definition that ruled out whales as fish, and even if most people agreed with Melville at the time.

Our assessment of this situation depends in part on our own contemporary knowledge of the difference between fish and whales. We look into the past and judge that past users of "fish" may have had an incomplete understanding of what we now take ourselves to understand. We see that we had created the words "fish" and "whales" before we fully understood the difference between fish and whales. We slowly pieced together evidence that whales were not fish, that "Whales are fish" was and always had been false. Externalism allows for "Whales are not fish" to be true before anyone clearly understood that whales are not fish. It also shows how someone like Melville (or Ishmael) could have vehemently defended the false notion that whales are fish. He was able to think and talk about whales and fish, even though he was confused about the difference between them, in part because his ability to refer to fish using the word "fish" and whales using the word "whales" does not depend on his inner understanding of the difference between them.

Likewise, externalism will allow us to understand how someone could vehemently defend a false conception of racism. Even a person who does not understand what racism is can refer to racism using the word "racism," and in doing so they can say false things about racism. On an externalist view, the word "racist" can have a semantic value that is independent of the thoughts or opinions of any particular person, or even a group of people within a language-using community. People are able to say false things *about racism*, because their ignorance about racism does not preclude them from referring to racism. Externalism also shows how people could have false beliefs about *racism*, as opposed to having beliefs about other phenomena that are superficially similar.

Notice that externalism encourages us to formulate our ontology (our theory of what exists) separately from our semantics. It is one thing to theorize about what fish are; it is another to theorize about what people mean by "fish." It's one thing to theorize about what racism is; it is another to theorize about what people mean by "racism." The metasemantic theory is a distinct third theory that connects these two. It's a third thing to understand why "racism" refers to racism, what the connection is between the community of speakers and the phenomena of racism in virtue of which they use "racism" to refer to racism.

This tripartite investigation helps us to keep our theoretical inquiries separate. Our investigations into racism are not essentially tied to a semantic theory of what the word "racist" means. We can investigate the phenomenon itself without studying how people use words. By the same token, in principle when theorizing about the semantics of "racism," we do not need to suppose the meaning of this word is essentially tied to our theory of racism. We could speculate about groups who refer to something other than racism using that word, theorize about different possible worlds in which the word means something different, and so on. But at the same time, our inquiry into the actual semantics of "racism" as it is currently used cannot be totally distinct from our theory of racism itself on an externalist approach, since an externalist metasemantic theory establishes the meaning of "racism" as a function of the relationship between communities of speakers and racism itself. A metasemantics for "racism" must presuppose a theory of racism in order to theorize about the meaning-making connection between the community of speakers and racism itself.

6.3.3 *Famous Arguments for Externalism*

Externalism has historically been supported by thought experiments, such as the one I gave when I suggested that "fish" would not have referred to fish if the scaly creatures that swim in the water were all mammals. The original and most famous version of this thought experiment is Putnam's (1975) Twin Earth case: imagine a planet just like Earth with people exactly like humans, speaking a language that sounds just like English, but on this Twin Earth there is no H2O—all the rivers, lakes, clouds, and organic beings are composed of some other chemical substance dubbed XYZ which functions biologically for creatures there in a way that is analogous to the way water functions for us here and which cannot be distinguished from water by any ordinary observation. XYZ is clear, tastes like water, boils at the same temperature, and so on. Putnam argued "water" as used on Twin Earth can't refer to water, because there is no water on Twin Earth, even though every person on Twin Earth is internally mentally organized the same way we are. This argument convinced many philosophers to accept the externalist position.

The Twin Earth thought experiment helps us articulate what internalism is. Historically, internalists maintained that "water" means the same thing on Earth and on Twin Earth. The external differences between the two environments do not suffice for a difference in the semantics of "water." Sociologically, internalists have historically been philosophers who were not convinced by the externalist thought experiment arguments.

Externalism became widely accepted in part because it fits nicely with scientific realism, the view that our best scientific theories give us accurate depictions of objective reality. On a scientific realist picture, fish and whales are distinctive groups in and of themselves. Scientific inquiry reveals the true nature of the difference between them. Externalism allows that we can construct scientific theories about things we incompletely understand. Because we can think and talk about things we don't yet understand, we are able to formulate and test false hypotheses about all kinds of natural phenomena we wish to investigate. We can talk about matter and force, light and gravity, atoms and black holes, whales and fish, racism and gender, while our theories about these things are not yet completely accurate. If our ability to refer to things depended on antecedently knowing exactly what they are, we wouldn't be able to refer to them in the course of formulating what turned out to be false hypotheses about them. Scientific theorizing thus depends on being able to talk about and represent things we have limited understanding of.

The fact that the word "water" referred to H2O even before we discovered that water is H2O is partly due to the fact that we stood in external, meaning determining relations to H2O when we introduced the word "water" for it. These relations let us refer to it before we understood what it was. I think we should say something similar about racism. We were able to think and talk about racism before we understood exactly what that was. People were being racist before we understood clearly what racism is. People introduced a name for racism; they called it "racism." They started labeling incidents of racism, identifying racist practices, and figuring out what crucial features were common among different examples of racism. Some false theories were proposed, such as the theory that racism includes any and all differential treatment on the basis of skin color. This earlier theory does not get at the nature of racism. Not yet having an adequate understanding of racism, people often called things "racist" which were not in fact racist. Although people have disagreed about the nature of racism, with some people having false theories of it and mislabeling things as "racist" that are not racist, they were all talking about the same thing.

Later, more sophisticated and more accurate theories of racism were developed, incorporating more evidence and making finer distinctions. According to these more advanced theories, racism is recognized as a form of systemic domination embedded in the social fabric, organizing social power relations in a wide range of areas. These more advanced theories are about the same thing as earlier theories, namely racism. "Racism" refers to racism on both the earlier inadequate theories and the more advanced later theories. The difference is that the later theories do a better job of explaining what it is. Externalism allows less advanced theories of racism to refer to the same thing as more advanced theories.[8]

So how should externalism be explained metasemantically? What external factors make it the case that "fish" refers to fish, when the internal features of the speaker are not sufficient in and of themselves to secure that referent? In Putnam's thought experiment, the reductive naturalistic metasemantics program found a reason to see causal connections to the physical environment as partly constitutive of the semantic content of an expression. The difference between Earth and Twin Earth seemed to have something important to do with the difference in what substances the people on those planets come into causal contact with. The people on Twin Earth come into contact with XYZ, while people on Earth come into contact with H2O, and this difference in causal interactions appeared to be crucial for determining the meaning of "water." Similarly, in my scenario where the animals in the oceans and lakes are all mammals, the case

---

[8] There is a concern (sometimes raised by white academics who are opposed to applying critical race theory) that such a picture encourages a kind of intellectual elitism where academics, a predominantly white community, are legislating what "racism" means to non-academic folks of color who may not share the same academic theory and who may even be opposed to the critical race theory understanding of racism. Why should academics, especially white academics, be telling non-academic Black folks what racism is? My reply to this worry is that the critical race theory understanding of racism is created by Black, Indigenous, and other theorists of color within the academy and outside of the academy, in conversation with non-academic folks of color, and reflects an understanding of racism that has developed in communities of color over centuries. Even if that understanding is not ubiquitously accepted, it is coming from communities of color, not white academics. See Chap. 8 for more detail.

suggests that the meaning of "fish" has something to do with which kinds of animals the people are catching and eating.

Kripke's (1980) very influential *Naming and Necessity* also contributed to the idea that causal relations were involved in fixing the semantic properties of expressions. Kripke's central thesis was that the content of a name is not a description of the thing it names; rather a name directly refers to the thing and contains no descriptive element of meaning. But how does the reference of a name get fixed? Kripke suggested that a name is introduced through an initial baptism—someone identifies the person they mean to name and says something like, "We'll call her *Holly*," or whatever name they choose. Then the name is passed from person to person by interactions in which one person tells another the name, creating a causal chain of events linking the community of name users back to the initial baptism. Chains of causal relations were suitable for the reductive naturalist because they could (purportedly) be described without appealing to the semantic features of the expressions under use. This causal picture of reference was developed and defended extensively by Devitt (1984).

The picture of causal chains fixing the reference of a name also fit with something Putnam had suggested, viz. that communities make use of a division of linguistic labor. Not everyone in a community must know how every term is applied; as long as someone knows, the community can rely on that person to supply the meaning of the word. Or if causal contact is all that is required to fix the referent of, for example, "fish," it need not be that each individual who uses the word "fish" has come into contact with fish. A person can pick up the word from another member of the community who has seen a fish. This other person also need not have a perfect understanding of the nature of fish or the distinction between fish and whales. Even the initial reference fixers, the people who first started using "fish" as a word for fish, might not know what fish are. They just need to have had perceived some particular fish and named their kind "fish" so they could tell their friends and family members about them.

Much of the discourse around externalist metasemantics was part of the reductive naturalist program.[9] But not every form of externalism must be reductive or naturalistic. The intersectional metasemantics I will propose in Chap. 10 is externalist but does not adhere to the restrictions of reductive naturalism, so I want to spend some more time exploring this idea.

---

[9] See Putnam (1975), Dretske (1987), and Fodor (1998).

6.4 Externalist Metasemantics Without Reductive Naturalism

Burge (1979) was an early dissenter from the reductive program. He wrote, "[T]he assumption that psychological terminology will be ultimately non-intentional and purely functional seems without strong support." In other words, the science of psychology appeals to representations and semantic content, and there seems to be no scientific reason to believe that a more advanced, future psychology would eliminate these features from its discourse.[10] Why then should philosophers presuppose that a more advanced science of psychology or linguistic meaning would be fully reducible to non-semantic terminology?

I agree with Burge that a successful metasemantics for English does not need to eliminate all reference to semantic contents or explain meanings purely in terms of non-semantic phenomena. For example, an explanation of what a word means in a community may invoke semantic notions such as belief or knowledge about the domain of discourse, where belief and knowledge involve representational contents of the same kind as the meanings of words used to express them and the metasemantic origins of these mental contents may be elucidated by reference to the meanings of words as they are used in the community the agent belongs to.

Is such an explanation problematically circular? It depends on how we conceive of the explanatory aims of the metasemantic program. Once we set aside the reductive naturalistic program, there is no longer a very strong reason to explain meanings in terms of non-meanings.

Consider by analogy a theory of physical dynamics. The distribution of force vectors of a system at a time T is a function of the distribution of force vectors in that system at time T-1. What is happening force-wise at any given moment is explained by the distribution of forces at the preceding moment. Is a dynamic physical explanation of this kind problematically circular? Certainly not. Forces are explained in terms of other forces and there's no need for a deeper explanation of what a force is or why there are forces at all. If there were someday a reductive explanation of forces in terms of something else, that would be an interesting breakthrough. But such a breakthrough is not a prerequisite for theorizing about dynamic forces. We don't even expect such a breakthrough.

---

[10] Burge (2010) provides an extended argument for this conclusion.

If a dynamic metasemantics can be constructed in a similar vein, even roughly similar, then there is no reason to eliminate meanings from explanations of meanings. For example, we could provide legitimate explanations about how meanings come into existence, how they spread, and how they are sustained, by giving a theory that appeals to the distribution of semantic properties at earlier times without thereby giving a circular explanation. We might postulate that the word "racist" got its meaning on the basis of things people were saying about racist things and events, where these sayings were themselves semantically interpreted. This kind of explanation does not require us to say what meanings are in some ultimate metaphysical sense, and certainly does not require us to do so in a way that avoids any and all reference to semantic features in the environment.

We could also explain how word meanings spread from person to person in a similar way, viz. by postulating that the first person uses an expression with some semantic property and then another picks up that usage with the same semantic features. Or we can postulate that a group uses a word in a particular way and that individuals pick up the meaning from the group, where the group usage is not merely identical with the individual usage patterns of the group members. This is analogous to views on which groups themselves are not identical with the sets of individuals that compose them (Ritchie, 2013, 2020). Likewise, we could explain what a group means at time T by appealing to what members of the group used that word to mean at time T-1. Insofar as these explanations make no explicit mention of any reductive bridge laws from the semantic to the non-semantic, they enable us to get some distance away from the naturalistic reductive program.

Someone might object that physics is different because it is *the* fundamental science. The correct metasemantics isn't like this—it's not the ultimate theory of reality—so there must be some explanation of how meanings exist in a physical world. But if this is understood as an a priori requirement that the meaning of every expression is explained in virtue of some series of physical events (described without mention any meanings), then as I argued earlier, we do not have strong reason to accept this requirement. If we suppose there is a cogent explanation of meanings in terms of other meanings, this fact by itself may undercut the cogency of reductive explanations that don't mention meanings. If the meaning of expression E depends on patterns of meaningful word uses at other times and places, and if these patterns are essential for explaining why E has the meaning it does, then any theory that refuses to incorporate meanings into its explanation of E's meanings cannot be correct.

Suppose that current meanings are explained in virtue of the recent history of semantically interpreted uses of expressions. Then it's also reasonable to assume that the semantical interpretations of those expressions used in recent history are the result of what words meant in history a little further back, and those word meanings are in turn explained by earlier meanings; on and on back to the earliest days of semantics. Let's suppose that current meaning-making chains go all the way back to early humans over two hundred thousand years ago. It might be that way back then there were some meaning-making events that were part of the origin of language use. It may be that these semantic genesis events could be explained in reductionist terms—some story about how an animal first creates a meaningful symbol. But once there are some meanings, the causal story may involve those meanings in ways that diverge from any cogent or illuminating reductive story. The picture I mean to convey is one in which the causal order of word meanings cannot be traced by looking at generalizations about the underlying physical events without attending to the semantic properties of those events.[11] The metasemantic explanation for every contemporary word meaning on this kind of theory would involve reference to other meanings.

Word meanings don't need to be explained by non-semantic causal relationships between speakers and the things they refer to, as has been suggested by causal chain theories of reference and other kinds of reductive naturalistic metasemantics. Instead, the meaning-determining relationship may involve semantically interpreted acts, like people saying what they think words mean. It also might depend on what they would say about things in the environment, like what they would say counts as a good example of a fish. It might involve reaching agreements about semantic facts, like that "fish" does not refer to mammals. Agreements of this kind involve saying meaningful things.

We use words to explain what we think words mean. If coordination on meanings requires talking meaningfully about meanings, we surely cannot expect a reductive metasemantics to explain how we do it. Again, this is not a problematically circular kind of explanation. We can postulate that word meanings at a given time are partly determined by what people say

---

[11] This picture is akin to Davidson's (1995) anomalous monism, but for semantic properties rather than mental states.

and think about word meanings at earlier times. We can also postulate that what people mean now is a function of what people in their community *would* say under various possible circumstances, but don't actually say. What I mean by "fish" might be determined by what people would say "fish" means, even if they never actually talk about it.

How does a non-reductionist metasemantics account for the fact that a community may not understand what water is and yet refer to it anyway? Reductive naturalistic externalism has to try to explain this feature of language by appeal to causal relations: it's because Earthlings are causally in contact with H2O and not XYZ that explains why the word "water" refers to H2O and not XYZ. Non-reductive metasemantics can say that too, and much more besides. In addition to causal contact, the non-reductionist can appeal to the meaningful speech people use to coordinate their uses of "water," including people's informed reflective agreements about what they think "water" refers to. The fact that people think and say that "water" refers to H2O can be part of the explanation of the fact that it does. Likewise, non-reductive metasemantics can explain how "racism" refers to racism, that it is partly due to the fact that people think and say that "racism" refers to racism. The non-reductivist can also appeal to what people should say about word meanings, as I will explain in detail shortly.

But here political disagreement is once again foregrounded. What happens when people think and say conflicting things about what "racism" means? The metasemantics I argue for in Chap. 10 does not entail that if a population thinks and says that "racism" refers to mere race-based discrimination in the absence of systemic oppression, then they are right. A non-reductive metasemantics can account for such widespread error based on misinformation in many different ways. My approach has a strong affinity for what I take to be Frege's approach to semantics for mathematical languages. The semantic features of our language are not determined by how people actually think and talk about word meanings. They are determined by how people should think and talk about word meanings, given how reality really is—and, I will add in Chap. 8, given the political exigencies we face as a society beset by interlocking systems of oppression.

6.5 Ideal Language Metasemantics

On the non-reductionist approach, externalist meanings may be partly determined by modal facts about what people would say about word meanings under various conditions. We need not postulate that the reference-fixing relation depends only on what people *actually* say or think about the meaning of "fish." The more relevant thing might be what people *would* say or think if prompted to think and talk about it. Most people probably do not talk or think about the meaning of "fish" very often, but they would have a lot to say if you asked them. The same goes for all other words and expressions, including "racism" and "woman." The amount of talking and thinking people actually do about word meanings is not nearly so large as what they would be able to do if prompted. Plausibly these robust modal facts are more relevant for determining the meaning of words than the little bit people actually say.

This opens a wide range of questions concerning which possible thoughts and conversations bear on the externalist determination of word meanings. Which possible thoughts and assertions determine the meaning of "racist"? I suggest that the possible thoughts and statements of people who are misinformed about the nature of racism are not relevant to the meaning-determining relation. Only people who know what they are talking about make a meaning-fixing contribution to the communal metasemantic profile. This holds generally. Those who know what they are talking about contribute to the fixation of reference, both in terms of their actual behavior but even more so in what they would say about the meanings of words if they were asked to explain them. Those who do not know what they are talking about do not contribute in the same way. The presence of misinformation within a community thereby disables people from being contributors to meaning making.

Misinformed people make a contribution to meaning making only in an idealized sense: it matters what they *would* say if they were no longer ignorant or misinformed about the domain in question. So, the way a white supremacist uses the word "racist" is not completely irrelevant to what the word means; the meaning of that word depends on what the white supremacist would say about racism if their ignorance were dispelled. Likewise, the usage patterns of "woman" by transphobic enforcers of cisnormativity matter to some degree. But what matters is how these people would use the word "woman" if they understood more about gender. Misinformed people don't use words *completely* wrongly. The bits they get right help to determine that their words are aimed at representing a part of reality that they incompletely understand, but what really matters is what they would say if they were better informed.

When we give our assessment of the metasemantic determinants of a word like "racist," the perspective I am proposing requires us to endorse an antecedent understanding of racism in order to ascertain who is misinformed about it. This is similar to all forms of externalism. We utilize a background theory concerning the domain of discourse in order to assert what the meaning-determining relationships are. It is part of the externalist metasemantics for "fish" that there are fish swimming in the water, and we draw on our non-semantic theory of fish to specify what fish are. For "racism," we utilize our sociological theory of racism to specify the meaning-fixing relationship between the community and racism itself. The externalism I have in mind relies on what an informed version of the community would say about the meaning of "racism," and given that racism involves systemic oppression, a well-informed community would say that "racism" refers to a form of systemic oppression.

The idea that reference is fixed by what the well-informed would say, and that we ascertain who counts as well-informed based in part on our theory of the reality to which the words refer, sits very well with popular externalist intuitions about Putnam's Twin Earth thought experiment. Everyone knows that "water" refers to water, but only the experts know what water really is. They are the well-informed ones, and so their understanding of the meaning of the word determines its referent. But this was true even at a time when no one understood the nature of the referent. In Putnam's original thought experiment, he points out that people in the 1700s referred to water with the word "water," even though they did not yet understand fully what water was. A person who was more completely informed about the nature of water would have been able to say more clearly what the word referred to, that is, H_2O, even though no one at the time was sufficiently well-informed.

On this basis we postulate that at a given time, the modal facts that determine what a word refers to include what a better-informed person would say the word referred to. So even if the community is in a state of confusion at the present moment, reference can be determined by the thoughts and statements of a better-informed person, even if no such actual person exists at present. The meaning of "water" in 1700 was determined by what a better-informed person would have said it refers to, even though this person did not exist yet. Equivalently in this case, the referent of "water" was fixed in 1700 by the thoughts and statements of a merely possible person who understood better what water was. This dependence on counterfactual knowledge is not really so strange; it fits nicely with the scientific realism intuition. Our scientific terms presently refer to what a (perhaps merely possible) better-informed scientist would say they refer to.

In the case of "racism," things are perhaps a bit trickier. According to intersectionality and critical race theory, there is a great deal of misinformation about racism at work within the social fabric. The function of this misinformation is to obscure the nature of racism in order to facilitate its propagation into the future. Misinformation about racism is part of what Charles Mills (1997) calls white ignorance, the socially sanctioned bad epistemic practices that mask the existence and operation of white supremacy as a political system. Due to the presence of this misinformation, many people's thoughts and statements are inert with respect to the reference-fixing relation for "racism," namely those people who are in the grip of white ignorance. Their counterfactual thoughts and statements contribute to the reference fixing relation, but only at possible worlds where they are no longer misinformed.

Those who more accurately understand racism, saying and thinking true things about racism, more closely enact the usage patterns of the ideal linguistic community. By emulating those who understand racism and accepting corrections from them, we adjust our own usage to accord with what the ideal community would say the meaning of "racist" is.

The anti-reductionist externalist metasemantics fits neatly with the social epistemology of word meanings. Our best estimation of what "racist" currently means is guided by our estimation of who best understands what racism is. Those who know what racism is are the best guide to how we should use the word "racist" because their linguistic behavior will most closely resemble the linguistic behavior of the ideal linguistic community, and the meaning of "racist" is determined by the practices of the ideal version of our linguistic community (including their statements about what "racist" means). At the same time, our estimation of who counts as an expert on racism is partly conditioned by our understanding of racism itself. And all of these features of our epistemic situation are conditioned by politics. I will not treat a critical race theorist as an expert on racism if I agree with the Trump administration's view of critical race theory and intersectional identity politics as a "creed [that] creates new hierarchies as unjust as the old hierarchies of the antebellum South,"[12] literally asserting that Black feminist politics around racism are the moral equivalent of chattel slavery.

The meaning of "racist" is not determined by what anyone presently thinks it means, unless someone presently has a perfect understanding of the phenomenon of racism. "Racist" means what a fully informed speaker

---

[12] President's Advisory Committee (2021), that is, *The 1776 Report*, Appendix III pp. 33.

would take it to mean. We therefore work toward understanding what "racist" means by working to understand what racism itself is. Understanding what "racist" means requires, minimally, not believing that critical race theory is the ideological equivalent of white supremacist antebellum South.

Surely there must be some relationship between truth and power, because the spread of ignorance and misinformation is a political tool for controlling what passes for truth within a social fabric. How can a metasemantics provide a theoretical framework for postulating objective truth in English and provide for the possibility that "BLM is racist" is objectively false, while still recognizing the influence of power over people's belief systems? I have already begun in earnest to address that question by formulating a metasemantics on which truth is not susceptible to semantic corruption by the production of ignorance. The next chapter builds on this theory by providing a thorough account of social power and interrogating the way in which power is related to truth and misinformation.

References

Burge, T. (1979). Individualism and the Mental. *Midwest Studies in Philosophy*, 4, 73–121.
Burge, T. (2010). *Origins of Objectivity*. Oxford University Press.
Burgess, A., & Sherman, B. (2014). A Plea for the Metaphysics of Meaning. In A. Burgess & B. Sherman (Eds.), *Metasemantics: New Essays on the Foundations of Meaning*. Oxford University Press.
Carnap, R. (1936/2002). *The Logical Syntax of Language*. Open Court Publishing.
Carnap, R. (1950). Empiricism, Semantics, and Ontology. *Revue internationale de philosophie*, 1, 20–40.
Chomsky, N. (1959). A Review of B F. Skinner's Verbal Behavior. *Language*, 35(1), 26–58.
Davidson, D. (1995). 5 Mental Events. *Contemporary Materialism: A Reader*, 107, 1.
Dennett, D. (1987). *The Intentional Stance*. MIT Press.
Devitt, M. (1984). Designation.
Field, H. (1972). Tarski's Theory of Truth. *The Journal of Philosophy*, 69(13), 347–375.
Field, H. H. (1977). Logic, Meaning, and Conceptual Role. *The Journal of Philosophy*, 74(7), 379–409.

Fodor, J. A. (1974). Special Sciences (or: The Disunity of Science as a Working Hypothesis). *Synthese*, 28(2), 97–115.
Fodor, J. A. (1975). *The Language of Thought (Vol. 5)*. Harvard University Press.
Fodor, J. A. (1987). *Psychosemantics: The Problem of Meaning in the Philosophy of Mind*. MIT Press.
Fodor, J. A. (1997). Special Sciences: Still Autonomous After All These Years. *Philosophical Perspectives*, 11, 149–163.
Fodor, J. A. (1998). *Concepts: Where Cognitive Science Went Wrong*. Oxford University Press.
Greenberg, M., & Harman, G. (2005). Conceptual Role Semantics.
Hempel, C. (1949). The Logical Analysis of Psychology. In H. Feigl & W. Sellars (Eds.), *Readings in Philosophical Analysis* (pp. 373–384). Appleton-Century-Crofts.
Lewis. (1983). New Work for a Theory of Universals. *Australasian Journal of Philosophy*, 61(4), 343–377.
Loar, B. (1981). *Mind and Meaning*. Cambridge University Press.
Melville, H. (1851/1992). *Moby Dick, or, The whale*. Modern Library ed. New York: Modern Library.
Mills, C. W. (1997/2014). *The Racial Contract*. Cornell University Press.
Neurath, O. (1937). Unified Science and Its Encyclopaedia. *Philosophy of Science*, 4(2), 265–277.
President's Advisory Committee. (2021). The 1776 Report.
Putnam, H. (1975). The Meaning of 'meaning'. *Philosophical Papers*, 2, 1.
Putnam, H. (1981). *Reason, Truth and History*. Cambridge University Press.
Quine, W. V. O. (1951). Two Dogmas of Empiricism. *Philosophical Review*, 60(1), 20–43.
Quine, W. V. O. (1960). *Word and Object*. MIT Press.
Ritchie, K. (2013). What Are Groups? *Philosophical Studies*, 166(2), 257–272.
Ritchie, K. (2020). Social Structures and the Ontology of Social Groups. *Philosophy and Phenomenological Research*, 100(2), 402–424.
Sarkar, S. (1992). Models of Reduction and Categories of Reductionism. *Synthese*, 91(3), 167–194.
Schiffer, S. (1972). *Meaning*. Clarendon Press.
Schiffer, S. (1987). *Remnants of Meaning*. MIT Press.
Skinner, B. F. (1957). *Verbal Behavior*. Appleton-Century-Crofts.
Stich, S. P. (1983). *From Folk Psychology to Cognitive Science: The Case Against Belief*. MIT Press.
Wittgenstein, L. (1953). *Philosophical Investigations*, G.E.M. Anscombe and R. Rhees (eds.), G.E.M. Anscombe (Trans.), Oxford: Blackwell.
Yalcin, S. (2014). Semantics and Metasemantics in the Context of Generative Grammar. In A. Burgess & B. Sherman (Eds.), *Metasemantics: New Essays on the Foundations of Meaning* (pp. 17–54). Oxford University Press.

CHAPTER 7

Power and Regimes of Truth

7.1 Situated Skepticism About the Concept of Power

The concept of power is integral to intersectionality studies and critical theory. Power is the fundamental unit in terms of which systems of oppression are understood. Racism, patriarchy, heterosexism, neoliberal capitalism, and cis supremacy are all fundamentally about power, the power vested in systems that exploit, exclude, and oppress some for the benefit of others. These systems of oppression are sustained by the production and distribution of misinformation and ideology, and this production is also a function of power. Power is the subject matter of political struggle.

The possibility of operating our political machine on the basis of truth is also a question of power. Social justice movements struggle for the power to inform our political institutions in light of what is true about the systems of oppression that organize our society. This includes a struggle over control of the diffuse social epistemic apparatus that ascertains what the words of public language mean. The power to shape public opinions about the meanings of words is thus an object of political struggle. But when we realize that public opinion does not metasemantically determine the meanings of words, we can separate the power struggle from the semantics. Truth itself is not an object of political struggle.

In this chapter I develop a theory of power and its relation to truth based on the ideas of the foremost theorist of power—Michel Foucault. The concept of power is widely regarded with suspicion within the world of analytic philosophy. My aim is to develop a view of power and its relationship with truth that fits within both the critical theory tradition and the analytic tradition. My view sees power as holding influence over what is considered to be true. It aims to validate Michel Foucault's methodology of interrogating the ways in which power influences operations of the words "true" and "truth" within political, academic, and scientific discourses, and the ways power flows from those discourses back into the social and political spheres (Foucault 1980). At the same time, my view represents truth itself as an objective property which can be ascertained through evidence and argument.

When I talk about the operation of truth in a discourse, I am referring to the operation of symbols—the word "truth" and its mental analogue, the concept of truth. These symbols operate within a social fabric in virtue of people saying and writing things to one another, institutions sending official emails, grant proposals being accepted or rejected, governmental agencies writing intelligence briefings, police signing affidavits, journal articles being published. Truth itself is a property of representations, sentences, thoughts, and beliefs that is not tied essentially to the use of the word "truth" within a social fabric. Truth itself is not a matter of what people say is "true." How a society uses the word "true" and how it interprets its meaning do not determine what is actually true. Power affects what is taken to be true, what is believed to be true, what is treated as true, what is sanctioned as true by officially recognized institutions, what the official and unofficial conditions for accepting a statement as true are. It affects which statements function as true. But power does not ultimately determine what *is* true.

I believe this is how Foucault understood his own theory of the connection between truth and power, not as a theory of truth itself but of how our representations of truth influence and are influenced by the grid of social power. My view of power and its relation to truth, inspired by Foucault's, is intended to allow a clear sense in which sentences have objective truth-conditions that are independent of the operation of power, even though the operation of power over how people use the concept of truth is a very significant aspect of the matrix of domination (Collins, 2002) and a central battleground in liberatory political struggle.

Why is Foucault's concept of power denigrated within the world of analytic philosophy? Part of the explanation has to do with the poststructuralist analyses that have been conducted using Foucault's ideas. These poststructuralist analyses invoke the concept of power to attack central propositions of European Enlightenment philosophy: that we can have clear and distinct ideas, that we can analyze our concepts a priori by reflecting on them (without, for example, considering the role they play in maintaining structures of oppression), that we can have objective knowledge of reality, that rationality is a universal and objective property that reliably leads to objective knowledge, and that there is a self that can be identified in abstraction from social constructions beset with power relations. To critique these ideas from the poststructuralist Foucauldian perspective involves showing how power has shaped the operation of concepts. Poststructuralist critique even extends to the concept of objective truth itself, pressing the concern that its deployment is merely the effect of the field of power relations.

The poststructuralist hermeneutics of power is antagonistic to the methodology of traditional analytic philosophy and its practitioners who mostly ignore power relations when doing conceptual analyses. Analytic philosophers typically argue about the correct application of concepts without any reference to how the deployment of that concept operates within the field of social and political struggle. Poststructuralist critique portrays the standard analytic philosopher as ignoring the influence of power over their own theoretical considerations and as thereby crucially missing the fact that their own conclusions are the effect of power.

Analytic philosophers tend to see poststructuralist criticism as fallacious, as theoretical puffery, and as lacking any substance. The analytic philosopher's methodology is supported by a background epistemology that legitimates ignoring sociology and contingent social situation. The critical theory objection contradicts that background epistemology by presupposing that sociological factors could be relevant for philosophical argumentation. From the analytic perspective, the poststructuralist critique fallaciously infers that something is false because it is sociologically problematic, and the poststructuralist covers up this fallacious argument with a flurry of muddled thinking and imperspicuous concepts.

The Foucauldian concept of power is often viewed as one of these sham concepts, failing to pass muster in the rigorous analytic discourse that refuses to admit any concept as legitimate that has not been thoroughly vetted through an extended process of giving and refuting necessary and sufficient conditions for the concept's application, this discursive process being the hallmark of analytic philosophy. Analytic philosophers legitimate one another in being skeptical about it. They license one another to not read Foucault and to be cynical about anything based on Foucault, again without reading or thinking hard about it.

Skepticism about the concept of power is spread through analytic philosophy departments among graduate students and teachers alike. Poststructuralism is disparaged as incoherent, as a false pretense to legitimate philosophy, and as the refuge of those who can't or won't think hard about a subject matter. The disparagement extends to the official processes that dispense power within the philosophy world: journal referees and PhD granting committees are well-trained in recognizing the alleged chicanery of poststructuralist critique. Consequently, whenever poststructuralist ideas appear within a piece of analytic philosophy writing or commentary, the highest standards of rigor and argumentation are applied to judge the project, arguably far higher than the standards used to judge more mainstream work.[1] This procedure culls most any project that relies on critical theory. Ironically, the social power vested in the analytic philosophy community exerts itself within the discourse to limit and marginalize the participation of poststructuralist ideas and critiques.

Part of my aim in this chapter is to take the analytic philosopher's challenge head on and provide an analytically acceptable theory of power and its relationship with truth, to satisfy the high degree of methodological rigor demanded within the analytic tradition for such a project as mine. I am giving what is called a *rational reconstruction* of Foucault's theory in terms the analytic philosopher can accept. Pursuing the project in this way is only a strategic approach to interfacing with the analytic philosophical discourse. I don't mean to suggest that poststructural analysis should or must conform to the strictures of analytic philosophy. I think the ways in which analytic philosophical discourse restricts engagement with critical theory can legitimately be critiqued as an exercise of oppressive power.

I agree with the perspective from which power pervades all aspects of discourse. Yet I do not think this fact destabilizes the crucial concepts of epistemology such as truth and knowledge. I also do not think it

---

[1] For example, the methods of mainstream analytic philosophy may be taken for granted, simply assumed, while a critical theory paper presented in an analytic context must justify and defend its methodology—against extreme skepticism—in addition to making its central point.

destabilizes the crucial concepts implicated in today's political struggles for social justice, such as the concept of racism or the concept of gender. In order to formulate and comprehend an intersectional theory of truth and its relationship with power, we need a theory of power on which the existence of objective truth is secured even as we recognize the ubiquitous influence of power within a discourse.

I will draw on Foucault's theory of power as my starting point. I think much of what I have to say is what Foucault said about power. I think Foucault's own understanding of power aligns with my understanding, but I will not be centrally interested in defending this historical interpretive claim. I will develop my view through a close reading of two of Foucault's writings on the subject of truth: the suggestively named "Truth and Power" (Foucault 1980) and Chap. 2 of *The History of Sexuality: An Introduction*.[2]

Section 7.2 gives the theory of power. Section 7.3 considers some objections to the theory I propose. I then go on to apply this theory of power in Sect. 7.4 to talk about the relation between power and truth. The conclusion of this chapter, Sect. 7.5, draws attention to how this relation between truth and power is connected with epistemic violence and intersectionality in the misinformation age.

7.2 FOUCAULT ON POWER

Foucault (1978) begins his exposition of the concept of power by saying what power is not. "[T]he word power is apt to lead to a number of misunderstandings ... with regard to its nature, its form, and its unity. By power I do not mean ...,"[3] and then he lists three things one should not mistake as the essence or nature of power.

Power is NOT "a group of institutions and mechanisms that ensure the subservience of the citizens of a given state." Power is not identical with the institutions that undergird the nation state. The institutions themselves—governing bodies, the lawmakers, the courts, the police, the military, and so on—are loci of power. They generate power and are created through the application of power. They apply force in various ways through the influence of power. But they are not power itself. They are more like generators and conduits of power.

---

[2] Foucault (1972/1980), Foucault (1978/1990).
[3] Foucault (1978), p. 92, including the following quotes to be explained.

Power is NOT "a mode of subjugation which, in contrast to violence, has the form of the rule." Power is not identical with or fundamentally grounded in the officially mandated rules and laws that subjugate people. A 'mode of subjugation' in the form of a rule of law—in other words, a system of oppressive laws—is a socially constructed entity that harnesses the power of such institutions as the state, the courts, the police, the military, and the prisons, in order to enforce a kind of social order. Again, power is more metaphysically primitive than the existence of laws.

Power is NOT "a general system of domination exerted by one group over another, a system whose effects, through successive derivations, pervade the entire social body." Power is not identical with or fundamentally grounded in the unofficial rules, customs, and relationships that pervade the social order and sustain social hierarchies and matrices of domination. Systems of domination that promote the interests of one group over another are constructed using power. Systemic oppression provides power to the privileged and deprives the marginalized of it. Power is thus a more basic concept than that of a system of domination. Systems of domination are built on the basis power for the sake of creating and controlling power.

Power is importantly implicated in all of these things. Foucault's point is we should not identify power as fundamentally constituted by any of these phenomena. Power is a more basic unit. Nation states, laws, and systems of domination are to be explained in terms of power, but they are not power itself. Foucault summarizes these points explicitly. "The analysis, made in terms of power, must not assume that the sovereignty of the state, the form of the law, or the over-all unity of a domination are given at the outset; rather, these are only the terminal forms power takes."[4]

A theory of power should explain how the state is formed, organized, and sustained; how the law is constructed, applied, and enforced; how systems of domination come into being and operate. It should not be done the other way around, explaining power in terms of social institutions. Assuming the existence of domination in giving a theory of power would put the cart before the horse in the order of explanation. Power is the more fundamental explanatory unit, the theoretical notion in terms of which more complex social structures are to be theorized.

To illuminate Foucault's theory of the social fabric, it is helpful to consider analogies and disanalogies between power and the concept of energy in physics. In some crucial respects, power is to the social sphere as energy

[4] Ibid., p. 92.

is to physics. Power is the determining property in the dynamic evolution of social systems, just as energy is the fundamental determining property in the dynamic evolution of physical systems. Power is the basis of force fields of interaction between social entities, just as energy is the basis of force fields of physical interactions. The potential force of a social entity—that which it has but is not currently applying—might be described as its rest power, the intrinsic constitution of that entity in terms of its potential force relations with respect to other social entities. This is analogous to the rest energy of a physical object. The rest energy of a physical object determines its invariant mass, which tells us the object's intrinsic energy content. The intrinsic power content of a social object is its resting potential for doing work in the social sphere, which is carried out through the application of power.

There are also crucial disanalogies between power and physical energy. Examining these helps illuminate what is distinctive about a dynamic theory of the social world, and the concept of power which is the fundamental determinant of dynamic social evolution.

Power, unlike energy, is not necessarily transferred to the object upon which it works. Often power works on marginalized groups and institutions to divest them of power, for example, when the KKK's paramilitary power worked to divest Black folks of their voting power during post-Reconstruction. In the dynamics of a Foucauldian power system, the power operative in one system can siphon power into itself or undermine the power of others. We need not conceive of this transfer as a zero-sum exchange, which leads us to the next disanalogy.

Power, unlike energy, is not conserved. The total energy in the universe never changes, but the total amount of social power does. Events in the physical, social, financial, and political world can produce increases in the total amount of power in the social system. The invention of new technologies, such as a cure for cancer or a vaccine for COVID-19, increases the total power within the community. This increase does not necessitate a decrease elsewhere in the system. When a group of people who were disorganized become more organized, their power to affect the system increases. This may decrease the power of others to some extent. Those who would oppose the will of the newly organized group may lose power. But there is no a priori reason to think the increase of power within the organizing group must be exactly counterbalanced by a net decrease in the power of all others.

There can also be total decreases in the power of the total social system. A war that kills many people, destabilizes governments, and destroys infrastructure decreases the total power in the system. Similar loss of power can happen through a pandemic. Lastly, consider that if all life in the universe were extinguished, all social power would be extinguished, while the total energy of the system would remain unchanged by such an event. Hence, social power, unlike physical energy, is not necessarily conserved.

The fact that social power is not conserved means there can be no analog in the social realm to a time-reversible dynamics like we have in physics. You cannot begin with the current distribution of power and trace the system backward to its beginning, because along the timeline there are sudden appearances of new power. This also means that a social system is not deterministic in the sense of a classical dynamic physical system. An omnipotent demon can't tell exactly what will happen in the social world by attending only to the power dynamics that exist within the social realm, since the events of the social world are also determined by physical forces that occur outside the explanatory domain of a social theory. This is also related to the fact that new forms of power can be created through the operation of non-social physical forces. When a community gains power through achieving access to the internet, this newly created power is partly a function of newly created physical systems—the systems that physically enable access to the internet. When a community is damaged through a natural disaster, this can cause its members and institutions to lose power. Obviously, landsides and wildfires and other natural events can't be predicted on the basis of social factors alone, so the evolution of the social world cannot be perfectly predicted on the basis of social factors alone.[5]

This fact has to do with yet another disanalogy between power and energy. While energy and power are both explanatorily fundamental within their own respective domains, power is not a metaphysically fundamental property, whereas physical energy might be. Events in the social realm are influenced and constituted by events within the physical world, but the physical world is not constituted by the social world in the same way. The physical world may be fully deterministic, and perhaps this means the social world is also deterministic in a sense, but a dynamic theory of social systems that postulates power as its fundamental explanatory unit is not

---

[5] Even the most powerfully predictive social dynamic theory ever imagined—psychohistory—falls prey to this essential shortcoming; see Isaac Asimov's (2004) *Foundation and Empire*.

itself a theory of physics and so does not account for every event that is relevant to the development of the social world.

Foucault recognized this autonomy of a theory of social dynamics. He writes, "power must be understood in the first instance as the multiplicity of force relations immanent in the sphere in which they operate and which constitute their own organization[.]"[6] The sphere in which they operate is the social world, the sphere of things and events that belong to the social order. In saying that power's characteristic force relations are "immanent" in that sphere, I read Foucault as avowing the idea just outlined that power is an explanatory concept of the social order that applies only within the domain of dynamical social interactions. This is not to say that power cannot be drawn from purely physical objects and events, as happens when a person fashions a tool or a weapon from physical components. It only means that the characteristic force relations that power enters into hold between things belonging to the social ontology. Here we also see Foucault affirming the analogy between power and energy when he says that fundamentally power should be construed in terms of force relations—the force relations of the social world. We also find an affirmation of the concept of resting power as the constitutive nature of a social entity when he writes that instances of power include the multiplicity of force relations that constitute the organization of social entities.

Foucault writes, "[power must be understood] as the process which, through ceaseless struggles and confrontations, transforms, strengthens, or reverses [the multiplicity of force relations in the social sphere.]" In other words, it is of the nature of power that it be the crucial determinant in the evolution of social systems, where that evolution is understood in terms of the transformation of power relations. The action of power is to affect the distribution of power within the system. This also can involve altering the composition of social entities, viz. by altering their potential power relations.

Foucault's idea that the nature of power is to affect configurations of power might sound problematically circular, but it isn't. In physics, one moment of the energy configuration determines the next moment of the energy configuration. Just as the physical dynamic transforms the system from one configuration of energy into another as a function of the distribution of energy in that system at a time, so too does the social dynamic transform the system from one configuration of power relations into

---

[6] Ibid., p. 92. The proceeding quotations are all from this passage.

another as the result of the distribution of power in that system. In the dynamic social theory, the power distribution at one moment leads to the power distribution at the next. The effect of power at time T1 is to bring about a new configuration of power at some later time T2. This dynamic function is the essence of power, just as the essence of energy is intimately connected with the effect of energy on later states of energy. The analogy shows why there is no circularity in saying that the characteristic action of power is to create new configurations of power.

Foucault says power must be understood "as the support which these force relations find in one another, thus forming a chain or a system, or on the contrary, the disjunctions and contradictions which isolate them from one another." Force relations are the fundamental constituents that make up social entities. Power relationships make compound social entities coherent when the parts of the compound social object lend support to one another. Meanwhile, social entities are made distinct from one another by the "disjunctions and contradictions which isolate them from one another." This is a principle of individuation between social objects. The unity of a social object consists in mutually supporting power relations between its parts, while the distinctness of two social objects consists in the potential for them to exert power in distinct and potentially opposing ways.

For example, to the extent that the Church and the State are distinct, this is because their internal systems of power are disjoint, and their strategic initiatives at least potentially contradict one another. Similarly, for the separation of the executive and judicial branches of the US government, the distinctness of these institutions is constituted by internally coherent but externally antagonistic power relations. Likewise, social identity groups are distinctively identified in terms of the internal coherence of their strategic goals and the oppositions they face from antagonistic groups and institutions. Even individuals themselves can be thought of as constituted (within the social sphere) by their power relationships to other social entities.

Elaborating the relationship between social entities and their underlying constitutive power relations, Foucault writes, "[power] is the moving substrate of force relations which, by virtue of their inequality, constantly engender states of power, but the latter are always local and unstable." The picture is analogous to the existence of macroscopic objects in relation to the physical forces that constitute them at a microscopic level. The social entities are like the macroscopic objects and the power relations that undergird their existence are like the microphysical forces. The macroscopic social entities are "local" in the sense that the underlying power relationships that constitute their existence are operative in a unique way surrounding their location in social space. They are "unstable" in the sense that they are liable to come apart, to decompose into their more fundamental constituents. In the social sphere, this means that macroscopic social entities can be decomposed into their microscopic constituents, or in other words, destroyed.[7]

Foucault's theory of power fits nicely with an intersectional framework that recognizes unique social roles for identities in the grip of intersecting systems of oppression. The social entities composed of social force relations are unstable in the sense that those underlying power relationships are always in flux. A large social entity such as capitalism or white supremacy or the male gaze is liable to change forms, shift its boundaries, encompass new forms of power, and so on. The matrix of domination changes constantly in its relation to all of the smaller social entities, such as people, families, local businesses and schools, affecting them in new and innovative ways as the power structure continues to evolve. Moreover, the relationships between individuals and groups can be very specific and nuanced in ways that reflect structural intersectionality. Racism and sexism are not wholly distinct forms of power.

What is the extent of power within the social domain? If this picture is accurate, then power is the very substance of the social world and constitutes its fundamental ontology. Foucault is famous for saying "power is everywhere," and this is the sense in which he means it. He writes,

> The omnipresence of power: not because it has the privilege of consolidating everything under its invincible unity, but because it is produced from one moment to the next, at every point, or rather in every relation from one point to another. Power is everywhere; not because it embraces everything, but because it comes from everywhere. (Foucault 1978, p. 93)

---

[7] This part makes me think of Hobbes's (1651) *Leviathan*. The sovereign or the state can be decomposed when the social order fails, in which case what remains is the power of the individuals in the state of nature. The microscopic constituents of macroscopic social entities like the sovereign or the state include the myriad power relations that exist in the state of nature among people, including their physical abilities, their weapons, and their knowledge. When these micro power relations are organized in a certain way through the social contract, the sovereign is created and imbued with power from below. Of course, Foucault's theory of power is much more generalized than social contract theory.

Every entity within the social sphere is a source of power, is constituted by social power, and also through its activities has the potential to generate new power. Power comes from everywhere, even from non-social entities—everything from sticks and caves to computers and vaccines—because of the way the social fabric makes use of everything. Laws, information, concepts, resources, land, weapons, doctorates, police badges, golf skills, math textbooks, expensive cars, backyard pools, and middle school lunch tables—everything is a potential source of social power.

There are mind-bogglingly many kinds of power that exist in the social sphere. The police have the power to arrest people and even kill them without repercussion under certain circumstances. The state has the power to eliminate homelessness. Some people have the power to express their gender or sexuality freely, while others do not. Some institutions have the power to control which bathrooms a person can enter. Some people have the power that comes with positive body image. The marketing sector has immense power to both reinforce and exploit peoples' need for positive body image. Developing new medical technologies increases our power to treat cancer and heart disease. Access to these technologies is restricted through social power. Smartphones give us the power to stay in contact with one another and access the vast stores of information connected through the internet. The internet lends power to disinformation brokers, hackers, and politicians. Dementia divests a person of the power to operate within the normal parameters of human interaction requiring memory and reasoning. The social fabric is made up of all of these social power relations and indefinitely many more.

One might think that because the concept of power is so all-encompassing, it is in fact meaningless. Everything is power, so the concept of power does not draw any distinctions. Everything falls under its extension. Some theorists think that for a word to be meaningful, it must divide the domain into distinctive parts.[8] I've heard it claimed, for exam-

---

[8] This idea is an artifact of De Saussure's (1916) linguistic theory, semiotics, which postulates that semantics depends on binary opposition: words only have semantic values insofar as their semantic function can be contrasted with an oppositional term. Binary opposition is also the precondition for deconstruction as that concept was deployed by Derrida (1967). Binary opposition is not entailed by model-theoretic semantics, which can assign meanings to terms which have no binary oppositional term. For example, the expression "trumpet" can be assigned an extension, the set of trumpets, without postulating that there is some term which is the binary opposite of "trumpet" (which I suppose would be a word for all and only non-trumpets?). Most analytic philosophers of language reject binary opposition as a precon-

ple, that if everything counts as racist, then "racism" is meaningless, and racism doesn't exist. But these are logical errors in reasoning. Just because everything has a property doesn't mean nothing has that property. If everything has energy, it doesn't logically follow that nothing has energy, or that "energy" is meaningless. It's logically possible that everything in the social sphere is or is composed of power.

Another crucial aspect of power according to Foucault, and another major disanalogy with physical energy, is that power has its own inherent rationality. In a sense, power is to be understood as having its own agency, its own directives, goals, and strategies. Of power itself, Foucault says, "there is no power that exerts itself without a series of aims and objectives. But this does not mean that it results from the choice or decision of an individual subject." The aims and objectives are attributed to power itself, not to the people who wield it or the institutions that are composed by it. As the undercurrents of power coalesce and act to bring about the existence of social institutions and entities, these underlying activities can (according to Foucault) be properly or helpfully thought of as intentionally directed, as if controlled by a mind acting on the basis of reasons, enacting its own strategies, even though this intentional and directed activity need not be housed in the mind of any individual and need not be rooted even in the collective conscious decisions of a group of individuals.

On the rational autonomy of power, Foucault writes,

> let us not look for the headquarters that presides over its rationality; neither the caste which governs, nor the groups which control the state apparatus, nor those who make the most important economic decisions direct the entire network of power that functions in a society (and makes it function); the rationality of power is characterized by tactics that are often quite explicit ... the aims [of power are] decipherable, and yet it is often the case that no one is there to have invented them, and few who can be said to have formulated them ... (Foucault 1978, p. 95)

There are two crucial claims here: (1) that power is intelligible only insofar as we attribute rationality to it, and (2) that its rationality cannot be traced or reduced to the individuals who are operating with it. Before asking whether this could be true—let's postpone that until Sect. 7.3—I will illustrate this idea using a couple of examples.

dition on semantic value. This fact has something to do with why analytic philosophers are typically baffled by Derrida's concept of deconstruction.

My first example comes from John Steinbeck's *Grapes of Wrath*.[9] Oklahoma tenant farmers are getting kicked off their land during the Great Depression. The landowner comes to tell the tenants they must vacate their home, which is to be bulldozed the next day. The landowner says, "We're sorry. It's not us. It's the monster. The bank isn't like a man." The tenant says, "Yes, but the bank is only made of men."

The landowner replies, "No, you're wrong there—quite wrong there. The bank is something else than men. It happens that every man in a bank hates what the bank does, and yet the bank does it. The bank is something more than men, I tell you. It's the monster. Men made it, but they can't control it."

When the man driving a tractor comes to bulldoze their house, the tenant threatens that he will shoot the tractor driver. The driver points out that the bank will just send another driver. Then the tenant asks, "Who gave you orders? I'll go after him. He's the one to kill." But as the driver points out, the one who told him to bulldoze their house got his orders from the bank.

Then the tenant suggests he will shoot the bank president and the board of directors. The driver tells him the bank is responsible to shareholders who will just fill those positions with new people. If he shoots the president and the board, they'll just be replaced by others.

Exasperated, the tenant asks, "But where does it stop? Who can we shoot?"

To which the driver gives the final answer, "I don't know. Maybe there's nobody to shoot. Maybe the thing isn't men at all."

Here the bank provides an example of an institution, a conglomeration of force relations within the social sphere both constituted by power and a user of power, which has definite and intelligible motives and rationality, but where those motives and rationality are not constituted by the people who work for the bank, or even those for whom the bank works. Perhaps all bank's employees are horrified by what it does and would oppose it if they had the power. Most beneficiaries of the bank, those who make money from the bank, who rely on it for loans, and so on, are not sure how it works. By and large, users of the bank have no hand in implementing or carrying out its strategies. The employees who carry out its strategies have little or no power to control what the bank does. To understand a bank we postulate procedures, economic strategies, and goals that

---

[9] Steinbeck (1939), Chap. 5.

motivate its actions, and this in fact does not require postulating any intentions or strategies of the individuals who work for the institution or derive benefits from it.

A person can become the CEO of a powerful bank like JPChase Morgan or a state can wield the power generated by a bank such as Chinese Construction Bank. Actors in the field of social power relations can gain access to the power of an institution. But the power doesn't reside essentially within these actors; rather, they wield it and it flows through them. But even then, the human's interests merely align with the interests of the institution as a precondition for their coming to power. If those interests should come apart, the CEO will be fired. If the head of a state should find themselves in opposition to the state itself, they will be divested of power.

I think this is what Foucault means when he says, "Power is not something that is acquired, seized, or shared, something that one holds on to or allows to slip away."[10] He means power is not *essentially* something possessed by a person, although people do acquire, seize, and share power. A person can acquire power in the sense of coming into a position to direct the operation of power in accord with their own will, but a person cannot have power in any inherent sense, beyond perhaps their own biological powers. Power should not be understood as fundamentally something individual people hold or use.

To vary the example from a bank to something of a larger ontological scale, lets focus on the phenomenon of white ignorance (Mills, 2007), which is an aspect of whiteness itself. White ignorance is a form of group-based miscognition about the nature and extent of racism that functions to preserve systems of domination and oppression that privilege those who are racialized as white at the expense of those who are racialized as nonwhite. White ignorance can appear at the individual level, as when a white person fails to recognize microaggressions or white privilege. It can pose as knowledge of social justice, as when someone says they are against all forms of racism including anti-white racism. It can appear within institutions, for example, as a ban on racial sensitivity training or a ban on teaching critical race theory at a university. In each case, the distinguishing feature of white ignorance is that it obscures the nature and extent of racism and supports white power by promoting ignorance of racism within the social, political, and economic landscape.

---

[10] Ibid., p. 94.

White ignorance embodies what Foucault describes as the rationality of power divorced from the rationality of individuals. The operation of white ignorance fulfills a strategic function on behalf of white power. It obscures power relationships that favor white people, shielding those relationships from scrutiny and activism directed at changing them. White ignorance thereby helps to preserve the status quo of racial inequity. White ignorance can thus be theorized as a strategic initiative of the political institution of white supremacy, a kind of strategy for camouflaging and protecting itself. It counters the attempts of people of color to shed light on systemic racial inequality through the use of misinformation and causes white people to fail to understand how the system of racialized power works. In many cases, it even causes white people to completely disbelieve in the existence of the racist system of which they are both benefactor and beneficiary.

Who is it that enacts this strategy? White people do. But do they know what they are doing? It is part of the strategic function of white ignorance that white people do not understand racial inequality or how they benefit from it. When white ignorance is functioning well, according to its own strategic goal, the white people who reinforce white ignorance do not know what they are doing when they are reinforcing it. Arguably the vast majority of white people are in the grip of white ignorance. Very few, if any, white people fully understand the extent to which they participate in and benefit from structural racism. The strategic function of white ignorance is the production of this very ignorance, which protects white power. The white people who participate in creating white ignorance therefore tend to be totally unaware of its operation or its strategic benefits for themselves and unaware of the harms it inflicts on communities of color. White ignorance is a great example of the autonomous, strategic rationality of power serving its own interests.

The last aspect of power I want to consider before moving on to think about objections is Foucault's proposition: "Power comes from below." The point of this proposition is to assert that power does not originate with the rulers, the wealthy, the powerful, and the people at the top of the social pyramid. Rather, it is generated from the circumstances of all the people and materials in the social domain. The large-scale effects of power are derived from the coordination of many small instances of power. Foucault writes about it this way:

> the manifold relationships of force that take shape and come into play in the machinery of production, in families, limited groups, and institutions, are

the basis for wide-ranging effects of cleavage that run through the social body as a whole. These then form a general line of force that traverses the local oppositions and links them together; to be sure, they also bring about redistributions, realignments, homogenizations, serial arrangements, and convergences of the force relations. Major Dominations are the hegemonic effects that are sustained by all these confrontations.[11]

The picture that emerges is one in which the massive social institutions, including nation states and powerful financial institutions but also even larger entities such as capitalism, white supremacy, patriarchy, and other things of that ontological magnitude, are constructed from large networks of smaller power relations. These Major Dominations compose what Collins (2002) calls the matrix of domination, which will be examined in great detail in Chap. 8 using the Foucauldian framework described here. The Major Dominations are social entities arising from the social force relations embodied at more microscopic scales, in personal relationships, families, small groups, and local institutions which compose the larger social structures we inhabit. Hence, the matrix of domination 'comes from below.' Racism and sexism are not imposed in the first instance by nation states and laws. Rather, they create nation states and laws.

7.3 Two Objections to a Foucauldian Theory of Power

Here I want to cover two objections to the conception of power I've just detailed. The first is a reductive naturalistic worry: should we really accept that power exists over and above the natural world, especially given its intentional or goal-directed character? The second regards its explanatory power. Should we really postulate that this single entity, power, is the crucial explanatory property of all social dynamics?

7.3.1 The Naturalistic Objection

The reductive naturalist insists that power can only be postulated insofar as it can be reduced to physical processes. This raises a worry for the *intentional character of power*—Foucault's conception of power as goal directed and intelligible in terms of strategy and tactics. How could power itself

[11] Ibid., p. 93.

have plans and intentions, where those plans and intentions are not identical with the plans and intentions of any physical person, perhaps not even supervening on all of our brains? How could white supremacy itself have intentions? It can seem as if white supremacy were some demon that pervades the social sphere and directs people's actions. But isn't this a wild metaphysical speculation? How could power have a mind of its own in a physical world?

Firstly, I would appeal to Fodor's (1974, 1997) notion of the autonomy of the special sciences in defending the idea that a theory of power need not be reducible to more fundamental scientific concepts. We do not require, for example, economists to justify the use of concepts such as supply and demand or the concept of money by providing reductive naturalistic definitions in terms of neuroscience or some other more fundamental science. The prospect of defining money or value or wealth in reductive physical terms is dim, and moreover, it is pointless. The concepts of economics operate in a way that is independent of the underlying physical reality that realizes economic activity. So too we might suppose the social sphere, which encompasses economics and many other human sciences in addition, cannot be reduced in any systematic way to the underlying physical medium in which social objects exist and social events transpire.

A science of social power may properly be seen as autonomous from more fundamental physical sciences. The intentional, rationalistic, strategic operation of power is a postulate of the theory of power relations, part of that explanatory theory. We can accept this theory without giving a reductive naturalistic specification of how it is related to physics and biology.

The social sciences are autonomous; they are free to postulate properties that are appropriate to their own domains of discourse. Perhaps the rational intelligibility of power is just one such property. A non-reductive theory of the rational agency of power might simply stipulate that power has intentionality and acts strategically. Then the acceptability of this theory is a matter of whether it helps illuminate the subject matter, makes accurate predictions, and so on. Postulating the intentionality of power is like proposing an axiom, Foucault's axiom for organizing the social sphere.

What does it mean to say that we can accept a non-reductive theory of power's intentionality? There are at least three ways to understand this.

The first way is to postulate that the intentional features of power are emergent metaphysical phenomena, existing in the social sphere but irreducible to properties of the underlying physical media. On this view, the distinctive theoretical apparatus describing the intentionality of social power corresponds to a metaphysically distinctive layer of reality, the social, in which such intentionality really exists. Power really exists and it really has a mind of its own. In fact, it has many minds, as many minds as it has configurations, each configuration (each bank, each nation state, and each matrix of domination) with its own beliefs, goals, and strategies. This will seem metaphysically hefty to some philosophers and frankly unbelievable to others, but the emergentist theory of the intentional character of power might be true.

The second possibility is we could become instrumentalists about postulating power as a non-reductive, intentionally directed entity. An instrumentalist denies that the non-observational vocabulary of a theory refers to any real objects or entities, but nevertheless regards their inclusion within the theory as justified on the grounds that they increase predictive power.

One kind of traditional instrumentalist denies the reality of the entities postulated by fundamental physics such as electrons and protons, speculating that the success of our physical theories in terms of making predictions does not require that "electron" and "proton" actually refer to anything. They simply enable us to make useful predictions. Hence, predictive success should not license us in accepting the reality of all of the theory's ontological postulates. We can use physical theory to make empirically adequate predictions without believing that electrons and their kin really exist (Van Fraassen, 1980).

Following this template, we might speculate that the Foucauldian theory of power is not literally true on the grounds that there really is no such thing as power as Foucault conceives it. Nevertheless, we may find instrumental value in using the word "power" in accord with Foucault's theory in virtue of its ability to predict patterns and outcomes in the social world.

I think Foucault himself may suggest a kind of instrumentalist perspective when he says (of power), "the viewpoint which permits one to understand its exercise ... makes it possible to use its mechanisms as a grid of intelligibility of the social order." One adopts a point of view which enables one to impose a grid onto the domain of social entities and relations. A grid here is a metaphor, alluding to the metric of spacetime, a system of coordinating, ordering, and calculating the procession of events. To say that we *impose* the grid makes it sound like it is something we bring to the world, like a tape-measure or a heads-up display through which we interpret events. We adopt the power framework in order to make the order of social events more intelligible. We adopt a perspective in order to see power as the fundamental property, to see power everywhere, controlling and constituting all social objects and events. This may be like applying an instrumental theory which need not necessarily capture something that is out there, existing in itself.

A third possibility falls somewhere between realism and instrumentalism. The third approach makes use of Dennett's (1989) concept of an intentional stance. The intentional stance is a way of treating an object or system as if it has propositional attitudes including beliefs, goals, and strategies in order to make predictions about what it will do. When one takes the intentional stance toward, for example, a chess-playing computer program, one attributes intentions, goals, motives, and other mental states to that program, in order to predict what it will do.

Dennett contrasts the intentional stance with what he calls the physical stance and the design stance. When one adopts a physical stance, one makes predictions on the basis of the physical features of the system such as its mass, its trajectory, and so on. When one takes the design stance, one makes predictions in light of the purported function of the object. The intentional stance goes beyond design to postulate rational agency.

According to Dennett, there are some real patterns that cannot be detected and predicted unless one applies the intentional stance. One certainly cannot (at present, anyway) predict what the biochemical human organism will do without using the intentional stance. As I understand him, Dennett takes a system to *really* have representational contents or intentional states if and only if one must take the intentional stance toward that system in order to predict what it will do. On Dennett's view a human really has contentful mental states in virtue of the fact that we must treat the human organism as if it had contentful mental states in order to predict what it will do. This is something of a middle ground between realism and instrumentalism about the science of cognitive psychology. It says that contentful mental states in humans are real because the intentional stance is necessary to predict human behavior, but the reality of contentful mental states and hence the truth of cognitive psychology as a scientific theory is tied to the instrumental success of those theories.

My third suggestion is to apply the intentional stance approach to Foucault's axiom of the rationality of power. Power really and truly embodies intentional states precisely because adopting the intentional stance toward the operations of power is the best way to predict what it will do. Because treating power as following goals and strategies is more predictive than not doing so, we are licensed to treat power itself as really embodying intentional states.

This depends of course on whether a Foucault theory of power understood in terms of strategy really is predictive and helpfully explanatory. This could be questioned on empirical grounds. How does one, for example, measure power? Are there any reliable predictions being made? But I think such criticisms are premature. We are only barely beginning to conceptualize power as the fundamental substrate of the social realm. Demanding that we be able to precisely measure and predict its operations now is asking too much. It may be sufficient for the time being that Foucault's notion of power allows us to formulate a grid of intelligibility, as he suggests, for the social world. Precision may come later. Ultimately, whether power really has intentions is a matter of whether a mature science of the social sphere postulates those intentions. Insofar as a Foucauldian science of power relations is the correct approach to studying the dynamic social world, it would seem appropriate to apply Dennett's criterion of the reality of intentional states to the operations of power.

7.3.2 The Overly-Reductive Objection

The second objection concerns the all-encompassing theoretical role of power. As I've presented it, the theory of power reduces all social relationships to relationships of power. But surely there is more to sociality than just power. A theory of the social world that is entirely focused on power leaves out bonds of affection and love, duty to one's family and friends, obligations to one's institutions, our interest in prosocial and altruistic behaviors like contributing and giving, and our interest in creating our own life narratives and being seen the way we want to be seen by others. If the Foucauldian theory of power does touch on these things, it seems to reduce them to power struggles, which surely misses the point.

Foucault offers a response to this objection when he writes,

> Relations of power are not in a position of exteriority with respect to other types of relationships (economic processes, knowledge relationships, sexual relations), but are immanent in the latter; they are the immediate effects of the divisions, inequalities, and disequilibriums which occur in the latter, and conversely they are the internal conditions of these differentiations; relations of power are not in superstructural positions, with merely a role of

prohibition or accompaniment; they have a directly productive role, whenever they come into play.[12]

Foucault recognizes other kinds of social relationships that are not fundamentally characterized in terms of power. Economics, knowledge, and sexuality are not merely power relations. It is a misreading to think everything reduces to power in the sense that nothing except power exists in the social world. Yet power relationships inhere within other kinds of relationships. Economic, epistemic, and sexual relationships (among many others) are sources of power, respond to power, have their character fixed partly by power relations, and are partly constituted by power itself. Additionally, power influences the development of these kinds of relationships. Differences in power, for example, can play a problematic role in sexuality, as is well known. Differences in power can bring about terrible injustice in the domain of economic relationships. Power is also necessary in order to create economic prosperity and power dynamics within relationships when understood and dealt with appropriately can help the relationship to flourish. Relationships are not simply power, but they contain, respond to, and produce power.

So Foucault's theory of power does not obliterate all other conceptions of social relationships. It interfaces with those conceptions and helps illuminate their features. It helps us see how various kinds of relationships exist among power relations.

It may also be helpful to recall the instrumentalist or quasi-instrumentalist position here. Insofar as power relations are part of a grid of intelligibility that we impose upon the social order for the purpose of making sense of its structures and making predictions about its dynamics, we can see it as but one of many lenses with which to view things. While it postulates power as the fundamental and all-encompassing phenomenon, we need not take this to be the ultimate metaphysical truth of the matter. Rather we can treat the application of the power framework as one way of carving up or interpreting the social order. Understood in this light, we can choose to use the power framework when it seems appropriate and put it away in contexts where viewing everything in terms of power would not serve our interests—in the context of our loving relationships, for example. Yet it is always available to provide an analysis if the need should arise, and as Foucault points out, there are no relationships in the social order for which

[12] Ibid., p. 93.

the power framework is wholly inappropriate or unilluminating, since power touches on everything and inheres in everything within the social domain.

7.4 Regimes of Truth

Foucault clearly sees truth as implicated in political struggle, and not just in the sense that there are objective facts about political struggle. Political struggle involves exerting power over and through the social institutions and practices surrounding the concept of truth. The way in which the concept of truth operates within the field of social power is what Foucault calls a *regime of truth*. He likens the struggle over this apparatus to a battle.

7.4.1 The Battle for Truth

> There is a battle 'for truth,' or at least 'around truth'—it being understood once again that by 'truth' I do not mean the 'ensemble of truths which are to be discovered and accepted' but rather the 'ensemble of rules according to which the true and the false are separated and specific effects of power attached to the true'...a battle about the status of truth and the economic and political role it plays.[13]

That there is a political battle over truth is in some sense obvious. Different political factions compete to put their view of reality and morality in the driver's seat of the political machine. The sense in which Foucault perceives there to be a battle for truth is more subtle than this. His theory attempts to identify the ways in which power operates on and through the social institutions that license the ascription of truth to various viewpoints and propositions, and how these truth-determining institutions in turn provide a source of power and influence within the social fabric.

The battle for truth is a struggle for control over an "ensemble of rules," those that "separate" the true and the false. This is not a metaphysical separation between the nature of the True and the nature of the False. The battle is waged for control over a vast and multifaceted sorting procedure embedded in the social fabric. The procedure sorts the true from the false by labeling some sentences as true and some as false. The sorting procedure also attaches power to these proclamations. It enables

---

[13] Foucault et al. (1980), p. 132.

socially sanctioned judgments of truth to carry weight and authority within the field of social force relations. The sorting procedure is a social entity that is realized or constituted by all of the individuals, groups, and institutions in the social fabric, insofar as every agent in the social sphere contributes their own force relations guided by their own epistemic rules to promoting or advocating for the truth or falsity of various sentences.

One very striking feature of this passage is the care Foucault takes to make sure we are not confused into thinking that truth itself is influenced by power. He says the struggle is not a battle over the "ensemble of truths which are to be discovered and accepted." What is not at issue are the truths that are *out there*, waiting for us to discover and accept them, that is, reality itself. Political struggle does not decide what is the case in any deep metaphysical sense. It only affects how we, as a society, represent and respond to reality. That is the function of the ensemble of rules for separating the true from the false—the embodiment of our epistemic procedures within the social fabric—to coordinate our conceptions of reality, our beliefs, and our actions in response to that perceived reality. It does not determine reality itself. Further, the idea of a battle for truth is "above all to be taken as a hypothesis."[14] It is meant to be an empirical question whether and to what extent power interacts with our discursive practices around the notion of truth. This is very far from an apodictic claim to the effect that reality itself is constructed through applications of power.

In the battle-for-truth passage Foucault puts the word *truth* in scare quotes. Someone might read this as suggesting he is cynical about the existence of truth, but that would be a misreading. Clearly Foucault believes there are real truths about the way power operates in the social order, objective facts about how societies operate and about the history of knowledge and oppression, about how institutions are set up and how their configurations evolve over time, about the history of prisons and clinical psychiatry, things which can be ascertained or verified to some degree through empirical inquiry. He is not a skeptic about objective reality. He is not asserting that our political struggles have the power to shape reality itself in any extraordinary metaphysical sense, as if there were no objective reality beyond whatever point of view the political power struggle produces. Rather, he is arguing that our linguistic and conceptual representations of truth are influenced by and implicated in political struggle.

---

[14] Ibid., p. 132.

The battle for truth is a sociological phenomenon, a political struggle for control over the word "true" or its analogues in other languages, taking place at particular times and places in history. It is a struggle over how the word "true" operates within discourses, where these discourses draw strength and authority from the power structures present in the society and also feed back into those power structures. It is not a struggle for control of truth itself, as if reality itself were socially constructed as the product of this political struggle.

The social epistemic apparatus is what Foucault sometimes refers to as the *episteme* of a society at a given time. What is the episteme? A society embodies a complex apparatus of various procedures—including the rules and procedures applied by scientists and scientific institutions, news, media, judicial bodies, governmental agencies, and the vast distributed networks of interpersonal relationships and their individual and collective methods of making judgments—which function together to sort the true from the false within the social fabric. The episteme as it relates to the concept of truth at a time and place in history is what Foucault calls a regime of truth.

The episteme embodies multitudes of power relations concerning a huge range of things, for example: the ability to send and receive information and misinformation, the distribution of credibility, the measurement of quantities by officially sanctioned calibration devices (such as the international prototype of the kilogram), and the creation of epistemic authority roles—detectives, judges, principle investigators, managing editors, teachers, oversight committees, census takers, and ballot counters.

The apparatus is not purely epistemic insofar as its judgments impose force within the social sphere. People and institutions are bound to act in accord with its judgments on pain of confronting the power that is embodied within the social fabric that channels the authority of the epistemic decision procedures. A company that lies about the amount of carbon it is emitting is subject in part to the scientifically sanctioned measurement procedures that are applied to measuring its carbon output. International relations are predicated on intelligence briefings produced by authorized governmental agencies. The outcomes of democratic elections are determined by vote counting procedures that purport to tell us the number of people who voted for each candidate. A police officer is given a special credibility status in court: what they say carries special epistemic status for the state and its relation to the ordinary citizen or non-citizen confronted with police power. The judgments of juries are binding in very physically powerful ways, as when a person is incarcerated. A person who has been labeled a felon has their credibility impugned from a thousand angles within the social network. The judgments of accredited teachers and degree-granting institutions constitute a gateway to obtaining an officially sanctioned education. The judgments of accredited scientists and economists operate to inform governmental policy. And who accredits these scientists and economists, these teachers, these degree-granting institutions? Their accreditation proceeds by means of other rules and procedures for adjudicating questions of truth and falsity concerning their credibility, merit, and trustworthiness. Who validates these institutions? Ultimately, there is a distributed network of individuals and groups whose combined patterns of judgments (and they are by no means uniform or consistent) provide the backdrop for the social sanction of epistemic authority. But this network is also influenced by those very socially sanctioned epistemic authorities, forming their opinions and beliefs on the basis of media, education, scientific discourses, governmentally disseminated information (or misinformation), and expert opinions from all fields, including legal opinions. At every place in this interconnected feedback loop of information and authority, power exists and interacts with judgments about truth and falsity.

That this apparatus can be contested, its power redirected or undermined, is clearly apparent in many political conflicts. One recent salient example is the attack waged by President Trump and his allies on the epistemic apparatus connected with the 2020 US presidential election. The attack was an effort to sew mistrust in the epistemic institutions that tally votes, spreading the idea of widespread voter fraud and simultaneously attacking the credibility of mainstream media sources in order to discredit the media's support for the integrity of the voting process as safe and secure from fraud. This was an unsuccessful but potentially very dangerous attempt to subvert and undermine the social power that undergirds the epistemic apparatus for counting votes. If the general population ceases to trust the vote-counting apparatus, this promotes a possible outcome in which that apparatus loses the social power that enables its political function, that is, the legitimation of the next incoming president. The attempt to subvert the epistemic authority of the vote-counting apparatus was unsuccessful due to the resilience of the system, which also includes the epistemic authority vested in other institutions, namely the courts and state governments that certified the election results. These institutions have their own rules for ascertaining the truth, which were applied to the claims of voter fraud themselves, and the determination was that those claims were untrue. This illustrates a crucial feature of the episteme: it has many parts and these parts operate in conjunction with one another, providing mutual support to one another.

This scenario illustrates how crucially the determination of truth and falsity can be in connection to social power. What is determined to be true, according to the social institutions that sort the true from the false, has immense impact in terms of the accumulation and distribution of social political power to one group versus another. Simultaneously, there are power relations that undergird the sorting process. The legitimation of one claim as true and the other as false depends crucially on the power behind the institution or group that certifies the claim. These certifications can be issued from many different components within the system, and their deliverances need not be coherent or even based on real information, as when those in power corrupt a democratic election process.

This must all be kept conceptually distinct from the idea that those in power determine the nature of reality itself. If the Trump administration had successfully undermined public faith in the vote-counting apparatus, this would not change the number of votes that were actually cast in favor of Joe Biden. Reality is not whatever the social epistemic apparatus—the episteme—proclaims it to be. The episteme is a complex physical machine that makes decisions (as a distributed network makes decisions) about what shall count as true and false, and then enforces those decisions through social power. This is quite distinct from having the power to determine what is really true. The beliefs and opinions of a small collection of animals living on one planet in a galaxy containing over one hundred billion planets do not have ultimate significance in determining reality itself on the whole. We are not even infallible authorities about our own social reality.

To be sure, Foucault says things which could be construed as suggesting that truth is constructed by us. For example, he writes, "Truth is a thing of this world: it is produced only by virtue of multiple forms of constraint. And it induces regular effects of power."[15] This sounds as if he is saying that the truth itself is produced by the operation of social power. But again, recall what he says about his talk of truth: "by 'truth' I [Foucault] do not mean the 'ensemble of truths which are to be discovered and accepted' but rather the 'ensemble of rules according to which

[15] Ibid., p. 131.

the true and false are separated ...'" The sense in which truth is the product of multiple constraints and induces effects of power is the sense in which the rules embodied in the social apparatus for truth determination are subjected to constraints and induce power.

Foucault goes on to describe the regime of truth as the social organization of power that embodies the relationship between all the various social entities and the concept of truth as it is deployed in that society. But before we explore that concept in detail, I want to first explain what Foucault means by a discourse.

7.4.2 What Is a Discourse?

Discourses are tactical elements or blocks operating in the field of force relations; there can exist different and even contradictory discourses within the same strategy; they can, on the contrary, circulate without changing their form from one strategy to another, opposing strategy.[16]

This is a very permissive definition of discourse. A discourse is individuated by its tactical function within the field of power relations. One might have expected him to say something about speech or texts, for example, 'the discourse around gender in society x is the set of all the speech acts, texts, and media about gender that are occurring or present in society x.' I think this is intuitively what a discourse seems to be: a set of texts, speech acts, and media, individuated by their content. Discourses will overlap to the extent that the topics of distinctive discourses overlap; for example, the discourse on gender and the discourse on sexuality will overlap.

But Foucault does not delimit the concept of discourse to a specific set of representation types; it's not limited to text and speech. This is because the 'conversation' around a particular topic extends to an open-ended range of forums and social entities. The discourse around gender includes laws about who can be drafted into military service. It includes bathroom signs. It includes color schemes, for example, pink for girls and blue for boys. It includes fashion. It includes gender confirmation surgeries. It includes body language and posture. It includes aspects of sexuality. All of these things have a shared content, in some sense. They are all bound up with the conversation around gender. Perhaps they are all 'texts,' as some deconstructionists like to say. But I think Foucault's open definition of

---

[16] Foucault (1978), pp. 101–102.

discourse is meant to capture the fact that a discourse can exist and operate in an unlimited number of formats.

How then should we understand Foucault's way of individuating discourses as tactical elements operating in the field of force relations? This way of individuating discourses is closely connected with Foucault's central idea that the operations of power can be made intelligible as having strategic goals and making tactical decisions. We can identify a discourse by first identifying some goal and attendant strategy connected with the operation of power. The discourse around gender is connected with a power struggle, a clearly identifiable one: the drive to retain a traditional conception of gender as binary and tied to biology and supporting distinctive social and sexual roles for men and women versus the drive to create a new conception of gender and sexuality that challenges traditional gender roles and which allows a multitude of gender identities beyond the binary and legitimates the reality of trans people's genders. The discourse about gender quintessentially includes speech, text, and media about ideas and questions relating to gender, but also extends to all the multiform ways in which gender is enacted and (de)legitimated within the social fabric.

We can identify the discourse about racism in the US as that tactical element quintessentially composed of texts, speech, and media about racism but extending to many other facets of social interaction which play a tactical role in the power struggle over the epistemic status of racism in the US. This discourse operates in one direction to solidify white ignorance by misrepresenting the nature of racism. The other direction includes critical race theory and intersectionality. The resistant side of the discourse aims to theorize and generate information about racism as it presently exists, expose and confront white ignorance, and destabilize the epistemic practices that undermine knowledge of racism.

Generally speaking, seeing discourses as individuated by both content and strategic value in the field of social power relations, we can conceive of them as large scale and defuse entities, not simply bound up with texts and speech acts but potentially extending to any aspect of social interaction. We can individuate and identify particular discourses by reference to their subject matter, while recognizing that distinctive discourses will often overlap. Most important for present purposes, this conception allows us to talk about the operation of the concept of truth within a discourse.

7.4.3 What Is a Regime of Truth?

Each society has its regime of truth, its 'general politics' of truth: that is, [i] the types of discourse which it accepts and makes function as true; [ii] the mechanisms and instances which enable one to distinguish true and false statements, the means by which each is sanctioned; [iii] the techniques and procedures accorded value in the acquisition of truth; [iv] the status of those who are charged with saying what counts as true."[17]

The regime of truth is the very large and diffuse social structure organizing the ways in which power relations support or countermand applications of the concept of truth within various discourses that pervade the social fabric. Foucault's initial description of the regime of truth is a statement of the trappings of power that are relevant to this apparatus.

Note that each regime of truth is specific to a particular society in a particular place and time. That is not to say that truth itself is relative to such a society. What is unique and relative to a given society is the way in which power is distributed in that society. It's not just about who has power, but also what institutions, laws, government, media, and so on exist there. The regime of truth for a given society encompasses all the social factors that influence applications of the concept of truth within that society.

How is the regime of truth related to Foucault's concept of an episteme? The regime of truth is centrally concerned with the operation of the word "true," whereas the episteme is a larger apparatus concerning all of the epistemological concepts at work in the social fabric. The episteme interacts with the regime of truth in many different ways and is partly composed by it, but they are distinct things.

Foucault indicates four components of the interaction between social power and the functioning of the word "true" within a social fabric. The first [i] is that power affects the kinds of discourses that persist within the society, which elements of discourses are acceptable, and which function as true. This notion of 'functioning as true' is crucial to understanding the regime of truth.

What is it to make a statement function as true? As a configuration of power relations, the regime of truth supports the application of the word "true" to a statement. It also enables that statement to influence others within the discourse as if it were true. For example, in his initiation of the

[17] Ibid., p. 131.

1776 Project, Trump asserted, "Teaching this horrible doctrine [Critical Race Theory] to our children is a form of child abuse in the truest sense of those words."[18] This sentence is false, but is made to function as true within the discourse around racism when it informs people's attitudes as if it were true. Part of its functioning as true is that large numbers of people believe it. The spread of this false belief is a consequence of the regime of truth insofar as Trump has the social power to appear credible and to spread his message and gain uptake. The statement also functions as true when it informs the attitudes and decisions of institutions. Acting as if the statement were true, Trump "banned trainings in this prejudiced ideology [Critical Race Theory] from the federal government and banned it in the strongest manner possible."[19] A sentence functions as true when it is treated as a justification for action. This function is enabled by power, the power that constitutes the regime of truth, when the epistemic authority that legitimates the statement as a justification for action rests on social power. A statement's being made to function as true is also a source of power, as when it enables the President to ban a certain theory of racism from being taught in governmental departments. Less than a year later, we are seeing critical race theory come under attack from conservative individuals and institutions intent on restricting the theory of racism from being taught in schools across the country; the impetus for this movement and its justification are partly sustained by false statements about critical race theory, which are circulated and made to function as true.

To say that a statement functions as true within the social fabric means it is treated as if it were true are across a wide range of contexts and social institutions within the society, that judgments of its truth are backed by epistemic authority enabled by social power, and that such judgments enable further beliefs and actions on the basis of that statement as if it were true, where these further beliefs and actions draw on the same social power that legitimated the statement as true in the first place.

In the example of gender, the regime of truth makes propositions entailing or supporting the idea that gender is biological and binary function as true. Let's consider one small part of the regime of truth around gender, the power vested in the Oxford English Dictionary. Its status is constituted in part by power—the fact that people and institutions will appeal to it for guidance and justification—and its definitions exert power

[18] Trump (2020).
[19] Ibid.

within discourses. The Oxford English Dictionary (2020b) defines "woman" as "An adult female human being" and defines "female" as "of or denoting the sex that can bear offspring or produce eggs, distinguished biologically by the production of gametes (ova) which can be fertilized by male gametes" (Oxford, 2020a). This combination of definitions exerts an influence on people and institutions. It functions as part of the regime of truth with respect to the discourse around gender on behalf of that strategic initiative that aims to retain a traditional biological conception of gender. It justifies people's belief in biological definitions of gender and legitimates further beliefs and actions, such as the belief that trans children should be forced to use bathrooms for genders they do not belong to, for example, trans girls should be forced to use the boy's bathroom, and it supports the policy actions that follow from this belief.

Crucially, the fact that a regime of truth makes statements of biological gender essentialism *function as* true does not entail that biological gender essentialism *is* true. Gender is non-binary and non-biological even though the social power that constitutes the regime of truth in the US supports and enforces patterns of applying the word "true" to such statements as would entail that gender is binary and biological. These include such statements as "Women are adult human beings biologically distinguished as belonging to the sex that can produce eggs." We can recognize those statements as false, even as we recognize a multitude of ways in which cisnormative power structures operate to reinforce acceptance of those sentences as true.

The regime of truth in the US strongly supports white ignorance insofar as it makes statements function as true which, if accepted, obscure the nature and extent of racism in the US—statements like "Anti-white racism is real." When a statement about racism functions as true when it is in fact false, the regime of truth acts as a source of misinformation. This fact highlights the difference between a sentence's being true and its functioning as true. There are many ways for statements that constitute misinformation to function as true, especially when those in power make such statements, as when the president of the US falsely claims that "Critical race theory … is toxic propaganda, ideological poison that, if not removed, will dissolve the civic bonds that tie us together. It will destroy our country." Critical race theory's central definition of racism is not toxic propaganda—it's the truth. Insofar as critical race theory is regarded as false propaganda, and statements from the highest seat of political power lend sociological force to this perspective, the truth about racism is obscured through the use of power.

We can represent the truth conditions of statements like "Critical race theory is toxic propaganda" using models from model theory. Some models of that statement make it true; others make it false. I argued in Chap. 5 that we should interpret such sentences of English using models that render them false, because they constitute misinformation about the nature of racism. How can this square with the recognition that the regime of truth makes that statement function as true? Whether the operation of the regime of truth determines the semantics of English is a metasemantic question. The fact that the regime of truth makes statements like "Anti-white racism is a big problem in the US" function as true has no bearing on the meaning of "racism," on any acceptable metasemantics, as I will argue in Chaps. 9 and 10. The fact that a statement functions as true does not make it true.

There is still a lot to say about what it means for a statement to function as true. We will continue to fill in this conception as we investigate further properties of the regime of truth. Let's turn next to component [ii] of the regime of truth: the mechanisms and instances which enable one to distinguish true and false statements, the means by which each is sanctioned. What are these mechanisms and what exactly do they do?

These mechanisms are the acts and procedures for judging the truth and falsity of statements. They are properly described mechanistically insofar as they have causal implications. They cause or causally facilitate judgments to happen, to be recorded, published, broadcast, publicly affirmed by teachers, judges, government officials, or socially legitimated in any number of other ways. These epistemic mechanisms are connected to power in the sense that their dictates are given legitimacy in the direction of public thought and given weight in deciding individual, collective, or institutional actions.

The regime of truth influences how epistemic judgments are actually made within the social fabric; it does not determine how they *should* be made. There are objectively true epistemic facts about who has knowledge, what evidence is good, what is misleading, and what beliefs are really justified. The fact that Trump thinks he is justified in believing that critical race theory is propaganda, and the fact that his belief in his own justification is supported by a large network of social power and people who agree with him, does not mean that he is in fact justified. In objective reality, he lacks good evidence for his belief, which is in fact the product of white ignorance. The reality of who is justified and who is not is objective and the same for everyone, even though we cannot all see the truth about who is justified from our situated perspectives.

The mechanisms we actually use for arriving at judgments of truth and falsity are not necessarily those we *ought* to use in deciding truth or falsity. The regime of truth is constituted by the mechanisms which are *in fact* in effect within our social fabric. It's important to distinguish between how we actually do things and how we should do things. Our society should be using different mechanisms for making judgments, given the objective truth about epistemology. It is possible for the power structure within a society to support objectively good epistemic practices. For example, if the regime of truth in the US were reconfigured so that power supported the elimination of misinformation and active ignorance about racism, gender-based oppression, capitalist exploitation, and so on, this would improve the quality of the epistemic decision procedures that saturate the social fabric. Changing the episteme in this way is crucial for addressing social injustice.

Closely related is [iii], the set of procedures and techniques accorded value in the acquisition of truth. These are not the procedures by which we decide on the answer, but they are contributories to the decision procedures. They include measurements, investigations, observations, studies, and interviews. They are facilitated by technologies such as telescopes, particle accelerators, thermometers, censuses, polling apps, data collection software, medical tests, body cameras, and orbital reconnaissance vehicles.

These procedures and techniques for gathering information with their attendant technologies may or may not be good means of actually ascertaining the truth. What makes them part of the regime of truth for a given society is that they are used, trusted, and function as valued sources of evidence within that society. We can attempt to ascertain the epistemic virtue or lack thereof of our socially sanctioned epistemic procedures and techniques. This kind of criticism, which is crucial to any critical theory, attempts to root out the ways in which evidence, observations, studies, and so on can be misused to create the misinformation and active ignorance that sustains the matrix of domination.

I want to emphasize that evidence, observation, and science can be objectively good sources of information and justification, even though all evidence, observation, and science participate in complex networks of social power. When scientists make observations and construct theories about the human causes of climate change, their conclusions may be objectively justified. This fact is distinct from the further objective fact that huge systems of power are battling to legitimate or delegitimate those findings. The creation of new technologies and new scientific theories is also a source of power. Which humans will benefit from scientific progress and which will be subjugated by it? This question cannot be addressed without recognizing the connection between the regime of truth and objective reality. The regime of truth produces real knowledge. That knowledge is a source of power, and it can sustain oppression as well as oppose it. Knowledge of racism, sexism, and other forms of oppression is also scientific, objective, and produced through the regime of truth.

The last component Foucault mentions is [iv] the status of those who are charged with saying what is true. I take this category to encompass both expert opinion and public trust. They might be scientists or priests, politicians or philosophers, family members or newscasters. A person's status as an epistemic authority may be conditioned in part by race or gender or ability or sexual orientation or educational status or any number of other features. The regime of truth gives people epistemic power. It gives some people's beliefs and pronouncements more weight than others. Again, the epistemic status conferred on a person by the regime of truth may or may not match their actual reliability as a producer of knowledge. A person can be made to function as a truth-teller even if they are misinformed, even if they are a liar or a bullshitter.

A lot of recent discussion in social epistemology has been focused on credibility and the ways in which social power can unjustly affect the distribution of credibility (Fricker, 2007; Govier, 1993) and the ways in which systemic oppression facilitates epistemic violence in the form of silencing (Dotson, 2011). These critiques may be seen as focused on this component of the regime of truth and the way in which it produces injustice and oppression. The same literature aims to correct our practices, to implement different social structures that redistribute credibility in ways that allow those who are marginalized within the system to be sustained at a more equitable level of credibility. This is an initiative to modify the regime of truth to make it more epistemically virtuous, to enable the marginalized to have more epistemic power, more input to collective knowledge, as they objectively should be given their objective status as virtuous epistemic agents who are unjustly and inaccurately accorded lower epistemic status.

7.4.4 Political Struggles for Truth and Justice

It is possible for a regime of truth to embody mechanisms for deciding truth and falsity that consistently fail to track truth but serve some other goal, such as keeping a political party or social identity in power. But it is also possible for a regime of truth to be virtuous, as when power backs procedures for adjudicating truth from falsehood which actually embody good epistemic principles. This is crucial for any society that would oppose systemic oppression, for systemic oppression subsists on misinformation, propaganda, and active ignorance.

To transform the regime of truth into a force for good, we must recognize that our current epistemic decision procedures are implemented within a social fabric that is beset with social inequality and controlled by power structures which use them to their own advantage. But we must not mistake this fact for the claim that there is no objective truth, that there are no objective epistemic virtues, or that every society will necessarily be epistemically corrupt. Social justice initiatives depend on making accurate information and true sentences about racism and gender function as true. The promise of a better society requires generating knowledge of oppression within a social fabric that is strongly antagonized by such knowledge.

Our understanding of what is wrong with the current regime of truth and what is required to improve it for the sake of social justice are, of course, conditioned by the social fabric and bear the mark of the influence of power. We are not in a position to extricate ourselves from the web of power relations in order to determine, in a way that is totally removed from the influence of power, what the correct epistemic principles are, who the objectively good epistemic authorities are, or what objective reality looks like. Our epistemology is inherently conditioned by our deepest political commitments and our ability to know is limited by the extent to which we engage in shared political struggle.[20]

Nevertheless, it is important to recognize that just because we cannot step outside our own situatedness and ascertain the correct epistemic principles, it does not follow that no such principles exist. This point bears some emphasis. It can be obscure if one assumes that one must be able to determine the objective truth-conduciveness of one's epistemic methods from within one's own subjective perspective.

---

[20] See Code (2012), Harding (1995), and Scheman (1995).

This view is known as internalism about justification (Chisholm, 1977; Cohen & Lehrer, 1983). According to internalism, one must have 'internal' access within their own subjective experience to the factors that justify their beliefs, if those beliefs are to count as justified. Justification depends on your own internal reasons, those that seem to you to be good reasons. If I am dreaming that I am on a boat, then I'm justified in believing I'm on a boat because it seems to me, internally, as if I am perceiving the boat and the water.

An externalist (Bach, 1985; BonJour, 1980), on the other hand, thinks that whether one's beliefs are justified is a matter of whether their belief-forming mechanisms are truth-conducive, whether or not they have any internal warrant for ascertaining this fact. If I am dreaming that I am on a boat, then I am not justified in believing I'm on a boat; I am not seeing any boat or any water because my eyes are closed. I have no evidence that I'm on a boat, even though it seems to me as if I do. I dreamed that I had evidence, but in fact I didn't.

The view of justification I am proposing for intersectional epistemology is externalist. One group may be justified in their beliefs about racism and another may not be, even though within their own experiences each group takes itself to be justified. One group may be subjected to extensive misinformation, propaganda, and active ignorance, while another group may be informed by good information, even if both groups think they are the one with the good information and the other is the one in the grip of misinformation and propaganda. Externalism tells us that who is really justified is not a matter of what things look like from within a particular politically situated worldview. It depends on whether the information those groups rely on in fact track reality.

There is an objective truth about who is a liar, who is a bullshitter, who is misinformed, and who really knows what they are talking about, even though some who really know are deprived of epistemic power, and even if liars and bullshitters are popped up by an oppressive regime of truth. We can likewise believe there are objectively good scientific theories as well as objectively bad, pseudoscientific ones that propagate racist and sexist beliefs, even if the regime of truth supports the pseudoscientific theories and treats them as real science. Foucault's concept allows for us to distinguish between the order of things which is supported by the regime of truth and things as they actually are, apart from our contingent view of reality conditioned by prevailing systems of power and technology.

Power exists within a reality that contains many objective facts, including objective facts about power itself and the social world which it constitutes. Humans have the power to represent this reality accurately as well as the power to obscure it through ideology and misinformation. I think Foucault's own understanding of truth and power is close to mine. I do not think he intended his theory of power to undermine objective knowledge, but rather to complicate our epistemic relationship with it by drawing our attention to the multiform ways in which power interacts with epistemology.

7.4.5 Syntacticism About the Regime of Truth

Foucault summarizes his view with two propositions[21] about truth that are meant to clarify the role of the concept of truth as it operates within the field of social power relations:

[I] 'Truth' is to be understood as a system of ordered procedures for the production, regulation, distribution, circulation and operation of statements.

[II] 'Truth' is linked in a circular relation with systems of power which produce and sustain it, and to effects of power which it induces and which extend it. A 'regime' of truth.

Notice again that Foucault identifies his target as 'Truth' with scare quotes. I think some have interpreted this as a cynical way of referring to truth itself—the representation of reality—in such a way as to suggest that there really is no such thing. I believe, however, that Foucault's aim in using scare quotes is to refer to "truth" the syntactic device: the word itself, the rules for its application within the language, its logical syntax, and the way it operates with respect to the system of ordered procedures Foucault refers to in [I].[22]

That he has a syntactical concept of truth is suggested by his claim that these procedures are implemented on *statements*, pieces of language. This syntactic conception focuses our attention on the machine of language

---

[21] Ibid., p. 133.
[22] The syntactical conception I am presenting is very much influenced by Neurath's (1983) conception of the operation of statements within a social fabric (see also Anderson, 2019). As far as I know, it is an unexplored question whether Foucault ever read Neurath's work. It would not be completely surprising given that Neurath was a Marxist philosopher of science with an interest in the role of truth in politics.

and its relationship to power and the influence of power over the rules for the application of the truth predicate. The confusion of thinking Foucault disavows objective reality itself arises when Foucault's statements about the influence of power on uses of the words "true" and "is true" are misinterpreted as claims about truth and reality itself. If you think Foucault is talking about the referent of "truth," rather than a syntactic symbol, then you will read him as saying that truth itself is shaped by power.

Proposition [I] gives us a theory of what "truth" is, namely a predicate identified by its role in certain ordered procedures concerned with the regulation, distribution, circulation, and operation of statements. This role constitutes the identity condition of the predicate, which is essentially constituted by its role within the socially regulated order implementing the ways in which the truth predicate functions in discourses. Proposition [II] then gives the relationship between this predicate so constituted and other wider systems of power. Let's spend a little more time with proposition [I] before turning to proposition [II].

Proposition [I] identifies five characteristic functions of the truth predicate: production, regulation, distribution, circulation, and operation of statements. The first is the production of statements, literally the creation of sentences under the guise of asserting them as truths. The second is concerned with the regulation of statements. The truth predicate regulates the behavior of other statements by sorting them into the categories "true" or "not true" (i.e., "false"). It functions as a marker for the treatment of statements. It also controls connections between statements, by controlling which inferences are licensed.

Distribution and circulation of statements are a matter of where those statements appear and how they are presented. Statements labeled "true" are presented as to be circulated and tend to have wider distribution than statements labeled as false, although of course questions of what is "true" and what is "false" will be hotly contested especially within the political sphere. But even the presentation of statements on news programs, in Reddit forums, in official letters from the Dean of the University, in emails from your grandmother, all count as part of the circulation of statements.

The operation of statements refers to their causal efficacy in the open-ended field of discourse, how they are combined with other statements within the logical syntax of the discourse to produce new statements and new concepts, and how they interact with larger chunks of representational material within the social fabric (anything from laws to bathroom signs to bedroom decorating schemes). These operations can occur through institutions according to rules, as in courtrooms, scientific journal reviews, and official government reports. Or they can operate through private and unofficial channels. In any case, operation means causation: what the statements *do* in terms of affecting the course of events.

Since so much of the social world enters into discourse, the constitutive function of the truth predicate is tied to a very wide range of phenomena. It includes all the ways in which truth is thought to properly inform discourse and the course of social evolution. The apparatus that embodies the constitutive function of the truth predicate is ontologically vast.

Proposition [II] then concerns the reciprocal relationship between this ontologically vast apparatus and other equally vast but metaphysically distinct social power structures: police, prisons, legislative bodies, media platforms, degree-conferring institutions, hospitals, and military forces, to name a few institutions that Foucault himself was particularly interested in, as well as an open-ended list of other institutions with which the truth predicate might interact.

To call this relationship "circular" is to say the functioning of the truth predicate contributes to the power of other institutions, which in turn contribute to the power of the truth predicate. The regime of truth vests institutions with power by legitimating their fundamental operations by rendering key presuppositions and pronouncements as true. These institutions make use of the truth predicate to coordinate their efforts and draw on epistemic support for their activities, both in terms of justification and also through the use of information to become more effective. These institutions then reinforce the power of the truth predicate and the apparatus which determines its proper applications. The power to inform and justify decisions is sustained through the power of the institutions that make use of the truth predicate. It is a circular relationship because the power of the "truth" predicate is sustained through its connection with powerful social entities, while at the same time it lends its own power to those entities.

The regime of truth can be organized so that it makes sentences that are actually true function as true. Therefore, the word "truth" has the potential to organize and communicate good information, to express what is really true, and to organize and support the circulation of true statements about things such as racism, mass incarceration, gender-based oppression, homophobia, and other forms of real, objective inequality. Oppressive power works hard to prevent the regime of truth from doing this.

The struggle over the word "true" is a struggle over the system of procedures that embodies the constitutive function of the truth predicate, a political struggle over the means of regulating, distributing, circulating, and controlling the operation of statements, as well as the interactions between these procedures and the broader social institutions in which the apparatus sustaining the truth predicate is embedded. The power infused in the truth predicate is an important site of political contestation because the truth itself matters. Not just the deployment of the truth predicate, but what is actually true matters. We want to be in touch with reality. In order for this to happen, political struggle is necessary, because the regime of truth is contested.

7.4.6 Truth, Science, and Democracy

Foucault says that "In societies like ours, the 'political economy' of truth is characterized by five important traits." These traits characterize the organization of social practices around the application of the words "truth" and "true" within modern settler-states and European states, which Foucault sees as centered on scientific discourses. The five traits are as follows:

> [1] 'Truth' is centered on the form of scientific discourse and the institutions which produce it; [2] it is subject to constant economic and political incitement (the demand for truth, as much for economic production as for political power); [3] it is the object, under diverse forms, of immense diffusion and consumption (circulating through apparatuses of education and information whose extent is relatively broad in the social body, not withstanding certain strict limitations); [4] it is produced and transmitted under the control, dominant if not exclusive, of a few great political and economic apparatuses (university, army, writing, media); [5] lastly, it is the issue of a whole political debate and social confrontation ('ideological' struggles).[23]

Trait [1] identifies science, and the institutions that draw on the expert knowledge produces by the conglomerate of scientific fields as well as those that fund the scientific endeavor, as the primary arbiter of truth in modern political economies. Science holds a special place in determining what we do and how we are organized. Its measurements, theories, and judgments are treated as having paramount epistemic importance and

---

[23] Foucault (1980), "Truth and Power," pp. 131–132. Bracketed numbers added.

therefore given prominence within the systems of power, including within the democratic system of government.

To say that science plays a social role as arbiter within political power structures is not to denigrate science as non-objective or to suggest that somehow scientific truth is socially constructed. It is possible for social power to be organized around epistemically virtuous institutions. It is a separate question whether the scientific institutions we have, embedded within systems of power, are in fact epistemically virtuous. It may be that they are corrupted; they might serve white supremacy and patriarchy, and so on. My point is that scientific institutions are not *necessarily* corrupted by their interactions with power.

Anyone can recognize that scientific institutions can enter into power relations in both honest and dishonest ways, that they can be more or less accurate in their efforts to uncover reality, and that they can be more or less biased. The idea that a science might be biased or inaccurate presupposes that there is an objective reality that our sciences can do a better or worse job of uncovering. Foucault was well aware that scientific institutions could be used to subjugate people, as when scientific institutions licensed the belief that homosexuality was a form of mental illness. But it would be a mistake to infer from the power-based criticism of science that he thought science was necessarily oppressive.

The second trait [2] is that there is a demand for truth, and this demand acts on and through the institutions that produce and regulate the production of "truth"—sentences labeled "true," which may also be true. The demand is due to the ways in which ascriptions of truth generate both economic and political power. Calling some things true and others false creates economic and political conditions of operation. Our politics and economics move in accord with what the regime of truth says is the case. Furthermore, economic and political powers rely on knowledge of what is really true, and so the demand for truth is partly a demand for real, objective knowledge. We want to produce statements about the spread of COVID-19 infections and the effectiveness of vaccines that are objectively true and justified, while at the same time those who would rather see the economy reignited at whatever cost might prefer simply to have statements about low infections and effective vaccines function as true, regardless of their actual truth, in order to enable a return to business as usual.

In some cases, statements that are made to function as true are in fact false, such as the statement that white people are oppressed in the US. This false statement is made to operate as true and thereby generates white ignorance and sustains white power, so there is a demand for such statements. The demand comes from those who are aligned with white power against the anti-racism movement. It is a demand for misinformation, even though those who demand it may think they are demanding the truth. Misinformation has great potential to generate power and is thus in high demand.

But just as surely as misinformation generates power, so too does accurate information. The power of knowing the actual truth about objectively verifiable matters of fact is made abundantly clear throughout Foucault's writing. For example, in *Discipline and Punish*, Foucault (1975) describes the draconian epistemic function of the pandemic lockdown during the Black Death, in which each household and neighborhood of the city was meticulously locked down and monitored for any deviant movement outside of the occupant's prescribed location. Here there is a great concern to generate accurate information about where people's bodies are, in the interest of controlling their movements and punishing violations—those found where they were not supposed to be were put to death. The power of surveillance, draconian or otherwise implemented, comes from its ability to find out what is *really* going on, in order to implement systems of control. By the same token, all technological power is based on knowledge. Knowledge is power in part because it is factive.

For social justice movements, there is a very strong demand to uncover the truth about how the racist matrix of domination operates and functions, how it evolved, and what strategies are effective in combating it. There are objective truths to be discovered and disseminated, such as how the matrix of domination that undergirded chattel slavery was transmuted into the system of Jim Crow apartheid and then into the system of mass incarceration (Alexander, 2020). Anti-racism advocates and those who are opposed to the prison industrial complex ought to recognize this information as objective truth, not merely the product of their own politics but something that really happened. The truth of it exists, even if it is covered up or erased (Arendt, 1967). Those who oppose the matrix of domination demand the truth, while those who work in favor of the matrix of domination label true statements as "false" and get misinformation to function as "true."

The third trait [3] of contemporary regimes of truth is that statements labeled "true" are generated and circulated widely, in response to the great demand for truth. This means the widespread availability of a certain slate of representational artifacts and media that are signified as true.

Many of the statements which are made to function as true really are true. Sometimes power and truth align such that power facilitates the spread of true statements; in these scenarios, information is transmitted through the media, through education, through the government, and so on. The possibility of objective truth circulated by the operations of power allows us to formulate questions about how much of that which is made to function as true is really true, how much is misinformation or ideological propaganda, and how does the configuration of the present matrix of domination contribute to and depend upon misinformation and ignorance.

The fourth trait [4] expresses that the wide circulation of "true" statements is facilitated through a small number of powerful social entities. These include such entities as the academy, the scientific community, the media, and parts of the government—the courts, the ballot counters, the census takers, the surgeon general, the attorney general, the intelligence community, and others. What is characteristic of modern civilizations is that the power to distribute information and misinformation has been centralized, infused into organizations of power that constitute these megalithic truth regulators.

This centralization is not necessarily a bad thing. Witness the fear that the internet is destabilizing democracy by allowing statements to circulate and function as true which have not been vetted by the more traditional institutions of epistemic regulation we have come to rely upon. I think this is a legitimate fear precisely because our megalithic epistemic institutions serve a vital function. We want our information to be vetted by experts and systems that implement good epistemic practices. When propaganda and misinformation are used to discredit the epistemic institutions on which the democracy operates, it hurts people. It hides wrongdoers from accountability. It destabilizes and fragments the narratives we use to organize ourselves around important ethical themes. It is therefore dangerous to attack the megalithic information structures upon which information-age democracy is based, and the danger is strongest for those who are most marginalized.

On the other hand, these very powerful, centralized epistemic institutions also play a central role in creating ideology and misinformation about things such as racism and gender. The ordered regulation of ignorant beliefs and the creation of a mainstream dominant consciousness proceeds by the operation of the regime of truth and its megalithic truth/power broker institutions. If the matrix of domination is to be transmuted into something resembling a fair and equitable society, the institutions that circulate statements of truth for public consumption must be reformed and reorganized. This must take place at small scales in millions of locations within the social sphere. As Foucault notifies us, power comes from below.

Social justice might require the total reorganization or dissolution of the megalithic truth broker institutions. As I mentioned, this is a risky road. A safer strategy might involve the subtle modification of those institutions in myriad small ways over an extended period of time. It's a big ship and it could take a long time to turn it safely. Safety comes at a cost, though. Justice delayed is justice denied, so taking a slow and subtle approach may be morally inexcusable. And yet a blitzkrieg against our truth-sorting institutions may do more harm than good for the very marginalized groups it is meant to help. It's an empirical question what we should do, and we may not have time to gather all the evidence we need before deciding. In any case, the goal is to produce a more truth conducive political consciousness, one that abolishes white ignorance and other forms of active ignorance that are the basis of oppression.

Lastly, [5] is the issue of political debate and social confrontation. In the abstract, this means that our societies are politically organized around ascertaining the truth. The truth matters to politics, at least nominally. This is a contingent, sociological state of affairs. The fact that political goals and activities are beholden to the operation of the apparatus that makes statements function as true is the result of the contingent organization of power. It might someday be otherwise, and in some places and times it has been otherwise.

The question of whether a given society does or does not function such that truth and reason inform its politics is related to the Platonic ideal that reason and truth should be made to govern politics. Foucault's understanding of the relation between truth and politics is the non-ideal theoretical version of the Platonic inquiry. Foucault is describing social power dynamics and their relation to truth, giving us a way to survey the contingent configuration of the social order, while Plato is describing how a society should be organized so that truth becomes the guide to politics.

Both Foucault and Plato may be right. That truth functions to regulate the political machine in a democracy may be an engineering accomplishment in terms of the struggle to organize social power relations so that truth is relevant to politics. I agree with Plato that a society whose contingent organization of power enables truth to govern is both epistemically and politically virtuous in an objective sense. The truth literally sets people free, which is why systems of oppression thrive on active ignorance and misinformation.

It is a separate question whether any actual society meets the Platonic ideal. Surely, none does. Foucault's theory of power provides a grid of intelligibility for understanding how and why our actual society fails to reflect the truth about things like racism and gender. But the Platonic ideal may be useful insofar as it enables us to conceive and advocate for a political goal. We should want to construct a more epistemically virtuous political system and we should want to criticize any political organization of power that puts misinformation and ignorance in control of the state apparatus and other institutions of social power.

7.5 Epistemic Violence and Intersectionality in the Misinformation Age

What is characteristic of the misinformation age, or the sense that such an age is coming into existence, is the concentrated attacks on the central megalithic institutions of the regime of truth, the creation of a multitude of alternative sources of truth regulation and dissemination, and the fear that the power vested in the previous regime of truth might be undone. To take a recent example, consider the Trump administration's attacks on the institutions that have been the backbone of the regime of truth during the twentieth and early twenty-first centuries. Trump has denounced the media and had strong effect in undermining confidence in traditional news sources. The Trump administration flagrantly attempted to undermine confidence in the voting process and the truth-aptness of our ballot counting procedures. Trumpism is very antagonistic to the academy, portraying it as a source of ideological misinformation and un-American propaganda. It has worked to undermine climate science in order to promote the economic and political power of the US fossil fuel industry. Trump repeatedly took aim at the US census, attempting to implement new policies that would force census takers to undercount the number of migrants in the country in order to deprive them of governmental representation. Trump also worked to undermine confidence in the intelligence community, repeatedly purging US intelligence agencies of their expert leadership and denying the validity of its reports. Trump infamously worked very hard to undermine the credibility of medical experts in the face of the COVID-19 pandemic. His efforts arguably created a much worse pandemic. By the end of his presidency, Trump had not yet taken aim at the truth-aptness of the court system. That might seem to have been the next logical target, given that the court system ultimately sided against him in his attempt to undermine the epistemic credibility of the election process. But Trump was very focused on appointing conservative and ideologically aligned judges and took great pride in his accomplishments on that front, so he might have been hesitant to invoke skepticism about the court system itself. But it is predictable that the epistemic legitimacy of the court system will come under pressure from Trumpism if public trust in the courts fails to advance its strategic ends.

These examples illustrate some ways the regime of truth can and has become a political battlefield. The radical left already knew it was a battlefield. The regime of truth in its current configuration is part of the matrix of domination. The central pillars of the regime of truth have functioned to promote the well-being of more dominantly situated groups. The regime of truth surely requires social justice initiatives to address grave systemic issues around racism and gender-based oppression, around ablism, around poverty and classism, around cis-supremacy and fat-phobia, around homophobia and sexism. There are many ways in which the regime of truth constitutes the matrix of domination we live in. I will elaborate in the next chapter.

An oppressive regime of truth is the apparatus that makes misinformation about gender and racism function as true and empowers active ignorance about systems of oppression. Misinformation and active ignorance are the lifeblood of systems of oppression, as I will argue in the next chapter. Reinforcing an oppressive regime of truth constitutes a form of epistemic violence. It harms marginalized epistemic agents in their capacity to act as producers of knowledge. Epistemic violence is intimately connected with the physical, material, and psychological violence of the interlocking systems of oppression themselves: racism, misogyny, homophobia, and so on. Linguistic acts that spread misinformation, such as linguistic hijacking of the word "racist," draw on and reinforce the power of an oppressive regime of truth that sustains and protects racism itself. Thus, Foucault's understanding of power and truth enables us to give an epistemic violence model of misinformation. The regime of truth is an engine of misinformation, and therefore, it is an engine of epistemic violence.

But the regime of truth is also a source of stability, a vehicle for change and accountability, and at least in principle functions as a bulwark against even more complete and violent forms of oppression. Think of the totalitarian surveillance state that strictly controls all information and quashes the flow of all dissenting opinion, that hides all information about sexual abuse and governmental corruption, that tightly controls media representation, imprisons dissenters, and completely undermines education and free speech. The democratic institutions of a free press, a free academy, a free speech, a transparent government, and a transparent and accountable police force and justice system are important ideals for intersectional struggle. Government action on climate change informed by a thriving, credible, and accurate scientific community is crucial. Accurate sociological data about the intergenerational effects of slavery, Jim Crow apartheid, and mass incarceration are crucial for appropriately addressing past injustices and dismantling current systems of oppression. The connection between truth and political action is crucial precisely because we want our political initiatives to be responsive to reality. This is why an intersectional theory of objective truth is necessary in light of the Foucauldian critique of truth and power.

The theory of intersectionality developed in the next chapter is very much aligned with this Foucauldian understanding of power and its relationship with truth. The production of truth and its operation within the field of power relations is closely connected with the matrices of domination that constitute structural intersectionality and give rise to the many aspects of intersectional oppression, political intersectionality, and the intersectional identities that exist in the midst of intersecting systems of oppression. Collins (2002) is clearly engaged in a Foucauldian analysis of power when she develops her concept of the matrix of domination. The Foucauldian relationship between truth and power and the way this relationship shapes the matrix of domination is thus a central commitment of intersectionality theory. I do not mean to claim that the details of the theory of power I have sketched here are necessary for every acceptable theory of intersectionality—I mean only to suggest one way of thinking about power that captures what is important to a theory of intersectionality. But what is necessary is that some similar theory of the relationship between truth and power is part of the theory of intersectionality.

Thus, intersectionality constrains the theory of truth. Insofar as we need a view of truth as objective—and we do need that, badly—it must be an intersectional theory of truth. This means it must incorporate a clear view of the relationship between truth and power, specifically the way that misinformation and falsehood sustain the continued existence of intersecting systems of oppression.

REFERENCES

Alexander, M. (2020). *The New Jim Crow: Mass Incarceration in the Age of Colorblindness*. The New Press.
Anderson, D. (2019). Rejecting Semantic Truth: On the Significance of Neurath's Syntacticism. In *Neurath Reconsidered* (pp. 363–382). Springer.
Arendt, H. (1967). Truth and Politics. *Truth: Engagements Across Philosophical Traditions*, 295.
Asimov, I. (2004). *Foundation and Empire* (Vol. 2). Spectra.
Bach, K. (1985). A Rationale for Reliabilism. *The Monist, 68*, 246–263.
BonJour, L. (1980). Externalist Theories of Empirical Knowledge. *Midwest Studies in Philosophy, 5*, 53–73.
Chisholm, R. (1977). *Theory of Knowledge* (2nd ed.). Prentice-Hall.
Code, L. (2012). Taking Subjectivity into Account. In *Education, Culture and Epistemological Diversity* (pp. 85–100). Springer.
Cohen, S., & Lehrer, K. (1983). Justification, Truth, and Knowledge. *Synthese, 55*, 191–207.
Collins, P. H. (2002). *Black Feminist Thought: Knowledge, Consciousness, and the Politics of Empowerment*. Routledge.
De Saussure, F. (1916/2011). *Course in General Linguistics*. Columbia University Press.
Dennett, D. C. (1989). *The Intentional Stance*. MIT Press.
Derrida, J. (1967/2016). *Of Grammatology*. Jhu Press.
Dotson, K. (2011). Tracking Epistemic Violence, Tracking Practices of Silencing. *Hypatia, 26*(2), 236–257.
Fodor, J. (1997). Special Sciences: Still Autonomous After All These Years. *Philosophical Perspectives, 11*, 149–163.
Fodor, J. A. (1974). Special Sciences (Or: The Disunity of Science as a Working Hypothesis). *Synthese*, 97–115.
Foucault, M. (1975/2012). *Discipline and Punish: The Birth of the Prison*. Vintage.
Foucault, M. (1978/1990). *The History of Sexuality: An Introduction*. Vintage.
Foucault, M. (1980). *Power/Knowledge: Selected Interviews and Other Writings, 1972–1977*. Vintage.
Foucault, M., Rabinow, P., & Martell, L. (1972). Truth and Power. In Foucault, M. (1980). *Power/Knowledge: Selected Interviews and Other Writings, 1972–1977*. Vintage.
Fricker, M. (2007). *Epistemic Injustice: Power and the Ethics of Knowing*. Oxford University Press.
Govier, T. (1993). When Logic Meets Politics: Testimony, Distrust, and Rhetorical Disadvantage. *Informal Logic, 15*(2). https://doi.org/10.22329/il.v15i2.2476

Harding, S. (1995). "Strong objectivity": A Response to the New Objectivity Question. *Synthese, 104*(3), 331–349.

Hobbes, T. (1651/1980). Leviathan. *Glasgow 1974.*

Mills, C. (2007). White Ignorance. *Race and Epistemologies of Ignorance, 247,* 26–31.

Neurath, M. (1983). *Philosophical Papers 1913–1946: With a Bibliography of Neurath in English* (Vol. 16). Springer Science & Business Media.

Oxford English Dictionary. (2020a). "female, n." OED Online. Oxford University Press, December 2020. Oed.com.

Oxford English Dictionary. (2020b). "woman, n." OED Online. Oxford University Press, December 2020. Oed.com.

Scheman, N. (1995). Feminist Epistemology. *Metaphilosophy, 26*(3), 177–190.

Steinbeck, J. (1939/2006). *The Grapes of Wrath.* Penguin.

Trump, D. (2020). Remarks by President Trump at the White House Conference on American History, September 17, 2020. https://www.whitehouse.gov/briefings-statements/remarks-president-trump-white-house-conference-american-history/ [Removed by Biden Administration].

Van Fraassen, B. C. (1980). *The Scientific Image.* Oxford University Press.

CHAPTER 8

An Analytic Philosopher's Unified Theory of Intersectionality

The political reality that centrally informs the arguments of this book is the existence of intersectionality. Abstractly, intersectionality involves the way in which different forms of oppression co-constitute one another and interact with one another to produce unique forms of oppression where they act in tandem (Collins, 2002). More concretely, intersectionality is the phenomenon whereby white supremacy, patriarchy, sexism, heterosexism, heteronormativity and homophobia, cis-supremacy and transphobia, fatphobia, ablism, neoliberal capitalism, imperialism, settler-colonialism, and Western cultural domination emerge from, converge with, reinforce, and co-constitute one another. These phenomena can helpfully be described within the Foucauldian power framework introduced in the preceding chapter, along with their interactions with the regime of truth (Foucault, 1980) that helps to sustain their existence.

But the theory of intersectionality goes beyond describing interlocking systems of oppression. It provides tools for understanding complex social identities, as well as conceptualizing the tensions that arise within political movements. Intersectional theories are critical theories, which means they have a pragmatic social and political function of describing and effectively dismantling the ideological systems that perpetuate oppression. Intersectional frameworks put interactions between systems of oppression at the center of political analysis, while also providing tools for conceiving of social identities as multifaceted and integrated.

My presentation of intersectionality is intended to provide a concrete and particular theory. I'm not saying this is the only accurate theory of intersectionality. Intersectionality may be understood as an entire field unto itself (Cho, Crenshaw & McCall, 2013), which interacts with other fields such as philosophy in an interdisciplinary way. I aim to present the ideas developed in intersectionality studies for an audience of analytic philosophers and also to contribute to intersectionality studies by applying the analytic lens to the topic at hand.

My project requires stating a definitive theory of intersectionality, which will then interact with the General Metasemantic Adequacy constraint I introduce in the next chapter to give an Intersectional Metasemantic Adequacy constraint. Then in Chap. 10 I will give a metasemantics that satisfies that constraint.

8.1 A Methodological Worry

The attempt to state a definitive theory of intersectionality poses a methodological problem. Intersectionality studies as a discipline is characterized in part by extensive "discursive debates about the scope and content of intersectionality as a theoretical and methodological paradigm" (Cho et al., 2013). It is self-reflective and self-critical and makes room for many perspectives concerning its own theoretical nature. Stating a definitive, totalizing theory threatens to delimit this self-reflection. It also threatens to exclude large swaths of intersectional work and foreclose new possibilities for expanding and applying the concept.

My theory risks being what Dotson (2012) calls a closed conceptual structure, a framework or theory that presents itself as total or complete and thereby excludes or restricts expansions of the structure's domain, but which in fact fails to capture the whole phenomenon under investigation. Dotson maintains that a catchall theory of a given phenomenon is unrealistic to achieve whenever that phenomenon is extremely pervasive, which surely intersectionality is. The solution according to Dotson is to develop open conceptual structures, theories that do not foreclose alternative understandings of the phenomenon under investigation.

Cho et al. (2013) argue in a similar spirit that intersectionality studies must endeavor to achieve "greater theoretical, methodological, substantive, and political literacy without demanding greater unity across the growing diversity of fields that constitute the study of intersectionality." The demand for greater unity puts pressure on various theoretical projects to conform to a totalizing central conception, and this pressure destroys the crucial flexibility of the intersectional framework to address theoretical questions and political needs in the huge diversity of circumstances in which intersectionality is needed. Thus, we should not demand unity.

Analytic philosophy as a discipline is very interested in developing and defending totalizing, unified theories. I am self-consciously constructing a theory within this discipline as a contribution to intersectionality studies. Cho, Crenshaw, and McCall warn that this kind of methodology is inherently in danger of misrepresenting intersectionality, because "disciplinary conventions import a range of assumptions and truth claims that sometimes contribute to the very erasures to which intersectionality draws attention ... Pressure to locate a project firmly within a conventional field when part of the project is directed precisely at that field's conceptual limitations replicates on an academic level the same constraints that confronted plaintiffs who challenged the categorical apparatus in antidiscrimination law [in Crenshaw's (1989) discussion of the inability of courts to conceptualize the unique circumstances of oppression that Black women face]." The worry for me is that by attempting to articulate intersectionality firmly within the analytic philosopher's framework, just by conforming to that framework I will undermine my own project's goals.

One could see analytic philosophy with its disciplinary strictures as functioning as part of the regime of truth that obscures understanding of intersectionality. I recognize that intersectionality is multiform and inherently resists being accurately formulated as a discrete and determinate theory, that it must be stated as a kind of open conceptual structure, and that analytic philosophy as a discipline is ill-suited for formulating open conceptual structures since it is constantly attempting to give totalizing, unifying necessary and sufficient conditions in order to define once and for all its objects of study.

Yet Cho, Crenshaw, and McCall also concede that "[a]t the same time, efforts to produce new knowledge cannot dispense with the apparatuses through which information is produced, categorized, and interpreted." The regime of truth in its present configuration cannot be totally dispensed with, even if it is problematic in certain regards. The discipline of analytic philosophy is part of the apparatus we have to work with. Sociologically speaking, it is a power structure which legitimates and makes certain statements function as true in a very contested way governed by philosophical discourse itself. While the apparatus of philosophy may be deeply flawed in its connection to an oppressive regime of truth, this does not entail that philosophy as an institution cannot take on an emancipatory function or that its methods when explicitly situated in a field of power relations can't be put to use in theorizing about intersectionality. I see my project as an experiment in attempting to formulate a picture of intersectionality within the methodological framework of analytic philosophy.

Even though the theory I am presenting is a totalizing, unifying theory, I do not think anyone should treat the theory as if it is in fact *the* total, unified truth. Rather, my aim is only to develop one possible determinate picture with which to illustrate the main themes of this book and to convey my own understanding of the topic. My aim is not to *defend* the view developed here as The One True Theory of Intersectionality. I mean to offer it as one might offer a novel or a painting portraying a complexity that goes beyond what the medium can possibly hope to capture. The medium of analytic philosophy is the totalizing theory. That's the paintbrush I know how to use, but I do not mean to insist that the painting is the reality.

The view developed here is a synthesis of the main ideas presented by the foundational thinkers in intersectionality theory, reconstructed as a unified theory. But that unified theory has five aspects: (i) intersectionality as structural oppression, (ii) intersectionality as the division of political energy, known as political intersectionality (Crenshaw, 1990), (iii) intersectional identities, (iv) intersectionality as critical theory, and (v) intersectionality as praxis.[1]

My methodology is that of an intellectual historian in the analytic philosophical tradition, so I will proceed by doing close readings of

---

[1] On my analysis the word "intersectionality" is ambiguous across these five aspects of theory. For example, intersectionality is a critical theory about the oppressive system that shares its name. "Intersectionality" refers both to interlocking systems of oppression and to the theoretical frameworks that investigate and resist those systems. The ambiguity is striking because in one sense "intersectionality" refers to something bad and in another sense refers to something good. When Flavia Dzodan (2011) famously asserted, "My feminism will be intersectional or it will be bullshit," she meant feminism must be informed by intersectionality, the critical theory, which is good. But when Crenshaw (1990) writes that "Many women of color, for example, are burdened by poverty, child-care responsibilities, and the lack of job skills. These burdens, largely the consequence of gender and class oppression, are then compounded by the racially discriminatory employment and housing ... These observations reveal how intersectionality shapes the experiences of many women of color," she is referring to intersectionality, the system of interlocking oppressions, which is bad. A theory of intersectionality ought to recognize some version of this ambiguity.

foundational texts and synthesizing a unified theory from the ideas located there. The rest of the chapter proceeds in six parts. The first part presents a brief history of intersectionality. The remaining five parts present each of the five aspects listed above.

One last caveat: your author closely approximates what Audre Lorde (1980) refers to as the 'mythical norm.' According to Lorde, "In america, this norm is usually defined as white, thin, male, young, heterosexual, christian, and financially secure." We might add: able-bodied, cis, settler/non-native, neurotypical, and a US citizen. While I do not fit comfortably into every one of these categories, my experience has largely been one of fitting into the norm, at least close enough. When I reflect on the norm, I do not strongly experience what Lorde describes when she writes, "each of us in our hearts knows *that is not me*." I grew up feeling that I was subsumed by the mythical norm, even when I deviated in various categories. So, I come to intersectionality as an epistemological outsider. I have not lived a life that puts me into much direct contact with structures of oppression within my own experience. My understanding of the phenomena of intersectionality comes through the experiences of the marginalized and oppressed, their testimony, and the theoretical perspectives they have developed.

My access to this knowledge is limited by my willingness and ability to engage effectively with the political causes that underlie the theory and praxis of intersectionality. This is part and parcel with the epistemic aspect of intersectionality theory itself: each intersectional social identity provides its own specialized knowledge of social reality, and we can only know across political divides insofar as we are in political solidarity with other groups. For this reason, belonging to the mythical norm tends to promote an affinity for the kinds of ideological misinformation that promote the interests of dominant groups and obscures knowledge of intersectionality. My epistemic access is recognizably imperfect, from the perspective of intersectionality theory itself. My view should thus be understood as that of a member of the dominant group, hopefully an effective ally, trying to provide a perspective developed from a social position from which the concepts of intersectional theory sometimes seem alien and counterintuitive.

8.2 A Brief History of Intersectionality

Intersectionality as an intellectual movement is widely recognized as having its roots in US Black feminism. My analysis will focus primarily on Black feminist texts, but as Collins and Bilge (2016) note, "African-American women were part of heterogeneous alliances with Chicanas and Latinas, Native American women, and Asian-American women ... these groups were also at the forefront of raising claims about the interconnectedness of race, class, gender, and sexuality in their everyday life experiences." Many scholars have noted that the history of intersectionality is both contested and perspectival, that it arises from many identities and many theoretical needs and answers to many different narratives (Collins & Bilge, 2016; Grzanka, 2018; Nash, 2018). Intersectional theorizing itself stresses the importance of recognizing a plurality of knowledge-generating perspectives, both present and historical. It will therefore be important to draw on these interconnections in giving my brief historical overview and in adducing the details of the theory.

Awareness of intersectionality is as old as intersectionality itself. As Patricia Hill Collins (2002) notes in *Black Feminist Thought*, "On some level, people who are oppressed usually know it. For African-American women, the knowledge gained at intersecting oppressions of race, class, and gender provides the stimulus for crafting and passing on the subjugated knowledge of Black women's critical social theory."[2] The oppressed develop awareness of the contours of their oppression and develop a shared understanding among others who are similarly oppressed.

The Combahee River Collective (Collective, 1977) raises the same point when they write, "we find our origins in the historical reality of Afro-American women's continuous life-and-death struggle for survival and liberation ... Contemporary Black feminism is the outgrowth of countless generations of personal sacrifice, militancy, and work by our mothers and sisters." Because the struggle is life and death, everyone participating in it must deeply understand what's going on. This kind of knowledge is not academic. It is rooted in the work of mothers and sisters, family-based knowledge about how to live one's life in a community beset by imposed hardships. It is rooted in militancy, the armed and organized opposition to racism and sexism. These are also locations of sacrifice, of people giving up parts of themselves to help those in their families and

---

[2] Collins (2002, p. 11).

communities, sometimes even sacrificing life and limb. Countless generations of these practices!

The point of noting the deep history of intersectional knowledge at the outset is to emphasize that intersectional theorizing predates any academic discourses about intersectionality. It arises within every community that is subjected to intersecting systems of oppression. The communities who have historically experienced intersecting oppressions have been theorizing about it since the beginning out of necessity for survival. Knowledge of intersectionality therefore dates back at least to the origins of racial and colonial oppression, by which point women were simultaneously being subjected to racism, imperialism, and gender-based oppression.

Black women in the US were publicly discussing intersectionality in the nineteenth century. Free Black women, working as abolitionists as early as 1830, discussed feminist themes in the context of racism and slavery. They saw the importance of advocating for the lives of Black women specifically.[3] Wherever these conversations became public, they faced pushback and delegitimation at the hands of the dominant power structures that decide what counts as knowledge. This renders Black feminist thought a form of what Foucault calls *subjugated knowledge*.[4] Famous early statements of intersectionality from the nineteenth century were delivered by Maria Stewart (1831), Sojourner Truth (1851), and Anna Julia Cooper (1892) who published the first book-length Black feminist text (Guy-Sheftall, 1995). These women publicly articulated the existence of Black women and girls as their own distinctive social and political group, facing distinctive challenges and developing their own knowledge of the oppressive social order and their own strategies of resistance.

---

[3] See B. Guy-Sheftall (1995). Chapter 1 is focused on the period from 1830 to 1900.

[4] See Collins (2002), chapter 1, Footnote 2. Collins (2002) cites Foucault (1980) as the source for her term "subjugated knowledge," but distinguishes her concept from Foucault's arguing that Black feminist subjugated knowledge is not deficient knowledge—as Foucault seems to think subjugated knowledge typically is—but rather "has been made to seem so by those controlling knowledge procedures." Collins also critically notes that Foucault himself omitted Black feminist knowledge from his analysis because it is not "particular, local, regional" or "incapable of unanimity." I would argue that Foucault's account would recognize that Black feminist knowledge is not actually deficient, only made to seem that way by dominant power, and that subjugated knowledge is also only made to appear provincial by the same dominant power when in fact (especially when) it has potential significance to upend the status quo. But then, my reading of Foucault is strongly influenced by my reading of Collins!

The vast majority of women who participated in creating the theory and praxis of resisting intersecting oppressions during the nineteenth century had no voice to articulate those ideas within public spheres. Nevertheless, their knowledge feeds into academic theorizing about intersectionality in the twentieth and twenty-first centuries, as it was developed and transmitted through communities of women of color, passed down and developed intergenerationally (Collins, 2002).

Women of color slowly gained access to higher education beginning in the nineteenth century despite institutional pressures aimed at keeping them out. But it was not until the 1960s with the successes of the civil rights movement and the women's movement that women of color began to occupy prominent places within the academy. The emergence of intersectional theorizing within the academy occurs when women of color come to have an academic voice, beginning in the 1960s and 1970s.

This coming to academic voice coincided with a time where women of color in the US were confronting sexism in the Civil Rights movement and racism in the second wave of the American women's movement.[5] The male-led Civil Rights movement embodied certain patriarchal and heteronormative ideals, while the white-led women's movement inevitably failed to interrogate its racism and classism. Women of color participating in these movements were painfully aware of the intersectionality involved in political struggle that was being overlooked by Black men and white women, and these experiences fueled the growing academic theoretical articulations of intersectionality.[6]

It was in this context that the Combahee River Collective formed. Keanga Taylor (2017) writes, "It is difficult to quantify the enormity of the political contribution made by the women of the Combahee River collective, including Barbara Smith, her sister Beverly Smith, and Demita Frazier, because so much of their analysis is taken for granted in feminist politics today."[7] Taylor points out that the Combahee River Collective were the first to describe intersecting systems of oppression as interlocking. The Combahee River Collective was a loose-knit collection of Black women academics, poets, activists, and community builders based in the Boston area. The Combahee River Collective Statement, their manifesto, articulates many of the central themes of intersectionality, including the

[5] Smith (1977) and Crenshaw (1989, 1990).
[6] Collective (1977).
[7] Taylor (2017).

need to engage in identity politics, the need for addressing multiple forms of oppression simultaneously, and the need for self-care and community when engaging in political action against intersecting oppressions.

Barbara Smith said of their objectives at that time, "When we started talking about Black feminism in the 1970s, we were trying to assert that Black women had a right to define their own political destiny, their own political issues ... we were trying to carve out a place for ourselves [i.e. poor or working-class Black lesbians], but we also understood that if we were successful, if we were able to do that, then we would have carved out a space for every other kind of individual, every other kind, because even though we did not encompass every single identity, we had an analysis and a practice that said that, wherever you come from, Be You ... we knew that if we could get a foothold and get this rolling it would make space and revolution for everybody."[8] This is a perfect articulation of the sense in which intersectionality done right must start from the experiences of a particular localized social identity and work outward, but at the same time this process is and always has been understood as a movement for everyone, from multiple places at once, from every location within the matrix of domination. As such it has always been a kind of universal movement which was meant to build bridges and recognize situatedness and connect across the epistemic and pragmatic limitations that occur within the social fabric.

Getting the history of intersectionality right means both seeing it as a movement that originates in Black feminism and also as a kind of coalitional politics that was meant to encompass every form of intersectional resistance to oppression. Intersectionality is meant to help build alliances between social justice movements, which are in fact one and the same movement because all forms of oppression are co-constituted.

Through the theory and activism of the Combahee River Collective and through its connections with the emerging sphere of women of color gaining access to academia, these perspectives became highly influential in guiding the academic discourse in the decades to come. The Combahee River Collective statement is a powerful moment in the beginning of the transformation of the academic apparatus into something capable of recognizing and theorizing about intersectionality.

---

[8] From the panel Black Feminism & the Movement for Black Lives: Barbara Smith, Reina Gossett, Charlene Carruthers. January 21, 2016. Accessed 1-10-21 (https://www.youtube.com/watch?v=eV3nnFheQRo&t=435s).

In the early 1980s we see a proliferation of central intersectional texts within the academic discourse. bell hooks's (1981) *Ain't I a Woman?: Black Women and Feminism*, which she wrote as an undergraduate, provides an important critique of sexism in the Civil Rights movement and racism and classism in the Women's Rights movement. In her follow-up book *Feminist Theory: From Margin to Center*, hooks (1984) introduces the term "White Supremacist Capitalist Patriarchy" as a descriptor of the unity of the system of intersecting oppressions. Angela Davis's (1981) landmark study *Women, Race, and Class* presents an in-depth historical analysis of Black women's oppression under US chattel slavery and the continuity of transformation of the matrix of domination from the days of slavery through the late nineteenth and early twentieth centuries and theorizes the persistence of these patterns into the latter half of the twentieth century. Another influential work from the early 1980s is Moraga and Anzaldúa's (1981) collection *This Bridge Called My Back*, which presented critical essays and emancipatory poetry from Native and Chicana feminists alongside contributions from Black feminists and members of the Combahee River Collective—this collection includes the Combahee River Collective Statement as well, reprinted. Alice Walker (1983) published *In Search of Our Mother's Gardens*, a collection of prose and poetry that, among other things, coined the term *Womanist* as a name for the Black women's movement which is inherently intersectional and stands in opposition to the whiteness and heterosexuality of mainstream feminism. Audre Lorde's (1984) collection *Sister Outsider* is also published at this time, which introduced the concept of the mythical norm, the concept of epistemic exploitation, presented a powerful defense of the use of anger about racism, defended the power and legitimacy of Black lesbian sexuality, and furnished one of intersectionality's greatest proverbs: "The master's tools will never dismantle the master's house." Gloria Anzaldúa's (1987) *Borderlands/La Frontera: The New Mestiza* is another a highly influential work of this time, describing the intersections of racism, colonialism, and gender-based oppression as they influenced Chicana and Latina women. These works and many others mark the occurrence of the first large wave of intersectional scholars responding to one another in print within the apparatus of the academy. They form the backdrop of the theoretical development of intersectionality studies within academic discourses.

The late 1980s and early 1990s see the theory of intersectionality take on its most influential and widely cited forms. Kimberlé Crenshaw (1989, 1990) introduces the term "intersectionality" as a name for the phenomena involving interlocking systems of oppression, the ways in which they give rise to intersecting forms of political pressure, and the way these aspects of social life form the locus of intersectional identity politics. In 1990, Patricia Hill Collins (2002) writes a magnum opus, *Black Feminist Thought: Knowledge, Consciousness and the Politics of Empowerment*, which develops the concept of the matrix of domination as the ontological structure that embodies intersectional oppression at a given time and place. Collins also discusses the situatedness of knowledge within interlocking systems of oppression and applies the Black feminist identity politics of the Combahee River Collective to epistemology to develop Black feminist standpoint theory. The works of Crenshaw and Collins, as with the works of their academic peers, provide crucial concepts and frameworks that go on to inform the discourse within the academic sphere and beyond in the coming century.

From this point the academic discourse around intersectionality accelerates exponentially as the academy becomes more diverse. By the first decade of the twenty-first century, intersectional frameworks are being used in many domains of socio-political thought, and the framework itself has become widely recognizable outside of the academy. The expansion of intersectional frameworks can be seen to be coextensive with the steady increase of influence of women of color within the academy. This expansive and accelerated age of intersectional scholarship is largely traceable in its academic and intellectual heritage to the writings of the early Black feminist and intersectional woman of color scholars of the 1970s, 1980s, and 1990s.

A student of history is much better equipped to understand the present state of systems of intersecting oppressions. For example, reading and understanding Angela Davis (1981) on the history and evolution of Black women's oppression makes it very hard to deny that many of the same sociological forces that have kept Black women in check in the past are still with us today. Yet such claims are often presented as ideological misrepresentations through the influence of white ignorance, made to function as false; they are rendered obscure and intangible through lack of education or through the creation of counter-narratives; they are treated as of less than 'universal' significance in fields such as political science or philosophy; these are examples of the operation of a regime of truth that functions to preserve the status quo in its racist and sexist configuration of power.

Knowing the historical development of the frameworks of intersectionality is crucial for developing philosophical theories that properly incorporate the knowledge of a huge swath of philosophers, albeit philosophers who are by and large denied the status of philosophers by the discipline of analytic philosophy. The exclusion of the conceptual frameworks of intersectionality from the discourses of analytic philosophy perpetuates ignorance within that discipline and serves to reinscribe its own self-centered perspective.[9] The discourse in analytic philosophy is thus complicit, is part of this pattern of enforcing ignorance, insofar as it perpetuates ignorance of intersectional frameworks developed in response to the historically situated perspectives of marginalized groups. Analytic philosophical methodology renders intersectionality irrelevant to deep questions of philosophy. It excludes intersectional theory from mainstream philosophy, from what is considered 'real' or 'deep' or 'fundamental' philosophy.[10] One way forward, which I am pursuing, is to try to incorporate the insights of intersectionality theory into a framework formulated within the norms of the analytic tradition.

In the next five sections, I lay out what I take to be the five aspects of intersectionality theory: (Sect. 8.3) structural intersectionality, the theory of intersecting oppressions; (Sect. 8.4) political intersectionality, the phenomena whereby oppressed groups facing intersecting systems of oppression typically face competing political exigencies; (Sect. 8.5) intersectional identity, the phenomena whereby individual and group identities are conditioned through their shared struggle to exist amidst intersecting systems of oppression; (Sect. 8.6) intersectionality-as-theory, the sense in which intersectionality is a critical theory, an evolving discourse aimed at emancipation; and (Sect. 8.7) intersectionality-as-praxis, the sense in which intersectionality is a way of living and acting in opposition to structures of oppression, to bring about emancipation.

8.3 Intersectionality as Structural Oppression

Although intersectionality is widely perceived to be a theory of social identity, this is not its sole or primary aim (Collins & Bilge, 2016). Intersectionality is primarily a theory of oppression. Specifically, it is a theory about systems of interconnected, mutually reinforcing and mutually co-constituted forms of structural oppression. The relevance of social

---

[9] See Thani and Anderson (2020) for extensive discussion.
[10] See Dotson (2016) for a critique of the concept of fundamentality in philosophy and its role in perpetuating active ignorance.

identity within intersectional analyses arises due to the impact of interlocking systems of oppression upon people of various social identities. That intersectionality theory is focused primarily on structural oppression is clear in the early academic texts about intersectionality. The Combahee River Collective writes,

> The most general statement of our politics at the present time would be that we are actively committed to struggling against racial, sexual, heterosexual, and class oppression, and see as our particular task the development of integrated analysis and practice based upon the fact that the major systems of oppression are interlocking. The synthesis of these oppressions creates the conditions of our lives.[11]

The Collective identifies "the major systems of oppression" as the primary focus of their political analysis and asserts that they are interlocking. These interlocking systems are also the focus of political struggle and create the conditions of life for those living under them. It is because of the overlapping existence of racism, heterosexism, class-oppression, and gender-oppression that poor Black lesbians face the conditions they do and engage in the political struggles they engage in.

Audre Lorde repeatedly frames the central issue of intersectionality as a confrontation with massive, dehumanizing forces. In her 1981 keynote presentation at the National Women's Studies Association Conference, "The Uses of Anger: Women Responding to Racism" (Lorde, 1981), she makes reference to "the size and complexities of the forces mounting against us and all that is most human in our environment," and in the closing lines of the address identifies the primary enemy as

> [that which] launches rockets, spends over sixty thousand dollars a second on missiles and other agents of war and death, slaughters children in cities, stockpiles nerve gas and chemical bombs, sodomizes our daughters and our earth ... which corrodes into blind, dehumanizing power, bent upon the annihilation of all unless we meet it with what we have, our power to examine and to redefine the terms upon which we live and work[.]

Lorde presents a bold and grim picture of the full system of interlocking structures of oppression, which connects racism with capitalist exploitation, violence against women, environmental destruction, and the

[11] Collective (1977).

military industrial complex. This might be called the holistic picture of structural oppression, in which the many interlocking systems are conceived as a kind of single, unified machine with many components. Resistance must proceed by examining and reorganizing the conditions of life and work in a way that undermines the functioning of this machine. This is the primary goal of intersectional theorizing.

In Kimberlé Crenshaw's (1989) article introducing the term "intersectionality," in the first statement of the article that employs that term, again the focus is on interlocking systems of oppression:

> Because the intersectional experience is greater than the sum of racism and sexism, any analysis that does not take intersectionality into account cannot sufficiently address the particular manner in which Black women are subordinated.

The issue is framed in terms of Black women's subordination, which is identified through reference to an experience of oppression that goes beyond the sum of racism and sexism. The focus is on the plurality of distinctive ways in which discrimination is produced and experienced as the effects of discriminatory practices that target people in a variety of ways. The aim of the theory is to address the "particular manner in which Black women are subordinated." Black feminist praxis requires focusing on Black women in particular, but it simultaneously provides a model for a general approach to intersectional theorizing: any adequate theory of oppression must address the experiences of those who experience multiple forms of oppression.

8.3.1 Single-Axis Frameworks

Crenshaw contrasts intersectionality with what she calls a 'single-axis framework' for understanding discrimination. A single-axis framework represents each form of discrimination as operating independently of the others and renders the class of oppressions (racism, sexism, ablism, etc.) as conceptually analyzable into distinctive and non-overlapping categories. On a single-axis approach, one thinks about racism as separate from sexism, as separate from transphobia, as separate from class-based oppression, and so on. On an intersectional approach, one thinks of a theory of racism as being responsible for explaining ways in which, for example, racism can affect women and men differently, how it affects gay people of color and straight people of color differently, how it affects gay women of color differently from gay men of color, and so on.

Lorde (1980) articulates the distinction between intersectional and single-axis thinking by reference to what she calls the mythical norm. She identifies the mythical norm in the US as white, thin, male, young, heterosexual, Christian, and financially secure, and as I mentioned above, we can add able-bodied, cis, settler/non-native, and a US citizen. "It is within this mythical norm that the trappings of power reside within this society." The mythical norm is defined in terms of an identity, but the identity is a proxy for power in the Foucauldian sense. It is not the group of elite white men who constitute the power, but rather the power embodied in the system that supports white male dominance.

Lorde uses the mythical norm to identify and critique single-axis thinking embodied in white feminism. White feminism is aimed at addressing the struggle of a group of people who almost fit the mythical norm: women who are wealthy, straight, white, and heterosexual. Lorde addresses her white feminist audience saying, "Those of us who stand outside that power [the power embodied in the mythical norm] often identify one way in which we are different, and we assume that to be the primary cause of all oppression, forgetting other distortions around difference, some of which we ourselves may be practicing." The wealthy cis straight white feminist experiences a limited kind of oppression, marked off by the one way in which she is different from the mythical norm. Lorde is saying, the mistaken perception of white feminism is to identify this one aspect of difference as marking the essence of oppression and thereby neglecting intersecting forms of oppression.

Single-axis feminism ignores differences between dominant women and more marginalized women. "By and large within the women's movement today, white women focus upon their oppression as women and ignore differences of race, sexual preference, class, and age. There is a pretense to a homogeneity of experience covered by the word *sisterhood* that does not in fact exist" (Lorde, 1980). It's not that there is no sisterhood whatsoever, but rather that a homogeneity of experience does not exist. The pretense to homogeneity is a way of ignoring differences concerning the ways in which racism, homophobia, classism, and age affect how women's oppression operates.

Crenshaw (1989) describes how single-axis thinking obscures the complexity of oppression through her discussion of what she calls the 'but-for' model of discrimination. On the but-for model, each form of oppression is specified with regard to a person who would not be oppressed *but for* one aspect of their social identity. Racism is what afflicts a person who *but for their race* would be non-oppressed. Sexism is what afflicts a person who *but for their being a woman* would be non-oppressed. Oppression is thus understood as connected with deviations from a norm—Lorde's mythical norm.

Crenshaw (1989) describes how the but-for model works within legal contexts. In Degraffenreid v. General Motors, the plaintiffs alleged that their employers discriminated against Black women because all the Black women at the factory had been fired. The defendant contested they did not discriminate against women, because they had white women working in their office, and they did not discriminate against Black people because they had Black men working on the factory floor. The court agreed with the defendant, saying in effect that Black women could not form a distinctive oppressed group of their own. Here single-axis thinking precluded justice from being served, and in a way that was hard-coded into the standard interpretation of anti-discrimination law.

The but-for model embodies single-axis thinking because it represents oppression as that which afflicts the most privileged among the oppressed, those marginalized people who most closely approximate the mythical norm. Consequently, racism in its 'pure' form is that which afflicts men of color who are heterosexual, cis, financially secure, able-bodied, male US citizens. Sexism is what afflicts heterosexual, cis, able-bodied, and financially secure white women. Black women struggle to be included under legal protections aimed at serving Black men and white women when sexism and racism are understood according to the but-for model in this way. Gay Black men, trans white women, disabled queer people, and a myriad of other marginalized groups who face multiple forms of oppression will find themselves left out of legal protections and social safety nets that are designed to serve the most privileged among the marginalized.

The but-for model produces an absurd theoretical picture for understanding intersecting oppressions. Consider a person who simultaneously faces sexism, racism, and homophobia, such as a Black lesbian. On the but-for model, she experiences a combination of three things: the experience of a straight white woman, plus the experience of a gay white man, plus the experience of a straight Black man. But obviously what it's like to be a Black lesbian is different from being a straight white woman plus a gay white man plus a straight Black man.

The ways in which racism, sexism, and heterosexism stack up is not simply the sum of oppressions understood according to the but-for model.

We must use an intersectional framework according to which forms of oppression like racism and sexism produce unique effects when they interact with one another. In fact, we must go even further, because to say that racism and sexism 'interact' presupposes that they can be analyzed into separate categories, but how are these categories to be individuated if we do not apply the but-for model?

In contrast with the single-axis framework, Crenshaw presents her eponymous metaphor for intersectionality.

> Discrimination, like traffic through an intersection, may flow in one direction and it may flow in another. If an accident happens in an intersection, it can be caused by cars traveling from any number of directions and sometimes from all of them.[12]

The metaphor describes an interaction between systems of social force relations causing damage. A person can be subjected to interactions between distinctive systems. Crenshaw tells us to imagine coming upon the accident after it has occurred. Sometimes the direction of force can be distinctly identified, but when a car is hit from multiple angles simultaneously, the forensic evidence may be difficult to decode. This represents the idea that the oppressive conditions faced by women of color cannot easily be analyzed into separate vectors of sexism or racism.

Although in real traffic accidents we can usually reconstruct all the force vectors involved in the accident, the difficulty of this task is much greater and perhaps impossible when assessing the forces issuing from social structures. The metaphor also suggests a sense in which events that involve both sexism and racism can involve a kind of complex damage analogous to being hit simultaneously from two directions at once in an intersection.

But intersectionality is even more complex than the eponymous metaphor suggests, for two reasons. First, as noted above, even conceptualizing separate roads, for example, one for racism and one for sexism, proves problematic if we are not allowed to appeal to a single-axis model of oppression. Women of color can be affected by racism alone in the absence of sexism, the very same racism as men of color, but the racism road represents racism itself, the whole of racism, and an analysis of racism must incorporate recognition of the role sexism plays. We can't define the racism road without incorporating the sexism road. Likewise, for

---

[12] Crenshaw (1989).

sexism—sexism is racialized. If we try to say what *pure* sexism is, sexism that is not racialized, then we end up describing the experience of people who are oppressed as women but not as people of color, that is, white women. Hence, any attempt to state a theory of *pure sexism* or *pure racism* leads back to the single-axis framework.

Crenshaw addresses a second way in which intersectionality is more complex than the metaphor suggests. If we picture a two-way intersection of one-way roads, for example, the force vectors of racism and sexism somehow suitably individuated, then the metaphor provides three possibilities: you're hit from one road, you're hit from the other road, or you're hit from both simultaneously. But Crenshaw describes four possibilities:

> Black women can experience discrimination in ways that are both similar to and different from those experienced by white women and Black men. Black women sometimes experience discrimination in ways similar to white women's experiences; sometimes they share very similar experiences with Black men. Yet often they experience double-discrimination—the combined effects of practices which discriminate on the basis of race, and on the basis of sex. And sometimes, they experience discrimination as Black women— not the sum of race and sex discrimination, but as Black women.[13]

In the first three cases, Black women are being subjected to forces similar to those experienced by Black men and white women. Black women come in for a share of discrimination aimed at or designed for Black men, or a share of that aimed at white women, or they can be caught simultaneously in that pair of forces. But in the fourth kind of scenario, Black women experience a unique form of oppression that is geared specifically to their social identity. This is not an experience of 'trickle down oppression' where they are caught in nets that were prepared for Black men and for white women, but rather they are caught in nets that were designed specifically to catch Black women. This fourth form is not merely the sum of racism and sexism, but discrimination aimed specifically at Black women. In some sense this goes beyond the intersection metaphor, since it is not a collision of the distinctive forces aimed at Black men and white women.

The fact that racism and gender-based oppression are co-constitutive entails there is no adequate theory of racism that ignores how racism affects people of different genders differently and no adequate theory of

[13] Crenshaw (1989).

gender-based oppression that ignores how people of different races are differently affected by sexism. A theory of racism that fails to engage with the racialized ways women of color experience sexism and misogyny is incomplete, as is a theory of gender-based oppression that ignores systemic race-based differences in the treatment and life outcomes of women of color. Racism and gender-based oppression are conceptually interconnected in such a way that one cannot be accurately theorized without attending to the other.[14]

Of course, the theoretical picture is even more complicated than this delimited example suggests. For example, racism is also co-constituted by settler-colonialism, cis-supremacy, ablism, heterosexism, and the oppressive processes of neoliberal capitalism, among an indefinite and expanding list of further forms of structural oppression. And each of these other forms of structural oppression is conceptually implicated with every another. Heterosexism involves cis-supremacy, capitalist exploitation involves ablism, and so on. Highlighting this point, Collins (2002) writes, "Intersectional paradigms remind us that oppression cannot be reduced to one fundamental type, and that oppressions work together in producing injustice."[15] There can be no reductive or general theory of intersectional oppression. The phenomena under investigation are always giving rise to unique circumstances at highly specific intersections of social identities and institutions. Plausibly these highly particular circumstances cannot be derived, extrapolated, or predicted from any general principles.

Must all feminism be intersectional? A non-intersectional feminist wants to ask: Why do we always have to be focusing on some particular group—Black women, gay women, gay black women, trans Latinx women … can't we have a feminism that addresses the oppression that *all* women experience? The white feminist response to Black feminism is to assert that all women's lives matter.

---

[14] Presumably this theoretical interdependence reflects a kind of metaphysical interdependence, but the metaphysical nature of intersectionality has not been worked out. Co-constitution involves relations between properties; for example, being racist is sometimes a matter of being sexist in a certain way and vice versa. Hence, a theory of the metaphysics of intersectionality belongs to third-order logic or higher. Moreover, because intersectionality is anti-foundational, the relations between properties cannot be well-founded in the logical sense. Therefore, the logic of intersectionality also must conflict with the logic of grounding, which is well-founded. The metaphysical details are not pursued further in this book.

[15] Collins (2002, p. 18).

But focusing on the oppression that all women experience leads directly to feminism that is focused on white women who approximate the mythical norm. Non-intersectional feminism cannot be concerned with *racism* because not all women experience racism, specifically white women do not. Non-intersectional feminism cannot be concerned with *homophobia* because not all women experience homophobia, specifically straight women do not. Non-intersectional feminism cannot be concerned with *disability* because not all women experience disability, specifically able-bodied women do not. Non-intersectional feminism cannot be concerned with *transphobia* because not all women experience transphobia, specifically cis women do not. Non-intersectional feminism cannot be concerned with *poverty* because not all women experience poverty, specifically rich women do not. So the only kinds of sexist oppression that all women experience are those forms of sexism experienced by rich, able-bodied, straight, cis, white women.

From within the intersectional perspective, there can be no adequate non-intersectional analysis of women's oppression or any other form of oppression.[16] Intersectionality is necessary for accurately representing any form of oppression because forms of oppression interact and create novel circumstances for members of different intersectional identities. To analyze racism without intersectionality simply leaves out a wide range of experiences of racism. The same goes for analyzing gender-based oppression and every other kind.

8.3.2 What Is a Matrix of Domination?

At this point we have identified the phenomena of intersectionality and described the sense in which structures of oppression are co-constitutive. Next I will explain what I think is the most powerful concept for describing the ontology of intersecting systems of oppression, Patricia Hill Collins's concept of a *matrix of domination*. The concept of the matrix of domination is a way of describing the contingent configuration of power relations within a society that gives rise to structural intersectionality. It is one of the most detailed and powerful ontological concepts of intersectionality studies. The following discussion is derived largely from Collins (2002) in Chap. 10.

---

[16] For a canonical argument, see Dzodan's (2011) "My Feminism Will Be Intersectional or it Will Be Bullshit."

Collins (2002) introduces the notion of a matrix of domination to characterize the ways in which intersecting oppressions are organized at particular places, scales, and times. "The term matrix of domination describes an overall social organization within which intersecting oppressions originate, develop, and are continued." Social organization extends to every form of social relationship, from formal institutions to personal relationships. Racism and sexism are developed and continued through policy decisions that enable racist and sexist discrimination, but they are also developed and continued over dinner tables and in locker rooms and at water coolers.

Collins writes, "In the United States, such domination has occurred through schools, housing, employment, government, and other social institutions that regulate the actual patterns of intersecting oppressions that Black women encounter." She is not claiming that the matrix of domination is identical with these institutions, but rather that it operates *through* them. This is a very Foucauldian way of talking, where the institutions provide a channel for the operation of power. Here she is also saying that the institutions *regulate* patterns of intersecting oppression. These patterns exist in the social fabric beyond the institutions themselves, but the institutions function to coordinate oppressive behaviors.

Institutions are a means of using power. Insofar as elite white male power wants to subvert knowledge of racism, for example, it is strategically advantageous to control the schools, affect the housing policies, challenge employment laws that prevent discrimination, occupy seats of government, and so on, because these institutions influence the form and extent to which the matrix of domination that serves white male power can operate. The matrix of domination potentially encompasses and operates through every social institution within the society, because every social institution can operate in ways that enable, draw on, reinforce, and create forms of oppression.

Crenshaw's (1990) discussion of structural intersectionality illustrates how oppressive power can operate through institutions and illustrates the role that white ignorance plays in this operation. Crenshaw investigates the circumstances faced by poor women of color and their interactions with battered women's shelters in the poor neighborhoods surrounding Los Angeles. The battered women's shelters she investigated were designed to serve the interests of white women who faced no challenges from racist policing or from language barriers. They were designed for women who had citizenship and did not rely on their abusive partners to legitimate their presence in the US or provide legal advice, women who have extensive social networks and generational wealth to fall back on in order to escape abusive partners. Crenshaw notes how the white women who created these shelters made them to serve white women, consistently misperceiving or completely ignoring the plight of poor women of color, not bothering to address their needs. The ignorance involved is facilitated and propagated via a regime of truth that circulates an image of women's oppression that centers the needs of white women and obscures and misinforms about the circumstances underlying more complex and compounded forms of oppression.

The matrix of domination exists on personal levels, within networks of friends and family, even within individual minds. Collins (2002) writes, "As the particular form assumed by intersecting oppressions in one social location, any matrix of domination can be seen as an historically specific organization of power in which social groups are embedded and which they aim to influence." Being embedded in a matrix of domination means that all of your thoughts, words, and interactions take place against the backdrop of oppressive patterns of thought, speech, and action, encoded and shared through the social institutions that compose the broader culture and civilization in which you live.

The matrix of domination encompasses the social hierarchies that exist within the society. Hence, the matrix of domination explains the fact that, for example, men tend to talk over women, that men tend not to recognize the existence of emotional labor or recognize when women perform it for them, and that women tend to seem less qualified for positions in workplaces traditionally dominated by men. It explains why white people tend to feel fear when they see Black men on streets, why Black women are perceived as overly aggressive by white people, why trans people make cis people uncomfortable, and so on for the whole wide range of deeply problematic social prejudices that flow from oppression. These prejudices are created and reinforced through the operation of the matrix of domination within personal psychologies. The matrix itself is not reducible simply to prejudice and bias, but it is the source of those psychological attitudes.

The matrix of domination is sustained by elements of public discourse that function to justify the prevailing system of interlocking oppressions. Collins writes, "Intersecting oppressions of race, class, gender, and sexuality could not continue without powerful ideological justifications for their existence." The existence of the matrix of domination must be continually refined and reinscribed within the social fabric through the operation of images, ideas, and propositions that make sense of the system, make it acceptable, organize it, and justify its existence. In this crucial function, the matrix of domination is closely intertwined with the regime of truth.

Collins's discussion of the ideological elements of public discourse centers on the use of controlling images, which are elements of public discourse that function to portray members of oppressed identities in ways that divest them of power and authority. Collins discusses controlling images of Black women that include the mammie, the welfare queen, the jezebel (sexually uncontrollable Black woman), and the matriarch (the Black woman who refuses to let the Black man assume the natural role of patriarch). These images become widely shared and embedded in the culture, in politics, and in the collective unconscious as quick heuristics by which Black women are interpreted. They function to control perception of Black women's credibility, intelligence, work ethic, their perceived moral standing, and their perceived value (or disvalue) to society. They are used to justify policies such as limiting access to welfare, controlling reproductive freedom (see especially Roberts, 1999), limiting access to education and jobs, and limiting access to political power and influence.

Crucial to this perspective, controlling images are not accurate or true. They are false representations. This kind of use of misinformation is crucial to the operation of the matrix of domination. The matrix of domination runs on false representations. The regime of truth operates hand-in-hand with the matrix of domination. It provides the bones of the matrix through its power to make false images and statements function as accurate representations. To make an image function as accurate is to invest it with the power to affect how things operate, what happens, who is perceived as justified, and so on.

Collins clearly recognizes and articulates this connection between the operation of controlling images and the role of the central institutions that constitute the regime of truth in modern democracies, according to Foucault. She writes, "Schools, the news media, and government agencies constitute important sites for reproducing these controlling images." According to Collins, these megalithic loci in the regime of truth are centrally responsible for producing and circulating elements of public discourse that undergird the matrix of domination. Collins goes on to add other sources, including the internet: "The growing influence of television, radio, movies, videos, CDs, and the internet constitutes new ways of circulating controlling images." She notes that these "new global technologies" allow elements of the local US matrix of domination to gain wider uptake in cultures around the world. She also identifies government agencies, community organizations, churches, civic institutions, universities, families, and political movements as locations "where the controlling images of Black womanhood become negotiated."[17] By extension these are locations where the regime of truth operates to spread, reproduce, and evolve the controlling images that undergird the matrix of domination.

We might introduce another notion, perhaps coextensive with the idea of a controlling image: the controlling proposition. These are statements (maybe different from images) that function in exactly the same way that controlling images do *vis a vis* their role in creating ideological justifications for the perpetual reproduction of the matrix of domination. Among these, I would argue, are the statements "Trans women are men" and "Anti-white racism is a problem in the US." These statements are circulated and reinforced through the same avenues that Collins discusses. They are made to function as true in much the same way as controlling images are made to function as true, through the operation of the regime of truth. Just as controlling images are false representations made to operate as true in order to serve the interests of dominant power, controlling propositions are false statements that are made to operate as true.

Controlling images and controlling propositions are crucial components in the creation and maintenance of the matrix of domination. Understanding them as representations which are in fact false, but which are made to function as true, is crucial for understanding the way in which the matrix of domination rests on misinformation and active ignorance. The lifeblood of oppression is misinformation and active ignorance.

This is what James Baldwin meant when he wrote, "It is the innocence that constitutes the crime."[18] He is referring to the fact that white people maintaining their innocence is identical with denying the existence of oppression and refusing to allow the truth to be legitimated, refusing to let true statements about racism operate as true within the social and political power structures. Maintaining innocence while reaping the benefits of an unjust system requires using misinformation and sewing ignorance. This claim is closely related to Collins's claim that intersecting oppressions cannot continue without ideological justifications. The falsity of these

---

[17] Collins (2002, pp. 93–97).
[18] Baldwin (1963).

ideological justifications is, as I will argue in Chaps. 9 and 10, crucial data for any intersectional metasemantics to account for and incorporate.

The concept of a matrix of domination is at once a generalization of the concept of intersectionality and a way of referring to specific, detailed intersectional situations characterized by the contingent organization of power relations at particular times and places. Each matrix of domination is associated with a particular society or social order at a given period of time, characterizing the local organization of power relations among social identities within that social location.

Different nation-states embody different matrices of domination. For example, the ways that gay people are oppressed in Russia may not be the same as the ways in which they are oppressed in the US. Russia has recently implemented laws that criminalize any media that portrays homosexuality as normal; no such law exists in the US.[19] But the US still marginalizes gay people. All nations marginalize and oppress people on the basis of race, gender, ethnicity, class, and so on, but do so through different kinds of cultural and social institutions. This means that each nation state has its own distinctive matrix of domination, its own particular ways in which power relations are organized.

A single nation-state can also embody different matrices at different times. The ways in which Black folks were oppressed in the US in the early twentieth century is different from how they are oppressed in the early twenty-first century, although these distinct matrices are related and one may be seen as an evolution of the other. As social circumstances change, forms of intersectionality tend to mutate in order to survive and thrive in the new climate. Michelle Alexander gives a particularly striking characterization of this process in her book *The New Jim Crow*.[20] Alexander describes how racialized forms of control evolved into the Jim Crow laws after the end of slavery and then continued to evolve after the Civil Rights movement into the system of mass incarceration.

Just because we see an old matrix breaking down does not mean progress is being made. As our present matrix evolves in the face of social justice movements, it can become more hidden, more resilient, more difficult to pin down, and more deeply woven into the fabric of mainstream society in ways that are difficult to identify. It is not unreasonable to predict, based on observations of the past, that racism will continue to adapt and

[19] Human Rights Watch (2018).
[20] Alexander (2012).

become more subtle and harder to root out as anti-racism initiatives progress.

Within a large nation like the US, different geographical regions can realize different matrices. The oppression of Black folks in the South West may have different characteristics than the oppression of Black folks on the East Coast, which may be different from the Deep South. Different regions can embody different cultures, different histories, different kinds of relationships, different education systems, different kinds of social prejudice, different forms of local government, and so on. These different matrices can be interrelated and influence one another.

There can be different matrices of domination nested within one another. They can exist at different spatiotemporal scales. Boston might have its own matrix of domination, nested within the US matrix, nested within a global matrix. There might be towns or schools or living rooms where class or race or gender power differentials are muted or in which they operate differently. The matrix at one scale might be in tension with the matrix at another scale. It is even possible for a very localized area to present conditions of difficulty for dominant groups. For example, you might find a school in which it is hard to be white. But it would be inaccurate to view such a place as one in which 'reverse racism' is in operation, because racism exists at much larger scales. The white kids who are a minority in their school still benefit from the power differentials embodied in the larger matrix of domination.

Plausibly white supremacy, patriarchy, and capitalism are part of a global matrix of domination that is present everywhere on Earth, even though we might find specific locations or societies in which these factors do not strongly impact daily life. The population of China for example is majority non-white, yet the controlling images of white supremacist culture may still have a strong influence there. Chinese grandparents sending their grandchildren to universities in America may warn their progeny to avoid Black people.[21] Or, for an example at the state level, white supremacist controlling images of Muslims as dangerous terrorists arguably function to undergird the perception in China of Uyghurs as inherently dangerous, enabling and 'justifying' the use of concentration camps. For another example, the inherent valuation of whiteness underlies colorism in South American nations in which people of color are large majorities.

---

[21] This is a true anecdote relayed by one of my students.

8 AN ANALYTIC PHILOSOPHER'S UNIFIED THEORY OF INTERSECTIONALITY 209

In her chapter on US Black Feminism in a Transnational Context, Collins (2002) argues that the US nation state inherently serves elite white male interests. It follows on her view that a failure to interrogate the privilege that comes with US citizenship is a failure to interrogate one's role in perpetuating the matrix of domination. This suggests a kind of critique of any form of social justice activism in the US context that purports to embody intersectionality but fails to adequately recognize how much privilege exists for all US citizens in virtue of their implicit alignment with the US nation state. The US exerts global power and maintains its dominance in ways that benefit all of its citizens, even those who are marginalized and oppressed within US society.

Arvin et al. (2013) make a related critique from an Indigenous feminist perspective. They argue that the US as a European settler-colonial state—a nation whose very existence illegitimately dispossesses Indigenous peoples of their ancestral land and occupies it for the benefit of the settlers—inherently draws on and reinforces white male power to sustain its existence. Therefore, anyone who contributes to and benefits from the continued existence of the settler state partakes of whiteness and patriarchy. This is a surprising and radical view, for it entails that even Black feminists can benefit from participating in whiteness and patriarchy insofar as they do not push back against the existence of the settler state. A thoroughgoing intersectional critical analysis that recognizes Indigenous feminist concerns about native sovereignty and the role of the settler state in creating whiteness and sustaining patriarchal domination must recognize that any adequate reformation of the matrix of domination in order to sustain a real end to oppression must end white settler control over the land, either through the dissolution of the settler state or through some other kind of radical change that enables Indigenous sovereignty.

Collins recognizes the US settler nation state as constituting a matrix of domination that serves elite white male interests, but this is only a contingent fact of history. Counterfactually, there could have existed a totally different matrix of domination. White people could have been subordinate to Black people, men might have been subordinate to women, and so on. The actual forms that intersectionality assumes are contingent. They depend on social power dynamics and only exist where those dynamics produce systemic injustice and oppression. Collins writes that "regardless of how any given matrix is actually organized either across time or from society to society, the concept of a matrix of domination encapsulates the universality of intersecting oppressions as organized through diverse local realities." The concept of a matrix of domination is universal insofar as it can be applied to any possible configuration of interlocking systems of oppression.

Collins maintains that every oppressive society can be characterized by a matrix of domination. "All contexts of domination incorporate some combination of intersecting oppressions, and considerable variability exists from one matrix of domination to the next as to how oppression and activism will be organized." Every oppressive society gives rise to multiple intersecting oppressions. This might be a surprising claim, since someone might think there could have been a society which was *only* racist, not sexist or homophobic, and so on. Collins believes that it is a matter of sociological fact, a law of oppression, that systems of domination always develop by enforcing multiple forms of oppression at once. Oppression is necessarily intersectional.[22]

This makes strategic sense. In the Foucauldian sense that power can be understood in terms of strategic objectives and tactics, oppressive power wants to divide and conquer. It is compelled by its own interests to dominate by means of creating conflicting exigencies for those who are in its grip. Therefore, any dominating power will create rifts and irresolvable conflicts among the subjugated, as a matter of strategic expediency. So every system of domination will involve multiple forms of oppression that interact to produce exponentially difficult circumstances and difficult-to-resolve challenges for any would-be coalitions among the oppressed. This directly results in political intersectionality (Sect. 8.4).

Lastly, I want to emphasize that Collins sees the matrix of domination as closely connected with the regime of truth. Collins writes,

> despite the U.S. Constitutions stated commitment to the equality of all American citizens, historically, the differential treatment of U.S. Blacks, women, the working class, and other subordinated groups meant that the United States operated as a nation-state that disproportionately benefited affluent White men. Because this group controls schools, the news media, and other social institutions that legitimate what counts as truth, it possesses the authority to obscure its own power and to redefine its own special interests as being national interests.[23]

---

[22] The necessity is nomological, a ceteris paribus law of sociology. For an argument that ceteris paribus laws can be necessary, see Berenstain (2014).
[23] Collins (2002, p. 248).

Collins's concern with "social institutions that legitimate what counts as truth" exactly reflects the analysis of truth and power offered in the previous chapter. These institutions control public conceptions of truth, justice, prosperity, and so on, so that the social and political agenda favors elite white male interests, while being made to seem as if they promote the well-being of everyone. The regime of truth "obscure[s] its own power" through its power to promote ignorance and misinformation about its own functioning. The institutions that recreate the conditions of oppression obscure their own role in this process. If an oppressive regime of truth functions strategically to promote dominant power by obscuring the existence of dominant power, then part of its strategic function is to obscure knowledge about its own strategic function, viz. its role in creating the conditions of oppression.

Collins says the oppressive role of the regime of truth is a matter of redefinition. Without stretching Collins's words too far, we can say that part of what the regime of truth does in order to "redefine its own special interests as being national interests" is to redefine crucial terminology such as "racism" and "woman" to promote its own conceptions of the social order. Definitions of "racism" that promote white welfare and obscure the nature of racism as systemic oppression, and definitions of "woman" that promote a cis-normative conception of gender, are made to function as true, are circulated by "schools, the news media, and other social institutions that legitimate what counts as truth." This process creates the ideological justification for the matrix of domination. The strategic redefinition of terms includes acts of linguistic hijacking, when dominant agents appropriate the core terminology of successful critical theories in order to subvert and undermine those theories in ways that promote the power of dominant groups. We can see linguistic hijacking as serving the strategic function of countering critical theories within discourses centered on social justice.

But crucially, we should not concede that the oppressive and self-serving definitions produced by dominant groups in the course of justifying the matrix of domination *are true*. There is no strong metasemantic reason to grant dominant groups the power to stipulate their own meanings and there is strong reason to deny that they have that power. The ideological justifications that undergird the matrix of domination are false. They are constantly being revealed as false through the tireless efforts of marginalized groups, but of course, these efforts are met by the strategic active ignorance of dominant power.

8.4 Political Intersectionality

Crenshaw (1990) introduces the term *political intersectionality* to describe the way in which members of marginalized groups situated at the intersection of multiple forms of oppression are forced to decide between competing political exigencies. Black women, for example, often find themselves put in a position where their feminism is seen to conflict with the needs of anti-racism, and vice versa. More generally, this occurs whenever the needs of multiply oppressed marginalized groups conflict.

Crenshaw gives an example connected with her study of poor women of color seeking shelter at the battered women's shelters in LA. She tried to get statistical data about how many women of color were suffering from domestic abuse, but found that her attempts to get this information were being thwarted by anti-racism advocacy groups who did not want that information to be made available due to the accurately perceived threat that such information would be marshaled by white supremacist power as misinformation in support of the false controlling image of the violent Black male. By seeking to release accurate data about domestic abuse to help women of color, Crenshaw must risk throwing fuel on the fire of racism.

Diverse forms of oppression produce divisions and internal conflicts among those who would mount a resistance to the machine. This is a strategy. Lorde (1981) asserts, "Mainstream communication does not want women, particularly white women, responding to racism. It wants racism to be accepted as an immutable given in the fabric of your existence." Lorde is identifying one strategic function of racial division, to disrupt feminist efforts to move "toward coalition and effective action." Racism prevents white women and women of color from forming coalitions and acting effectively. In analogous ways, sexism, transphobia, and homophobia function strategically on behalf of white power to hinder people of color from forming effective coalitions across genders and sexualities.

The intersectional system employs a variety of oppressive structures to strategically divide marginalized groups and set them in opposition to one another in order to prevent them from acting coherently in unison. The effect is confusion, mistrust, disharmony, and even animosity among marginalized groups. The means of achieving this effect is to develop conditions of oppression such that working toward one group's goals involves sidelining or working against another group's interests. Collins's law of oppression, that oppression will always be intersectional, follows from the strategic effectiveness of this policy. Oppression will always be intersectional because divide and conquer is always strategically advisable. It would never be advantageous for dominant power to allow its adversaries to unite against it.

The appearance of conflicting political exigencies is the result of the regime of truth creating a false picture of reality, creating misinformation and conceptual confusion. White feminists, for example, believe that promoting Black women's interests is not in the interest of all women and think therefore that feminism cannot effectively be pursued in an intersectional way. This active ignorance is partly achieved through power sharing. White feminists do not want to criticize racism because it is against their interests, because they benefit from white power. Likewise, trans exclusionary radical feminists do not want to share power with trans women. This strategic initiative favors cis women and excludes trans women from benefitting from cis feminism. Non-intersectional anti-racism movements fear that focusing on feminist and LGBTQ issues will divide their movements and diminish their effectiveness. This active ignorance is partly motivated by the refusal to give up the power that comes from being male and straight. It is part of what keeps feminist and anti-racist movements caught in the grip of single-axis thinking, which reinforces the dominance of the more dominant subgroups among the marginalized.

Single-axis thinking is reinforced through the deployment of racist and sexist controlling images. The controlling image of the angry Black woman functions to divest Black women of credibility when they express legitimate anger about racism within the feminist movement (Collins 2002, Lorde 1981). The controlling image of the angry Black feminist does similar work on behalf of power within anti-racism movements. These controlling images provide justifications for discounting Black women and feminists, who are portrayed as irrational, self-serving, over-emotional, and failing to track with reality. It is one of the great ironies about political intersectionality that white feminists can criticize anti-feminists for their active ignorance about feminism while enacting strongly analogous attitudes toward Black feminists. From an abstract epistemological perspective, you would think learning how active ignorance works in one social domain would translate instantly and effortlessly to understanding how it works in other social domains, but this does not happen.

Both single-axis thinking and the deployment of racist and sexist controlling images are forms of misrepresentation and misinformation about the actual state of affairs. The single-axis anti-racist movement conceives of its own goals as in tension with the goals of Black feminism in part because it does not recognize that both are being confronted with a strategic initiative on the part of dominant power that is designed (although perhaps not by any human mind) to divide and conquer. Likewise, trans exclusionary feminism aims to make feminism centered on cis women, in a move to divest trans women of the power and protection by deploying the controlling image of a man disguised as a woman, tends to align with dominant cis-normative patriarchal power against its own interests in opposing the patriarchy.

Political intersectionality is often backed up by the threat of misinformation. For example, uncovering domestic violence statistics about communities of color in an attempt to help women in those communities will be used to reinforce controlling images of the violence inherent in communities of color. The oppressive regime of truth thereby poses a dilemma to the intersectionality movement: leave the truth about one form of oppression covered up in order to combat misinformation about something else, or else try to fight on two fronts against two aspects of active ignorance at once.

The intersectional way through the trap of political intersectionality is to battle misinformation on all fronts, not to sacrifice the more marginalized group in order to counter the tactics of the oppressor. In this case, that means exposing the truth about domestic violence in order to better address the injustices facing women of color, while redoubling efforts to combat the controlling image of the inherently violent Black man. The reason intersectionality always calls for fighting all battles at once is that whenever a strategic concession is made to fight less than an all-out battle, it is the more marginalized group whose interests are put on hold, sacrificed.

Tuck and Yang (2012) identify another case of political intersectionality that occurs in the tension between calls for decolonization and for reparations for slavery. Decolonization is the immediate repatriation, or rematriation, of all stolen lands to Indigenous sovereign control. All of the land owned by the US is stolen Indigenous land. Therefore, if the US were to comply with the demand for decolonization, it would immediately lose all of its land and natural resources. The US would no longer have physical borders, and it would have lost unfathomable wealth in the form of land, resources, the value of all of its infrastructure, its buildings, its power stations, its power of taxation, everything. In effect, decolonization would destroy the US outright. But if the US were destroyed in this way, it would be unable to pay reparations for slavery. Reparations essentially depends on settler futurity, on the indefinite continuation of the settler state, in order to pay back what the state owes to present day communities that have descended from communities of slaves. This form of political intersectionality presents a tension within intersectional politics.

The oppressive function of the regime of truth is central in creating this kind of political intersectionality, in limiting our ability to conceptualize and pursue effective remedies to past and present injustices. The world is made to seem as if the problems cannot be resolved, or as if any resolution of continuing injustice would cause harms to other marginalized groups. Strategically, the creation of these limitations and blockages of imagination is part of the function of the regime of truth. The idea that solutions to injustice are impractical, uncalled for, or too complicated to be implemented is the result of misinformation and active ignorance. The idea of repatriating stolen land or paying reparations seems impossible and unwarranted from within the mainstream US consciousness, let alone trying to do both at the same time.

Similar impossibilities, or blocks on imagination, are created in defense of the system of mass incarceration. Efforts to address problems with policing practices, reduce prison populations, end the war on drugs, and defund the massively overbudgeted militarized police forces are met with misinformation and controlling images. We find depictions of cities and states that have entirely disbanded their police forces and suddenly released all prison populations into the suburbs. Images are conjured of 911 calls going unanswered.

These imposed limitations on understanding and imagination are circulated by the regime of truth. From within the mainstream's version of commonsense, the kinds of radical solutions being called for seem impossible, crazy, dangerous, and ultimately hopeless. Initiatives to work through complexities of political intersectionality are stonewalled with flatfooted and simplistic counterarguments, misrepresentations about what is being proposed and why, and refusals to think long and hard about practical solutions. I am not saying solutions will be easy, or even that every problem on the agenda has a solution. What I am saying is, the regime of truth plays a powerful role in undermining our attempts to address these problems. It rushes to generate and spread rationales, controlling images, and concepts that aim to circumvent the attempt to address the problems at hand, even the attempt to conceptualize a solution or think clearly about the problem.

Combating political intersectionality requires battling these imaginative and conceptual limitations imposed through ideological means. Finding a way through the competing exigencies created by the matrix of domination must involve addressing the ignorance and misinformation embodied in the regime of truth at every level of ontological organization. This means addressing problems at the national state level. For example, we should form a congressional inquiry into reparations, and perhaps even an inquiry into the possibility of decolonization—what is required, what are the pitfalls, what solutions could be pursued?[24] It also means thinking things through carefully in more personal contexts, over dinner tables and in locker rooms and at water coolers, and not allowing shallow arguments and what might pass for 'commonsense' to derail important thought processes and conversations.

Dealing with political intersectionality also clearly requires social movements to adopt intersectional frameworks for understanding oppression. Single-axis approaches to feminism, anti-racism, homophobia, and so on are highly likely to produce political intersectionality, while more intersectional approaches are designed to unravel the knots and make progress through difficulties. Here again we find that the regime of truth plays a pivotal role in opposing progress, insofar as intersectionality is made to seem obscure, counterproductive, divisive, or disabling within political movements themselves. Nothing could be further from the truth. Statements to the effect that intersectionality destabilizes political movements rather than strengthening them are false but made to function as true in many conversations around political initiatives and grassroots movements.

8.5 Intersectional Social Identities

The combined effects and co-constitutive nature of intersecting forms of oppression become most apparent when examined in the context of the lives of people that experience multiple forms of oppression. Intersectional critical theories require us to begin our analyses from the lives of those who experience multiple forms of oppression because other approaches tend to produce mistaken theories of oppression by centering more

---

[24] See H.R. 40, a congressional bill for the formation of a commission to study the possibility of a national apology and a plan for reparations for slavery, here: https://www.congress.gov/bill/117th-congress/house-bill/40/text.

privileged groups. The methodological imperative of beginning with the lives of the most marginal is generated because of the way intersecting systems of oppression produce ignorance about oppression that grips even those who are oppressed, so long as those oppressed groups are relatively close to the trappings of power, i.e. close to the mythic norm.

The aim of this section is not to give a comprehensive theory of social identity, but rather to distinguish the aspect of intersectionality concerned with identity from the aspects of intersectionality developed in the preceding two sections and discuss how it interacts with them. Collins and Bilge (2016) write,

> Increasingly, many people who are involved in intersectionality understand it as a theory of identity ... But intersectionality also means much more than this. To understand intersectionality primarily as a theory of individual identity, often with the goal of criticizing it, overemphasizes some dimensions of intersectionality while underemphasizing others.

It is important to recognize that intersectionality is not, in the first instance, a theory of social identity. Social identities arise for many reasons. They are contextually salient properties that unify groups of individuals. Intersectionality is a theory of systems of oppression. Groups of individuals can be unified by their shared struggle within intersecting systems of oppression.

The existence of intersectionality also tends to produce practices of identity politics, the political praxis of organizing political movements around social identity, because it is often advantageous for people who are afflicted by certain intersecting oppressions to practice political solidarity with one another (Crenshaw, 1990). But it is important not to conflate intersectionality-as-structural-oppression with identity or identity politics.[25] There are three things: racism (structural oppression), race (social identity), and racial identity politics (a political praxis)—the same, mutatis mutandis, for other social identities.

What are social identities? The concept of a social identity is very abstract. It encompasses many different kinds of properties: race, gender, ability, sexuality, nationality, economic status, many others. These social identity properties may be deeply different from one another. For example, it may be that one can belong to a gender by identifying as that gender

---

[25] For an excellent discussion of this topic, see Chap. 5 in Collins and Bilge (2016).

(via some kind of psychological or social act); perhaps a person can belong to a sexuality by engaging in that sexuality, or by being disposed to engage in it under certain circumstances. These ways of belonging to an identity are extremely implausible for race or economic status or ability status. A white person cannot become Black simply by identifying as Black. A rich person cannot become financially vulnerable simply by acting as financially vulnerable people act. This shows that group membership in different identities is controlled by different kinds of factors. Social identity properties may all be socially constructed in some broad sense, but that does not mean they all function within the social fabric in the same way or that they are constructed in similar ways. It definitely does not entail that membership conditions are the same or even similar across groups.

Social identity properties involve complex relationships between individuals, communities, and prevailing matrices of domination. One of the central ways of viewing social identities within an intersectional framework is as political units or coalitions that form partly in response to political needs facing marginalized groups. So social identities are thought of partly as constituted by identity politics. Collins and Bilge (2016) describe the relationship between identity and identity politics as follows.

> Identity is central to building a collective we. Identity politics rests upon a recursive relationship between individual and social structures, as well as among individuals as an existing collective or a collective that must be brought into being because they share similar social locations within power relations.[26]

Collectives come into existence because of similarities of individuals existing within a matrix of domination. For example, the Black identity historically arises within the context of the US where being Black is socially constructed as a marker for subordination and where this subordination is justified by a complex and evolving racist ideology that permeates the culture. Simultaneously, communities of Black folks have always evolved their own resistant cultures to survive and thrive in this context. Individual identities are partly shaped by participation within the resistant cultures. Individuals then build and negotiate new coalitions, create new culture and community as time goes on. The coalitions and cultures developed are not uniform across the nation-state but develop differently in different

---

[26] Collins and Bilge (2016, p. 135).

regions, giving rise to distinctive Black identities that nevertheless share in the overarching Black identity that exists in the US (Robinson, 2014). The matrix of domination responds to this creative process with its own creative process, creating new controlling images and new ideological justifications for maintaining subordination.

Many social identity properties are thus intertwined with social customs and laws that are themselves intertwined with historically rooted systems of oppression. For example, Black racial identity is influenced by the 'one-drop' rule (Gotanda, 1991). To be Black, one has only to have one parent, or grandparent, or great-grandparent, etc., who is Black. This rule guarantees that the offspring of a Black person and a white person counts as Black. This conception of Blackness is part and parcel with the concept of whiteness as purity, which is destroyed if infused with any amount of Black ancestry. Hence, white racial identity is under threat of being destroyed through interbreeding with non-white groups. Except, confusingly, Indigenous identities are culturally and legally conceived in the inverse way (Tuck & Yang, 2012): the offspring of an Indigenous person and a white person is less Indigenous than their parent. In the mainstream imagination, eventually there will be no Indigenous people left due to interbreeding with white folks. Through interbreeding with whiteness, Indigeneity is destroyed and whiteness continues to exist.

Why is there this asymmetry between Indigeneity and Blackness such that Blackness destroys whiteness and whiteness destroys Indigeneity? If one were to try to do metaphysics in the absence of historical or political context, one would likely miss the obvious and brutal explanation (given by Tuck & Yang, 2012). In order to make the system of chattel slavery work, any child born of a Black person and a white person counts as Black and is therefore subjected legally and culturally to the condition of slavery, which enables white people to produce more slaves through rape and also prevents Black folks from gaining access to white power and wealth through marriage or interbreeding. Meanwhile, white settlers need to eliminate Indigenous populations who have a claim to the land on which the settler state exists; therefore, it benefits white settler power that Indigeneity should be eliminated through interbreeding. This clearly correct sociological explanation for the asymmetry of the descent rules for Indigenous and Black social identities highlights one way in which group identities can be bound up with historical practices of oppression.

Not every aspect of social identity is grounded in oppressive ideologies, however. Black social identities are partly a matter of culture, community, shared struggle, and shared history (Gotanda, 1991). Being Black involves standing in some relationship or other to Black culture and community, where there are a range of different Black cultures across the US giving rise to regional Black identities which a Black person can identify with (see Robinson, 2014). To some extent, of course, the culture and community of an oppressed group are related to intersecting systems of oppression, as these communities and cultures develop in the midst of those systems. Shared experiences and histories incorporate experiences of oppression. But oppressed communities are much more than their shared experiences of oppression.

8.5.1 Anti-essentialism About Social Identities

Even though we can make accurate observations about features of groups and conceptually explore the properties that constitute social identities and group membership, we should not immediately conclude that there is a true metaphysical theory that specifies necessary and sufficient conditions for membership in any social identity group. It is widely recognized within the feminist literature on womanhood and gender that theories purporting to specify the essence of gender are fraught. Spelman (1988) argued persuasively that attempts to give real definitions of womanhood tend to exclude more marginalized groups of women. Spelman wrote, "Any attempt to talk about all women in terms of something we have in common undermines attempts to talk about the differences between us, and vice versa." Spellman also argued that "[t]he more universal the claim one might hope to make about women ... the more likely it is to be false." Similar arguments could be developed, I think, for other kinds of social identities.

I understand Spelman's exclusion argument as a kind of pessimistic meta-induction. Every theory of womanhood we have constructed so far has been exclusive, has tended to center the experiences of more privileged women and make them the paradigm cases of womanhood while marginalizing or even totally excluding more marginalized women from the extension of "woman." The future will resemble the past; therefore, we have reason to believe that future attempts to construct inclusive theories of gender will center dominant groups and leave marginalized women out of the definition. We might conclude that no future theory will adequately define the nature of womanhood. Moreover, even if you think (as I suspect) that some future theory of womanhood or race could be fully inclusive and empowering to marginalized groups, the pessimistic meta-induction argument gives at least a prima facie reason not to pursue the development of such a theory, for we have strong reason to believe that creating an adequate theory will require developing and scrapping many inadequate theories along the way, and this process will be disproportionately harmful to the most marginalized.

This exclusion argument resonates strongly with intersectional theorizing, especially within Black feminism. Lorde (1980) recognized this kind of exclusionary thinking within white feminist circles when she wrote, "I believe one of the reasons white women have such difficulty reading Black women's work is because of their reluctance to see Black women as women and different from themselves." It is because white women have tended to represent themselves and their issues as paradigmatic of all women's issues that Black women's issues seemed to them to be not quite really women's problems at all but rather something else. The conceptual boundary of womanhood delimits what is seen as a feminist issue.

As Black feminism has gained a foothold in mainstream consciousness, white women are beginning to treat Black women's issues as part of their feminism, but we are still far from where Black women's struggles are seen as central to feminism within white feminist circles. Even today there are groups of women who are almost totally excluded in much the same way Lorde describes Black women's exclusion in the 1970s. Consider Lorde's statement, transmuted into one about cis and trans women: "one of the reasons [cis] women have such difficulty reading [trans] women's work is because of their reluctance to see [trans] women as women and different from themselves." Trans women are regularly perceived to be literally not women. An adequate intersectional feminism recognizes that just because a group of women does not have what mainstream feminism considers to be prototypical experiences of women's oppression does not mean they are not women. The experiences of oppression experienced by trans Black women are no less central to defining the interests or scope of feminism than the experiences of cis white women.

Typically, intersectionality avoids and condemns metaphysical theorizing about the nature of gender or other social categories on the grounds that such theorizing tends to center the experiences and properties of dominant groups and exclude more marginalized groups. It may be that this pattern is somehow inherent in the theoretical practice of formulating real definitions, although I don't think that has been demonstrated conclusively. It is possible we can create more and more accurate theories of social identity through trial and error.[27] This process may be harmful, perhaps so much so that it cannot be justified. But there may be a true, fully inclusive, and empowering intersectional theory of gender essence. If there is, then it must include trans Black women as paradigm cases of womanhood.

While I think there might be true, substantive metaphysical theories of social identities, I don't think having such a theory in hand is required in order to describe a semantic theory for social identity terms. On my preferred approach to the semantics of words like "woman," we identify their extensions in a deflationary way. I think that "woman" refers to women. I do not know if there is a true, substantive metaphysical theory of womanhood, but I know there are women and I know the word "woman" refers to them. There is no metaphysical hurdle for giving a model-theoretic semantics for this term. The extension of the word "woman" is the set of women.

In doing identity politics, sometimes people talk as if social identities were metaphysically substantive. Collins and Bilge (2016) recommend understanding essentialism talk as a strategic way of mobilizing political units. "[S]trategic essentialism is best thought of as a political practice whereby an individual or group foregrounds one or more aspects of identity as significant in a given situation." This approach postulates essentialist talk as a kind of political activity, a way of using features of one's identity to organize politically.

Collins and Bilge also maintain that identities should be understood as de facto coalitions. Social identities are groups of people who are disposed to form political alliances to help each other survive and thrive in the midst of intersecting systems of domination. What shapes social identities on the intersectional praxis conception of identity is a pressing political need to unify in order to resist oppression.

De facto coalitions co-constitute one another. Black people as a de facto coalition is made up of both men and women, of queer and straight people, of able-bodied and disabled people, of trans and cis people. But then every group is similarly co-constituted by every other group: the LGBTQ coalition is partially constituted by members of the Black coalition, as is the coalition of working-class folks, as is the coalition of women. We need not postulate any metaphysical essence associated with each

---

[27] This is structurally analogous to the realist response to the pessimistic meta-induction argument against scientific realism (Laudan, 1981).

identity, no set of necessary conditions had by all and only members of each identity. Moreover, we can grant that each individual is unique; no two people have exactly the same experiences. Belonging to a social identity is a matter of having a shared interest in creating a community and resisting oppression. The typical individual falls into a range of de facto coalitions because the typical individual is subjected to multiple kinds of oppression.

It is strategically important for marginalized groups to form alliances in the ways recommended by intersectionality politics. It is a survival strategy and a means of attaining some level of power within an oppressive system. As Crenshaw (1990) observes, "At this point in history, a strong case can be made that the most critical resistance strategy for disempowered groups is to occupy and defend a politics of social location rather than to vacate and destroy it."

Calls to abolish identity politics therefore function to attack and undermine an important source of resistance to domination and oppression. Any attempt to force marginalized groups to stop practicing identity politics, or to stop organizing around social identities, is therefore accurately perceived as a strategic move to disempower those groups. The regime of truth plays a crucial role in this discourse, providing opponents of identity politics with the epistemic high ground. The regime works hard to make identity politics seem vindictive, divisive, un-American, irrational, and unnecessary. It spreads the controlling image of 'victimhood mentality'—the false image that proponents of intersectionality inhabit a kind of mentally ill mindset that is actually fixated on attaining undue benefits through misperceiving itself as a victim—and portrays social justice movements centered around race or gender as themselves "racist" and "sexist." As with other aspects of the oppressive function of the regime of truth, these processes should be understood as spreading misinformation and false statements.

Marginalized social identity groups are locked in a battle for the power of self-definition against the regime of truth, which creates and propagates controlling images and propositions. These controlling images and propositions function to objectify, denigrate, discredit, and disempower their targets. They are false representations made to function as true, so opposing their operation means fighting misinformation and active ignorance. According to Collins (2002), this active resistance means "not being passive consumers of controlling images of Black womanhood." Collins describes resistant communities of Black women as "craft[ing] identities designed to empower them[selves]." This process of resistant redefinition fits with what Collins and Bilge (2016) call the transformative nature of social identity. As the struggle for existence against the matrix of domination proceeds, social identity groups develop new conceptions of themselves, their strength, and their culture.

The creative and transformative processes by which marginalized groups resist controlling images and exert control over their own self-concepts are an important aspect of what determines the semantic extension of the social identity terms that denote those groups. Controlling images and controlling propositions are false; they embody active ignorance and spread misinformation about the essence of social identities as well as spreading misinformation about the extension of the terms that denote members of those groups. It is only through actively interrogating and resisting the ideological effects of controlling images that an accurate view of the semantics of social identity terms can be achieved. For example, an accurate theory of the semantics of "woman" must account for the false controlling image of the trans woman as a man. Given a trans inclusive intersectional theory of social identity as background, the existence of such a controlling image is part of the data a metasemantic theory must account for.

8.6 Intersectionality as Critical Theory

Intersectional theories are critical theories as conceived by the Frankfurt School. Critical theories are essentially aimed at emancipating human beings from conditions of oppression (Horkheimer, 1972). A critical theory is a form of criticism insofar as it is aimed at criticizing the ideology that maintains the status quo. This tradition of criticism comes from Marxist theory, in which the ideology to be criticized was the Bourgeoise ideology that helps the worker accept the status quo, makes him accept his lot in life as fair or natural or inevitable (Lefebvre, 1982). The success of a critical theory depends on disrupting the status quo. A Marxist critical theory must shake the worker free of the active ignorance imposed by capitalism. If a Marxist critical theory does nothing to disrupt the worker's acceptance of the ideology undergirding the status quo, then the theory fails. It becomes an addition to the cultural milieu, another piece of the ideology, that keeps the worker working. Imagine a worker reading Das Capital but still showing up to the factory every day to chat about Marxism with his fellow workers. Insofar as the text becomes integrated into the status quo, insofar as it is not disrupting things, it is not succeeding as a critical theory.

Intersectionality as a critical theory is essentially aimed at disrupting the matrix of domination that constitutes our present intersecting systems of oppression. Its success or failure is not merely a matter of describing things accurately. Success requires more than truth. It must contribute to resisting and ultimately dismantling systems of oppression. Any piece of intersectional theorizing that merely describes how things are without providing impetus for emancipatory change is just another part of the regime of truth that sustains the matrix of domination. One can even imagine a kind of intersectionality theory—or something that purports to be intersectionality—that reinforces dominant power structures. For example, insofar as white feminists working within a single-axis framework manage to co-opt the term "intersectionality" and apply it to concepts and frameworks that marginalize women of color within feminist movements, their 'intersectionality' would be deeply defective.

The emancipatory function of critical theory is not merely pragmatic. Opposing the regime of truth and its ideological function of preserving the status quo of domination and oppression is inherently an epistemic endeavor as well as a pragmatic one. Resisting oppression goes hand in hand with the pursuit of truth. Critical theory is aimed at overcoming the ideological distortions imposed by mainstream dominant consciousness, improving our awareness of reality, and attacking concepts and epistemological norms that function to obscure the truth. The epistemic aim of critical theory, which is inherently part of its pragmatic aim, is to interrogate and dismantle the ideologies that promote ignorance and sustain the matrix of domination, which includes the ways in which the prevailing regime of truth propagates misinformation and active ignorance in order to maintain the matrix of domination. Since emancipation requires combating ignorance with knowledge of reality, the pragmatic and epistemic aspects of critical theory are inherently intertwined.

The regime of truth influences epistemic attitudes. It causes people to draw bad inferences and base their world views on misinformation and conceptual errors, while legitimating these practices as epistemically virtuous. Critical theory aims to identify bad reasoning and misinformation. However, it does so from a position that assumes there are forces of active ignorance at work in the social fabric. If you disagree with the fundamental social reality perceived by intersectionality theory that our institutions—including our epistemic institutions—are influenced by power in a strategic way that functions to promote the welfare and epistemic authority of dominant groups, then you will likely see critical theory as based on unfounded assumptions.

From this skeptical perspective, people—typically more dominantly situated people—tend to see critical theory as attacking objectively rational practices on the basis of politics. They will conclude that critical theorists are more interested in justice than truth. But this is a misunderstanding. Truth and justice are intertwined because the creation of perpetual injustice is predicated on the perpetual creation of falsehood and misinformation. The pursuit of justice therefore requires the pursuit of truth. It requires interceding on a massive scale to disrupt patterns of active ignorance that sustain the oppressive matrix of domination. But when a person's cognition is embedded within patterns of active ignorance, when their epistemic authority is vested in such patterns, they will tend to perceive attacks on those patterns as attacks on virtuous epistemic practices. Part of the function of the regime of truth is to discredit and marginalize any attempts to dislodge its own preferred epistemic practices.

Hence, insofar as a piece of theorizing counts as intersectionality theory, it must interrogate the oppressive regime of truth, its methods of recreating systems of domination as well as its methods of protecting itself by creating screens of misinformation and ideological misconception. This involves identifying and attacking whatever controlling images and whatever false or misleading pieces of misinformation function to obscure the truth of intersecting systems of oppression, as well as those that produce a lack of accountability among dominant agents.

When a dominantly situated group produces a narrative or explanation enabling it to rest comfortably with the current system, that is a way of reinforcing the dominant system. It's part of the function of critical theories to criticize and interrogate any such strategic moves to innocence (Tuck & Yang, 2012), and not just to describe them as problematic but to actually intercede aggressively to disrupt their function in preserving the comfort the dominantly situated group is seeking.

This aggressive pragmatic imperative, to not only describe but to *disrupt* the oppressive status quo, is one reason why opponents of intersectionality find it so uncompromising and undiplomatic. Centrists will often complain that intersectionality is causing divisions within left-leaning political groups by alienating white people, men, heterosexual people, and so on. These complaints are of a piece with complaints from white feminists about Black feminists within white feminist circles, that they are too angry, disruptive, or uncompromising.

Dominantly situated agents get the impression of being under constant attack from intersectionality. The sense of being attacked is actually the sensation of being prodded at every point where the dominantly situated group wishes to rest on the prevailing matrix of domination for support. Proponents of intersectionality will sometimes describe these points of rest as elements of privilege, because only dominantly situated groups can use the matrix of domination for support.

It's very comfortable to rest on the matrix of domination when it supports you. Dominant agents don't want to be made uncomfortable. Dominantly situated groups wish social justice advocates would ease up about certain things. These are the things the dominant group wants to take for granted as permanent parts of their lives, aspects of their lives they don't want to change—at least not yet! These are things they don't want fuss over, worry about, or give up. But meanwhile these very things constitute the sharp points of marginalization, the things marginalized groups cannot count on because the system leaves them out of those benefits, or they are benefits derived for the privileged at the expense of marginalized groups. Marginalized groups cannot rest on the matrix of domination or rely on it for support. It treats them badly and inflicts damage at precisely the points where dominant groups wish to rest.

In his Letter from Birmingham Jail, Dr. Martin Luther King, Jr., cited the white moderate as the greatest obstacle to Black equality and freedom. What is characteristic of the white moderate, King (1963) says, is that the white moderate "prefers a negative peace which is the absence of tension to a positive peace which is the presence of justice[.]" The absence of tension is equivalent to resting easy. The white moderate is willing to grant the existence of systems of oppression, but only up to the point where it requires immediate change. Immediate change requires giving up the support of the matrix of domination. The white moderate does not want that. But granting that change must happen while working to resist any change that upends privilege is just a clever way of resisting the change altogether.

King adds that "[s]hallow understanding from people of good will is more frustrating than absolute misunderstanding from people of ill will." What is characteristic of the moderate approach is shallow understanding. There is some degree of recognition of the matrix of domination, but that understanding conveniently stops short of understanding why immediate change is required. What is especially effective about this strategy, from the point of view of the strategic interest of white power, is that it recognizes some of the truth and grants some of the evidence about racism. It absorbs and incorporates a limited amount of information about oppression, while depriving the critical theory of its transformative impetus. It's like theoretical judo; white ignorance attempts to absorb the incoming blow and flip intersectionality onto its back while maintaining its own balance.

The situation is compounded by the fact that people who are dominantly situated tend not to recognize their privilege and so will often not see what marginally situated people are talking about (Pohlhaus, 2012). For example, white people tend to disbelieve in the existence of racial microaggressions and so think people of color are creating problems out of thin air when they discuss such microaggressions. We will talk about this in more detail in Chap. 11. The big picture is the regime of truth makes intersectional critique seem extreme and inappropriately uncompromising by obscuring the extent of domination and oppression. Dominant groups maintain their innocence by maintaining their ignorance. False statements made to function as true are a big part of how this works. The regime of truth supports dominant conceptions of reality, which exclude or preclude recognition of intersecting systems of domination. This is another sense in which intersectionality is strategically embattled by the regime of truth and why an effective intersectional theory must always be struggling to overturn received epistemic 'wisdom.' It also helps to illustrate the sense in which misrepresentation and falsehood facilitated through the regime of truth are the backbone of the matrix of domination.

The regime of truth undergirds the dominant response to intersectionality and constitutes the ideological system which intersectionality as critique is aimed at disrupting. Intersectionality as a critical theory is essentially concerned with overturning the ideological defenses of patriarchy, white supremacy, cis het supremacy, capitalist domination, ablism, and settler-colonial domination. This picture requires a theory of objective truth on which the ideological defenses of the prevailing systems of domination are objectively false, misrepresentations of reality.

8.7 Intersectionality as Political Praxis

Praxis is theory put into action. It has to do with how one lives one's life. A political praxis is concerned with how one comports oneself, how one organizes one's life, in the social and political sphere. Having an intersectional praxis means living in accord with an intersectional view of reality. A group embodies an intersectional praxis insofar as they live and act in accord with intersectionality as theory and enable one another to better embody such a theory in their everyday and political lives.

The preceding sections already outlined many ways in which praxis is crucially integrated into other aspects of intersectionality. Praxis involves how one builds and participates in communities in the midst of interlocking systems of oppression. It is part of what is involved in the creation of social identities, insofar as social identities are constituted through identity politics, which is a kind of intersectional praxis. It is involved in theorizing about intersectionality. Intersectional theory without intersectional praxis results in no change and therefore results in a failed critical theory. An adequate critical theory must motivate and provide guidance for developing an effective praxis. Intersectionality as critical theory is thus constantly refining and motivating intersectional praxis. It is part of the theory itself that people must engage in social change in order to bring about emancipation, such that a lack of practical engagement amounts to failing to really understand or accept the theory.

For most of its practitioners the praxis of intersectionality is nonnegotiable, since it is the praxis of survival in an unjust and dangerous social reality. More dominantly situated groups can ignore the need for intersectional praxis insofar as they do not face the injustice and danger of intersecting systems of oppression. Intersectional praxis is not second nature to those who do not naturally understand or recognize the existence of intersectional oppression due to prevailing misinformation and active ignorance embodied in mainstream consciousness via the regime of truth. Instead, more dominantly situated groups need to develop a praxis through understanding intersectionality more deeply, which requires deference to more marginalized perspectives and groups.

Even people who face multiple forms of oppression will sometimes find themselves in contexts where they have privilege. Even a person who experiences many forms of oppression will not automatically understand what another person at a different location in social space is going through. The possibility for misrepresentation and active ignorance is always live. In "Uses of Anger," Lorde (1984) says it plainly. "The woman of Color who is not Black and who charges me with rendering her invisible by assuming that her struggles with racism are identical with my own has something to tell me that I had better learn from, lest we both waste ourselves fighting the truths between us."

This fact is intimately connected with the situated knowledge postulated by Collins's (2002) Black feminist standpoint theory. Every group faces unique circumstances when confronting intersecting systems of oppression, and the failure to recognize differences in experience of oppression is always a failure of intersectional praxis. Intersectional praxis requires what Maria Lugones calls complex communication (Lugones, 2006), which involves refusing the illusion that I can transparently know and interpret your word meanings by reference to my own understanding of reality. No one can be sure they know exactly what another person is talking about when they say they experience racism, because no one knows the full extent of what racism is. This is consistent with the possibility that in using the word "racism" we all refer to the same thing. Even though none of us knows everything about racism, because there are crucial differences in how racism manifests across social identities and no one can know everything about every group's experiences, we can still all refer to the same thing—racism—which each of us grasps incompletely. In correcting one another's usage of terms through complex communication, we help our linguistic community move toward using the language of "racism" in accord with how it should be used, to represent racism in a way that is free of misinformation and ignorance.

The situation is compounded by the operation of misinformation within the social fabric. To communicate accurately, we must address false presuppositions and false images. Bringing the community as a whole into greater intersectional praxis therefore requires dealing with the regime of truth and confronting the inaccurate statements and controlling images that it makes operate as true.

8.8 Toward an Intersectional Theory of Truth

Throughout this chapter I have attempted to highlight the role of objective truth in theorizing about intersectionality, both by describing what is objectively true on an intersectional theory of social reality and by highlighting the ways in which the regime of truth supports the matrix of domination by making false statements operate as true. The actual objective truth about the existence of interlocking systems of oppression in the US and in transnational contexts, and the ways in which the regime of truth supports these systems by making false statements function as true, is the central political reality that informs the development of an intersectional metasemantics in Chaps. 9 and 10. I start with the truth of intersectional political and social theory and use this to argue that the semantics of English expressions as entailed by intersectionality theory generates a constraint on any acceptable metasemantic theory. Our theory of where word meanings come from, for someone who accepts the picture of intersectionality sketched in this chapter, cannot entail that Trump speaks truly when he says that Ocasio-Cortez is "racist."

For some philosophers my approach will appear to beg the question, since I am assuming there are definitive political truths and definitive political falsehoods before giving a theory of truth. But I maintain it is legitimate and in fact crucial to do philosophy *in media res* in this way. I take the existence of intersectionality to be established on independent grounds. The point of this book is not to begin at first principles, derive a theory of objective truth, and then apply it to politics and prove that intersectional theories are objectively true. Rather, I begin with a set of facts about oppression and social power dynamics that are well-attested by many sources and then describe how truth is relevant for understanding and changing the circumstances we find ourselves in. The methodology of assuming the truth of intersectionality as a starting point is defensible, indeed indispensable for one who accepts that truth.

The particular matrix of domination we are dealing with extends through the academy and is active within academic philosophical spaces. In recognizing that the power dynamics that undergird active ignorance are at play within philosophical discourse itself, it is clear or at least arguable that the professional philosopher's methodological objections against assuming the truth of intersectional political and social theory function to obscure the existence of interlocking systems of oppression. Thus, the charge of question begging in this context is itself a form of active ignorance and a means of controlling the flow of information in ways that harms marginalized groups and furthers the interests of the powerful.

REFERENCES

Alexander, M. (2012). *The New Jim Crow: Mass Incarceration in the Age of Colorblindness*. The New Press.
Anzaldúa, G. (1987). *Borderlands/La Frontera: The New Mestiza*. Aunt Lute Books; 4th ed. edition (June 12, 2012)
Arvin, M., Tuck, E., & Morrill, A. (2013). Decolonizing Feminism: Challenging Connections between Settler Colonialism and Heteropatriarchy. *Feminist Formations, 25*, 8–34.
Baldwin, J. (1963/2013). *The Fire Next Time*. Vintage.

Berenstain, N. (2014). Necessary Laws and Chemical Kinds. *Australasian Journal of Philosophy, 92*(4), 631–647.

Cho, S., Crenshaw, K. W., & McCall, L. (2013). Toward a Field of Intersectionality Studies: Theory, Applications, and Praxis. *Signs: Journal of Women in Culture and Society, 38*(4), 785–810.

Collective, C. R. (1977/1983). The Combahee River Collective Statement. In *Home Girls: A Black Feminist Anthology* (pp. 264–274). Kitchen Table—Women of Color Press.

Collins, P. H. (2002). *Black Feminist Thought: Knowledge, Consciousness, and the Politics of Empowerment.* Routledge.

Collins, P. H., & Bilge, S. (2016). Intersectionality. John Wiley & Sons.

Cooper, A. J. (1892/1988). *A Voice from the South.* Oxford University Press.

Crenshaw, K. (1989/2018). Demarginalizing the Intersection of Race and Sex: A Black Feminist Critique of Antidiscrimination Doctrine, Feminist Theory, and Antiracist Politics [1989]. In *Feminist Legal Theory* (pp. 57–80). Routledge.

Crenshaw, K. (1990). Mapping the Margins: Intersectionality, Identity Politics, and Violence against Women of Color. *Stanford Law Review, 43,* 1241.

Davis, A. Y. (1981/2011). *Women, Race, & Class.* Vintage.

Dotson, K. (2012). A Cautionary Tale: On Limiting Epistemic Oppression. *Frontiers: A Journal of Women Studies, 33*(1), 24–47.

Dotson, K. (2016). Word to the Wise: Notes on a Black Feminist Metaphilosophy of Race. *Philosophy Compass, 11*(2), 69–74.

Dzodan, F. (2011). My Feminism Will Be Intersectional or it Will Be Bullshit! Tiger Beatdown. http://tigerbeatdown.com/2011/10/10/my-feminism-will-be-intersectional-or-it-will-be-bullshit/

Foucault, M. (1980). *Power/Knowledge: Selected Interviews and Other Writings, 1972–1977.* Vintage.

Gotanda, N. (1991). A Critique of "Our Constitution is Color-Blind". *Stanford Law Review, 44,* 1–68.

Grzanka, P. R. (2018). *Intersectionality: A Foundations and Frontiers Reader.* Routledge.

Guy-Sheftall, B. (1995). *Words of Fire: An Anthology of African-American Feminist Thought.* The New Press.

hooks, B. (1981/2014). *Ain't I A Woman: Black Women and Feminism.* Routledge.

hooks, B. (1984/2000). *Feminist Theory: From Margin to Center.* Pluto Press.

Horkheimer, M. (1972). *Critical Theory: Selected Essays* (Vol. 1). A&C Black.

Human Rights Watch. (2018). No Support: Russia's "Gay Propaganda" Law Imperils LGBT Youth. HRW.org. https://www.hrw.org/report/2018/12/11/no-support/russias-gay-propaganda-law-imperils-lgbt-youth#

King Jr, M. L. (1963). Letter from Birmingham City Jail.

Laudan, L. (1981). A Confutation of Convergent Realism. *Philosophy of Science, 48*(1), 19–49.

Lefebvre, H. (1982). *The Sociology of Marx*. Columbia University Press.
Lorde, A. (1980). Age, Race, Class, and Sex: Women Redefining Difference. In *Women in Culture: An Intersectional Anthology for Gender and Women's Studies* (pp. 16–22). Wiley-Blackwell.
Lorde, A. (1981). The Uses of Anger: Women Responding to Racism. In *Sister Outsider*. Penguin Classics.
Lorde, A. (1984). *Sister Outsider: Essays and Speeches*. Penguin Classics.
Lugones, M. (2006). On Complex Communication. *Hypatia, 21*(3), 75–85.
Moraga, C., & Anzaldúa, G. (Eds.). (1981/2015). This bridge called my back: Writings by radical women of color. Suny Press.
Nash, J. C. (2018). *Black Feminism Reimagined: After Intersectionality*. Duke University Press.
Pohlhaus, G., Jr. (2012). Relational Knowing and Epistemic Injustice: Toward a Theory of Willful Hermeneutical Ignorance. *Hypatia, 27*(4), 715–735.
Roberts, D. E. (1999). *Killing the Black Body: Race, Reproduction, and the Meaning of Liberty*. Vintage.
Robinson, Z. F. (2014). *This Ain't Chicago: Race, Class, and Regional Identity in the Post-Soul South*. UNC Press Books.
Smith, B. (1977). Toward a Black Feminist Criticism. In *African American Literary Theory: A Reader* (pp. 132–146). New York University Press.
Spelman, E. V. (1988). *Inessential Woman: Problems of Exclusion in Feminist Thought*. Beacon Press.
Stewart, M. W. (1831). Religion and the Pure Principles of Morality. In *Maria W. Stewart, America's First Black Woman Political Writer* (pp. 28–42). Indiana University Press; 2nd Edition (November 22, 1987).
Taylor, K. Y. (Ed.). (2017). *How We Get Free: Black Feminism and the Combahee River Collective*. Haymarket Books.
Thani, Z., & Anderson, D. (2020). Third-Order Epistemic Exclusion in Professional Philosophy. *Symposion, 7*(2), 117–138.
Truth, S., (1851). Ain't I a Woman?
Tuck, E., & Yang, K. W. (2012). Decolonization is Not a Metaphor. *Decolonization: Indigeneity, Education & Society, 1*(1), 1–40.
Walker, A. (1983/2004). *In Search of Our Mothers' Gardens: Womanist Prose*. Houghton Mifflin Harcourt.

CHAPTER 9

Intersectional Metasemantic Adequacy

9.1 Taking Stock

This chapter brings together ideas introduced in the preceding chapters to argue for a constraint on metasemantic theories informed by intersectionality. This constraint says, roughly, that any acceptable metasemantics must be consistent with a wide range of first-order truths about intersectionality, including truths about matrices of domination, the power that constitutes them, and the ways in which oppressive political realities feed into and are sustained by a regime of truth that produces epistemic oppression and active ignorance about racism and misogyny. Before getting into the argument for the Intersectional Metasemantic Adequacy (IMA) constraint, I will briefly recap the ideas this argument is drawing on.

The first is a theory of truth from model-theoretic semantics. Truth and other semantic properties are objective features of natural language.[1] There is always an objective fact about which of two semantic models is more accurate for a given language. Speaker judgments are a source of information about semantics, but not when speakers are misinformed about first-order truths.

---

[1] See Kamp (1981) for a canonical statement of this view, which is an evolution of Tarski's (1933) concept of truth for formalized languages.

Second, I introduced the idea of a metasemantic theory. This kind of theory is concerned with where meanings come from, i.e. what determines the semantic features of a language.[2] I argued that we need not give a reductive naturalistic theory. Our theory need not reductively explain semantic properties in terms of non-semantic properties discovered by natural sciences like biology and chemistry. It also need not expunge all talk of semantics from its explanations—an acceptable metasemantics can, in the general case, appeal to semantically interpreted representations as part of the explanation for the content of other representations, as when we explain the meaning of a word by appealing to what a community says the meaning of the word is. I also argued that an intersectional metasemantics should be externalist; it should not postulate that sameness or difference in meaning is a matter of how things are within the minds or brains of the people using the language; it should incorporate broader usage patterns within the social fabric to determine meaning. Lastly I argued that an intersectional metasemantics should be a form of ideal language metasemantics, where the meanings of words are a function of how words should be understood given the target domain. At the end of Chap. 6 I began to sketch a metasemantics on which the meanings of "racist" and "woman" are determined by truths about racism and woman as those are understood by an ideal intersectional critical theory; this chapter argues that any acceptable metasemantics must do this.

Next, I described a Foucauldian theory of power (Foucault, 1978) and the ways in which configurations of social power affect and are affected by the operation of the word "true" within the social fabric (Foucault, 1980). Crucially, this theory distinguishes between power making a sentence *function as* true and power making a sentence literally true. On the view I defended, uses of the word "true" to create misinformation and promote ignorance do not affect what is actually true in the language, nor do they have any special metaphysical role in shaping reality itself. I argued that an intersectional understanding of the relationship between truth and power must preserve the sense in which important statements about oppression, such as statements about the harms and injustices of racism, sexism, and transphobia, are objectively true, while recognizing that statements expressing misinformation are objectively false.

---

[2] For extensive discussions about what metasemantics is, see the edited collection Burgess and Sherman (2014).

Lastly, I gave a theory of intersectionality.[3] According to this theory, intersectionality has five aspects: structural intersectionality, political intersectionality, intersectional identity, intersectionality-as-critical-theory, and intersectionality-as-critical-praxis. The form these aspects take is conditioned by the prevailing matrices of domination within which we are living. Knowledge of intersectionality is deeply political and contested, but this does not mean there is no objective truth. Minimally, there are objective truths about the existence of intersectionality and the extent to which it shapes people's lives, including the extent to which structural oppression creates and thrives on misinformation and ignorance. These are fundamental truths to which any acceptable metasemantic theory must be responsive, or so I will argue. An intersectional metasemantics must represent, *inter alia*, the ways in which misinformation is circulated and ignorance maintained by virtue of false assertions.

Now I will bring these elements together to argue for an intersectional metasemantic constraint. Section 9.2 argues for a powerful constraint on models of truth in natural language called *general metasemantic adequacy* (GMA). The constraint says that a metasemantic theory is only acceptable if it is consistent with our strongest first-order commitments, whatever these might be, including potentially first-order commitments about moral and political truths. Section 9.3 considers some objections. Then Sect. 9.4 derives a more specific version of the general constraint: intersectional metasemantic adequacy. The next chapter goes on to introduce a metasemantic theory that satisfies the intersectional metasemantic adequacy constraint.

9.2 General Metasemantic Adequacy

A condition of adequacy for metasemantics is a restriction on the class of acceptable metasemantic theories. It is not itself a theory. It states a necessary condition on being an acceptable metasemantics. A famous example of an adequacy condition on metasemantics is Tarski's (1933) Convention T, which is a condition of adequacy on the definition of truth in a language. Tarski's Convention T says that a definition of truth is adequate only if it entails, for every sentence S in the language, S is true if and only

---

[3] The theory developed was most centrally based on my readings of Collective (1977), Lorde (1984), Crenshaw (1989), Crenshaw (1990), Collins (2002), and Collins & Bilge (2016).

if P, where P is a copy of S in the metalanguage. The definition must entail e.g. "Snow is white" is true if and only if snow is white, "Grass is green" is true if and only if grass is green, and so on for every sentence in the object language. Convention T is not itself a truth definition but a necessary condition on being an acceptable truth definition. The following constraint, which I will argue for, exists at this level of abstraction.

General Metasemantic Adequacy (GMA)

A metasemantic theory M for natural language L is acceptable only if M entails that the semantics of L at the actual world substantiates our strongest first-order commitments, including the truth of our strongest first-order moral and political commitments.

Examples of some very strong first-order commitments include the following:

- Whales are mammals.
- The US gave women the right to vote in 1920.
- No particle moves faster than light.
- There is no set of all sets.
- Every real number is a complex number.
- Evolution explains speciation.
- Global warming is occurring as a result of human activity.
- Fewer people attended Trump's inauguration than Obama's.

These are sentences of English. We have very good reasons to think they are true. Our reasons are first-order reasons. They are concerned with extra-linguistic reality, not with the semantic or metasemantic features of English sentences. The truths they express are not universally known. Some are controversial. Some are the subject of misinformation campaigns. Yet the truth-values of these sentences do not depend on whether they are controversial or widely believed.

The truth of these sentences is data for both semantic and metasemantic theorizing. An accurate semantic theory reflects the actual truth-values of English sentences. A semantic theory that assigns *false* to "Whales are mammals" is inaccurate given the meanings of English words and our evidence about whales. A metasemantic theory that gives an inaccurate semantic theory for English is itself inaccurate, so assigning a semantic interpretation on which "Whales are mammals" is true in English is a minimal adequacy condition on being an acceptable metasemantic theory.

It may be that one of our example sentences is not true despite our strong reasons for believing it to be true. For example, perhaps evolution is not the correct explanation of speciation. In that case, the most accurate semantic theory interprets "Evolution explains speciation" as false. We do not know with absolute certainty what reality is like, and so we do not know with absolute certainty which sentences are true.

Nevertheless, despite our fallibility we must trust our best evidence for deciding what is true and what is false. Even though we are fallible and "Evolution explains speciation" might be false, we still have strong reasons to believe it is true. These are also good reasons to accept a semantic and metasemantic theory on which that sentence is true. Our best justified truths properly guide our theories of semantics and metasemantics, even though we lack absolute certainty.

The case is especially clear for scientific truths, historical truths, and truths of commonsense like "This tomato is red" (while holding up a red tomato) and "Here is a hand" (while holding up your hand like you're G.E. Moore). But our focus in this book is moral and political truth. Commitments to moral and political truths are more contentious. There is often disagreement about what is right or wrong or what is the case in the domain of politics. We cannot appeal to our common belief or commonsense when the truth of a statement is disputed, and in many cases there is no uncontentious way to settle disputes using empirical evidence.

Yet there may still be real objective truths about political realities even if there are politically situated differences of opinion about the truth-values of such statements. Consider the statement "Free markets promote prosperity." Even if there are politically situated differences of opinion about its truth-value, this sentence might be objectively true and might be objectively supported by strong empirical evidence. People disagree, but there may still be a fact of the matter.

A disagreement over the truth of S does not mean the sentence cannot serve as part of the fundamental data set for metasemantic theorizing, especially if the disagreement is caused by misinformation. Even if water's chemical nature were hotly debated, say by Flat Earthers, the truth of "Water is H2O" would still hold significance for metasemantic theorizing. Disagreement does not necessarily undermine strong evidence. Likewise, if the proposition that free markets promote prosperity was extremely well-supported by evidence, then we would have strong evidence to think that "Free markets promote prosperity" is true in English. Such a sentence may provide semantic data for metasemantic theorizing even if it is contested.

By the same token, that "Black women are more oppressed than white men" is true may be a fundamental datum for metasemantic theorizing, insofar as there is very strong evidence to support the proposition that Black women are more oppressed than white men. I would personally rank this proposition as equally certain with the proposition that water is H2O, even though I know many would disagree with me. I do not take such disagreements to undermine my confidence in the proposition that Black women are more oppressed than white men because I have good evidence that such disagreements are the result of active ignorance.

Consider next the metasemantic status of English sentences such as "Murder is wrong" and "Women deserve the right to vote." These are ethical statements, and their truth-values and truth-conditions are hotly contested within metaethics—but contested because of the metaphysical status of moral and legal truths. But despite metaethical controversies, such sentences may still constitute fundamental data for metasemantic theorizing. Consider the following sentences of English:

- Murder is wrong.
- Women deserve the right to vote.
- Very young children aren't morally or legally responsible for their actions.
- Free speech should be protected.
- Racism is a form of oppression.
- Unjust laws should be abolished.
- The right to abortion follows from the right to privacy in the US.

The fact that these sentences make moral, political, and legal claims does not make their truth or falsity any less relevant for metasemantics. Insofar as we have good reasons to think these sentences are true, we have good reasons to count the accurate assignment of truth to these sentences as a condition of accuracy on semantic theories. An accurate metasemantic theory must entail an accurate semantic theory, so any acceptable metasemantic theory must make "Murder is wrong" and "Women deserve the right to vote" come out true in English. Hence, moral and political commitments constrain metasemantic theory.[4]

General Metasemantic Adequacy codifies this epistemic constraint. Our first-order judgments about moral and political reality are reflected in our judgments of the truth-values of sentences appearing in moral and political discourses. These judgments are data for metasemantic theorizing. The true metasemantic theory of a language must comport with the true semantic theory for that language. When we have good reason to be strongly committed to the truth or falsity of a sentence, we are committed with roughly equal force to a restriction on metasemantic theorizing to verify our first-order judgment.

The same argument applies to more controversial political commitments, so long as these commitments are in fact strongly supported by evidence. The controversy surrounding such statements should not necessarily erode our confidence in their truth, since such controversy may be explained as an effect of active ignorance. Insofar as we may be strongly justified in believing the truth or falsity of politically contested claims, those claims may function as semantic data for metasemantic theorizing. Consider the following list of English sentences:

- Trans women are women, not men.
- Racism against white people is impossible in contemporary US society.
- Affirmative action for Black academic opportunity is anti-racist, not racist.
- Trigger warnings and safe spaces promote learning objectives.
- Mass incarceration is a mechanism of white control over Black bodies.
- Norms of knowledge legitimation reflect elite white male interests.

Because these claims are highly contested, we shouldn't say they reflect *our* strongest political commitments, where "our" suggests something like a consensus view.[5] But these sentences represent very strong commitments for some people, including me; moreover, I take myself to be strongly epistemically justified in believing they are true. A speaker of English who

---

[4] Note that this is a constraint even for error theorists and non-cognitivists, insofar as they must do work to explain away or incorporate the strong prima facie semantic evidence that these statements have straightforward truth-conditions and, moreover, that they appear to be straightforwardly true. It is also true for deflationists.

[5] See Code's (2012) discussion of 'we-saying,' which highlights the political nature of asserting what 'our' views are.

strongly believes that affirmative action is anti-racist believes and takes herself to have strong epistemic reason for holding that belief should accept that "Affirmative action is anti-racist" is true in English. One who takes themselves to know that trans women are women should likewise believe that "Trans women are women" is true in English.

The truth of a sentence is a check on the accuracy of a metasemantic theory. Thus, a strong commitment to the truth of "Trans women are women" is a commitment to a particular check on the adequacy of a metasemantic theory for English. Generally, when a person has good reason to accept a first-order political truth, one has roughly equally strong reason to treat this first-order truth as informing both their semantic and metasemantic beliefs. This is so even if the claims are contested or even highly controversial, as long as the controversy does not provide a defeater for the knowledge claim.

If our aim is a theory of truth that transcends political position, this is a crucial desideratum. The fact that some statement is contested or controversial is not in itself an overriding reason to regard it as uncertain, nor is it automatically sufficient reason to call its representational properties—its semantics—into question. Even highly contentious claims about political reality can be objectively true, objectively justified, and have determinate meaning, even if their truth, justification, and/or meaning are disputed. Natural languages are capable of representing reality even where there is disagreement over the truth or meanings of sentences.

Insofar as we (whichever group this might refer to) find a set of moral or political statements to be among the most certain truths of our language—the best supported, the most difficult to doubt, the most trustworthy, the most central to our worldview in a way justified by evidence—then we must treat the truth-values of these statements as part of the semantic bedrock for our metasemantic theorizing. This is the General Metasemantic Adequacy (GMA) principle in a nutshell.

9.3 Objections to GMA

At this point it will be helpful to address two pressing objections to the General Metasemantic Adequacy principle. Stating and responding to these objections helps clarify what the principle means, shows how GMA works, and elaborates on the argument for accepting it.

9.3.1 Objection 1: The Argument for GMA Confuses Sentences with Propositions

The above argument for General Metasemantic Adequacy might appear to confuse evidential support for the truth of natural language sentences with evidence for the propositions those sentences express. What about the possibility that one could be justified in believing the *proposition* that trans women are women without being committed to interpreting this proposition as the meaning of the English *sentence* "Trans women are women"? Perhaps I do not believe that "Trans women are women" in English expresses the proposition I believe. I might put it this way: "women" *should* denote trans women as well as cis women, but given historical usage patterns, cis-normative prejudices, religious attitudes, laws, and so on, "women" as it is used in mainstream English actually refers only to cis women. Perhaps the meanings of expressions used in mainstream contexts always reflect such dominant cultural assumptions, as Bettcher (2013) contends.

If we can accept the truth of the proposition that trans women are women without being thereby committed to interpreting "Trans women are women" as true in English, this considerably weakens the force of General Metasemantic Adequacy. It's not just a point about the semantics of "women." Believing that racism is a form of oppression would be consistent with accepting any number of semantic interpretations for the word "racism" in English, including interpretations on which Donald Trump speaks truly when he says critical race theory is "racist."

Responding to this objection requires thinking about object languages and metalanguages. In speaking about propositions, we always use a language. Perhaps the same goes for thinking about propositions, too, which may involve using a language of thought (Fodor 1975, 2006). When I say that I believe the *proposition* that trans women are women without believing that the sentence "Trans women are women" is true, what language am I using to express the thing I believe?

Unlike formal model theory in which the *object language* (the language being studied) and the *metalanguage* (the language in which we construct the model) are different by definition, the above statement uses English as both its object language and metalanguage. If I assert (in English) both that trans women are women and that "women" does not refer to trans women, I have said something confusing. When I use the word "women" in the first conjunct to assert that trans women are women, I am using "women" with a certain meaning which I then go on to deny. This might make sense if I am speaking a different language, not English, in describing my belief about trans women—more on this shortly. But if I am speaking English as my metalanguage, then I have stated a contradiction.

This is related to a very clear constraint on semantic theories: natural language semantics need to satisfy disquotational principles in straightforward cases.[6] It must entail, for example, that "Richard Nixon" refers to Richard Nixon, that "dogs" denotes dogs, that "Snow is white" is true if and only if snow is white; an acceptable semantics must do this for indefinitely many expressions. Call this *disquotational semantic adequacy*. Any adequate semantics for English must entail that "women" refers to women, however else its semantic features are described. If your view is that trans women are women but that "women" in English doesn't refer to women, then you are committed to the view that the semantics for English fails disquotational adequacy on pain of contradiction.

If I deny that "women" refers to women in English, then how do I express the proposition I claim to believe, namely that all trans women are women? How do I express the view that "women" in English fails to denote all women? Note here I used the word "women" to say what the word women fails to denote, but then what did I mean by "women" in that sentence? There seems to be no straightforward way to affirm that trans women are women using English and simultaneously deny that trans women are in the extension of "women" in English. By the same token I cannot use English to express the difference between believing the proposition that trans women are women and believing that the sentence "Trans women are women" is true in English.

Suppose instead I use a different metalanguage to express my propositional belief that trans women are women. Instead of using English, I might create an artificial language in which "Trans women are women" is true by definition. In my artificial language, the word "women" has a distinct meaning from the homophonic word "women" in English which

---

[6] For a thorough discussion of disquotational schemas, including a thorough discussion of the difficulties of making a fully disquotational semantic theory, see David (1994). I am not proposing that the semantics for English is exhausted by disquotational principles. My semantics is not deflationary, it's model-theoretic. My point is that any semantics for English must satisfy the disquotational schemas in straightforward cases. It must entail, for example, that "Trans women are women" is true if and only if trans women are women. But unlike a deflationary disquotational semantics, I am not saying this biconditional exhaustively specifies the semantics of that sentence.

excludes trans women from its extension. "Women" in my artificial language refers to the group that I believe trans women belong to.

Shifting the metalanguage to an artificial language might help state the objection. I could then say the sentence "Trans women are women" is false in English but true in the artificial language I have constructed. Or I could maintain that "Trans women are women" is true in a certain dialect of English spoken in trans subcultures but not in the mainstream dialect, as Bettcher (2009, 2013) maintains. Then I am not speaking the version of English I am critiquing when I say I believe that trans women are women; I'm speaking Trans-Friendlier English.

Let us begin by thinking about the version of the objection that appeals to two natural languages, two dialects of English, and then return later to the artificial language version. Bettcher (2013) writes,

> Frequently, in dominant cultural contexts, the expression "trans woman" is understood to mean "a man who lives as a woman." [And men are not women; hence trans women are not really women on this understanding.] Is this a case in which an individual merely misunderstands the meaning of the expression? No, because that meaning is accepted by many people and, indeed, often by the media, law enforcement agencies, domestic violence and homeless shelters, and so forth. Yet when I use that expression ("I am a trans woman") in trans subcultures, it simply *does not* mean that.[7]

Bettcher postulates there are two natural languages in play, a dominant version of English and a subculture version, Trans-Friendlier English. People who speak Dominant English and say "Trans women are men" speak truly. People who speak Trans-Friendlier English and say "Trans women are women" speak truly. So, there are two different languages with two different meanings of "woman."

This lets us state the objection as follows: couldn't someone believe the proposition that trans women are women, where that proposition is expressed by the trans-friendlier English sentence "Trans women are women," while denying that "women" refers to trans women as used in mainstream English? Then this person's political commitments do not immediately constrain what metasemantic theories of mainstream Dominant English they should find acceptable. This is Bettcher's position. I think it is plausible, but I don't think it is the right view of things.

---

[7] Bettcher (2013). See also Bettcher (2009) for development of related themes.

Notice that Bettcher's conclusion is being driven by a metasemantic principle, something like the following. A word's meaning in a context is determined according to what the majority of people, the media, the law, and/or social institutions interpret it as meaning in that context. But why should we accept this metasemantic principle? A person committed to the first-order claim that trans women are women need not accept this metasemantic principle.

Consider the opposing perspective. Given that I speak English and believe that trans women are women, I count the sentence "Trans women are women" as true in mainstream English. I therefore see mainstream transphobic interpretations of the semantics of "woman" that exclude trans women from its extension as *inaccurate*. I perceive there to be widespread false beliefs about the meaning of the word "woman" driven by widespread transphobia and its attendant widespread ignorance and misinformation about the nature of gender. These false views inform the oppressive practices of the media, law enforcement agencies, domestic violence and homeless shelters, and so forth. A proponent of this perspective has a strong reason to reject Bettcher's metasemantic presupposition that the widespread (mis)use of the word "woman" in dominant contexts produces a dominant meaning of "woman" in those contexts such that trans women really are excluded from its extension.

I have not yet stated my argument for this position, but I think the argument is straightforward and surprisingly powerful. If you think trans women are women, then the disquotational adequacy principle puts strong pressure on any metasemantic principle that purports to exclude trans women from the extension of "woman" in mainstream English. Consider the following first-order argument.

First-Order Slingshot

1. Trans women are women,
2. "women" in mainstream English refers to women,
3. Therefore, trans women are in the extension of "women" in mainstream English.

Given the conclusion of the First-Order Slingshot, it follows that "Trans women are women" is true in mainstream English. Then since "Trans women are women" is true in mainstream English, an accurate metasemantics of English must entail a semantics that agrees with this. The conclusion entails we should reject Bettcher's metasemantic principle that the semantics of speech in mainstream contexts reflects transphobic ideology.

Against this slingshot argument, what premise can be resisted? The reasons in support of premise 1 are the same reasons in support of the proposition Bettcher accepts, which she expresses in trans-friendlier English by saying, "Trans women are women," in trans-friendlier contexts. To argue against premise 1 is to engage in a first-order debate about womanhood, not a second-order debate about meaning. Premise 2 follows from disquotational adequacy. It is the assertion that "women" denotes the property of being a woman, whatever that *is* (the italics here is to emphasize the metaphysical nature of this question—it is not a question of semantics). Rejecting this premise is also very difficult. Why should the correct metasemantics for English assign anything other than the set of women as the extension of the predicate "women"?[8]

---

[8] To give Bettcher (2013) the full attention her work deserves, I should emphasize that my view fails to come to terms with certain elements of her view. Her theory is one on which the metaphysical construction of gender is done differently within different cultures, and so there is an attendant metaphysical difference between the way gender is constructed within the mainstream culture as opposed to the way it is constructed within trans-friendlier communities. The meaning conflict, the struggle between the two ways of using the word "woman," is part of this larger conflict between two ways of constructing gender. Bettcher draws on Lugones (1987) in describing different worlds of sense in which we can find ourselves, some trans friendly and some transphobic. It is part of the trans person's struggle that the world of sense in which they have the gender they identify as is constantly antagonized and sometimes destroyed by enforcers whose role is to impose the cis-normative world of sense on everyone. For Bettcher, conflicting meanings are part of this larger conflict between different cultures.

I am not arguing against this picture of the struggle for trans inclusion within mainstream consciousness. I do believe there are different cultures that are in a sense at war with one another, that transforming the mainstream culture to accommodate trans friendly worldviews is crucial for the survival and flourishing of trans folks, and that trans gender identities can be delegitimated or even metaphysically destabilized by hostile enforcers who are wielding the power of a cis-supremacist matrix of domination. I want to disentangle these phenomena from a theory of metasemantics in the following way. I don't think we must see this process as one in which the enforcers speak truly when they claim that trans women are men. We can see such linguistic violence as an attack on the metaphysical underpinnings of trans women's identities while interpreting the shared public language in such a way as to recognize their statements as false, as ideological misinformation about gender that spreads ignorance and misunderstanding about gender and its relation to biology. A grocery store clerk acting as a cis enforcer might destabilize a trans woman's gender in that context by calling her a "man," even if what the clerk says is (unbeknownst to her) false.

The slingshot argument applies to the artificial language version of the objection with equal force. Suppose you maintain that the English word "women" excludes trans women from its extension, so you construct an artificial language in which "Trans women are women" is true. Whatever reasons are given in support of the truth of this artificial sentence is support for the relevant proposition expressed by premise 1 above. After all, the point of constructing the artificial language was to express the proposition you thought you couldn't express in English, the one supported by the reasons for believing that trans women are women. If you haven't expressed the proposition that trans women are women, you can't claim to have believed that which you said you believed. But the construction of an artificial language does not affect the disquotational requirement for the semantics of English, so it cannot impugn premise 2 either. Whoever the women are, whatever they are, the English predicate "women" refers to them.

The general problem with the proposition-versus-sentence objection is it presupposes an ability to think about relevant propositions while denying that those propositions just *are* the meanings of the salient natural language sentences we would use (in fact, *do* use) to express them. We seem to lack an ability to think about propositions that are both closely related to the meanings of natural language expressions in crucially important ways and simultaneously different from those meanings. The closeness of the discourse to representing the subject matter accurately, together with our background understanding of the subject matter and our assessment of the ways in which misinformation, lack of understanding, and in many cases active ignorance contribute to the lack of fit between discourse and reality, are all components of our interpretation practice. This interpretive practice in some sense forces a certain interpretation that aligns with one's first-order views. When an English speaker's first-order belief is that trans women are women, their interpretation of "woman" in English is forced to include trans women. This kind of intersectional reference magnetism is a crucial aspect of the metasemantic theory proposed in the next chapter.

9.3.2   Objection 2: The Revisionist's Objection

According to the revisionist's objection, we can recognize defects in our representations. This is why we are compelled to engage in conceptual engineering. Cappelen (2018) calls this 'the revisionist's basic assumption':

The terms or concepts which we use to talk and think about a particular subject matter can be defective and can be improved to address these defects.

According to the revisionist's perspective, we can recognize that (for some metasemantic reason or other) trans women do not fall into the extension of "women." From this together with the disquotational principle, we are forced to infer that trans women are not women. But we also realize that trans women should be included under the extension of "woman" even though they are not, so we set about trying to change the meaning of the word "woman." This way of thinking is reflected in some Haslangarian ameliorative projects (see Haslanger & Haslanger, 2012), including possibly Jenkins (2016).

The revisionist, unlike the objector from objection 1, thinks that we do not yet have the cognitive or linguistic resources required to think or speak the propositions we want to think and say. We don't even yet have an artificial language that expresses the proposition we believe. We wish to say and believe that trans women are women, but we cannot because for some reason or other we do not have the means to express this proposition. A defender of this position sidesteps the reply to argument 1 because they are able to deny premise 1 of the slingshot, albeit with the caveat that premise 1 should be made into a truth through conceptual engineering.

In order to believe that "women" in English does not refer to women, we must be committed to some metasemantics or other that makes "woman" trans exclusionary in English. There must be some metasemantic explanation for why we cannot use "woman" to express our trans inclusive belief that trans women are women. The revisionist thinks we cannot at present properly even *believe* that trans women are women because we lack the proper concept. It's as if the metasemantic properties involved with the word "women" force our thought (expressed in English) onto a different subject matter. When we try to think that trans women are women, we end up thinking the false thought that trans women are cis women. Being a revisionist means working to change the content of the word "woman" in order to make the sentence "Trans women are women" true, through effecting some kind of sociological change.

The metasemantics presupposed by a revisionist entail that we could in principle need to regard our firmest first-order political commitments as false for metasemantic reasons. Someone firmly committed to "Trans women are women" could nevertheless regard this statement as false, if they thought that "woman" presently excluded trans women from its extension on the basis of a metasemantic principle that undergirds the possible need for content revisions. Their commitment to the truth of "Trans women are women" is a commitment to make a social change, to make it become true. If a revisionist's metasemantic principle is true then GMA is false, because it would provide an example of an acceptable metasemantics that is consistent with treating some of our own firmest first-order political commitments as false.

The revisionist argument against GMA presupposes a metasemantics that undercuts the semantic interpretation of our first-order commitments as true. But under what conditions could a candidate metasemantic theory rationally compel a trans inclusive feminist philosopher to treat "Trans women are women" as false in English? I suppose there is a metasemantic theory that entails "Trans women are women" is false in English, but what is the evidence in favor of accepting that metasemantics? And how could that evidence be stronger than a trans feminist's evidence that "Trans women are women" is true?

Let us say that *direct evidence* for a metasemantic theory is evidence that is not about the semantic features of the natural language under consideration. This is evidence that does not rely on or involve semantic theorizing; it bears on metasemantics *directly*. Direct evidence supports one metasemantic theory over another without appealing to semantic facts. *Indirect evidence* is semantic data that a metasemantic theory is responsible for explaining. Arguing indirectly for one metasemantic theory M1 over another M2 involves arguing that M1 fits the semantic facts better than M2, while arguing directly for M1 over M2 would be an argument that proceeds without appealing to semantics.

GMA says your strongest evidence for metasemantic theorizing is indirect evidence, including the semantics of your strongest moral and political commitments. These are, by assumption, among your strongest commitments to semantically interpreted parts of your home language, so it should be difficult or impossible to muster other stronger semantic considerations into an indirect argument against GMA (at least for someone who has very strong moral and political commitments). Hence, the revisionist must provide direct evidence for a metasemantic view that would contradict GMA. It needs to be direct insofar as there are no other semantic data stronger than our strongest first-order commitments.

But direct evidence for metasemantic theorizing is necessarily very weak, perhaps non-existent. Only indirect evidence generates epistemic friction in metasemantics. This means our strongest semantic judgments weigh more than any direct considerations in assessing the acceptability of a metasemantic theory. Consequently, the revisionist's objection to GMA cannot be maintained where the sentences to be revised are among our strongest first-order commitments. We cannot have sufficiently good non-semantic reasons to believe such metasemantic principles *over* our strongest first-order judgments. If someone has very strong first-order reasons to believe that trans women are women, they cannot have overriding metasemantic reasons for believing that "women" does not refer to trans women in ordinary English.

Why is direct evidence metasemantics vanishingly weak? The very notion that we need a metasemantic theory is predicated on the existence of semantic features of language. There's just no reason to postulate metasemantic properties apart from our semantic commitments. Insofar as we can have direct evidence in metasemantics at all, it must be based on theorizing about semantic features of the language and extrapolating from the empirical circumstances in which those features exist. But any such empirical evidence must be tentative when it is used to challenge semantics, as the justification for the relevance of that evidence is predicated on presuppositions about semantics, especially if that evidence is being used to challenge our strongest commitments. Direct empirical evidence for a metasemantic view cannot undermine semantic commitments unless the relevance of that evidence is supported by other propositions about semantics which are themselves more certain than the commitments being undermined.

It may be that the revisionist presupposes somehow that reductive naturalistic metasemantics lends some reason to doubt that "woman" refers to woman, but such an argument would be susceptible to a strong modus ponens counterargument. For if there were an argument which used reductive naturalistic metasemantics as a premise and concluded that "trans women are not women" was true, this would constitute a reductio of reductive naturalistic metasemantics for anyone who strongly believes the truth that trans women are women. This is for the same reason given above: our strongest first-order commitments epistemically outweigh any other evidence for metasemantics, including reductive naturalistic metasemantics.

If the revisionist is going to mount an argument that some of our strongest first-order political commitments must be abandoned for metasemantic reasons, the argument must somehow leverage semantic commitments that are stronger than our strongest first-order political commitments. This kind of argument we have not yet seen spelled out in detail, and the burden of proof is on the objector to provide such an argument. Speaking for myself, I cannot imagine how the evidence for some highly abstract principle about conceptual roles or causal chains of reference could undermine my confidence in the truth of the statement "Trans women are women." In general, people should be skeptical about metasemantic challenges to the truth of "Trans women are women" or whatever sentences of their home language express their strongest political commitments.

9.4 Intersectional Metasemantic Adequacy

General Metasemantic Adequacy entails that your political commitments constrain the set of possible metasemantics you can accept for your language. It does not tell you what political commitments you should have. What follows in this section is a description of what GMA becomes when you are strongly committed to a theory of intersectionality of the kind developed in the previous chapter. This second, more determinate constraint is the result of combining the general principle with the specific commitments of intersectional social theory and its epistemological entailments.

Intersectional Metasemantic Adequacy (**IMA**)

A metasemantic theory M is acceptable only if M entails that the semantics of English at the actual world substantiates the truth of the first-order commitments of our best theory of intersectionality, as that theory is expressed in English.

What does this principle entail about the metasemantics of English? There are indefinitely many first-order commitments that come with accepting intersectionality. These indefinitely many commitments have the potential to constrain the class of acceptable metasemantics in many ways. The scope of the constraint could be a subject of debate even within intersectionality studies. Here I will focus on what I take to be the central implications of IMA for metasemantics.

I have argued that intersectionality should be understood primarily as a form of structural oppression embodied by a matrix of domination (Collins, 2002) and that the matrix of domination is sustained by the regime of truth (Foucault, 1980), specifically the sociological patterns that make misinformation, false statements, and controlling images and propositions function as true which are in fact false. These systems—which exist at the individual, group, and institutional levels—promote misinformation and bad reasoning where information and good reasoning would threaten existing power structures. It works to undermine the epistemic agency of marginalized groups by discrediting them, obscuring their conceptual frameworks through linguistic hijacking, and doing all it can to diminish their epistemic power. The lifeblood of racism, sexism, homophobia, and so on, is misinformation, ignorance, and epistemic oppression.

A critical theory of intersectionality analyzes the production, distribution, and the consequences of ignorance, misinformation, and epistemic oppression. It is therefore always relevant to ask when judging the acceptability of an intersectional metasemantic theory: how is this metasemantics representing facts about ignorance, misinformation, and epistemic oppression? Does this metasemantics adequately describe the spread of false beliefs that maintain interlocking systems of oppression? Does it capture the ways in which misinformation is obscuring the reality of oppression and the experiences of marginalized groups within mainstream discourses? Does it capture how false statements are functioning as true in order to create and perpetuate prevailing conditions of oppression and exploitation? Does it accurately represent the relevant ways in which the epistemic agency of Black women is being affected by social power dynamics and prevailing epistemological systems?

On a metasemantics that answers these questions adequately, statements like "Trans women are really men" and "Anti-white racism exists" must be rendered as false, because intersectionality represents these statements as controlling propositions made to function as true in order to sustain an oppressive matrix of domination.

An adequate metasemantics must also render the semantic values of words in ways that accord with our best understanding of intersectionality. The extension of "woman" must include trans women, the extension of "racism" must include racist policing practices and other social institutions that promote white domination, and so on. It must also entail that the extensions of these words are the same for all users of the language, both the ignorant and those who know what they are talking about. When Trump uses the word "racist" it refers to racism, even though he does not know what racism is.

Intersectional Metasemantic Adequacy is not itself a metasemantic theory. It is a restriction on acceptable metasemantic theories. It says that the only theories of metasemantics that are acceptable are those that provide a certain semantic interpretation of English, one that renders political opponents as speaking in a shared language, in which false statements function as true to spread misinformation. It requires that, for example, hijacking misuses of "racist" must be rendered as false on any acceptable metasemantics. We have yet to give a metasemantic theory that actually satisfies the intersectional metasemantic adequacy constraint. That will be the aim of Chap. 10.

Whereas General Metasemantic Adequacy is politically neutral, Intersectional Metasemantic Adequacy is not. This metasemantic principle says that any acceptable metasemantic theory must comport with the indefinitely large list of highly contentious and hotly contested political commitments. Yet in this discourse, even the most antagonistic political adversary of intersectionality must recognize that *if* the first-order political commitments of intersectionality are true, then there are objective facts about whose beliefs and whose rhetoric is veridical.

There are objective facts about the flow of information and the flow of misinformation. The opponent of intersectionality must also recognize that rejecting the framework of intersectionality requires defending the objective veridicality of his own opposing views and beliefs. Thus, the intersectional metasemantic constraint does not make truth and falsity into just whatever it says they are. It is part of the intersectional metasemantic constraint that truth must be objective, not politically constructed, because that is what first-order intersectionality theory requires.

9.5 Objections to IMA

In this section I will briefly consider five objections to the intersectional metasemantic adequacy constraint.

Objection 1: This starting point puts you in a weak dialectical position because you are simply assuming that intersectionality exists.

Reply 1: I am not assuming anything. I'm relying on the work of scholars and thinkers who have developed the framework of intersectionality. As I argued in Chap. 8, there is a very long and robust intellectual tradition theorizing the existence and reality of intersectionality on the basis of strong empirical evidence, collected and systematized over many generations from many social locations. Objecting to this starting point requires arguing against the many social critical theorists who have developed the theory of intersectionality.

Objection 2: You missed the point of objection 1. The point is: from a philosophical perspective one cannot simply assume the truth of Black feminist social theory or any other social theory.

Reply 2: This version of the objection relies on certain disciplinary norms about what counts as a legitimate starting point within a professional philosophy setting. But the notion of a legitimate starting point is contested in the current dialectical setting. Traditional disciplinary norms are being interrogated.[9] Seen from the Black feminist perspective developed by Collins, this objection itself is a manifestation of the way traditional white male dominated academic discourses reinforce a regime of truth that subjugates and marginalizes Black feminist thought. By insisting that philosophical treatises cannot begin from an intersectional framework, one draws on the institutional power of academic philosophy to shut down conversations that center the discourses and theoretical perspectives created by Black women and other marginalized groups.

Objection 3: Well it won't convince anyone! If you won't start from universally accepted premises, how can you expect anyone to believe or care about your conclusions?

Reply 3: Starting from 'universally accepted premises' in this context means starting from premises that are accepted by dominant and marginalized groups alike.[10] Because of the influence of the regime of truth, premises that are generally acceptable or intuitive to dominant agents will tend to be antithetical to the propositions supported by subjugated knowledge, including knowledge of intersectionality.

It is a dictum of intersectional epistemology: universally accepted premises do not support knowledge of oppression. The claim that 'no one' will believe or care about the conclusions reached from an intersectional starting point really means that incredulous dominant agents will not believe or care about such conclusions. This is an unavoidable fact within a matrix of domination. Dominant agents will typically (although not always) refuse to believe, in many ways and for many reasons, in the conditions of oppression and domination that characterize their world. The intersectional theorist therefore should not start from propositions that are accepted by her political opponent, because such a starting point will obscure the nature of social reality.

[9] For an extensive discussion of this idea, see Dotson (2013).
[10] This reply owes its form in rough outline to Annas (2008) in her reply to an analogous objection to virtue ethics.

Objection 4: You are in a weak dialectical position because your political opponent can adopt your strategy and use it to argue against you. Given their starting points, everything you believe about intersectionality and its role in politics and metasemantics is false.

Reply 4: The fact that my political opponent can advert to their own first-order beliefs to argue for their position does not put me in a dialectically weak position. Rather, it puts me in the same position I am always in, that of arguing with someone who disagrees with me.

I recognize that my political opponents disagree with me about important first-order truths about things like gender, social identity politics, racism, and intersectionality. From my perspective, this is the result of ignorance, misinformation, and epistemic oppression. They may hold similar views about my position. But at least we are both interested in finding out who is objectively right. And I maintain that I have better reasons to believe I am right. Moreover, I think focusing on first-order evidence about racism and gender and refusing to let the conversation devolve into a debate about semantics is the best way to argue for the truth of the intersectional framework. Intersectional metasemantic adequacy promotes first-order discourses about systems of oppression insofar as it refuses to allow any metasemantics that misconstrues political opponents as speaking truly in their own languages. So intersectional metasemantic adequacy facilitates political discourse within the democratic space of reasons.

Objection 5: But your opponent could use your theory to promote and pursue harmful political agendas! Suppose they take on board General Metasemantic Adequacy and then argue that the word "woman" excludes trans women, "racist" includes affirmative action, and "marriage" excludes all but cis heterosexual couples. This framework gives reactionary groups a means of arguing for their views.

Reply 5: No theoretical resources are immune to co-optation in the service of harmful political agendas. A true theory can be co-opted and used to spread ignorance and misinformation. For example, some men's rights activists have used feminist concepts to argue against feminist conclusions. But this is not in itself a reason to abandon feminist theory. It is certainly not an argument that feminist theory is false. More generally, there is no way to prevent theories that promote social justice from being used by those who would oppose it.

9.6 SATISFYING IMA

The intersectional metasemantic adequacy constraint is not itself a metasemantic theory. It's a condition on something being an adequate metasemantic theory. In the next chapter, I introduce a metasemantic theory designed to satisfy IMA. This theory is also intended to be a metasemantics for the epistemic violence model of misinformation. It represents the semantics of English, a common language shared between political opponents, as determined by features of what a more ideal version of the English-speaking community would say about racism, gender, and the meanings of words like "racist" and "woman." On the metasemantics to be proposed, misuses of words that function to spread misinformation and active ignorance count as false.

REFERENCES

Annas, J. (2008). Virtue Ethics and the Charge of Egoism. *Morality and Self-interest*, 205, 1.
Bettcher, T. M. (2009). Trans Identities and First-person Authority. *You've Changed: Sex Reassignment and Personal Identity*, 1, 98–120.
Bettcher, T. M. (2013). Trans Women and the Meaning of 'Woman'.
Burge, T. (1979). Individualism and the Mental. *Midwest Studies in Philosophy*, 4, 73–121.
Burge, T. (2010). *Origins of Objectivity*. Oxford University Press.
Burgess, A., & Sherman, B. (Eds.). (2014). *Metasemantics: New Essays on the Foundations of Meaning*. Oxford University Press.
Cappelen, H. (2018). *Fixing Language: An Essay on Conceptual Engineering*. Oxford University Press.
Code, L. (2012). Taking Subjectivity into Account. In *Education, Culture and Epistemological Diversity* (pp. 85–100). Springer.
Collective, C. R. (1977/1983). The Combahee River Collective Statement. *Home girls: A Black Feminist Anthology*, 1 264-274.
Collins, P. H. (2002). *Black Feminist Thought: Knowledge, Consciousness, and the Politics of Empowerment*. Routledge.
Crenshaw, K. (1989/2018). Demarginalizing the Intersection of Race and Sex: A Black Feminist Critique of Antidiscrimination Doctrine, Feminist Theory, and Antiracist Politics [1989]. In *Feminist Legal Theory* (pp. 57-80). Routledge.
Crenshaw, K. (1990). Mapping the Margins: Intersectionality, Identity Politics, and Violence Against Women of Color. *Stan. L. Rev.*, 43, 1241.
David, M. A. (1994). *Correspondence and Disquotation: An Essay on the Nature of Truth*. Oxford University Press on Demand.

Dotson, K. (2013). How Is This Paper Philosophy? *Comparative Philosophy*, *3*(1), 121–121.
Foucault, M. (1978/1990). *The history of sexuality: An introduction*. Vintage.
Foucault, M. (1980). *Power/knowledge: Selected Interviews and Other Writings, 1972-1977.* Vintage.
Haslanger, S., & Haslanger, S. A. (2012). *Resisting Reality: Social Construction and Social Critique*. Oxford University Press.
Hill, C. S. (2002). *Thought and World: An Austere Portrayal of Truth, Reference, and Semantic Correspondence*. Cambridge University Press.
Jenkins, K. (2016). Amelioration and Inclusion: Gender Identity and the Concept of Woman. *Ethics, 126*(2), 394–421.
Kamp, H. (1981). A Theory of Truth and Semantic Representation. *Formal semantics-the Essential Readings, 1*, 189–222.
Lorde, A. (1984/2020). *Sister Outsider: Essays and Speeches*. Penguin Classics.
Lugones, M. (1987). Playfulness,"world"-travelling, and Loving Perception. *Hypatia, 2*(2), 3–19.
Tarski, A. (1933/1956). The Concept of Truth in Formalized Languages. *Logic, Semantics, Metamathematics, 2*(152-278), 7.

CHAPTER 10

A Metasemantics for Intersectionality

10.1 The Plan

My plan is to sketch a metasemantics for an intersectional theory of truth that satisfies the following principle, which I argued for in the preceding chapter:

Intersectional Metasemantic Adequacy (**IMA**)

> A metasemantic theory M is acceptable only if M entails that the semantics of English at the actual world substantiates the truth of the first-order commitments of our best theory of intersectionality, as that theory is expressed in English.

In previous chapters I have laid out a number of first-order commitments that I take to be part of the best theory of intersectionality. Among these commitments are the claims that ignorance and misinformation quintessentially involve false statements, that these statements are made to function as true through the operation of the regime of truth (Foucault, 1980), and that the matrix of domination (Collins, 2002) constituted by intersecting forms of oppression is sustained and reproduced in part through the effects of these false statements made to function as true. IMA is expansive because it imposes semantic interpretation criteria for all of the false sentences that are made to function as true as part of the matrix of domination, as well as imposing restrictions on how the referents of words like "racist" and "woman" are to be interpreted.

An intersectionally adequate metasemantics must entail a semantics for actual English that renders all statements that constitute misinformation about intersectionality and related topics as false in ordinary, mainstream English. It also must represent politically contested terminology as referring in accord with our best intersectional understanding of the domain of discourse. "Racism" should refer to racism as it is understood on our best theory of racism, "woman" should refer to women as that category is understood on our best theory of gender, and so on. This means assigning trans inclusive meanings to the words "women" and "men." It means assigning an extension to "racism" that only includes actual instances of racism and excludes so-called anti-white racism, which is not really racism. And IMA requires that indefinitely many other words also receive the correct interpretation—correct, according to our best theory of intersectionality.

But how is it that we manage to refer to racism and women as a community if the community is divided in its opinions and beset with misinformation and active ignorance? That is a central metasemantic question for intersectionality theory which I will attempt to answer here.

10.2 Constructing an Intersectional Metasemantics

I will focus on two politically contested statements which I believe, according to the best theory of intersectionality, constitute misinformation that functions to reproduce and maintain cis-het white supremacist structural oppression. These statements are false in regular old English but made to function as true in order to promote the strategic aims of cis-het white supremacy: "Trans women are men" and "Racism against white people is rampant." There are indefinitely many false statements that are made to function as true as part of the regime of truth that keeps the matrix of domination in working order but focusing on these two should suffice to give a picture of how the metasemantics works for other statements.

10.2.1 Preliminaries

The metasemantics I am constructing assigns model-theoretic semantic theories to fragments of English (see Chap. 5). It assigns set-theoretic semantic values (sets and functions) to each of the basic expressions of the language and gives rules for combining basic expressions to make more complex expressions, including sentences. The truth conditions of a statement are given by the semantic interpretation of the component expressions together with a definition of satisfaction, i.e. a rule for interpreting the truth-value of the sentence given a model or domain of discourse.

There are many possible semantic theories that a given metasemantics could assign, depending on facts about how speakers use their words and depending on facts about the realities they are talking about. Each semantic theory is a model-theoretic construction that gives its own distinctive assignment of meanings to the words and expressions of the language. An intersectional metasemantics picks out one of these possible semantic theories as the correct interpretation of the sentences and expressions of actual English.

Giving a complete metasemantics would require, among other things, having a complete semantics, which we have not got. It would include an assignment of meaning to every word and every semantically simple expression in the language, as well as telling us what the grammatical rules are and why they are what they are. My goal is much more modest. I want to focus on the metasemantics for the words "woman" and "racism" and indicate how I think the meanings of those words are determined. In the grand tradition of metasemantic theorizing, I will let the metasemantics I propose for that very limited fragment of English be suggestive of a larger, more complete metasemantic theory.[1]

One more preliminary: as I argued in Chap. 6, an intersectional metasemantics should be externalist and does not need to be reductive or naturalistic. This means that unlike many previous attempts to give a metasemantic theory, my metasemantics does not assign a semantic theory on the basis of naturalistic, non-semantic factors. I take it that people's thoughts and speech acts might be relevant for fixing the meanings of words, even when those thoughts and speech acts are presupposed to have semantic contents themselves. What a person means now by a word might be determined in part by what they meant earlier by it, or by the meanings

---

[1] See Fodor (1990) for an example of this methodology.

of other words they use, or by what others in their community say their words mean, or what people said they meant in the past. Meanings are not in the head (Putnam, 1975) because they are partly determined by such external factors. I also think that what a person means now by a word can depend crucially on how they and others in their community would have used the word under different counterfactual circumstances.

This last proposition is of central importance for the metasemantics I am proposing. The meaning determining relation I will argue for crucially involves deference to a counterfactual linguistic community. What a person means when they say "woman" has to do with how they and others would use that expression under circumstances in which misinformation about gender were removed from the social cognitive economy. Likewise, "racism" refers to racism because of how it would be used by the community if misinformation and active ignorance about racism were removed from the social cognitive economy. Roughly, the meanings of "woman" and "racism" (and other politically contested words) are fixed by patterns of usage in nearby possible worlds in which speakers by and large understand and accept the best theory of intersectionality.

10.2.2 Externalism

The word "woman" denotes both cis and trans women, despite the fact that perhaps a majority of the linguistic community think it denotes only cis women. The word "racism" refers to a form of structural oppression, even if the majority of the community does not understand what structural oppression is and thinks "racism" refers to something else. An intersectional metasemantics therefore must be an externalist metasemantics. The meanings of words, especially politically contested ones, must be determined by facts that go beyond individual thought, understanding, or linguistic behavior. Moreover, they must go beyond even what whole communities think, understand, and say, because whole communities can be mistaken in their utterances about gender and racism.

As I explained in Chap. 6, externalism is not a new or contentious view in the philosophy of language. Externalism is widely accepted for terms that refer to natural kinds, such as "water" or "cat" (Putnam, 1975). It is also widely accepted that the linguistic communities a speaker belongs to can play a role in determining what that speaker means by their words for a broad range of expressions (Burge, 1979). Kripke (1980) famously initiated a doctrine on which the referents of names are determined by causal chains that stretch back into history, of which the users of those names may be unaware. This causal theory of names was extended to other parts of speech by Devitt (1981). So there is a long and influential tradition within analytic philosophy of understanding semantics as depending on external factors.

To elaborate a bit more on what externalism is in the present context, think of Ben Shapiro. When Shapiro says that the Obama administration was "racist," he has certain thoughts, beliefs, and strong feelings about what that word means. He has dispositions to use it in certain ways. He has brain states that underlie his thoughts, feelings, and linguistic dispositions. The kind of semantic externalism I am adopting says that none of these properties suffice to determine what Shapiro means when he uses the word "racist." The metasemantic determinants that fix the meaning of the word when he uses it include factors outside of his physical and mental self. This allows us to see Shapiro's uses of "racist" as a form of linguistic hijacking, as attempts to use politically contested terminology to make false assertions that promote misunderstanding and thereby further the interests of dominant groups.

When a transphobic airline attendant insists that a trans woman passenger is a "man," the attendant has certain internal states of his brain and mind that produce this piece of linguistic behavior. He has thoughts, beliefs, and strong feelings about the proper use of this word "man" and strong dispositions to aggressively apply it to trans women. Semantic externalism says that none of these features are sufficient to determine what the flight attendant means by "man." Externalism makes it possible to systematically misapply the term "man," to assert falsehoods about gender in a systematic way that produces active ignorance against trans communities.

The most famous arguments for externalism have relied on thought experiments, such as Putnam's Twin Earth thought experiment and Burge's arthritis man. More recently, Yli-Vakkuri (2018) has argued for semantic externalism on logical grounds that don't appeal to intuitions about thought experiment cases. I take these arguments to lend credence to the externalist metasemantics I am developing.

But my argument for externalism is different from both of these approaches. It is an additional kind of argument. Mine is more like an inference to the best explanation. I argued that we have good reason to accept IMA, and IMA entails that an acceptable metasemantics must render such sentences as "Trans women are men" as false even when many people who assert them believe they are true, are disposed to use the words "women" and "men" in trans exclusionary ways, believe their misuses are true by definition, and where communities of such people corroborate one another's transphobic beliefs and assertions. My argument for externalism is that only an externalist metasemantics can satisfy IMA by rendering these systematic misuses as false, even though all internal indicators within those individuals who misuse them would suggest that they are speaking truly in accord with their own linguistic understanding.

It is one thing to say that we need an externalist metasemantics to satisfy IMA and another to describe one that actually does the trick. What kind of externalism will suffice to satisfy these desiderata?

10.2.3 Deference-Based Metasemantics

Recall in Chap. 2, I described a model of deference-based metasemantics first developed in Anderson (2020). On that model, what a person means is a function of their deference relations to others in their linguistic community. Linguistic deference is a disposition to conform one's linguistic behaviors to those of another person or group. We can imagine that each person has a disposition toward each other person in their community for each word or expression they use that reflects their willingness to adopt that person's usage of that word or expression. On a deference-based metasemantic model, what a speaker means by "woman" or "racist" is determined by patterns of use across their community, not just what is in their own individual mind/brain. This model is inspired by Burge's (1979) argument for social semantic externalism.[2]

I went on to argue (in Chaps. 2 and 3) against a kind of deferential metasemantics on which a group is able to mean whatever they want by a word so long as they form an insular deference network. This kind of deferential metasemantics, which I called the semantic corruption model, postulates that if all of the people who use "men" and "women" in a transexclusionary way defer only to one another and not at all to trans-friendlier communities who use "men" and "women" in a trans-inclusive way, then the trans-exclusionary sub-communities of English speakers can use

---

[2] Note that Burge's picture is anti-reductionist, insofar as deferring to another speaker regarding a word is a matter of using that word with the same *meaning* as that of other speaker. My metasemantics has the same feature. See Greenberg (2014) for discussion of how Burge's social externalism is non-reductive in this way.

"woman" with their own meaning and thereby truly assert that "Trans women are men" in their own language.

The semantic corruption model fails to satisfy IMA. It entails that when certain speakers of English speak the sentence "Trans women are men" it is true. Similar considerations show that on the semantic corruption model, English speakers can truly assert that "Racism against white people is rampant" in virtue of adopting a meaning of "racism" on which this sentence is true. So, insofar as IMA is correct, the semantic corruption model must be rejected.

Similar considerations tell against adopting any metasemantics on which the meaning of a word is determined by how it is used in mainstream discourses such as the media, the law, the government, programs such as domestic abuse shelters, and so on, where the linguistic behaviors enacted by these institutions are theorized as grounding oppressive or exclusionary meanings of words. For example, we should not accept any view where the meaning of "woman" is trans exclusive because of the way "woman" is used in mainstream discourses (see Bettcher, 2013 for an appeal to such a metasemantics). If a metasemantics entails that "Trans women are men" is true in English, even a dialect of English, then that metasemantics should be rejected, for it fails to capture how the regime of truth makes false sentences function as true—in subcommunities of dominant agents as well as within the broader linguistic community—to generate and maintain the matrix of domination.

In order to construct a deferential metasemantics that satisfies IMA, we must theorize a different kind of deference relation. My proposal is to understand the meaning-constituting deference relation as aimed at a merely possible or hypothetical group: the group that uses the words we currently use as part of the best possible theory of the target domain that could be constructed using those words given their history of usage. This deference relation involves deferring to past usage in a sense, because the ideal version of our current language is not a radical departure from past usage. It also involves the communal aspiration to speak our historically given language in a way that would be spoken if the community as a whole knew what it was talking about, how it would speak if it were free of ignorance and misinformation, if it were tracking the important truths that the oppressive regime of truth endeavors to obscure.

The ideal linguistic community for a given domain of discourse understands the reality they are dealing with and speaks according to the best possible theory of that reality. Part of what makes a theory the best theory is that it is true. Another aspect of the best theory is that it systematizes and explains the phenomena in the target domain. Yet another aspect of the best theory is that it is free from misinformation and ideological distortions. So, on the intersectional metasemantics I am proposing, the meanings of "men" and "women" are determined by reference to a merely possible community that uses the words "men" and "women" according to the best possible theory of gender. The meaning of "racist" is given by how the ideal community would understand and talk about racism.

Notice there is a connection between this way of conceiving of natural language semantics and Frege's (1879) way of understanding the semantics of a formally precise language for mathematics. We see our linguistic practices as conforming to a potentially unrealized ideal language, which does the best possible job of expressing the truths of the target domain. But unlike Frege's conception, the intersectional version of ideal language metasemantics is historically situated. The meanings of words are partly tied to historical usage. The idealized version of our language represents the best possible development of our language from where we are at now, our present historical starting point, which might leave us far from the most perfect language imaginable.

The linguistic practices of the ideal community include speech about the meanings of words themselves. Part of what makes "racism" refer to race-based systemic oppression is that, in an ideal version of our historically situated community, people say that "racism" refers to systemic racism. People in the ideal linguistic community say that "women" includes trans women in its extension. This is one way in which the intersectional metasemantics is non-reductive and non-naturalistic. It appeals to what people would meaningfully say about the meanings of the words we use to determine what those words mean. The meanings of gender terms refer in accord with the best intersectional theory of gender because, in the ideal linguistic community, that is how they are understood to refer.

Of course, what the best possible theory of gender is will be a matter of political dispute. Accordingly, the character of the ideal linguistic community will be a matter of political dispute. Trans exclusionary feminists, for example, will think that an ideal linguistic community would not use the word "woman" to refer to trans women (e.g., see Stock, 2018). Trans inclusive feminists think that "woman" should refer to trans women and cis women alike (e.g., see Bettcher, 2013; Jenkins, 2016). On the metasemantic view I am offering this dispute is about the character of the ideal linguistic community. But unlike theorists who see this dispute as concerning what the word "woman" *should* mean, my view entails that this is a dispute about what the word actually *does* mean. The word already means what it should mean, because the meaning of a word as it is now used depends on how it is used in the ideal linguistic community.

There are many details to fill in. How do we defer to a merely possible community? How do we know what a merely possible ideal community would say about racism or gender? Most pressing, why should we believe that transphobic communities would defer to a merely hypothetical community that uses the words "men" and "women" according to an intersectional theory of gender? All of these questions are answered by thinking about how language use aims at truth.

10.2.4 *Deferring to Ideal Linguistic Communities*

David Lewis, in his famous paper "Languages and Language" (Lewis, 1975), argues that truthfulness is the norm that governs our conventional adoption of an abstract language. We coordinate on a way of using sounds and shapes in order to implement a model-theoretic semantics for the purpose of expressing and communicating true propositions. The point of using a language is to create true representations of reality. Although this fundamental purpose can be corrupted for many other purposes—lying, deceiving, and misinforming—the power of language to deceive or misinform is parasitic on its fundamental purpose of communicating truth. It is because language aims at representing truth that it can be misused to transmit falsehood.

We are not free to use words in whatever way we choose because speaking a public natural language is a matter of solving a coordination problem and solving it in accord with the way the language has developed in the past. To use words meaningfully as part of a public language requires using them in a way that is coordinated with others. To say that we coordinate around truthfulness is to say that our efforts to speak the language are aimed at representing reality in tandem with other language users who are constructing the language along with us. Our present coordination is based on the linguistic practices of those who coordinated to construct our language in the past.

Deference is part of this coordination scheme. We defer to one another in order to coordinate on a shared language. But we aren't interested in simply matching our sounds and shapes with those made by our community members—that would create a mad community where people just mimic the sounds and scribbles of their friends. We want to coordinate on the way we use sounds and shapes to represent reality. That means we coordinate semantically, i.e. in ways that can only be described by referring to semantic properties themselves.

We defer to one another in our usage patterns in order to create a stable link between language and reality, one that is reflected not just in private thought but in communal discourse. In the process of coordinating, no one person or group is treated as the ultimate arbiter or authority about the correct way to use a word. We treat some as experts, others as competent guides, and still others as bad guides to how a word should be applied. Being seen as authoritative or reliable is a politically situated matter; politics will affect who is perceived to be a credible guide for representing reality. But as a matter of principle, no person or group is regarded as infallible or as holding absolute authority. This is because any person or any group—even one's own most credible authorities—may be found to use a word or expression in a way that fails to accord with the representational objective of the communal language-construction project. None of us is omniscient about reality, so no one is an infallible guide as to how our words are best used to represent reality.

In effect, as we move around and interact within our linguistic community, each person is generating an internal picture of what they take 'the community' to mean. There is no ultimate or final arbiter of what 'the community' actually means by any expression. If someone is found to deviate strongly from our internal picture of what the linguistic expression means in the public language, we may gently (or forcefully) nudge the speaker to adjust their usage. If many people nudge you in the same direction, you're likely to comply, unless you also have many supporters nudging you in the opposite direction. In this way, our acts of deference and our refusals to defer are practical demonstrations of what we take the community as a whole to mean. They express our beliefs about what the semantic features of the shared language are. Everyone is engaged in this nudging practice and everyone is receptive to correction from the community as a whole, with the crucial caveat that each of us will only receive corrections from someone if we think they know what they are talking about.

But there may be no such thing in actual reality as 'the community,' understood as a unified group coordinated on a single uniform way of using the language. We each imagine it exists and we are nudging one another to conform our usage to it, but the thing we are trying to conform to may be only an imagined ideal. Perhaps the actual community does closely conform to the ideal, but probably it doesn't. In either case, the thing we are striving to conform our usage to, and which we are encouraging and helping our fellow language users to conform to, is an image of a well-constructed community that we imagine or believe to exist. But whether it actually exists doesn't really matter. What matters is that the ideal is guiding our communal practices. We have an evolving coordination scheme that is bringing us into new and improved contact with reality. This process is essentially truth-seeking, as it is essentially guided by the need to construct and share accurate representations of reality.

Our communal practices of deferring and encouraging deference and conformity are aimed at producing conformity to an ideal language-using community, not conformity with our actual practices. The ideal community uses language in a well-coordinated and accurate way to truthfully describe the reality we are engaged in talking about. Our actual community is not well-coordinated and largely not accurate. We are fragmented and contradictory in our usage patterns, riddled with false belief and misinformation. If the actual linguistic community is very far from ideal, then surely our communicative practices aim at conforming to the *ideal* linguistic community, not the shabby, incoherent, and misinformed community we are actually participating in. The ideal community is consistent in usage and understanding, accurate in its beliefs, and circulates nothing but good information about reality. Our deference to that community represents our pursuit of the goal of attaining truth through linguistic representation.

This is true for everyone, regardless of their situated political perspective. Everyone is trying to produce a coherent and accurate linguistic community, regardless of whether you are a racist or an anti-racist, a trans feminist or a transphobe. There are major differences between these groups in terms of how they understand reality, thus they differ dramatically about what they think a coherent and accurate linguistic community looks like. But at the meta-level, everyone who speaks a shared language is engaged in a singular, unified truth-seeking practice. I follow Lewis (1975) in supposing that this is of the essence of what it is to speak a shared language.

Now let us return to the central questions raised at the end of the previous section. How do we defer to a merely possible community? How do we know what such a merely possible community would say about racism or gender? And why should we believe that transphobic communities would defer to a merely hypothetical community that uses the words "men" and "women" according to an intersectional theory of gender?

We defer to a merely possible community by deferring to what we imagine to be our actual community, but which is in fact a hypothetical community—the best, most coherent version of our present community that we can imagine. When one person defers to another, as when a white person defers to a person of color about what counts as "racist," the deferrer takes the deferree to be a good guide to what the ideal community means by "racist." This requires deferring in terms of both linguistic and factual belief. The deferrer takes the deferree to be a guide to what racism in fact is, and also a guide to what the ideal community would say the word "racist" means in accord with the best theory of that reality.

We defer to those we judge to be competent users of the language. But our judgments of competence are thoroughly infused with our judgments about reality. In judging that a person is competent, we judge them to have an accurate view of reality, as we understand reality. This means that our deference is guided in large part by our understanding of non-semantic reality.

As I will argue in the next chapter, our understanding of non-semantic reality is very much influenced by politics and social situation. Accordingly, our judgments of peoples' conceptual and linguistic competence are affected by factors related to social justice and social identity (Anderson, 2017). Thus, our perspective on what an ideal linguistic community would be like, how they would use language, and who is a good guide to follow in establishing a more ideal community, are all socially situated. This explains why different political groups tend to form distinct and mutually antagonistic deference networks, even though—as speakers of a single shared language—they are simultaneously engaged in a cooperative project with all other speakers of their language of arriving at an ideally accurate and coordinated version of their linguistic community. Political divides are concerned with the nature of reality, what should be done, and assessments about who knows what they are talking about, but these divides do not ground distinctive meanings sustained within the mutually antagonistic communities.

White ignorance motivates many people, especially within insular white communities, to insist on inaccurate definitions of racism. Such linguistic communities may strive to create a unified consensus around uses of "racism" that do not refer to systemic oppression, and they may succeed in influencing other groups to conform to their usage patterns. But although such groups might succeed in convincing large swaths of the community to use "racism" in a way that does not accord with our best theory of racism as structural oppression, the intersectional metasemantics renders this as a practice of systematically making and endorsing false statements about racism. This is because actual patterns of misuse, linguistic hijacking, and misinformation do not affect how the ideal linguistic community uses the word "racism." The ideal linguistic community uses "racism" in accord with the best and most accurate theory of racism, on which racism is a form of structural oppression, so the word "racism" refers to a form of structural oppression even if the vast majority of English speakers do not know this and actively resist knowing it.

How do we know what a merely hypothetical ideal community would say about racism and gender? We know what the ideal community would say insofar as we know the truth about racism and gender. The ideal linguistic community is by definition the most accurate in its usage patterns. Therefore, they use the words "racism" and "woman" in the ways that most accurately capture the reality of racism and the reality of gender. The only way for us to know how an ideal community linguistically behaves is to develop true theories of reality and use our language in the most accurate way to describe that reality while expunging misinformation and active ignorance from our linguistic practices. Therefore, part of figuring out how to use words accurately is figuring out what the best theory of reality is and use our words in accord with that theory, because that is what the ideal linguistic community would do, and by identifying and resisting misuses and misinformation that function to prevent the community from accurately representing reality.

Why should we believe that transphobic communities would defer to a merely hypothetical community that uses the words "men" and "women" according to an intersectional theory of gender? This follows from the broader project of language construction. Everyone who speaks the English language, or any shared public language, is invested in creating a coordinated and coherent practice of representing reality accurately (even though languages can be used to do other things such as lie or perform or create poetry or a million other things). In this sense, even the transphobic community is committed to speaking the language of intersectional gender theory insofar as that theory, unbeknownst to them, is the most accurate. This commitment is not realized within the hearts and minds of the transphobic community, but it is given by reality itself as the goal of their linguistic practice. The situation is roughly analogous to the person with COVID-19 who refuses to heed medical experts and doses themselves with hydroxychloroquine. In some sense, they are committed to NOT taking hydroxychloroquine insofar as they are attempting to do what is good for their body, although they whole-heartedly disagree with this assessment. Participating in a linguistic community involves being committed to speaking that language in a way that best represents reality, even and especially when groups within the community disagree about what reality is like.

Transphobic people strongly disagree with trans people about where the English language should be headed. This means that they also disagree about what the word "woman" presently means in English. The reason transphobic people think "woman" refers only to cis woman, and hence would be used to refer only to cis women in the ideal linguistic community, is because transphobic people have false beliefs about the reality of gender. Trans women and transphobic enforcers both want the language to accurately reflect the reality of gender, so they both defer to the ideal community (whatever that might be), which is why both trans friendlier communities and transphobic communities use the word "woman" with the same meaning, despite the fact that they vehemently disagree about what that meaning is.

Yet I contend there is an objective fact about what gender really is. Trans women are women. The ideal linguistic community understands this, and their use of the word "woman" reflects this understanding. Transphobic assertions like "Trans women are men" are therefore false, even though the speakers who assert those statements think they are true, because the transphobic enforcer defers to the ideal linguistic community. But the transphobic enforcer does not know how "woman" is used in the ideal linguistic community because they do not know the truth about gender, so they end up saying false things about trans women.

10.2.5 Languages as Historically Rooted

Someone might have the following worry. What if the ideal linguistic community speaks a completely different language from English? How can we suppose that the semantics for our language is determined by the practices of the ideal linguistic community if the ideal linguistic community might be totally alien and incomprehensible to us? What if they have totally different words? What if their theories of reality are so far advanced beyond ours that we have no idea what they are saying?

In responding to this worry I want to highlight an important sense in which, although I am appealing to the concept of an ideal linguistic community, I am not appealing to an ideal that is totally disconnected from our history or our present state of linguistic usage. I am not saying we defer to an ideal linguistic community which developed in isolation from our own community or which advanced so far beyond us that they are no longer intelligible. I am saying that we defer to a close variant of our actual linguistic community, a community that is similar to our actual community in crucial ways including their ability to speak intelligibly with one another, and also including having our shared history of oppression, domination, and privilege.

The ideal community has many linguistic usage patterns in common with us, but their linguistic practices are informed and coordinated in ways that our actual community is not. The ideal we defer to is not a totally alien far-flung possibility. It is the best version of our community as it currently exists. This allows us to recognize the semantics of our language as historically located and culturally embedded, while at the same time conceiving of it as determined by more accurate usage.

In the past the meanings of words were given according to what was, at that time, the best possible development of their current language. In most instances, except where there are very disruptive or radical changes in the language, the past linguistic community and the present linguistic community defer to the same ideal linguistic community. This is part of the explanation of why people in the past and people in the present speak the same language. We and those who came before us are part of the same project of developing a shared language that we all count as speaking because we are all engaged in developing it into an accurate and coordinated system.

This concept accords with traditional semantic externalism. Consider, for example, Putnam's (1975) argument that English speakers in the seventeenth century referred to H2O with their word "water," when speakers of English didn't know that water was H2O. Their word "water" still referred to H2O without their knowledge. On my view, this semantic fact is explained by the metasemantic fact that, as speakers of a language essentially aimed at coordinating on the best theory of reality, the meaning of their word "water" accorded with the usage patterns of a merely possible community of speakers that spoke their language but was better informed about the nature of water. That "water" referred to water was partly because there was water in their environment and they needed to talk about it, and "water" was the best word to use for it given historically situated patterns of linguistic behavior. Likewise, for Herman Melville's use of the word "fish" when he called whales "fish." What Melville said was false because his word "fish" meant what a better-informed community of English speakers would use "fish" to mean, given the historical patterns of use which existed in Melville's day.

In the past, speakers deferred to their ideal linguistic community, which was a possible development of the communities they occupied at the time. Some of these possibilities became actual. The ideal community Melville deferred to concerning "fish" resembles our current scientifically informed linguistic community, which identifies whales as mammals and denies that they are fish. This is why whales were not in the extension of "fish" as Melville used the word. It's not that Melville's usage was determined by the future, though. If science had never progressed and our current civilization was still confused about whether whales are fish, Melville still would have spoken falsely in the past when he said that whales were fish. In Melville's actual case, however, the future did resemble a more ideal community from his point in history.

At least, so we think. We think we know that whales are not fish. We might be wrong—maybe the idea that whales are mammals is some elaborate hoax created by a secret cabal of cetologists who control the scientific journals, the media, and the government? But probably not. Insofar as we think we now have the correct theory of whales and fish, and insofar as we think our current community is well-coordinated with this fact in terms of its linguistic usage, we are licensed to think of our current community as close to the ideal. At the same time, we are licensed to think of our present-day community as instantiating the ideal that people in Melville's time deferred to. In this way, communities in the past and their relation to communities that presently exist give us a model within the actual timeline of the way in which the ideal community determines the meaning of the actual community at a time. Putnam's case of the word "water" and its meaning in the seventeenth century provides a similar example.

By the same token, in any domain where we think our actual community resembles the ideal, we can take ourselves to be actually speaking the truth about that domain. If you believe as I do that intersectionality theory is roughly correct, then you should also believe that anyone whose assertions accord with that theory speaks truly about things like racism. If you think our best climate science is accurate, then you think people who speak in accord with the theory of human-caused climate change speak truly. Moreover, you should think that evidence in favor of these theories is also evidence in favor of the view that statements of the theory are true.

These may sound like simple truisms, but they are actually important desiderata for a metasemantics to capture. If we think our present-day best theories are accurate, then they had better count as true!

How similar to our actual language does the ideal language have to be in order to count as a version of our historically situated language? I do not have a complete answer to this question. But one necessary condition suggests itself: the language as spoken by the ideal community must be intelligible to actual speakers of the language. The ideal community of twenty-first-century US English speakers must speak a language that actual twenty-first-century US speakers are capable of understanding and speaking themselves. More generally, an ideal version of a historically rooted linguistic community must be similar enough to the actual historically rooted linguistic community as to be able to communicate with speakers of the actual language, albeit a bit differently.

Because the meanings of words are fixed by an idealized version of the linguistic community, it is possible for everyone in the actual community to believe and say something false. There may have been a time when every single person believed that whales were fish. They were all wrong. I also think there may have been a time when everyone believed that women necessarily have uteruses. This would be another example of a time when everyone in the community had a false belief. In the first case, the community probably expressed this false belief by uttering the false sentence: "Whales are fish." In the latter case, they might have said falsely: "Being a woman requires having a uterus." In both cases, the intersectional metasemantics offered here gives a clear explanation of how an entire community could use its words inaccurately and thus say false things.

Because the function of linguistic coordination is to represent reality accurately, we do not need to limit our interpretation of the language to how those in the past understood the meanings of their words, for their understanding of reality may have been limited and consequently their understanding of the meanings of their own words would have been incomplete or inaccurate. Likewise, we may regard many of the definitions in the dictionary—either now or in the past—as false. This is closely connected with the informed speaker constraint. Only the usage patterns of those who are informed about the target domain can be treated as reliable guides to the semantics of the word.

Consider that the word "racist" was employed during the 1970s largely in ways that accorded with the dictionary definition available at the time: "Prejudice, discrimination, or antagonism directed against someone of a different race based on the belief that one's own race is superior."[3] This definition obscures the crucial reality that racism is a form of oppression. Muhammad Ali might have satisfied this 1970s dictionary definition of "racist" by virtue of proclaiming that "the white man is the Devil." According to a more accurate theory of racism, such an attitude (while it might be problematic in some ways) is not racist, because it does not contribute to the oppression of white people. It may even be an anti-racist attitude, insofar as it functioned to promote resistance to white supremacist domination.

Was it true in 1970 to say that Muhammad Ali was "racist," because his attitudes satisfied the dictionary definition in use at the time? According to the intersectional metasemantics developed here, "racist" meant the same thing in 1970 as it does today, because the ideal linguistic community relative to the 1970s means the same thing by "racist" as what it means in the ideal version of our contemporary community, because both our past and present communities were engaged in talking about racism. The ideal linguistic community uses the word "racist" in accord with the best possible theory of racism developed from and intelligible from within our historically situated language. Racism is systemic oppression then, now, and always (and in all possible worlds), and "racism" refers to racism then, now, and in any version of our linguistic community in which "racism" has the semantic function of representing racism. So, it was false in 1970 to say that Muhammad Ali was "racist."

The point extends to contemporary definitions. The definition of "woman" according to Oxford Languages is "adult human female," and the definition of "female" is "of or denoting the sex that can bear offspring or produce eggs, distinguished biologically by the production of gametes (ova) which can be fertilized by male gametes."[4] If the metasemantics on offer here is correct, then given that the ideal community uses "woman" in accord with the best intersectional theory of gender, and given that according to this theory being a woman is not identical with the biological property of belonging to a biologically defined sex that bears offspring or produce eggs, the conjunction of these two definitions is false.

The fact that the word "racism" is used to refer to systemic racism, as opposed to using some other word for racism in the ideal community, is

---

[3] This definition is taken from McWhorter's (2019) "Racist is a Tough Little Word," published in *The Atlantic*.
[4] See Oxford English Dictionary (2020a, 2020b).

because "racism" is the best suited term for referring to this phenomenon among our historically given stock of linguistic representations. Actual attempts to use "racism" to refer to a slightly different phenomenon such as prejudice or race-conscious attitudes that are not essentially connected with systemic oppression deviate from the use of "racism" within the ideal community insofar as those uses promote an inaccurate understanding of the phenomenon of racism (which is a form of systemic oppression). This is why such misuses are false at the actual world. When one says that it is "racist" to implement programs that benefit Black lives specifically or that it is "racist" to say that Black lives matter, one speaks falsely precisely because to use it that way is a way of obscuring or misrepresenting the reality we have a strong pragmatic need to represent, that is, the reality of race-based systemic oppression.

10.2.6 Semantics Guided by Communal Goals

Creating an ideal linguistic community involves creating a community that tracks reality in both epistemically and politically virtuous ways. The character of the ideal linguistic community depends in part on what reality is like, and it also depends on what the community's best interests are. Which aspects of reality should the community be representing, and which of its historically given expressions are ideally suited for representing those aspects of reality given past usage? These pragmatic concerns are given in part by our political and moral convictions, as well as our scientific and logical convictions.

For example, the community of English speakers has a strong interest in representing the natural environment accurately in order to facilitate its survival and flourishing. This includes accurately representing things like the spread of viruses and the effects of human-induced global warming. The pragmatic need requires that we have linguistic representations that enable us to theorize accurately about these phenomena. It also requires that we not engage in linguistic practices that circulate false belief and misinformation about global pandemics and global climate change. In the ideal community, words are applied in such a way that widespread misinformation and ideology is not occurring. The linguistic representational need for eliminating misinformation and ignorance about climate change is partly due to the pragmatic need we have to reform our energy sector and combat the effects of past climate damage.

Note that these are politically contested goals, at least as contested as the facts about climate change are. Depending on who you ask, climate science might be seen as accurate or it might be seen as misinformation, and these views are reliably coordinated with what the critic thinks about the need to reform our practices to combat climate change. On the picture I am defending, there is an objective fact about who is right and who is wrong about what is really happening with the climate and also about what our objective needs as a community are. Accordingly, there is an objective fact about which theories of climate change count as good science and which count as misinformation. These facts are also relevant for determining how the ideal community uses words.

The same goes for representing systemic racism and gender-based oppression. On my view there are objective facts about the existence and material effects of systemic oppression. There are also objective facts about how the community as a whole must act in order to rectify systemic oppression and improve the life chances of people who are marginalized in virtue of interlocking systems of oppression. The pragmatic imperative that the society must address systemic oppression influences what aspects of reality an ideal version of our historically situated linguistic community must have linguistic representations for.

It is because systemic racism exists and because the community has a pragmatic need to recognize and address it that the community has strong need of a word for racism. This is why the ideal version of our linguistic community does have a word for racism. For the same reason, our community has a very pressing need to eliminate misinformation and active ignorance about racism and gender. Hence, the ideal version of our linguistic community is one in which misuses of words like "woman" and "racist"—misuses that function to promote ignorance and misinformation—have been eliminated. The fact that white supremacists and transphobes work to maintain systemic oppression and resist change creates the conditions of struggle required to reach a more equitable and more epistemically virtuous community. An ideal linguistic community has overcome these obstacles to accurate thought and speech. This is closely tied to why "racist" is not ambiguous—more on this shortly.

What our actual moral and political goals should be as a community is a matter of moral and political, as well as scientific, debate.[5] Some white

---

[5] For discussion of the possibility of an empirical science for communal welfare, see Evans (2017).

supremacists want to create a white ethnostate. Does this mean that creating a white ethnostate is part of our shared communal goals? Certainly not. On the view I am defending, there is a slate of real objective facts about what will promote the well-being of the community. Courses of action that cause inequity, injustice, oppression, exploitation, mass suffering, and death are courses of action that we have objective reason to avoid, while courses of action that promote improved life chances, welfare, justice, opportunity, prosperity, and real equality under the law are to be pursued. Political discourse is partly a matter of figuring out which courses of action are good and which are bad.

There will be deep political disagreements about what we should be doing as a civilization. These disagreements will sometimes be over moral principles—should we protect the poor and vulnerable at the expense of the rich? Sometimes they will be disagreements about empirical facts—is climate change occurring and what dangers does it pose to the most vulnerable? But all legitimate political disagreements, those which are not merely ploys to take over or destroy a society but which are engaged in the collective process of steering the ship, have as their telos the pursuit of that which is good for the society as a whole. (This does not entail that everyone is a communitarian; some people think individualism makes for a better society.)

Intersectionality theory has its own telos, its own inherent political aims. Intersectionality is concerned with dismantling systems of oppression and providing justice and opportunity for members of marginalized groups. Any metasemantics worthy of being called an intersectional metasemantics must reflect this telos. The metasemantics developed here builds the political telos of intersectionality into the conditions that affix the meanings of words and the truth conditions of sentences. The function of language is partly to represent reality accurately for the purpose of addressing systemic inequality. Social reality and systems of oppression objectively exist. The intersectional telos guides our community concerning which aspects of social reality need to be represented and for what purposes.

This is not to say that intersectionality stipulates the existence of these purposes. It only identifies them. They are part of objective reality. Intersectionality as a critical theory exists because of the political need to combat oppression, not the other way around. If intersectionality presents reality accurately, including the existence and function of misinformation, then that is the reality we all live in. If the intersectional telos truly does lead to a better society, then it represents our communal goals, regardless of the fact that people have different politically situated opinions about what would make things go best. The ideal linguistic community reflects how we really ought to be thinking and speaking, so if intersectionality is correct, then ideal linguistic practices really do accord with its picture of reality, and this entails that the meanings of our actual words are guided by the pragmatic aims of our best theories of intersectionality.

10.2.7 Ambiguity and Multiple Definitions

It is because racism is a pressing social problem that we as a community need a word for racism. Given our historical usage, the best word for us to use now for racism is "racism." Someone who insists that we should introduce a new term for systemic race-based oppression and reserve the word "racist" for phenomena that include anti-white bias is engaged in a kind of obfuscation. They are promoting misinformation about the nature of racism because the word "racism" has been and continues to be the best potential linguistic tool for representing racism. Because it is the best candidate for representing racism, an ideal version of our linguistic community uses "racism" to refer to racism—that is, race-based structural oppression. Therefore, "racism" actually unambiguously refers to systemic racism. Anyone who proposes a different definition of "racism" that gets the extension wrong in crucial ways engages in a form of active ignorance. That kind of misuse would not be tolerated within the linguistic practices of the ideal linguistic community. Therefore, we should see such uses as false. Wherever "racist" is applied to something outside the extension of the word "racist" as used by the ideal linguistic community, that usage is false.

Someone who proposes that "racist" is ambiguous promotes misinformation. There cannot be two closely related and partially overlapping definitions of "racism" in the ideal linguistic community, one entry for systemic oppression and one that also includes race-conscious discrimination in the absence of oppression, because the second of these would constitute a form of misinformation—obscuring the nature of racism. An ideal linguistic community eliminates all such forms of misinformation. Similar considerations go for all politically contested terms. We are not free to postulate ambiguities where the existence of such ambiguities would promote or enable active ignorance or constitute misinformation given the

correct understanding of the target domain and the community's pragmatic objectives in representing that domain clearly and perspicuously.
That is not to say that politically contested words can never be ambiguous. For example, the word "feminist" is ambiguous between a noun and an adjective. The word "intersectionality" is ambiguous between referring to interlocking systems of oppression and referring to the critical theory that seeks to resist those systems (see Chap. 8 footnote 1). The necessary condition for such ambiguities to exist, on the metasemantics I am sketching, is that the existence of the ambiguity cannot contribute to patterns of misinformation or active ignorance. The ambiguities that are ruled out are those cases in which two or more purportedly distinct semantic meanings overlap to such an extent that one meaning partly obscures or confuses understanding of the word as used to represent the crucial feature of reality that the ideal linguistic community uses that word to represent.

10.2.8 Meaning Change

It is a consequence of the metasemantics on offer that words in the past meant what an ideal community would have used them to mean. In many cases this entails that people in the past used their words to refer to what people now mean by that word. For example, when people talked about "water" four hundred years ago, the meaning of that word as they used it accorded with the best theory of water and so referred to H2O even back then when no one understood that hydrogen and oxygen were the fundamental elements composing it. This is because speakers of English deferred to the ideal version of their linguistic community. That ideal community understood what water is and so used "water" in accord with the best theory of chemistry.

By the same token, when people used the word "woman" four hundred years ago, they meant the same thing as what an ideal version of their linguistic community would have meant by it. An ideal version of their linguistic community would have used "woman" in accord with the best theory of gender, and so the word "woman" included trans women in its extension four hundred years ago.[6] If words always mean what they mean

---

[6] On some views, for example, Butler (1988) and Ásta (2018), gender is constructed in a very historically located way in virtue of the performances or ascriptive practices of the time and place. It's possible, if such a theory of gender is true, that trans women did not exist in the distant past. Even if there were no trans women at the time, the word "woman" could

in an ideal version of our historically situated linguistic community, then how can meanings ever change?

The metasemantics on offer entails that many words are very semantically resilient. Terms have a strong propensity to hold a consistent meaning over time. But it is possible for meanings to change. A change in meaning concerning an expression E—a case in which the semantics of E at time T1 is distinct from its meaning at a later time T2—requires that the ideal version of the linguistic community at T1 would use E with semantics S1 at T1, but the ideal version of the linguistic community at T2 would use E with semantics S2 at T2. When this happens, it is a matter of the actual community adopting a new usage and understanding of E such that the character of the ideal version of that community changes.

Consider the history of the word "girl." According to Oxford Learner's Dictionary (2021), "girl" in Middle English denoted children of both sexes, possibly having been derived from the Low German word *gör*, meaning child. At some later point, the word "girl" shifted to have a connotation of gender such that in contemporary English "girl" refers to children who are of the female gender.[7] If this etymology is correct, then the ideal version (not just the actual version!) of the Middle English linguistic

---

have still referred to trans women in an intensional way. I have restricted attention to extensions for simplicity, but the word "woman" picks out a different extension in each possible world. The word "woman" I claim had trans women in its intension even if in the past there were no trans women. However, I personally believe there were trans women in the distant past.

[7] I should register the following fact about my usage here. On my view, the word "female" is a gendered term—it communicates a relationship with the gender of womanhood. Consequently, its use as a technical term in biology for a certain kind of biological role function is incorrect, this misusage being an effect of the exportation of gender roles onto biological theory. The idea that there are "male" and "female" plants, for example, is not a purely scientific fact, but rather involves the misuse of gender terminology appropriate to human social reality applied as if it were a scientific type. This misusage fuels misinformation about gender insofar as "male" and "female" are purported to pick out biological kinds. Being part of a practice that embodies misinformation and active ignorance about gender, these patterns of usage would not be found in an ideal linguistic community. Therefore, it is false to say of a plant that it is female. Likewise, it is false to say of a dog that it is female, insofar as calling a dog female connotes a gender which the dog lacks. Because "female" is a gender term coextensive with "woman," I think it is correct to say that a woman is an adult human female; ipso facto, it is also correct to say that a trans woman is an adult human female. Thus, I agree with Byrne's (2020) conclusion that women are adult human females but disagree with many aspects of his argumentation, including crucially his belief that trans women are not female.

community applied "girl" indiscriminately to children of any gender. This means either there was a different world for girl, or that children did not have distinctive genders at the time, or that there was no strong political or pragmatic reason for the linguistic community to distinguish between children's genders using the term "girl"; hence, the ideal version of that historically located community would not have used "girl" to make such distinctions. Sometime later, the community began applying the word "girl" exclusively to children of a female gender. It may be that children's gender was only just becoming part of reality, or the reality of children's gender was entering the public consciousness and political discourse, or "girl" took over the function of a different word that had been used to demarcate the genders of children. At the time of this change, representing distinctions between the genders of children became of social or pragmatic significance, for better or worse, and so the character of the ideal version of that linguistic community changed such that it now used "girl" to refer to female children.

It is possible for words to change meanings, but the changes have to be fairly drastic.[8] Since the needs and the reality to be represented are relatively stable, the ideal community does not change its character very easily. Consider what it would now take to shift the word "woman" away from representing women. That would be a scenario in which the community no longer had a social or political need to represent women as such. I can imagine a kind of future where gender is totally eliminated along with the politics of feminism and the cultural imaginary around gender. (I am not saying this would be a good thing!) If such a future occurred, the word "woman" might cease to refer to women.

But there is very little in the way of real politics that is likely to affect the meaning of "woman" on my view. No trans exclusive dictionary, no matter how popular, will make "Trans women are men" true. False assertions that trans women are men will not make "woman" cease referring to trans women, no matter how often they are repeated, so long as a better

---

[8] The metasemantics on offer thus has implications for the view that linguistic expressions have a high degree of semantic plasticity. For example, Williamson's (1994) view of vagueness as ignorance relies on the presupposition that words have highly exact meanings that fluctuate quickly as a result of use, for example, "bald" is constantly changing its meaning in small ways. I do not have a view of the semantics of "bald," but the metasemantics on offer entails that such fluctuations do not occur for "racist," at least not in ways that could have any political consequences. For other discussions of semantic plasticity, see Hawthorne (2006), Williams (2007) and Dorr and Hawthorne (2014).

version of our community would reject those assertions. Even if the entire community were in the grip of a cis-normative ideology, "trans women are men" would still be false, even if everyone asserted it every day, and even if that statement were roundly made to function as true by the social power of the regime of truth. As long as the ideal version of our linguistic community would eliminate such an oppressive ideology and use the word "woman" to pick out the class of people who are actually women, the word "woman" would continue to denote both cis and trans women. I see no reason to think that any amount of cis-supremacist ideology or misinformation would change the character of our ideal linguistic community in a way that would shift the meaning of "woman" as it is actually used. (For related reasons, there simply is no coherent project of socially engineering our usage of "woman" to shift its meaning to include trans women in its extension. It simply already means what it should mean.)

The same goes for "racism." It does not matter how many people might be convinced to adopt a usage of "racism" or "racist" that spreads misinformation and white ignorance about the nature and extent of racism. The word will continue to represent racism so long as it is in the community's best interest to use "racism" to refer to race-based systemic oppression. This is partly a matter of what racism really is and partly a matter of eliminating patterns of linguistic usage that function to obscure its nature from mass public comprehension. The regime of truth operates in such a way as to make false statements about racism function as true, but an adequate intersectional metasemantics represents these statements as false no matter how powerful those false statements become in their function of reproducing the matrix of domination.

10.2.9 Intersectional Reference Magnetism

The approach to metasemantics I have described presupposes certain aspects of reality. For example, it presupposes that racism exists and that the essence of racism is race-based structural oppression. It presupposes that trans women are women. These presuppositions figure in determining what the words "racism" and "woman" mean. It is because race-based structural oppression exists as a salient and important aspect of reality that an ideal version of our linguistic community must have a word that refers to racism. It is because trans women are women that our word "woman" refers to trans women and cis women alike in the ideal linguistic community.

Moreover, these reference relations are partly determined by the way words are actually (not just ideally) used. It is partly because the word "woman" is actually used in connection with gender that it refers to trans women. In a very different possible world, a very different linguistic community might have used the sound "woman" to refer to water. In that world, the ideal version of that linguistic community would not have used "woman" to refer to trans women and cis women alike, because their starting point is so different from ours. There might be other possible worlds in which gender never existed, where there are linguistic communities but no word for women. The intersectional metasemantics I've described presupposes a certain historical starting point, a historically located pattern of usage of a word, and then assigns that word a meaning as a function of the closeness of the actual pattern to a more ideal counterfactual pattern.

This type of metasemantics might be described as a form of reference magnetism (Lewis, 1984; Sider, 2013). Words acquire meanings that are the best candidate meanings for them to have, given local modal facts about linguistic usage and the relation between language and reality. But on this version of reference magnetism, which words are 'magnetized' to which semantic values is not determined according to which semantic values are the most natural or in any other way that abstracts from the politics involved in language use. The kind of reference magnetism I'm describing is one according to which words take on meanings in accord with the political, pragmatic, and epistemic needs of the community at a particular time in history. It is a holistic function that involves external reality, including the existence and nature of the prevailing matrices of domination the linguistic community is facing, which the language must represent, as well as the community's potential knowledge and the ways the regime of truth curtails and subjugates the epistemic powers of its marginalized communities.

Intersectional reference magnetism implies that words used in political discourses are 'magnetized' to have the semantic values they should have in order to accurately represent the nature of social reality and combat the misinformation that feeds into systemic oppression. It implies the kind of externalism I have been advocating that an intersectional metasemantics should have. There may be other theories of intersectional reference magnetism that do not work quite the way I have described here. For example, a theory of intersectional reference magnetism may not have to be a version of ideal language metasemantics. What all versions of intersectional reference magnetism have in common is that politically significant terms refer in accord with our best theory of intersectionality.

10.2.10 Intersectional Metasemantics in Action

Our political arguments can be couched in this metasemantics as debates about reality and the semantic function our words should have in order to best represent that reality, where this semantic function is partly responsive to the pressing moral and political needs of our community and also responsive to our best scientific theories and our philosophical judgments. The semantics of expressions can be understood model-theoretically in terms of truth-conditions that are the same for all users of the language. Debate over relevant features of reality and over what our moral and political objectives should be can thus be seen as answering to objective facts, even when the disputes are intractable due to situated social and political differences of opinion about what is the case and what is to be done about it.

Debates about semantics can take the form of debates about what our words should mean. But these are not necessarily to be understood as proposals for future developments of the language. Rather they can be seen as debates over what our words actually presently mean, where the semantic features of our actual language as it currently exists are determined in part by how we should use words. This captures a certain sense in which the true semantic theory is a normative theory. The norm of communally representing reality entails that our linguistic practices *should* conform to those of an ideal community which is purged of misinformation and active ignorance and which embodies the best theoretical understanding expressible within a language that is an intelligible expansion of our present historically situated linguistic practice, because that ideal community's linguistic practice is the most veridical and practically efficient way of achieving our most pressing goals.

There is an analogy between the correct practice of linguistic interpretation and certain practices involving the interpretation of laws within the US common-law framework. Interpretations of the law are partly seen as a matter of precedent, of how the laws were applied in the past, but interpretation is also sensitive to the usefulness or purpose of the law in promoting the aims of the society. When giving such an interpretation, we do not take ourselves to be stipulating a new meaning for an old law; rather, we see ourselves as interpreting what the law always meant for us. Likewise, linguistic interpretation is a matter of both how words have been used in the past, since adhering to past precedents is necessary for intelligibly speaking a historically rooted language and involves ascertaining what the representational functions of our shared linguistic representations have been, and also of what they are supposed to be doing for us in the future.

On this view, most conceptual engineering projects have nothing to achieve in terms of changing meanings. Interpreting how our linguistic representations should be applied given the furniture of reality and given our representational goals is a matter of ascertaining their *actual* meanings, not a matter of describing merely possible new meanings to assign to those expressions. Revision is therefore always or almost always unnecessary, since our words already mean whatever we think they should be revised to mean. There is still a sense in which conceptual engineering or ameliorative projects are important. They may be seen as attempts to reorganize the episteme to enable wider recognition of the correct way to use a word, to purge misinformation and enable the spread of true beliefs by reconfiguring the episteme and the regime of truth to become a more epistemically virtuous machine. It is not really about engineering or ameliorating a word or a concept, though; it's more about engineering and ameliorating the social fabric.

Intersectional metasemantics helps us characterize the regime of truth and its role in creating and sustaining intersecting systems of oppression. Those systems of oppression require a litany of false statements that are made to function as true, circulating widely and supported by institutions of power; these false statements function as presuppositions within individual psychologies that sustain active ignorance; their spread is coextensive with and facilitated by the spread of misinformation about such things as gender, race, racism, sexism, homophobia, transphobia, ablism, fatphobia, classism, and indefinitely many other aspects of social, political, economic, and physical reality. Opposing these intersecting systems of oppression requires opposing misinformation and active ignorance, addressing epistemic oppression by enabling the epistemic agency of marginalized groups, and spreading true beliefs and good information about the nature and extent of things such as racism and gender.

In summary, the falsity of statements that are made to function as true by the oppressive regime is grounded by the intersectional metasemantics on which the meanings of the words composing those sentences depend on the practices of an ideal hypothetical community. But although it is ideal in a certain sense, the ideal community is not a community which has never experienced or dealt with intersectional oppression. It is the idealized version of our actual historically situated community, a community of English speakers that has a long history of participating in and obscuring the existence of racism, sexism, class-domination, and so on. The ideal linguistic community for our historically located society is one which begins where we are, using the words we have, and then roots out and eliminates active ignorance and misinformation; it consistently deploys language we already understand and which has historical connections to the world in service of an accurate and liberatory representation of intersecting systems of oppression.

10.3 Objections

Objection 1: You say a linguistic community that organizes its linguistic practices to use "racism" as a word for prejudice and not for race-based systemic oppression—call it *the conservative community*—would still refer to race-based systemic oppression, even though that community coherently and consistently refuses to apply the word in accord with the view of racism as systemic oppression, on the grounds that the ideal linguistic community would use "racism" accurately and therefore would apply it to race-based systemic oppression. But why isn't the ideal version of the conservative community one that uses "racism" to refer to prejudice? Why is it any less accurate to have a word that refers to prejudice, rather than systemic racism, given that prejudice is a thing, and given that the conservative community wishes to talk about prejudice using the word "racism"? Why must a community have a word that refers to racism at all if it would prefer to talk about race-based prejudice?

Reply 1: The answer has to do with the historical situatedness of the word "racism" and the role that definitions of "racism" as mere prejudice as opposed to systemic oppression play in propagating white ignorance.

I concede that in the most abstract sense, there is no reason a language must have a word for racism. Abstractly a language can be composed of any words with any meanings. But this level of abstraction erases important details about the historical situation of our actual language, of the centrality of racism within the social fabric and the role that misuses of "racism" play in creating misinformation and false belief about that central organizing force of the social sphere. Racism is a central and crucial aspect of reality that must be recognized and confronted. Any ideal version of our present, historically located linguistic community must be able to clearly and coherently represent it. Attempts to misuse the word "racism" to deflect or undermine our ability to think clearly and accurately about race-based systemic oppression are aligned with white ignorance. They function to spread ignorance about a central aspect of reality. A possible linguistic community cannot be the ideal linguistic community with regard to racism if it facilitates widespread active ignorance about racism.

This is of course a situated perspective and not one that everyone will accept, particularly those who do not believe racism exists or that it features as a central factor in our social and political life that must be addressed. It is, nevertheless, true that racism exists, that it must be remedied, and that therefore an ideal version of our present linguistic community requires an unambiguous name for it.

Objection 2: You claim that racism is a central and crucial aspect of reality that any ideal version of our actual linguistic community must have the means to represent. But that's not something everyone believes. Not everyone thinks that racism exists or that it exists in the way you say it does.

Reply 2: Granted, but the fact that not everyone agrees with me does not mean I am wrong. The truth-conditions of the language fundamentally depend on politically contested realities. This does not entail that truth-conditions are subjective or that there is no objective fact about what the semantics of English really is. My opponent and I may differ in our opinions or in the evidence we have available, but these differences do not entail that racism is not objectively real, nor does it contravene the fact that our community has a strong need to represent it linguistically.

What racism is, the extent to which it orders the social and political sphere, and what must be done in order to promote a more just society are not merely matters of opinion. Consequently, how the ideal linguistic community would deploy its representations is not merely a matter of opinion, even though opinions about how our language should ideally be used are bitterly divided. The fact that someone disagrees with me along predictable political lines does not entail that they are right about reality or the character of the ideal linguistic community, nor does it entail that no one is right.

My opponent and I disagree about the nature of racism, the extent to which it exists in the US, and what is to be done about it. So be it. That is where we are at. What I am saying is, if they are right then racism is not what I thought it was and consequently the ideal linguistic community does not use "racism" as I think it would, i.e. "racist" actually refers to something other than systemic oppression. If I am right, then the ideal linguistic community uses "racism" to refer to systemic racism, and so it actually refers to systemic racism now. I think that we must agree on this abstract characterization, insofar as the truth matters to either of us. Both sides can see the debate this way.

Objection 3: You say that what we mean is a function of what the ideal community means, but what fixes the meaning of words in the ideal community? In the counterfactual world where the English speakers form a perfect version of our community, where do the meanings of words come from? Are they not the best version of their own community, by definition? But then your view entails that the meanings of words in the ideal community are determined by whatever the ideal community itself means by them, but that is circular in a bad way.

Reply 3: The ideal community is a kind of regulative fiction. It provides us with an epistemic guide for interpreting language. It characterizes an ideal for which we strive, which helps guide our linguistic practices, our theory construction and our everyday linguistic interactions. It helps us solve our coordination problems. It provides a conception of truth as a relation between representation and reality which is largely independent of beliefs or practical needs.

The function of the idealized hypothetical community is fulfilled in part because by and large we really believe in the possibility of actualizing it. Moreover, we really can actualize it or approximate it, insofar as our actual community can really be brought closer in line with the practices that we imagine an ideal community should embody. I think we can have good epistemic reasons to believe that an ideal linguistic community would say and believe certain things, insofar as we can have evidence and good reason to believe things about reality and insofar as we can identify ways that language use would provide better or worse representations of that reality. I think we can construct a mathematically precise theory of semantics for the ideal community using the model-theoretic approach. We can describe truth-conditions that hold for all users of the language and thereby conceptualize objective truth-values for statements. And I think we can and should identify the semantic theory of our own home language with that of the ideal community's in the way I've outlined above.

Beyond this, I think we should not expect a further explication of where meanings come from. On my view, there simply is no deep metaphysical explanation of where meanings in the ideal community come from. The felt need to give such a theory is, I think, the result of a mistaken commitment to a reductive naturalistic theory of semantics. It is an inclination to search for something natural and non-semantic to be the source of meaning. Intersectional metasemantics, at least the version I have to offer, does not answer the reductionist's felt need for such an explanation.

I think semantic reality is a kind of virtual reality sustained by our shared interpretive practices. It exists insofar as we act as if it exists and take it to order our thoughts and behaviors in accord with our presuppositions about truth and representation. This is a deep fact about human psychological organization. We rely on presuppositions about the nature of truth, representation, and reality in organizing ourselves, our epistemologies, our lives, and our social structures. The ascription of meanings to sounds and marks and brain states is, at bottom, a kind of interpretive stance. Even our thoughts are part of this virtual reality insofar as our thoughts are interpreted according to a semantic theory.[9] The virtual reality of semantics provides a grid of intelligibility for making sense of human thought and action which is (as far as I can tell) indispensable: given our social and psychological organization, we cannot make sense of thought, speech, and behavior without postulating semantic properties. But this indispensability does not guarantee that we will be able to come up with a satisfying reductive metaphysical explanation of where meanings come from.

[9] This may cause some head-spinning. If interpretations are themselves thoughts or some other kind of semantically interpreted mental state, then to be an interpretation is to represent the world as being some way. For example, a semantic interpretation is a mental state that represents the language as embodying a certain semantic theory. But the mental state itself must have semantic content in order to be an interpretation in this sense. Where does the mental content of the interpretive state come from? On my view, the mental content is part of a semantic theory and so it is an aspect of the virtual reality sustained by our interpretive practice. But the interpretive practice is sustained by the collection of interpretive thoughts. So, the basis on which the virtual reality exists is itself part of that virtual reality. The virtual reality is created by things inside the virtual reality itself. So how does this virtual reality obtain within the physical world, if there is no reductive explanation of where the reality takes hold outside of itself?

In short, my reply is: it's not really part of the physical world as the physical world is usually conceived. When you combine the view that semantics cannot be explained by a reductive naturalistic theory with the thought that all physical things must admit of a reductive, non-semantic explanation for their existence, you reach the conclusion that either semantic properties (including truth) do not exist or else semantic properties are non-physical (or at least not grounded in other physical properties). Since it is incoherent to say that truth does not exist (or at least it's very hard to make sense of that idea), I must conclude that either physicalism is false or that reductive naturalistic explanation is not a precondition for existence in a purely physical universe.

I do think that insofar as we can provide any explanation of where meaning originates within the idealized hypothetical community, that explanation must crucially draw on the actual history of the meanings of words. The meanings of words today depend in part on our deference to earlier linguistic practices, earlier versions of our linguistic community. The meanings of words as used in those earlier communities depended on features of what would have made their linguistic communities more ideal, as well as their deference to still earlier stages of the community. There is a chain of communities stretching back to the beginning, and the result of each later stage in the evolution of meaning partly depended on contingent historically located political and material struggles within the community to change their language in response to their social, political, economic, and virtual environments, including their semantic environments and their conflicting attitudes about which direction they should go in order to realize the ideal version of their historically situated (in the past) linguistic community. These struggles cannot be characterized in a reductive, non-semantic, or apolitical way, for the crucial explanations depend in part on what words meant in the past and on what the regime of truth at the time was doing with those meanings (propagating them, suppressing them, etc.). To give a full explanation of our current linguistic community and its idealized version, then, one would have to retrace all of the political and material struggles involving language, as well as the evolving semantic functions of those words, back thousands of years through who-knows-how-many iterations of non-ideal linguistic communities and their respective ideal-community aspirations.

Perhaps if you could trace this historical evolution of meaning back to the very beginning, you would find a point at which meaning originated from non-semantic properties in very simple cases. Maybe in that first case one cave person tried to convince another that this sound *blargh!* means *tiger right behind you!* Perhaps that sentential meaning was the first semantic property.[10] But at each stage, even this first stage, you would have to appeal to the ideal hypothetical community at that stage to explain what

---

[10] Probably not, though. I assume the origin of representation goes back further than the origin of public language. See Burge (2010) for an extensive philosophical and empirical defense of the view that objective representation exists in non-linguistic animals and thus presumably existed in our pre-human ancestors before the advent of language. Even in these cases, I think our understanding of the semantic contents of non- or pre-linguistic mental representation—in the animal world, including our own deep history as a species, as well as in pre-linguistic infants—proceeds via a kind of idealized interpretive practice that does not

the semantics of the language was. In the caveperson case, it would be an ideal caveperson community which is organized to use *blargh!* to mean *tiger right behind you!*

Objection 4: Your view depends heavily on the nature or character of reality. For example, you say that "racism" refers to structural oppression because structural oppression exists in reality and because our society has a vested interest in eradicating racism. But to say that racism really exists, you must first give us a theory of truth. You can't begin with reality and then give a theory of truth, for we must presuppose that your theory of reality is true.

Reply 4: This is another deep issue in the metaphysics of truth and realism. This kind of objection has been raised by a number of authors whose aim is to shake our conception of reality by highlighting our befuddlement about the nature of truth and representation.[11] I cannot fully address this worry, but I have something to say about how I think the response might go, and my answer helps to illuminate the methodology behind my approach to intersectional metasemantics.

I think we cannot neatly separate out our commitment to a theory of truth from our commitments to reality itself as we understand it. This is the sense in which my metasemantics is aligned with Quine's methodology; although I don't think he would agree with much of what I am proposing, it is Quinean in spirit. We have no guide to truth other than that which guides our understanding of reality. We cannot look for analytic truths that are known independently of our epistemic reasons for holding our first-order beliefs. In order to give a theory of truth, we must first have some ideas about what reality is like. We find that reality contains things and people and also the brains, models, and languages we use to tell each other what we think reality contains. As we gain evidence about the nature and extent of reality, including the brains, models, and languages located inside it, we are able to articulate theories of things like how our brains related to reality, how language encodes information, and so on. In order to understand truth in a natural language, then we must do a lot of science of the world around us.

necessarily admit of a reductive metaphysical explanation to neural states or molecules inside neurons or anything like that.

[11] For examples of this tradition, see Rorty (1979), Putnam (1981), Taylor (2006), and Button (2013). For a realist reply to these kinds of worries, see Devitt (1997).

Exactly the same thing is true for understanding the representational relationship between language and politically contested realities such as the nature and extent of racism or the legitimacy of trans gender identities. Insofar as we are able to ascertain the semantic features of our linguistic expressions "racist" and "woman," our ability is grounded in our ever-increasing understanding of the things those words refer to as they exist in reality and our relationship with their objective existence as a community of language users trying to understand themselves, their environment, and their place in it. These are big questions and the answers are hotly debated. The metasemantics I've sketched gives a way of thinking about the answers and their relation to semantics as part of an objective reality, no matter how heated the debate gets and no matter how much misinformation permeates the social fabric.

10.4 Truth, Democracy, and Epistemic Violence

A fascist in the mold of Hitler recognizes that mass interest in ascertaining the truth is antagonistic to the aim of destroying one's political opponents. Hitler (1939) wrote, "It is the responsibility of propaganda to emphasize exclusively the one cause it represents and not to evaluate other causes. It must not objectively explore any truth that favors the other side or fairly weigh the options ... It must not argue matters based on theoretical rules of justice. Propaganda must constantly endeavor to present only the aspect of the truth that is favorable to its own side."[12] Such a fascist sees the role of propaganda as unifying the masses in ideological objectives while preventing them from having any interest in finding the truth. The power of propaganda consists in its ability to divest people of any interest in sincere debate or inquiry.[13]

Intersectionality is not propaganda. It is a truth-seeking philosophy which aims to uncover the truth and hold it up to the public in the face of the overwhelming power to obscure truth that is vested in the white supremacist, capitalist, patriarchal regime of truth. The theory of intersectionality must encompass a theory of objective truth that places truth at the center of discourse, including the kinds of vibrant debates and academic discourses which are necessary to articulate the truth, to see it from

---

[12] *Mein Kampf*, chapter 6, "War Propaganda." It should be noted that *Mein Kampf* is itself fascist propaganda; hence, the veracity of the text is questionable.

[13] For a contrasting view of propaganda, see Stanley (2015).

all sides, and to strategically address the kinds of disinformation and ignorance that might be mustered against it. It must simultaneously identify and counter sources of misinformation. It must do this while authoritative voices call it propaganda, allege that it imposes ignorance and dogmatism of its followers, and paint it as if it were part of an oppressive regime of truth (one aimed at oppressing those who are in fact members of dominant groups).

The intersectional metasemantics I've just given is designed to explain how objective truth is possible in political struggle. It is meant to orient social justice movements within the post-structuralist landscape in order to claim the power of objective truth. We can conceive of political arguments as first-order disputes about the nature of things like racism and gender, rather than rendering them as semantic disputes. Intersectional metasemantics shows us how these disputes interface with empirical evidence and helps explain why obtaining the truth is relevant for political action. Only by seeing political disputes as substantive in this way can they be given their proper weight within the democratic space of reasons.

Lastly, the intersectional metasemantics provides a way of thinking about misinformation as a form of epistemic violence. Political discourses are situated within an objective reality characterized by social power. Linguistic hijackings, controlling images, and controlling propositions are false, are a source of misinformation, and function to obscure reality in ways that sustain the prevailing system of oppression. The harm that comes from misinformation is epistemological, material, and psychological all at the same time. It is not simple, or even theoretically important, to tease apart which harms of misinformation are epistemological, which are social, which are ethical, and which are physical, in part because these dimensions of human life are very much intertwined in the social epistemic sphere.

The metasemantics developed here allows us to take stock of these issues from a perspective that recognizes an objective truth about these social realities, while maintaining that our view of that truth may be conditioned by our social and political situatedness. Not every true belief about the social fabric will be acceptable or seem justified to all participants. Nevertheless, there are objective facts about who is justified and who has knowledge. These will be the themes of the final chapter.

References

Anderson, D. E. (2017). Conceptual Competence Injustice. *Social Epistemology*, *31*(2), 210–223.

Anderson, D. E. (2020). Linguistic Hijacking. *Feminist Philosophy Quarterly*, *6*(3). https://doi.org/10.5206/fpq/2020.3.8162

Ásta. (2018). *Categories We Live By: The Construction of Sex, Gender, Race, and Other Social Categories*. Oxford University Press.

Bettcher, T. M. (2013). Trans Women and the Meaning of 'Woman'. In The Philosophy of Sex: Contemporary Readings Sixth Addition. Eds. Power, Nicholas, Raja Halwani, and Alan Soble. 2012. pp. 233–250.

Burge, T. (1979). Individualism and the Mental. *Midwest Studies in Philosophy*, *4*, 73–121.

Burge, T. (2010). *Origins of Objectivity*. Oxford University Press.

Butler, J. (1988). Performative Acts and Gender Constitution: An Essay in Phenomenology and Feminist Theory. *Theatre Journal*, *40*(4), 519–531.

Button, T. (2013). *The Limits of Realism*. Oxford University Press.

Byrne, A. (2020). Are Women Adult Human Females? *Philosophical Studies*, *177*, 1–21.

Collins, P. H. (2002). *Black Feminist Thought: Knowledge, Consciousness, and the Politics of Empowerment*. Routledge.

Devitt, M. (1981). Designation. New York: Columbia University Press.

Devitt, M. (1997). *Realism and Truth*. Princeton University Press.

Dorr, C., & Hawthorne, J. (2014). Semantic Plasticity and Speech Reports. *Philosophical Review*, *123*(3), 281–338.

Evans, J. (2017). A Working Definition of Moral Progress. *Ethical Theory and Moral Practice*, *20*(1), 75–92.

Fodor, J. A. (1990). *A Theory of Content and Other Essays*. The MIT Press.

Foucault, M. (1980). *Power/Knowledge: Selected Interviews and Other Writings, 1972–1977*. Vintage.

Frege, G. (1879). Begriffsschrift, Concept Script, a Formal Language of Pure Thought Modelled Upon that of Arithmetic. Translated by S. Bauer-Mengelberg in J. van Heijenoort (ed.), From Frege to Gödel: A Source Book in Mathematical Logic, 1879–1931, Cambridge, MA: Harvard University Press, 1967.

Greenberg, M. (2014). Troubles for Content I. In *Metasemantics: New Essays on the Foundations of Meaning* (pp. 147–168). OUP.

Hawthorne, J. (2006). 10. Epistemicism and Semantic Plasticity. In *Oxford Studies in Metaphysics Volume 2* (p. 289). Oxford University Press; 1st edition (June 1, 2006).

Hitler, A. (1939). *Mein Kampf* (J. V. Murphy, Trans.). London: Hurst and Blackett.

Jenkins, K. (2016). Amelioration and Inclusion: Gender Identity and the Concept of Woman. *Ethics, 126*(2), 394–421.
Kripke, S. (1980). *Naming and Necessity*. Wiley-Blackwell; 1st edition (July 23, 1981)
Lewis, D. (1975). *Languages and Language*.
Lewis, D. (1984). Putnam's Paradox. *Australasian Journal of Philosophy, 62*(3), 221–236.
McWhorter, J. (2019, July 24). Racist is a Tough Little Word. *The Atlantic*.
Oxford English Dictionary. (2020a, December). female, n. OED Online. Oxford University Press. Oed.com.
Oxford English Dictionary. (2020b, December). woman, n. OED Online. Oxford University Press. Oed.com.
Oxford Learner's Dictionary. (2021, January). girl. n. Oxford University Press. https://www.oxfordlearnersdictionaries.com/us/definition/english/girl
Putnam, H. (1975). The Meaning of 'Meaning'. Language, mind, and knowledge. Minnesota studies in the philosophy of science, Volume 7 (1975), page 131–193.
Putnam, H. (1981). *Reason, Truth and History* (Vol. 3). Cambridge University Press.
Rorty, R. (1979/2009). *Philosophy and the Mirror of Nature* (Vol. 81). Princeton University Press.
Sider, T. (2013). *Writing the Book of the World*. OUP.
Stanley, J. (2015). *How Propaganda Works*. Princeton University Press.
Stock, K. (2018). Open Future—Changing the Concept of "Woman" Will Cause Unintended Harms. Economist.com. https://www.economist.com/open-future/2018/07/06/changing-the-concept-of-woman-will-cause-unintended-harms
Taylor, B. (2006). *Models, Truth, and Realism*. Oxford University Press on Demand.
Williams, J. R. G. (2007). Eligibility and Inscrutability. *The Philosophical Review, 116*(3), 361–399.
Williamson, T. (1994/2002). *Vagueness*. Routledge.
Yli-Vakkuri, J. (2018). Semantic Externalism without Thought Experiments. *Analysis, 78*(1), 81–89.

CHAPTER 11

Situated Knowledge and the Regime of Truth

11.1 OVERVIEW

This chapter turns to the question of knowledge. How can anyone know anything within a social and political climate that is riddled with misinformation, in which one's social and political alignment and social identity strongly affect what one is likely to believe, and in which even our conceptions of rationality, good evidence, and truth itself are conditioned by political factors?

The misinformation age is characterized by echo chambers and deference networks that function to reinforce situated worldviews that are out of touch with reality. Each political faction has its own basis for justifying its worldview, and we may suppose that each faction does a half-decent job of constructing its own justifications such that, by its own lights, people should believe in accordance with its worldview. How can anyone be objectively justified in believing that they have an accurate worldview when we see these opposing worldviews have their own internal logic of justification, such that if you belonged to that group you would adopt their worldview and take yourself to be justified? How do we know our own worldview is not the one in the grip of misinformation and ideology?

I think we can make use of an understanding of reason and evidence on which some groups have an objectively better claim to knowledge than others, even when each group appears to be justified to those who belong

© The Author(s), under exclusive license to Springer Nature Switzerland AG 2021
D. E. Anderson, *Metasemantics and Intersectionality in the Misinformation Age*,
https://Doi.org/10.1007/978-3-030-73339-1_11

to it. Specifically, I will argue that oppressed groups have more accurate knowledge of oppression than dominant groups, even though the status of that knowledge is bitterly contested and beset with active ignorance and misinformation.[1] This can be true even if members of dominantly situated groups cannot be rationally compelled to abandon their inaccurate worldviews. There's no guarantee that if a person is rational and good-hearted that they will be able to know what is really going on, because they may be trapped inside a social epistemic bubble sustained by the oppressive regime of truth that prevents them and everyone they trust from understanding reality.

Up to this point, the book has dealt primarily with the concept of truth and its relation to political struggle. I have described a theory on which truth is an objective part of reality—specifically, an objective property of the sentences that belong to our shared language—even within a linguistic community that is deeply torn and divided over politics, even when that community believes different things and accepts conflicting sources of evidence as reliable, even when misinformation and active ignorance pervade the social fabric, even when biased social and political powers infuse the institutions that circulate and legitimize statements as true or false.

The epistemology sketched in this chapter is an extension of the intersectional theory of truth. There is an objective truth about reality. This reality includes things like the nature and extent of racism and sexism and the ways in which these forms of oppression intersect and co-constitute one another. Reality also includes facts about who knows what is going on with these intersecting systems of oppression and who is ignorant, who understands the nature of oppression and who does not, what counts as misinformation about oppression, which practices constitute active ignorance, and what the really good evidence is. Both reality itself and the epistemic factors that enable us to know reality are politically contested, but just as with truth itself, the fact that the epistemological situation is under dispute does not entail that there is no objective fact of the matter. Some people really know what's going on and some people really don't, even though everyone thinks they know what's going on.

---

[1] The epistemology I am developing here is influenced by accounts of situated knowledge and standpoint theory; see Matsuda (1987), Roberts (1991), Harding (1992), Scheman (1995), Code (2012), Pohlhaus Jr (2012), and especially Collins's (2002) chapter Black Feminist Epistemology. Lastly, my ideas are strongly informed by Dotson's (2014, 2018) theories of epistemic oppression and epistemic power.

The aim of this chapter is to articulate a theory of situated knowledge that comports with the intersectional metasemantics sketched in the previous chapter. Section 11.2 lays out some general features of the intersectional epistemology and argues that the concepts of objective truth and rationality should play a crucial role. Section 11.3 describes how knowledge of intersectionality is both situated and objective and describes how epistemic oppression and active ignorance contribute to the perpetuation of the matrix of domination.

11.2 Truth, Knowledge, and Objectivity in Intersectional Epistemology

This section articulates some of the relationships between epistemological concepts including truth, knowledge, evidence, rationality, and objectivity within an intersectional approach to epistemology. These concepts as I think about them are broadly speaking part of what might be called traditional analytic epistemology, traditional in the sense that the concepts and their relationships will be familiar to students of analytic epistemology. Here I argue that traditional analytic epistemology can be an important contribution to an intersectional epistemology. My aim is also to explain how intersectional critical theory fits into and properly informs analytic epistemology.

Truth is not the same thing as knowledge. Truth goes beyond what is known. Truth might even go beyond what can be known. The concept of truth and its role within our cognitive economy is essentially tied to its ability to mark off sentences as having a special representational connection with reality that does not depend essentially on whether anyone knows or believes they are true. Truth is not dependent on political faction or social identity. It is not relative to persons or cultures.

The intersectional metasemantics of Chap. 10 satisfies this condition on truth. Truth in English is determined in part by the linguistic practices of an ideal version of the English linguistic community and in part by reality itself—that which does not depend on linguistic convention. The idealized version of our current linguistic practices determines the semantics of our actual language, including the truth-conditions of our sentences. The truth or falsity of these sentences depends on both their semantic properties—most importantly their truth conditions—and facts about reality that are independent of linguistic convention, although these cannot necessarily be teased apart insofar as we cannot ascertain the meanings of words independent of making our first-order judgments about reality.

Most cases of knowledge involve true justified belief.[2] In all but a few special cases, S knows that P if and only if S believes that P, P is true, and S is justified in believing P. Truth, belief, and justification are conceptually and metaphysically distinct. Something's being true does not entail that anyone believes it, or that anyone is justified in believing it. Believing something does not entail that it is true, nor does it entail that one is justified. Being justified in believing P does not entail P is true. Moreover, you could be justified in believing P without actually believing P; for example, if you have decisive evidence for P but refuse to believe it. Again, the intersectional metasemantics satisfies this picture of knowledge. Truth, belief, and justification are all distinct.[3]

The picture of justification and rationality I offer here comports in broad strokes with the traditional analytic philosopher's conceptions of justification and rationality. Sources of justification include observations, measurements, experiences, testimony, good reasoning, intuitions, proofs, and anything that counts as evidence. We can call these *epistemic reasons.* Whatever kind of thing can metaphysically justify a belief is an epistemic reason to hold that belief. Justified beliefs are held for good epistemic reasons. Whether something is a good epistemic reason for a given proposition P is an objective fact.

Whether a person takes something to be a good reason to believe that P depends partly on the person's background beliefs and overall cognitive organization. Due to politically situated differences in access to and appreciation of evidence, there will be differences in belief about what

---

[2] The caveat "most" is due to the very famous and influential Gettier (1963) argument that true, justified belief is not sufficient for knowledge.

[3] Code (2012) and Scheman (1995) raise important worries about S-knows-that-P epistemology and what Code calls 'generic man' epistemology. These worries are centered on the fact that genericity tends to track with the mythical norm. Epistemology that focuses on fully abstract agents, which does not make any reference to contingent social realities, tends to leave subjugated knowledge out of the conversation, especially subjugated knowledge that indicts the practices of S-knows-that-P epistemology on sociological grounds. My response to these worries is to proceed along the lines Scheman (1995) suggests when she points out, for example, that an answer to the Gettier problem must depend on situated perspectives about what counts as justification and what count as cases of knowledge. I believe these terms must be understood in accord with our best theories of intersectionality. In fact, on my view the language of epistemology itself—"rational", "evidence", "belief", and so on—is subject to the Intersectional Metasemantic Adequacy constraint.

propositions are supported by good evidence. Detractors of intersectionality tend to portray it as based on wishful thinking, or as a result of the will to power or so-called victimhood mentality, or on the basis of lies, rather than on good evidence. On the epistemology I defend here, these detractors are objectively wrong. There are facts about which political factions actually have objectively good epistemic reasons in support of their worldviews and which don't. Opponents of intersectionality are in the grip of misinformation. Intersectionality theory, on the other hand, is supported by objectively good epistemic reasons.

A belief is *rational* insofar as it is properly responsive to good epistemic reasons and irrational otherwise.[4] Only rational beliefs can be justified. Responding irrationally to good evidence undermines your justification even if it produces a true belief. But not all rational beliefs are justified. Specifically, if you base your conclusions on faulty evidence, then even though you have made a rational inference your belief can be unjustified on this basis. A person can rationally come to believe a falsehood if they are fed misinformation by sources they trust.

Unfortunately, active ignorance plays on this possibility. White ignorance, for example, crafts misinformation precisely so that rational white people can be made to believe false propositions about race and racism, which are made to function as true by the regime of truth in order to undergird the matrix of domination. It is rational for you to believe what the president of the US says when all of your most trusted sources assure you that the president knows what he is talking about, and yet the president may in objective reality be a liar and a bullshitter and a defender of white supremacist ideology.

When the social fabric is saturated with misinformation, and when this misinformation comes through trusted sources, people are put in a very difficult position. A human being must trust others in order to be a

---

[4] Rationality can be formally modeled, where this typically involves using probability theory and other mathematical tools to define rational and irrational inferences; being disposed to make rational inferences and avoid irrational inferences is what it is to be properly responsive to good epistemic reasons. Modeling rationality using mathematical tools is the domain of formal epistemology. However, I want to also flag that the word "rationality" has been coded language for a long time, used to represent women and Indigenous people as irrational and epistemically less virtuous than white men. Whether it is a good plan to go on using "rationality" to demarcate and epistemic virtue—and hence determining what it means to be rational—is up for debate in the present context. My mission here is to highlight the concept's good aspects, its potential for strengthening the intersectional perspective, and thus present an argument that the concept of rationality can be part of an empowering intersectional epistemology.

functioning epistemic agent. We also must decide who to trust on the basis of the information we have available. If we base our decisions about what sources of evidence to trust on misinformation, then we can be rationally led to form false beliefs. Part of the effectiveness of an oppressive regime of truth is that it subsists within trusted communities. It shapes who we trust and mistrust.

Moreover, our social epistemic relationships shape our attitudes toward epistemic practices. Science denialism is a social activity. Is science denialism irrational? From a certain perspective, that of the person who recognizes the epistemic value of science, it is definitely irrational to ignore and demonize science. Scientific practices are our best source of information about the natural and social world. If you believe this, then science denialism is irrational. You divest yourself of a crucial source of information. But what about people who believe that science consistently misinforms us and who are constantly reinforced in this belief by everyone they trust and love? Is it irrational for these people to deny that science is a source of knowledge? I grant that the belief is false and unjustified, but it may still be rational if it is supported by one's social epistemic network. We rely deeply on our social fabric for epistemic calibration. To imagine that we can rationally discard the epistemic principles embodied within our network of trusted epistemic sources is to apply an ideal, solipsistic epistemology that has little to do with actual human cognition, which is inherently social.

Echo chambers are not irrational. What is irrational is trusting people who have, from your point of view, deeply mistaken cognitions about reality supported by misleading epistemic principles. We cannot expect our political opponents to trust our information or our epistemic procedures, even if our information is objectively good and our procedures supply objective justification, precisely because they take us to be in the grip of misinformation and ignorance.

Can echo chambers and epistemic tribalism be addressed through the kinds of advice you sometimes find in critical thinking textbooks? We can teach people to identify fallacies, to check sources, consider possible biases, base beliefs on established facts rather than opinions, and so on. I do not believe, even if everyone had these skills, that it would end the spread of misinformation. There are very intelligent people with good educations in critical thinking who nevertheless believe and propagate misinformation. Partly this may be a matter of the selective applications of those skills in the service of supporting one's worldview. Typically, people will spend a great deal of effort to search for explanations and arguments that support what they deeply believe. They will expend mental energy, time, and bandwidth to combat the views and arguments of people they disagree with. Critical thinking skills are useful for all of these ends, even when they are pursued in biased ways based on misinformation. While critical thinking has the potential to dispel misinformation, simply teaching people critical thinking or insisting that they use it will not correct the much deeper problem of politically situated misinformation and misconception.

Part of my project is to defend the idea that traditional analytic epistemology can be fruitfully merged with an intersectional theory of truth for epistemic language. We cannot stem the flow of misinformation through the application of abstract epistemological concepts alone, because misinformation is a sociological problem. Misinformation requires a social engineering solution. It requires understanding how misinformation flows from power and how power stifles and discredits sources of good information. Then it requires intervening in those power dynamics. But this project may still be aided through the application of abstract analytic epistemology concepts.

How do we socially engineer a solution to the problem of misinformation? The solution I propose requires focusing on epistemic power. Epistemic power, according to Dotson (2018), is a kind of systemically imparted positive epistemic status that gives its beneficiaries greater standing and authority to adjudicate truth from falsehood. An oppressive regime of truth perpetuates epistemic oppression insofar as it systematically divests marginalized groups of epistemic power. It preserves the status quo, the matrix of domination in its present configuration, by stifling the epistemic agency of the marginalized groups working to dismantle it. It reinforces the epistemic power of dominant groups to make statements function as true that support the prevailing matrix of domination, including statements about who knows what, about who is rational, about whose experiences are veridical and what information should inform political action. This happens at the personal level in classrooms and at conferences, in public debates and in politics, at dining room tables and at high-school lockers. It also happens at the theoretical level whenever situated knowledge is attacked on the grounds that it is not objective or fully rational.

The best way to stem the flow of misinformation and improve our chances as a society of achieving both truth and justice through our discourses is to check the epistemic power of dominant groups and increase the epistemic power of marginalized groups. This cannot be done in a merely theoretical way. It must be accomplished through altering the social fabric in order to invest marginalized groups with greater epistemic power. But we also need good epistemology in service of this social engineering project. We need an epistemology on which knowledge of intersectionality is subjected to power but also objectively accurate. Intersectionality can and should embrace objectivity. As Patricia Hill Collins (1998) argues, Black feminist theory is not compatible with a post-structuralist rejection of objectivity because Black feminism entails that it is objectively true that intersecting oppressions exist and that Black women know about them.[5]

While the regime of truth does undergird oppressive power structures, it is also a potential source of power for marginalized groups. Intersectionality should not necessarily oppose the conceptual structures involved in conferring epistemic power on dominant groups. Rather, those conceptual structures might be better reinterpreted and redirected to provide marginalized groups with more epistemic power. This requires understanding the epistemic framework of objective truth, objective evidence, and objective rationality in a way that supports the situated knowledge and epistemic authority of marginalized groups.

11.3 Situated Knowledge, Situated Ignorance, and Epistemic Oppression

This section outlines a number of ways in which social situation, social identity, and politics can shape what one knows and what one is ignorant of, and the ways in which the regime of truth distributes epistemic power to the benefit of dominant groups and furthers the subjugation of marginalized groups. All of these cases depend upon a concept of truth, justification, and objectivity on which there is an objective fact about what is really true and who is really justified, but in which socially situated misinformation and active ignorance produce false beliefs.

The theoretical perspectives developed here about situated knowledge are meant to serve the pragmatic social engineering goal of checking dominant epistemic power and amplifying the epistemic power of marginalized groups to produce and distribute knowledge of intersectionality. They are meant to serve this goal in two ways. First, they are meant to help clarify social epistemic issues among friends and allies of intersectionality. They

[5] See Collins (1998), chapter 4.

are meant to explain how intersectional epistemology might be conceived within an analytic philosophy framework, with the goal of illuminating our social epistemic situation, among friends. Second, they are meant to operate as strategic elements in the discourse, engaging with political opponents of intersectionality. They are developed to confront dominant epistemic power on its own turf, using its own concepts, to defeat arguments against intersectionality couched in the language of analytic philosophy.

As with the theory of intersectionality I gave in Chap. 8, I do not mean for these epistemic considerations to be apodictic or to be taken in the spirit of The One True Epistemology.

11.3.1 Situated Linguistic Understanding

Understanding a language involves understanding (at least tacitly) the conventions of a community. One learns a language by deferring to those who speak it and adjusting one's personal usage patterns accordingly. Being part of a community gives relatively immediate access to that community's language, while being an outsider limits one's comprehension of what can be expressed using that language. Outsiders become insiders through deference and integration, matching one's patterns of speech and thought to the representational properties of the shared linguistic medium under development. This does not require adopting a community's beliefs, only its modes of representation, its semantics.

Burge (1979, 1982, 1986) argues that this kind of social externalism is an implicit commitment of traditional analytic epistemology. Acquiring concepts and learning a language both involve deference. As I argued in Chap. 10, the semantic values of the words and concepts themselves are determined via deference to an idealized community. But the process of forming our own beliefs about the correct application of words—our own image of what the idealized community would say—is driven by our actual interactions with people and groups we live among. We may or may not come to have an accurate understanding of the meanings of the words of our public language. It is possible to acquire a misunderstanding of the meaning of "woman," for example, especially if one acquires one's pattern of usage from a community that believes falsely that gender is biological.

Our judgments about who is competent with their words, about who knows what they are talking about, are situated in an important way. Social situation conditions our ability to speak accurately and understand the language by conditioning our judgments of who knows what they are talking about, as well as conditioning our understanding of the representational purposes for which the language is being developed. If I am part of a community that understands gender as biological, then it will be more difficult for me to learn the real meaning of "woman," as compared to if I grew up in or became part of a trans friendlier community with a more accurate view of gender.

Concept acquisition is relatively simple, if concept acquisition means gaining the ability to think and speak using the semantic properties of a word. A child who can ask, "what is racism?" already has the concept of racism in this sense, because they can use the word "racism" to refer to racism. Otherwise, they could not use it to ask for information about racism. We imbibe the concepts of our community in this sense without effort, as a natural consequence of speaking the shared language.

Things are more difficult when it comes to actually understanding the meaning of a word such that one can use it accurately. If one is not a member of a community that knows what racism is, then one will not have good guides as to how to apply the word "racism" or to understand what it means. In that case, one must make a concerted effort to think and talk in accord with members of a community one does not belong to, a community that does understand what racism is. Things are especially difficult if one is politically opposed to the community in question and unwilling to conform to its thought patterns. In that case, it is highly unlikely that the outsider will be able to think and speak as members of the community do. They still have the ability to think and talk *about racism*, albeit falsely, by using the word "racism," but they will have difficulty understanding what it means. Getting out of that predicament is very difficult.

Take a white man who is highly antagonized by intersectionality, trans feminism, and anti-racist thought. In order to understand what "woman" or "racism" means, that man will have to conform his thought and linguistic practices to those of the community who understands what gender and racism actually are. But this man does not agree that the critical intersectionality community knows what they are talking about. His skepticism aligns with his political commitments which are in support of the status quo and resistant to any radical trans feminist or anti-racist changes to the social fabric. This man will therefore be actively resistant to understanding the meaning of "woman" or "racism."

The situation is one in which the man is objectively and actively ignorant about the real meanings of those words. He may even work to attack and destabilize communities that use the words "woman" and "racism" to make true statements about women and racism, believing whole-heartedly that those communities speak falsely when they say that trans women are women and that racism against white people is impossible. He may even be acting rationally insofar as his worldview has been confirmed over and over by everyone and everything he trusts as a source of evidence. But this man's views are objectively false, he is misinformed, and his efforts constitute epistemic oppression and violence against trans communities and communities of color.

Of course, the situation he *believes* he's in is one in which he understands the meanings of "woman" and "racism" correctly and the intersectional feminist does not. He falsely believes that feminism and anti-racism promote injustice. This is why intersectional feminists must endorse objective truth and justification, so that we can say: even though from his own perspective he takes himself to be justified and to know the truth, in actual reality he does not know the truth and is not justified in his beliefs.

The fact of his believing what he does and the fact that he takes himself to be justified are (in all likelihood) to be explained as the result of a regime of truth that reinforces cis-normative and white-supremacist beliefs through the spread of misinformation and false definitions through a wide variety of channels, institutions, and mechanisms. His misunderstanding of the meanings of the words "woman" and "racism" are part and parcel with his misunderstanding of gender and racism, which are likewise the effect of an oppressive regime of truth.

Justification is external to the perspective of the individual, or even the group to which he belongs. This man's linguistic intuitions may be widely shared. He will find much support for his judgment that "woman" refers to a biological kind. Even the dictionary agrees with him, for God's sake! From his internal perspective, he has all the justification he needs to know that "woman" refers to cis women only, not trans women. But on the intersectional epistemology I am developing here, this man's internal perspective is systematically in error. He does not know what he is talking about, even though he thinks he does. It's almost like being in the grip of an evil demon. Everywhere he turns, he finds support for his own view of the semantics of "woman" and yet this support is, in actual reality, systematically deceiving him about the nature of gender.

Real justification (which is external justification) for one's semantic interpretation of the language requires having one's understanding stand in a certain kind of alignment with reality itself. One can only know what "woman" means if one is able to know roughly how that word would be applied in an idealized version of the linguistic community. Knowing this is a matter of knowing what gender really is and/or knowing enough to trust others who really objectively know what gender is. But there is no absolute guarantee, no perfect certainty from within one's own perspective that one has deferred to a linguistic community that knows what it is talking about. One must be lucky enough to be embedded in or somehow have the good sense to defer to a community of language users that really does know what they are talking about.

Suppose the community in question is a subset of English speakers who are marginalized within interlocking systems of oppression, a group of epistemic agents who are developing their own concepts and terminology in order to conceive of and describe the world as they experience it. For example, Black feminists have introduced terms and concepts within their various communities for describing intersecting systems of racism and sexism and the consequences these systems have for social, political, economic, and epistemic life. Access to Black feminist thought and language is mediated by political engagement.[6] A person who is a Black feminist will easily comprehend the thoughts and ideas of that community. A person who hates the theory of intersectionality, who thinks racism and sexism are non-existent, and who sees Black feminists as hostile and irrational, will find it impossible to conform to the norms and thought patterns of the Black feminist community. Between the Black feminist and the anti-Black-feminist, there is a range of cases representing intermediate degrees of potential uptake, differing in terms of political alignment and willingness to engage intellectually with Black feminism. The degree to which a person can access and use the concepts and linguistic knowledge of Black feminism is thus mediated by political alignment.

A person who is not fully aligned with Black feminism can gain more access to these concepts by engaging in political activism aligned with Black feminist goals. The process of working and thinking together, of sharing struggle with genuine conviction, interest, and effort, makes the acquisition of Black feminist concepts much more likely. Hence, for

---

[6] Pohlhaus Jr (2012) provides an excellent discussion of this phenomenon. It is also a theme that Collins (2002) discusses under the heading of transversal politics.

outsiders, getting involved in the struggle is a way of gaining access to knowledge.

More generally, the ability to comprehend and use the representational contents generated within a given socio-political group is mediated by political alignment and political efforts. Differences in political alignment or apathy generate rifts in conceptual tools. Being a member of the group makes access to that group's concepts easier. Belonging to a social identity means belonging to a de facto coalition, where this involves having common interests with other members of that coalition, including common interests in representing certain aspects of reality and common interests in shared political struggle. But belonging to a group does not guarantee access to conceptual resources because it does not guarantee political alignment or effort. Only through active participation in political struggle—by thinking and acting in accord with the needs and interests of the relevant group—do situated representations become available.

These facts represent obstacles for the social engineering project. The regime of truth supports widespread misunderstanding and false intuitions about the meanings of words. It reinforces the epistemic power of those who, conferring among themselves, insist that "woman" refers to a biological category and who discredit or delegitimize attempts to explain what "woman" really means. It supports the idea that "female" is a scientific category, that somehow biology and medical science would be set back hundreds of years if suddenly they were forced to stop using the word "female" for plants and dogs, and that "woman" simply refers to the human version of a universal biological category, female. The regime of truth reinforces the 'commonsense' notion that "racism" can be applied to someone who is mistrustful of white people on the basis of their being white. The fact that such an idea seems or feels intuitive (for those who experience such an intuition) is the result of psychological conditioning imposed through the regime of truth, imposed from a thousand angles including movies, news, old media, new media, governmental agencies and individuals, networks of friends, family, and colleagues. People are trained to have a feel for these words, but these feels are not the basis of semantics.

Promoting the epistemic agency of marginalized groups requires intervening in the ways that these epistemic patterns subsist within the social fabric. The challenge is strategic and innovation is needed. An epistemology on which truths about intersectionality are objective and justified helps us to steer the discourse toward a more equitable distribution of epistemic power, or at least that is my hypothesis and my hope.

11.3.2 Situated Evidence and Situated Information

Different people have access to different evidence in virtue of living under different social circumstances. Even where people of different social identities encounter the same evidence, there are often predictable differences in how that evidence is received and interpreted—whether it's noticed, whether it is treated as important or ignored, and what propositions the evidence is taken to justify can all depend on one's sociopolitical outlook.

bell hooks (1984) describes growing up in a small Kentucky town where the Black folks lived on the far side of the railroad tracks, away from the center of town. They could visit the white neighborhood and they could work there, but they could not live or belong there. "We always had to return to the margin, to cross the tracks to shacks and abandoned houses on the edge of town." hooks was acutely aware of her living conditions. The white people were not. Her perspective made salient aspects of the social rules that were necessary for her survival. For instance, don't linger too long in the white neighborhood or else risk being punished by law enforcement officers. In addition to knowing how to survive, she was aware of the vital role that Black folks played in the life of the community, certainly more aware than were the white people living there. She writes, "Our survival depended on an ongoing public awareness of the separation between margin and center and an ongoing private acknowledgement that we were a necessary, vital part of that whole." The white folks were largely unaware of these facts.

What accounts for these differences in knowledge between Black folks and whites in that Kentucky town? Intersectional epistemologists, as well as traditional analytic epistemologists, can point to socially situated differences in people's interactions with evidence. The white people did not have the same experiences. They also had no need to register and incorporate evidence that was crucial for survival for Black folks there. The white folks could ignore that evidence, they probably never noticed it, but Black folks could not afford to ignore it. Social situation thus affects one's experience and evidence. This is not a strange phenomenon; it's commonplace and commonsensical. Pohlhaus Jr (2012) refers to this as situatedness. According to Pohlhaus, shared challenges associated with living in a given social role tend to produce a shared pattern of cognitive activity: "habits of expectation, attention, and concern ... contributing to what one is more or less likely to notice and pursue as an object of knowledge in the experienced world." A person's awareness of and engagement with evidence is shaped partly by their social situation.

The effect of social role on available evidence is probabilistic, and this probabilistic influence is only nomologically necessary. It would be metaphysically possible for a white person from the center of town to know some or perhaps even all of what hooks knew. The important point is this knowledge was thrust onto the Black people living on the edge of town, but it was obscure to the white people living in the center.

Like situated knowledge of representational contents, the availability of situated evidence is a function of political alignment and engagement. A member of a community is typically aware of evidence that is relevant for that community's survival, while an outsider can become aware of the relevant evidence if the outsider becomes involved in that community's struggles. An outsider who cares nothing for the community and who is uninterested in its struggles will typically have little or no awareness of the situated evidence that crucially informs the community's knowledge of its own circumstances. Moreover, when dominant agents are hostile or resistant to the perspective of a marginalized group, they tend to interpret evidence in ways that conflict with the marginalized group's interpretation of that same evidence. For example, a member or ally of the Black community is more likely to see economic disparity between whites and Black folks as evidence of structural oppression, whereas white supremacists typically interpret the same evidence as supporting the superiority of white culture or biology.

The classical epistemologist can easily accommodate socially situated disparities in evidence, for it is not different in kind from the general fact that different people have different evidence. The classical picture can also capture the way that evidence can be interpreted differently across social positions. These variations can be represented, for example, as different credences in the conditionals that represent evidential relations. Or they can be represented in a Bayesian framework as systematic differences in conditional probabilities that are predictable on the basis of social identity. Such models do nothing to preclude the objectivity about evidence inscribed in the traditional picture of epistemology. There may be variations in subjective credences about evidential support relations, yet there could also be objective facts about what propositions a given body of evidence actually supports.

This way of conceiving evidential support relations again implies a kind of externalism about evidence. The fact that a person has a coherent internal picture on which he is justified does not guarantee that he is in fact justified. Being really justified is a matter of having good evidence and being free from misinformation, and what makes evidence good or bad, or what makes something count as information versus misinformation, is not decided by what goes on inside the mind of the individual. Whether something counts as good evidence depends on whether it actually carries information about what really happened or what really is the case. The quality of your information, or whether you are beset with misinformation, is not something you can always know from within your own situated perspective. Hence, we can have a conspiracy theorist who thinks they are justified, who thinks they have a lot of evidence for the conspiracy, who is nevertheless not justified because in objective reality their beliefs about the quality of their own evidence are based on misinformation.

Consider the Stop the Steal Skeptic who believes that Trump won the 2020 election. This person thinks the reported vote count is inaccurate, that Donald Trump in fact received more votes than Joe Biden. They think an act of deception was carried out by Democrat-leaning voters, hundreds of thousands of whom managed to submit falsified votes, perhaps supported by secret but very widespread illegal actions to destroy votes for Trump. The failure to find convincing evidence of these events is the fault of incompetent oversight officials and lax regulations, or perhaps there is an abundance of evidence but this evidence is being willfully neglected or covered up by the judicial branches of the various swing states that went for Biden, or perhaps the evidence was covered up by the media and Biden-supporting political power. All reports that there is no evidence of widespread voter fraud are therefore seen as part of the disinformation campaign that undergirds the Democrats' power move to steal the election. In these suspicions, the Stop the Steal Skeptic finds wide support from their community of politically like-minded friends, family, and internet associates, as well as from their own preferred sources of news, and even from some US Senators and of course the lame duck President himself who ultimately incited an insurrection in an attempt to stop the certification of the next president by force. Behind this search for corroborating evidence and the unwillingness to lend due credibility to sources of good information is the conviction that Trump was a very successful president with a wide base of support and that therefore it was very unlikely that Trump would lose the election. It is not altogether irrational to say,

"I'm not sure what happened, but I am pretty sure something fishy is going on," if you were convinced by all of your experiences, all of your trusted friends and family, all of your trusted news sources, and your elected officials themselves whom you take to have good intelligence on the facts, all of which indicate to you that there was massive voter fraud.

And yet Joe Biden won the election by more than seven million votes, in actual reality. The Skeptic's belief that Trump won is objectively false, in actual reality. The source of evidence for this fact consists in the physical information encoded by the voting process. This evidence is objectively there, it exists, regardless of whether the majority of people believe it. Anyone who believes that Biden won the election on the basis of this physical evidence—the ballots themselves and the reliable counting procedures that tallied the scores—has a justified true belief that Biden won. The source of the Stop the Steal Skeptic's belief, on the other hand, is an effective disinformation campaign. In actual reality, the Skeptic's beliefs are based on misinformation and lies. There is a real, objective disconnect between the Skeptic's beliefs and reality. This is why they are objectively not justified, even though they would of course disagree with everything written in this paragraph.

The Skeptic and his opponent disagree about who is misinformed—that's not news! But the important thing is, someone is objectively right. Even the Skeptic agrees with this point. He thinks *he* is objectively right and justified. So, we can at least agree that someone is objectively right. Hence, both sides really conform in their epistemic practices to this kind of objectivity. They only disagree about who objectively knows what is going on. Part of the dispute is over who objectively has good evidence.

The fact that a person's evidence is objectively bogus is not necessarily something she can be made aware of. Imagine providing argument after argument, evidence upon evidence, for the reality of the Biden victory and the fabrication of misinformation about the election by the Trump campaign. Now imagine the Skeptic formulating alternative hypotheses about the source of our (objectively good) information and arguments. She continues to incorporate the new evidence and arguments into her narrative of deception and misinformation. It is plausible that for at least some Stop the Steal Skeptics, no amount of good evidence or argument would overturn their view. Does this show that such skeptics are not rational? I don't think it does. If their internal story is consistent and if they have strong enough prior conviction in Trump's victory and the power of Trump's political opponents to produce misinformation and cover up a stolen election, then they could in theory consistently and rationally dismiss every piece of evidence we provide. Even if our arguments are logically strong, even if they are deductively valid, it is still not necessarily irrational to dismiss those arguments if by the Skeptic's lights they have good reason to reject one or more of the argument's premises. And yet, on the externalist conception of evidence and justification I am defending here, the Skeptic will still not be justified, even if they can rationally dismiss all the evidence and argument we have, because their worldview fails to informationally track what actually happened.

How can we socially engineer a solution to this problem? We must promote the effectiveness of good situated evidence, which quintessentially includes the experiences of marginalized groups. We must work to disempower situated misinformation, which quintessentially persists within dominant groups. Teaching abstract epistemology and critical thinking skills by itself won't do the trick, because a person equipped with those skills can still rationally disagree with intersectionality theory, can even maintain and defend a conspiracy theory through the application of those very skills. Rather, we must confront those aspects of the regime of truth that enable and empower the flow of misinformation.

This is a very difficult battle because the oppressive regime of truth operates within people's families and local communities as well as through politicians, media, and internet. The battle has to be fought at the macro level through institutional politics, but also must be carried on at the micro level, the level of family and community where false concepts and misinformation are shared and debated over dinner tables, in locker rooms, or at water coolers.

How do we carry out effective dis-disinformation campaigns within families and communities of friends? This is an empirical question and a strategic question. What strategies are effective? Should we fight tooth and nail with our friends and families over politics, give them no quarter, enact a scorched earth policy of canceling our closest friends, our parents and grandparents, our colleagues who are acting on behalf of misinformation and active ignorance? Here I'm thinking mainly about white people canceling white people over racism. Canceling people is part of the Black feminist practice of self-care, of cutting people out of your life when they are a drain because there is no spare energy due to living with intersecting oppressions. This is an important practice and should not be denigrated. But when, say, a rich cis-het white feminist cancels her white dude friend over his ignorant racism or stops talking to her racist uncle because she can't stand his politics, this cannot be justified in the same way. More generally, the problem is with dominant people who closely approximate the mythic norm practicing cancel culture—in many cases this is actually a problematic misappropriation of Black feminist praxis.

The pervasiveness of misinformation and the imperative to confront it at the personal level, which is part of intersectional praxis, has given rise to the controlling image of the social justice warrior. This controlling image helps enable privileged groups to ignore arguments and evidence presented in support of intersectionality theory. It is fed by the dominantly situated perception that people enacting intersectional praxis are fighting over nothing or over very small things as if they are fighting a war. They're not entirely wrong. Intersectional praxis recognizes that the very small things add up to give us a social fabric that produces the matrix of domination. Power comes from below, as Foucault says. Altering the regime of truth and destabilizing the matrix of domination requires that we continue to fight and win many small battles in the discourse. Intersectionality does advocate for us to fight small battles tenaciously.

But what is the effective strategy for winning many small battles? Here I want to float a hypothesis. I think our best weapon against misinformation is our close personal relationships with people who are beset with misinformation and active ignorance. Close personal relationships are an invaluable resource for intersectional praxis, especially close personal relationships that connect misinformed or actively ignorant people or communities with sources of good information and accurate concepts. In conducting dis-disinformation campaigns, therefore, we must be very careful not to damage or destroy the kinds of close personal relationships that provide channels for the flow of good information into misinformed communities.

This is exceedingly difficult because the kinds of confrontations needed to win battles against misinformation are also liable to damage personal relationships. Hitting a person over and over with facts that contradict their worldview is not a way to maintain a close friendship or family tie. But refusing altogether to confront ignorance and misinformation is just to go along with the matrix of domination. What is needed are subtle strategies and individualized approaches within particular relationships that allow the transmission of good information in a way that is low-key enough so as to preserve the relationship but also potent enough to disrupt oppressive worldviews. This is a long-term strategy which urges a balance of patience, leniency, decisiveness, and action when confronting active ignorance and misinformation in personal relationships.

As is often the case in social epistemology, both ethical and epistemological concerns arise when we think about how people should interact with one another in order to facilitate the social production of knowledge. The question of how we should interact in dealing with misinformation is both ethical and epistemological. I am arguing that our ethical duties are closely tied to our epistemological objectives in a way that depends on being strategically effective in combating misinformation. Doing the right thing ethically is a matter of doing what will, in the long run, be most effective for abolishing the matrix of domination through the elimination of misinformation and active ignorance within the social fabric. In assessing our ethical imperatives within personal relationships, we must constantly take this fact into account.

11.3.3 Situated Testimony

Social situation and political alignment predictably affect judgments about the credibility of testimony. An agent is disposed to trust and believe those who share their political alignment and to distrust and disbelieve those who are opposed to their political commitments. These attitudes manifest in judgments of the credibility of testimony, even when the testimony proffered is a potential transmission of knowledge. Political alignments are aspects of social situation and are often correlated with social identity. Hence, access to knowledge via testimony is socially situated.

Consider testimony from Black folks concerning police brutality in the US. This testimony is perennially shared within Black communities, but only ever gains limited uptake in white communities. In Black communities the reality and threat of police violence is well known and ever present, so testimony about police brutality is accepted as a matter of course. Yet many white communities denounce Black testimony concerning police brutality as lacking credibility. This disparity illustrates the situatedness of testimony.

Access to information through situated testimony comes with political struggle. Members of a marginalized group who participate in their own political struggle easily accept testimonial knowledge concerning that struggle. Outsiders who struggle in solidarity with a marginalized group will tend to ascribe higher credibility to testimony given by members of that group concerning its experiences and interests. Those who are indifferent or opposed to that group's political interests will tend to ascribe lower credibility to such testimony. Hence, white folks who are involved in or aligned with Black Lives Matter are more likely to assign high credence to Black testimony about police brutality, while opponents of Black Lives Matter tend to discredit such testimony or downplay its significance. This exemplifies one way that political involvement can affect credibility attributions.

The formal epistemologist has tools for modeling the way an agent's assignment of credibility can depend on the speaker's social identity and its relation to the topic about which they are speaking. Assignment functions can be sensitive to all kinds of features. A simple version takes an agent, a social identity, and a domain of discourse and returns a number, where this number represents a kind of probabilistic adjustment to the credibility the agent assigns to speakers belonging to that identity about that domain of discourse. For example, the formal epistemologist can represent the opponent of Black Lives Matter as having a low credence in Black testimony about police brutality.

We can also state generalizations about social identities in these terms. For example, we can say white people are on average more likely to be skeptical of Black testimony about police brutality than Black folks are. Such generalizations are defeasible. Some particular white person could be an exception to the rule. These generalizations are also non-monotonic. So, for example, white people who are actively engaged in prison abolition will not necessarily fall under the same generalizations as white people simpliciter. Traditional analytic epistemology is capable of developing formal models that reflect such claims and these may be of some use within an intersectional epistemology, minimally in showing that intersectional epistemology can be done in the 'rigorous' way that analytic philosophers typically aspire to.

11.3.4 Ideology

One very significant component of many critical theories is the notion of ideology, stemming from Marxist epistemology (Mannheim 1924, Lukács 1972, Althusseir 2011, Lefebvre 1982) and taken up by feminist standpoint theorists (Hartsock 1983), Black feminist standpoint theorists (Collins, 2002), and philosophers of race (Mills 2005). An ideology in this tradition is understood to be a system of ideas, values, and practices that functions to perpetuate structural elements of domination within a society by producing and legitimating a distorted view of reality that serves the interests of dominant groups by obscuring relations of oppression and exploitation. The traditional example of ideology from Marxist theory is the system of ideas that keeps the worker from rising up against the capitalist by making capitalist exploitation appear to be natural, equitable and just.

Within the conceptual framework of traditional analytic epistemology, an ideology might be identified simply as a theory or a set of propositions that informs an individual's epistemological practices. Such a theory is a component of an individual's total background beliefs and can be formally represented in just the same way as other sets of background beliefs. What makes an ideology different from other background theories is only a matter of its content, viz. the social and political implications it has and the effects of these implications on the individual's perspective on various politically significant elements of reality.

But a more expanded and adequate view sees an ideology not just as a set of ideas or commitments that live in the minds of individuals, but rather as a program of operation by which the regime of truth makes a certain set of statements function as true, viz. those statements that constitute the ideology. The pervasiveness of an ideology then consists in its key premises being made to function as true by a wide range of social institutions, backed by social power and enabled to inform policy decisions, as well as being spread through social power at smaller scales so that the ideological propositions are believed by large and powerful swaths of a given society. On this view widespread belief is not the essence of an ideology, but the regime of truth works to ensure that ideologies are widely believed and that they inform many people's background theories of reality, semantics, and epistemology.

Belief in an ideology can be explicit, as when its central tenets are expounded, or it can be largely tacit, as when its central tenets are held as background assumptions that are never consciously proclaimed or scrutinized. As Foucault (1980) emphasized, ideologies are not necessarily constructed intentionally with the purpose to do harm. Their authors may not even notice they are constructing or reproducing an ideology. Ideologies can arise and evolve organically as dominant groups create justifications and ultimately create whole cultures to facilitate their pursuits. This process needs no oversight or special attention, although surely those in power sometimes initiate strategic developments of ideology to consolidate their power.

The presence and operation of ideology within the individual psyche is predictable on the basis of social identity. White people are more likely than people of color to adopt a white supremacist ideology. Men are more likely than women to adopt a patriarchal or misogynistic ideology. These generalizations do not hold ubiquitously. Sometimes women promote patriarchal ideology, while some men are feminists; some white folks are anti-racist and sometimes people of color espouse white supremacist ideas. But such cases are noteworthy because they cut against the grain. They are exceptions to the rule that ideological commitments track social identity in obvious ways. All of this is intelligible to the analytic epistemologist, and all of it fits well into an intersectional epistemology that regards ideology as part of an objective reality.

The epistemological upshot is that ideologies qua programs of operation with the regime of truth influence what a person can know. Observation is often theory laden. Conceptual resources are often theory laden. Even testimonial uptake is theory laden, insofar as the interpretation of what is said depends on background theory. Thus, ideologies are a ground of situatedness for each of the preceding three aspects of knowledge production and transmission. Moreover, what one finds plausible is always a function of what one already believes, so postulating ideologies allow us to predict which propositions will be acceptable to people who conform to them.

Struggle for or against an ideology is always political. Access to socially situated resistant knowledge is always a struggle against prevailing dominant conceptions of reality that function to obscure such knowledge. From the traditional analytic epistemologist's perspective, this means that achieving a marginalized standpoint and thereby accessing situated knowledge requires rejecting, or at least resisting, many prevailing background theories that are widely believed by dominantly situated epistemic agents and within mainstream consciousness. It also requires struggling against the myriad avenues of epistemic power that flood in to support dominant worldviews and perspectives against opposing points of view.

For example, there is a prevailing ideological belief that academic success is purely a matter of intelligence and good character and not at all a matter of social identity. Consequently, an affirmative action program designed to promote good academic outcomes for members of a social identity *qua* their social identity is widely perceived to conflict with merit-based criteria for academic success. Moreover, the agents who wield epistemic power within departments and university review boards will be sure to flex that power to negate affirmative action initiatives to the extent they are capable. These same groups of people tend to reaffirm one another's justifications for resisting affirmative action initiatives. Thus, appreciating the reasons in favor of affirmative action inherently involves calling into question background beliefs about meritocracy in academia and requires challenging those who are in epistemic power who would defend the status quo. An agent who tacitly or explicitly maintains a belief in such meritocracy, or who benefits from the epistemic power that affirmative action would undermine, is unlikely to call those beliefs into question unless they are engaged in political struggle alongside advocates of affirmative action. This is true regardless of whether the agent is a member of a dominant or subordinate group. Hence, belonging to a marginalized social identity is not sufficient to obtain freedom from oppressive ideologies; one must also engage in political struggle.

11.3.5 Science and Situated Experience

Intersectional epistemology must make good use of science. It is on the basis of good science that we can know about the extent of gender-based oppression, the extent to which the effects of slavery have continued to negatively impact Black communities in the US, the extent to which fossil fuels are contributing to global warming and climate injustice, the extent to which corporations are polluting the water, the harmfulness involved in locking up drug offenders and separating them from their families and their children on the pretense of protecting them from harmful drugs, the extent to which economic interventions that purport to benefit everyone provide benefits to the rich only, and a million billion other issues that are relevant to justice and ending oppression. Science is crucial for understanding social injustice and for creating solutions.

But there is also a lot of empirical knowledge that is not scientific. You do not need to do science to know what color your house is. You just look at it and immediately know what color it is. If you are a person of color, you do not need to do science to know about racism. You just experience it, constantly. You confer with others who have experienced it and share insights. This is not The Scientific Method, but it is a good method of learning and systematizing experiences and empirical evidence. If you want to know what your gender is, you do not need to do science to figure it out. You don't need to do biology. Your exploration of your own gender is a different kind of empirical knowledge. You learn through experience and through interrogating your experience of gendered existence, in conversation and relationships with others.

I have seen a white male professor confront a woman of color who was giving a job talk. He pressed her to justify claims about her personal experiences of racism by supplying scientific data. The presupposition would appear to be that an individual's experience of racism, together with her conversations with others who have experienced similar phenomena, was insufficient justification for her to assert an empirical generalization about racism, on the grounds that any such assertion must be backed by scientific data. This is both an example of epistemic oppression and an example of how to flex your white male epistemic power.

It is objectively unreasonable to invoke a scientific standard of knowledge for ordinary every-day racism, because it is possible to know about such patterns of racism without having scientific data that justifies your belief. To impose such a criterion of justification from a position of systemic power in that context—for a tenured white male professor to invoke that criterion against a claim about racism made by a job candidate who is a woman of color—is an example of how invoking scientific standards of justification can function as a mode of epistemic oppression to delegitimate knowledge of racism and disempower a marginalized person.

Yet I think science can help us to formulate empirical theories of gender and racism that go beyond personal and communal experience. Our best theories of gender and of racism are scientific in the sense that they are responsive to a wide range of patterns that involve millions of people and take account of all the environments in which gender and racism exist and interact within the social fabric. These patterns are vast and complicated and go far beyond the ability of any individual or even any individual's immediate community to fully grasp in the absence of data collection and scientific theorizing. The nature and extent of gender and of racism are difficult to fathom and go beyond what personal or immediate-communal experience can systematize.

The best theory of gender systematizes everyone's experiences of gender and catalogues all the ways in which these features interact with other aspects of the social fabric including other social identities, laws, systems of oppression, material realities, biology, ideology, and everything else that influences how gender develops and changes over time. This will take a lot of science. The best theory of racism systematizes the experiences people have of racism across the full spectrum of social identities, including all the ways that racism interacts with sexism, classism, homophobia, fatphobia, transphobia, including all the ways it interacts with economics, education, nationalism, environmental damage, and many other factors as well. This too requires a lot of data and a lot of theorizing.

We can't avoid getting organized scientifically if we want to understand these phenomena. There is just no way of collecting and organizing this data without doing science. As we discover more about the complexity of things, we expand our scientific theorizing to interconnected domains. So, for example, when we systematically compare experiences of racist oppression, we discover that racism is connected with economics; then we use scientifically informed economic models to help us understand how racism interacts with economic factors to produce racialized economic oppression. We collect data about how women of color are systematically marginalized in ways that white women and men of color do not experience and thereby identify intersectional patterns of oppression.

Our means of systematizing the vast amount of information required for understanding gender and racism must ultimately be scientific, but this does not mean that gender or racism must be theorized in a way that is apolitical and value neutral. On the contrary, all of the theoretical terms involved in these scientific theories and the procedures for adjudicating their proper application must be interpreted in accord with the Intersectional Metasemantic Adequacy constraint. The truth of any scientific theory is therefore partially constrained to comport with our strongest moral and political commitments, for those are fundamental in assigning truth-conditions to the sentences of the language and extensions to our terms. Even the language in which the scientific method is discussed, including the word "science" itself, must be interpreted in accord with IMA. This is a powerful source of skepticism against the claim that science can demonstrate that "woman" denotes a biological concept, for example, for there is simply no scientific evidence strong enough to overturn our fundamental semantic commitments (see Chap. 9).

There is no doubt that scientific institutions can and have been used to promote racism, sexism, transphobia, homophobia, and every other aspect of the matrix of domination. They have also acted as gatekeepers that have refused access to marginalized communities for closely related reasons. Scientific inquiry is a social phenomenon and as such it is intimately connected with the regime of truth and is therefore subjected to the modulating and distorting forces contained therein. Creating accessibility for marginalized groups to the realms of professional science is very important for addressing these issues.

As I argued in Chap. 8, this does not entail that science is necessarily inaccurate or non-objective or that its pronouncements necessarily benefit those in power. But there is clearly a huge potential for scientific institutions to promote the interests of dominant groups, including quintessentially the potential to create and propagate misinformation about gender and race.[7] Science can be done poorly to produce results that benefit dominant groups, reinforce the matrix of domination, and undermine the political and epistemic agency of marginalized groups. Even science that is done well can produce misinformation—after all, there is always a chance that even a perfectly constructed scientific experiment could support a conclusion which turns out to be false—and when this happens, the misinformation can be propagated even more effectively as it was the result of good science; see O'Connor and Weatherall (2019). And there is also no escaping the fact that what a person regards as good science is inextricably linked to their social situation and their political commitments. Whether someone accepts the latest study on climate change is going to be highly dependent on their politics. Yet all of these factors can and should be accounted for against the backdrop of a scientific realism that recognizes a reality beyond the social, on which scientific progress is objectively possible, even if hard to attain due to the political and social power that operates within scientific institutions.

We cannot evaluate our scientific institutions without some eye toward whether those institutions are actually producing and propagating good information or whether they are producing and propagating misinformation and active ignorance, and there is no way to do this in a politically disengaged way.[8] Thus, scientific inquiry must be constantly checked from a sociological perspective that has one eye on objective reality and another on the political and social embeddedness of the scientific institutions and the operation of power on the legitimation and dissemination of what passes for scientific knowledge. This is the fundamental requirement of what Harding (1992) calls *strong objectivity*. In order to be maximally objective, we must constantly reflect on how social power might be affecting our scientific conclusions.

---

[7] For examples of how the institutions of science have propagated misinformation about gender, see Fine (2010). For examples of how it has propagated misinformation about race, see Gould and Gold (1996).
[8] See Harding (1992) and Scheman (1995) for extensive arguments.

11.4 Truth in Political Struggle

The preceding considerations all point to the way in which political struggle is relevant for ascertaining truth and the sense in which truth is central to political struggle. One can only gain access to the information generated from marginalized perspectives, information that the oppressive regime of truth is working to erase and obscure, if one is actively getting involved in political struggle in solidarity with the group that produces the information.

This information is highly particularized. As I will sometimes say to my students: if you want to understand the struggles of undocumented immigrants in the Boston area, the only way to do this is to either be an undocumented immigrant in the Boston area or to be actively involved in trying to solve the problems they are facing. One cannot access this information without being really involved; being only passively involved, say by reading a couple news articles on the internet, is not going to be sufficient to really understand the situation. Once one is really working in the trenches, trying to secure aid and protections and helping people who have been confronted with police power and bad landlords, then one becomes part of the communal struggle and gains deeper insights and perspectives into the matrix of domination and the ways it is effecting domination at that particular location in social space.

Because our time and energy are limited, none of us can be deeply involved in everyone's struggles. Because being deeply involved in political struggle in particular social locations is required for deep understanding of the relevant particular aspects of social reality, we all have strong limitations on what we can know about our society and about the matrix of domination that permeates it. Each of us can only attain a fragment of the larger picture.

This limitation on our ability to know is part of objective reality. It does not entail that truth is subjective or that everyone speaks different languages. It means that understanding social reality requires forming networks of political alliances, getting involved in creating change where we can, and facilitating communication between social justice movements. This also involves sending messages and information through the powerful networks of the regime of truth, which has the potential to facilitate the spread of knowledge as well as ignorance. The potential for mass knowledge of oppression can only be realized through mass political activism. We are seeing some of this today, there is no doubt, but more is required.

Knowing the truth is important because the system of oppression is built on misinformation. Our epistemic limitations therefore serve the interests of dominant power. As people become more confused, mistrustful, and misinformed about the matrix of domination, dominant power gains greater advantages in its strategic initiatives to create injustice and disparity that favors dominant groups. The operations of the regime of truth to divest people of the rationale for supporting social justice movements therefore also function to block knowledge of the matrix of domination. Even though we are limited in what we can know by our limited ability to participate in political struggle, these struggles are dramatically important, both socially and epistemically.

REFERENCES

Burge, T. (1979). Individualism and the Mental. *Midwest Studies in Philosophy, 4,* 73–121.

Burge, T. (1982). Other Bodies. In A. Woodfield (Ed.), *Thought and Object: Essays on Intentionality.* Oxford University Press.

Burge, T. (1986). Individualism and Psychology. *The Philosophical Review, 95*(1), 3–45.

Code, L. (2012). Taking Subjectivity into Account. In *Education, Culture and Epistemological Diversity* (pp. 85–100). Springer.

Collins, P. H. (1998). *Fighting Words: Black Women and the Search for Justice (Vol. 7).* University of Minnesota Press.

Collins, P. H. (2002). *Black Feminist Thought: Knowledge, Consciousness, and the Politics of Empowerment.* Routledge.

Dotson, K. (2014). Conceptualizing Epistemic Oppression. *Social Epistemology, 28*(2), 115–138.

Dotson, K. (2018). Accumulating Epistemic Power: A Problem with Epistemology. *Philosophical Topics, 46*(1), 129–154.

Foucault, M. (1980). *Power/knowledge: Selected Interviews and Other Writings, 1972-1977.* Vintage.

Fine, C. (2010). *Delusions of Gender: How Our Minds, Society, and Neurosexism Create Difference.* WW Norton & Company.

Harding, S. (1992). Rethinking Standpoint Epistemology: What Is "strong objectivity?". *The Centennial Review, 36*(3), 437–470.

hooks, B. (1984/2000). *Feminist Theory: From Margin to Center.* Pluto Press.

Gould, S. J., & Gold, S. J. (1996). *The Mismeasure of Man.* WW Norton & company.

Matsuda, M. J. (1987). Looking to the Bottom: Critical Legal Studies and Reparations. *HaRv. cR-cll Rev, 22*, 323.

O'Connor, C., & Weatherall, J. O. (2019). *The Misinformation Age: How False Beliefs Spread*. Yale University Press.

Pohlhaus, G., Jr. (2012). Relational Knowing and Epistemic Injustice: Toward a Theory of Willful Hermeneutical Ignorance. *Hypatia, 27*(4), 715–735.

Roberts, D. E. (1991). Punishing Drug Addicts Who Have Babies: Women of Color, Equality, and the Right of Privacy. *Harvard Law Review, 1*, 1419–1482.

Scheman, N. (1995). Feminist Epistemology. *Metaphilosophy, 26*(3), 177–190.

Index[1]

A
Accuracy duality, 50, 51
Active ignorance, 38, 47n2, 52, 55, 62, 94, 99, 166, 168, 169, 177–179, 206, 211, 213–215, 223–226, 229, 231, 235, 240, 241, 248, 257, 260, 262, 263, 271, 278, 280, 281, 282n7, 286–289, 300, 301, 303, 306, 316–318, 325
Alexander, Michelle, 175, 207
Ambiguity, 72, 92, 94, 97, 186n1, 280–281
Analytic, 2, 15, 16, 18, 19, 21, 37, 57, 77, 103, 105, 107, 108n4, 110, 114, 115, 134–136, 136n1, 144–145n8, 183–231, 263, 301, 302, 305, 307, 312, 319–321
Analytic sentence, 15, 16, 18
Analytic truth, 18, 19, 293
Anti-reductionist, 130, 264n2

B
Baldwin, James, 98, 206
Black feminism, 188, 191, 201, 209, 214, 221, 306, 310
Black Feminist Epistemology, 300n1
Black feminist standpoint theory, 193, 229
Boston, 190, 208, 326
Burge, Tyler, 28, 30–34, 105, 124, 262–264, 264n2, 292n10, 307

C
Carnap, Rudolph, 15, 18, 42, 42n1, 84, 117
Collins, Patricia Hill, 5, 18, 55, 59, 61, 134, 149, 180, 183, 188, 189n4, 190, 193, 194, 201–206, 209–212, 217, 218, 222–224, 229, 252, 255, 259, 300n1, 306, 310n6, 319

---

[1] Note: Page numbers followed by 'n' refer to notes.

Collins' law of oppression, 210, 213
Combahee River Collective, 188, 190–193, 195
Concept, 2, 5, 19n16, 32, 35n5, 37, 43, 49n3, 54, 58, 61, 65, 69, 70, 74n7, 76, 77, 79, 80, 103, 105, 106, 111, 112, 116, 133–139, 141, 144, 144–145n8, 150, 152, 155, 157, 160–162, 169–171, 180, 184, 187, 189n4, 192, 193, 202, 207, 209, 210, 215, 217, 219, 225, 249, 256, 272, 273, 287, 300, 301, 305–308, 310, 311, 316, 317, 324
Conceptual role semantics, 116, 116n7
Controlling image, 18, 55, 61, 63, 205, 206, 208, 212–215, 219, 223, 224, 226, 230, 252, 295, 317
Controlling proposition, 41, 206, 224, 253, 295
Crenshaw, Kimberlé, 5, 26n2, 184–186, 186n1, 192, 193, 196–200, 203, 204, 212, 217, 223
Critical theory, 2, 5, 55, 67, 92, 133–136, 136n1, 166, 183, 186, 186n1, 194, 211, 216, 224–229, 236, 253, 279, 301, 319

D

Davis, Angela, 192, 193
Decolonization, 214, 216
Defer, 30, 32, 36, 38, 63, 264, 267–273, 310
Deference, 30–32, 35–37, 229, 262, 264–270, 292, 299, 307
Deference magnet, 36, 37
Democracy, 45, 51, 53–57, 173–178, 205, 294–295

E

Empirical, 15, 16, 18, 37, 78, 92–97, 99, 110, 111, 153, 156, 177, 239, 251, 254, 278n5, 279, 292n10, 295, 316, 322, 323
Energy, 105, 138–142, 145, 186, 277, 305, 316, 326
Episteme, 57, 58, 60–62, 157, 159, 162, 166, 287
Epistemic reasons, 44, 242, 290, 293, 302, 303, 303n4
Epistemic violence, 41–65, 137, 167, 178–180, 257, 294–295
Epistemic violence model, 22, 41, 57–65, 179, 257
Epistemology, 59n10, 60, 62, 130, 135, 136, 166–170, 193, 255, 291, 300–307, 300n1, 309, 311, 313, 316, 318–322
Evidence, 14–16, 37, 43, 62, 68, 78, 92–99, 110, 119, 122, 134, 165, 166, 169, 177, 199, 228, 238–243, 241n4, 250–252, 254, 256, 274, 289, 290, 293, 295, 299–304, 306, 309, 312–318, 322, 324
Extension, 3, 18, 35, 35n5, 50, 81, 88, 89, 96, 104, 144, 144n8, 206, 220, 222, 224, 244–250, 253, 260, 266, 274, 280, 281, 282n6, 300, 324
Externalism
semantic, 28, 30, 117, 263, 264, 273

F

Feminism, 2, 186n1, 188, 192, 197, 201, 202, 212–214, 216, 221, 283, 308, 309
Feminist, 2, 3, 15, 17–19, 62, 64, 92, 130, 188–190, 189n4, 192, 193, 196, 197, 201, 209, 212, 213, 220, 221, 225, 227, 229, 250,

INDEX 331

255, 256, 266, 269, 281, 306, 308–310, 316, 317, 319, 321
First-Order Slingshot, 246
Fish, 97, 98, 104–106, 113, 115–123, 126–129, 274, 275
Fodor, Jerry, 106–108, 108n4, 111, 113n6, 150, 243
Foucault, Michel, 3, 57, 57–58n9, 58, 60, 79, 92, 105, 134–157, 159–162, 167, 169–175, 170n22, 177–179, 183, 189, 189n4, 205, 236, 252, 259, 317, 320
Frege, Gottlob, 69–80, 79–80n9, 80–81n11, 84n14, 86, 86n16, 87, 103, 127, 266

G

Gender, 3–5, 10, 12–20, 19n16, 20n17, 22, 25, 36, 37, 43, 45, 46, 46–47n2, 49–51, 55–57, 56n7, 61–64, 70, 97–99, 121, 128, 137, 144, 160, 161, 163, 164, 167, 168, 176, 178, 179, 186n1, 188, 200, 204, 207, 208, 211, 212, 217, 220–223, 246, 247n8, 256, 257, 260, 262, 263, 266, 267, 269, 271, 272, 276, 278, 281–283, 281n6, 282n7, 285, 287, 294, 295, 307–310, 322–325, 325n7
General Metasemantic Adequacy (GMA), 43, 184, 237–252, 254, 256
Gotanda, Neil, 7n3, 10, 219, 220

I

Ideal language
  community, 269
  metasemantics, 48, 127–131, 236, 266, 285

Identity politics, 191, 193, 217, 218, 222, 223, 229, 256
Ideology, 43, 56n7, 59, 62, 133, 163, 170, 176, 218, 219, 224, 225, 247, 277, 284, 299, 303, 319–323
Ignorance, 2, 5, 12, 14, 29, 38, 41, 47n2, 49, 52, 55, 58, 62, 64, 65, 73, 75, 76, 79, 94, 98, 99, 119, 128, 130, 131, 147, 148, 161, 164–166, 168, 169, 175–179, 194, 203, 204, 206, 211, 213–217, 223–226, 228–231, 235–237, 240, 241, 246, 247n8, 248, 253, 256, 257, 259, 265, 277, 278, 283n8, 289, 295, 304, 306–326
Indigenous, 3, 11n9, 61, 62, 122n8, 209, 214, 219, 303n4
Indigenous feminist, 209
Information, 4, 12, 18, 20, 38, 59, 93, 94, 96, 97, 111, 116, 144, 157–159, 161, 166, 168, 169, 172, 173, 175, 176, 180, 185, 212, 228, 231, 235, 253, 254, 269, 287, 293, 294, 304, 305, 308, 312–318, 324–326
Informed Speaker Constraint, 45, 97–99
Institution, 4, 17, 20n17, 38, 43, 49, 51, 55, 56, 58–61, 114, 133, 134, 137–140, 142, 144–149, 153, 155–159, 162–164, 172–174, 176–178, 180, 186, 201, 203–207, 210, 211, 225, 246, 253, 265, 287, 300, 309, 320, 324, 325, 325n7
Instrumentalism, 152
Intentions, 10n7, 46, 105, 112, 115, 147, 150, 152, 153

Interlocking systems
  of domination, 12
  of oppression, 41, 55, 62, 64, 65, 67, 79, 127, 179, 186n1, 193, 195, 196, 210, 229–231, 253, 278, 310
Internalism
  justification, 169
  semantic, 115
Interpretation, 22, 43, 47, 48, 56, 72, 73, 76, 78, 79, 81, 83, 84, 84n13, 85n15, 87–89, 92–95, 108, 126, 198, 238, 243, 246, 248, 250, 254, 259–261, 275, 286, 287, 291n9, 310, 313, 321
Intersectional identity, 130, 180, 186, 193, 194, 202, 237
Intersectionality, 2, 5, 7, 11, 45, 103, 130, 133, 137, 143, 161, 178–180, 183–231, 235, 237, 252–256, 259–295, 301, 302n3, 303, 306–308, 310, 311, 316, 317
Intersectionality as critical theory, 186, 224–229, 237
Intersectionality as praxis, 186
Intersectional Metasemantic Adequacy (IMA), 184, 235–257, 259–260, 263–265, 302n3, 324
Intersectional theory of truth, 137, 180, 230–231, 259, 300, 305

J

Justification, 14, 49, 55, 57, 80n9, 163, 165, 166, 169, 172, 204, 206, 207, 211, 213, 219, 242, 251, 299, 302–304, 302n3, 306, 309, 310, 316, 320, 322, 323

K

Knowledge, 15, 29, 30, 36, 41, 49–51, 53, 58, 61, 62, 64, 67, 67n2, 68, 71n5, 79, 83, 96–99, 104, 119, 124, 129, 135, 136, 143n7, 147, 153, 154, 156, 161, 165, 167, 168, 170, 173–175, 179, 185, 187–190, 189n4, 193, 194, 203, 211, 225, 229, 237, 241, 242, 255, 273, 285, 295, 299–327

L

Language of thought, 111, 112, 113n6
Linguistic community, 30, 32, 34, 35, 38, 54, 72, 130, 230, 262, 264–278, 280–285, 282n7, 288–290, 292, 300, 301, 310
Linguistic hijacking, 12–20, 22, 27, 52, 61, 62, 64, 103, 179, 211, 253, 263, 271, 295
Linguistic meaning, 110–115, 124
Logic, 68, 69, 69n3, 72, 73, 77, 78, 80, 81n11, 82, 82n12, 84, 86n16, 87, 88, 90–92, 201n14
Logical consequence, 80, 84, 91
Lorde, Audre, 187, 192, 195, 197, 212, 221, 229

M

Matrix of domination, 134, 143, 149, 151, 166, 175, 176, 179, 180, 191–193, 202–211, 216, 218, 219, 224–228, 230, 231, 247n8, 252, 253, 255, 259, 260, 265, 284, 301, 303, 305, 317, 318, 324–327
Meaning, 2–4, 9, 10n7, 11, 12, 15, 16, 18–22, 25–38, 41, 44, 46–54,

46–47n2, 56, 57, 63, 63n12, 64, 69–71, 73–76, 75n8, 83, 88, 89, 93–96, 105, 109–130, 116n7, 133, 134, 144n8, 165, 211, 230, 231, 236, 238, 242–249, 247n8, 257, 260–263, 264n2, 265–267, 270, 272–275, 279–288, 283n8, 290–292, 302, 307–309, 311
Meaning change, 46, 281–284
Melville, Herman, 104, 106, 116–119, 273, 274
Metasemantics, 4, 12, 14–16, 19, 20, 22, 27–38, 41–44, 48, 51, 56, 58n9, 64, 76, 103–131, 165, 184, 207, 211, 224, 230, 231, 259–295, 301, 302
Mills, Charles, 12, 98, 130, 147, 319
Misinformation, 1, 2, 4, 5, 10n7, 12, 14, 16, 17, 19–22, 38, 41–65, 73, 76, 79, 89, 99, 103, 127, 128, 130, 131, 133, 137, 148, 157, 158, 164–166, 168–170, 175, 176, 178–180, 187, 205, 206, 211–216, 223–226, 229, 230, 236–239, 246, 247n8, 248, 252–254, 256, 257, 259, 260, 262, 265, 266, 269, 271, 277–281, 282n7, 284–288, 295, 299, 300, 303–306, 309, 314–318, 325, 327
Model, 22, 22n18, 27, 35–37, 41–45, 48, 49, 51–53, 56–65, 80–85, 80–81n11, 85n15, 86n17, 87–89, 91, 93, 95–99, 165, 179, 196–199, 235, 237, 243, 257, 261, 264, 274, 293, 313, 319, 324
Model-theoretic semantics, 2, 35n5, 67–99, 103, 222, 235, 261, 267
Model theory, 65, 68–94, 165, 243

N
Nation state, 59, 137, 138, 149, 151, 207, 209, 210, 218
Naturalistic, 103, 105–110, 113, 115, 123–125, 127, 149–153, 236, 261, 290, 291n9
Naturalistic metasemantics, 108, 113n6, 114, 122, 126, 251
Natural language, 2, 5, 22, 63n12, 68, 69, 71n5, 73, 73n6, 76, 77, 86–87n17, 87–95, 91n18, 103, 105, 106, 110–113, 235, 237, 238, 242–245, 248, 250, 266, 267, 293

O
Objective
 objectively refers, 73
 objective meaning, 71
 objective truth, 2, 5, 12, 13, 48, 50, 64, 65, 67–69, 77, 79, 87, 92, 103, 131, 134, 135, 137, 166, 168, 169, 175, 176, 180, 228, 230, 231, 237, 239, 290, 294, 295, 300, 301, 306, 309
Objectivity, 2, 77, 78, 92, 301–306, 313, 315, 325
Ocasio-Cortez, Alexandria, 7–11, 13, 21, 26, 27, 29, 30, 33–35, 42, 44, 52, 64, 70, 116, 231

P
Political intersectionality, 180, 186, 194, 210, 212–216, 237
Politically situated, 5, 89, 94, 98, 99, 169, 239, 268, 280, 302, 305
Politically situated differences, 239, 302

Power
  epistemic, 62, 78, 79, 167, 169, 253, 285, 305–307, 311, 312, 321–323
  institutional, 255
  social, 37, 57–59, 61, 64, 67, 68, 79, 114, 122, 131, 134, 136, 139, 140, 144, 147, 150, 151, 155, 158, 159, 161–167, 170, 174, 177, 178, 209, 231, 236, 253, 284, 295, 320, 325
Propaganda, 18, 55, 164, 165, 168, 169, 176, 178, 294, 295
Public language, 11, 21, 72, 88, 89, 103, 115, 133, 247n8, 267, 268, 271, 307
Putnam, Hilary, 107, 118, 120–123, 129, 262, 263, 273, 274

R
Racism, 3–5, 7–14, 16, 18–22, 20n17, 25–27, 29–31, 33–37, 33n4, 41, 43–47, 49–53, 49n3, 52n5, 55–57, 56n7, 59, 60, 63, 64, 68, 76, 84n14, 87, 88, 93–99, 109, 112, 116, 117, 119–122, 122n8, 127–131, 133, 137, 143, 145, 147–149, 161, 163–169, 172, 176, 178, 179, 188–190, 192, 195–203, 206–208, 211–213, 217, 228–230, 235, 236, 240, 241, 243, 253, 256, 257, 260–262, 265–267, 269–271, 274, 276–278, 280, 284, 287–290, 293–295, 300, 303, 308–311, 316, 322–324
Realism, 108, 121, 129, 152, 222n27, 293, 325
Reductionism, 107–109

Reductive naturalistic metasemantics, 108, 114, 122, 126, 251
Reference, 29, 72, 83, 84, 93, 107–111, 113, 115, 117, 123–126, 128–130, 135, 161, 195–197, 230, 252, 266, 285, 302n3
Reference magnetism, 248, 284–286
Regime of truth, 57, 58, 61–63, 79, 95, 155, 157, 160, 162–174, 176, 178, 179, 183, 185, 193, 204–206, 210, 211, 213–216, 223, 225, 226, 228–230, 235, 252, 255, 259, 260, 265, 284, 285, 287, 292, 294, 295, 299–327
Reparations, 214–216

S
Satisfies, 82, 85, 86n17, 88, 136, 184, 237, 244, 244n6, 254, 257, 259, 264, 265, 301, 302
Semantic corruption model, 22, 27, 27n3, 30, 35–37, 41–45, 48, 49, 51–53, 56, 57, 58n9, 64, 264, 265
Semantics, 2–5, 9, 10n7, 11, 12, 15, 16, 18, 21, 22, 25–38, 42–50, 52, 53, 56, 60, 63–65, 63n12, 67–99, 71n5, 74n7, 103–117, 108n4, 113n6, 116n7, 119–127, 126n11, 131, 133, 144–145n8, 165, 222, 224, 230, 235, 236, 238–244, 241n4, 244n6, 246–248, 250–254, 256, 257, 259–261, 263, 264, 266, 268, 272, 273, 276–282, 283n8, 285, 286, 289–295, 291n9, 292n10, 301, 307–311, 320, 324
Settler, 61, 187, 197, 209, 215, 219

INDEX   335

Settler-colonialism, 183, 201
Sexism, 10, 12, 143, 149, 167, 179, 188, 190, 192, 196, 198–203, 212, 236, 253, 287, 288
Shapiro, Ben, 14–18, 21, 26, 27, 33–37, 42, 44, 77, 263
Single-axis framework, 196–202, 225
Situated
  evidence, 94–99, 312–318
  ignorance, 306–325
  knowledge, 67n2, 229, 299–327, 300n1
  perspective, 5, 64, 67, 68, 88, 94, 166, 194, 289, 302n3, 314
  political, 5, 269
  situatedness, 64, 67n1, 168, 191, 193, 288, 295, 312, 318, 321
Social fabric, 43, 58, 68, 122, 130, 131, 134, 138, 144, 155–157, 161–163, 165, 166, 168, 170n22, 171, 191, 203, 204, 218, 225, 230, 236, 287, 294, 295, 300, 303, 304, 306, 308, 311, 317, 318, 323
Social identity, 3, 67, 142, 168, 183, 187, 191, 194–195, 198, 200, 201, 207, 216–224, 229, 230, 256, 270, 299, 301, 306, 311–313, 318, 319, 321–323
Socially situated, 3, 5, 77, 103, 270, 306, 312, 313, 318, 321
Space of reasons, 45, 53–57, 256, 295
Strategic, 2, 47n2, 77, 136, 142, 148, 150, 161, 164, 179, 210–214, 222, 223, 226, 227, 260, 307, 311, 316, 320, 327
Strategy, 26n2, 56, 59, 145–149, 151–153, 160, 161, 175, 177, 189, 212, 223, 227, 256, 316, 317

Structural oppression, 1, 26, 26n1, 27, 33–35, 37, 60, 68, 78, 87, 94, 98, 186, 194–211, 217, 237, 252, 260, 262, 271, 280, 284, 293, 313
Syntactic, 34, 83, 170, 171
Syntacticism, 170–173

T
Tarski, Alfred, 80–92, 235n1, 237
Trans, 2–4, 13–19, 14n10, 19n16, 21, 36, 43, 44, 46, 46–47n2, 47, 55, 56, 62, 64, 68, 71, 98, 103, 161, 164, 198, 201, 204, 206, 213, 214, 221, 222, 224, 241–253, 244n6, 247n8, 256, 260, 262–266, 269, 272, 281, 281–282n6, 282n7, 283–285, 294, 308, 309
Trump, Donald, 7–12, 10n7, 19, 21, 27, 29, 33, 34, 36, 42–44, 52, 52n5, 64, 68, 70, 87–89, 94, 111, 112, 116, 117, 130, 158, 159, 163, 165, 178, 179, 231, 243, 253, 314, 315
Truth, 1–5, 9, 12–16, 18–22, 33, 37, 38, 41, 43–46, 48–65, 67–70, 73–81, 74n7, 75n8, 80n9, 84–97, 85n15, 86n16, 86–87n17, 103, 108, 110, 114, 131, 133–180, 183, 185, 186, 193, 204–206, 210, 211, 213–216, 223, 225, 226, 228–231, 235–243, 235n1, 248–252, 254–256, 259, 261, 265–267, 269, 271, 272, 274, 279, 290, 291, 291n9, 293–295, 299–327
Tuck, Eve, 61, 214, 219, 226
Twin Earth, 120–122, 129, 263

W

Whales, 97, 98, 104, 105, 113, 116–119, 121, 123, 238, 274, 275
White feminist, 197, 201, 213, 221, 225, 227, 316
White ignorance, 130, 147, 148, 161, 164, 165, 175, 177, 203, 228, 270, 284, 288, 289, 303
Whiteness, 33, 147, 192, 208, 209, 219
Woman, 3, 4, 10, 13–15, 19, 20, 22, 46, 46–47n2, 47, 50, 52, 56, 61, 62, 64, 68, 70, 71, 86, 89, 93, 96, 98, 103, 109, 112, 128, 164, 193, 198, 205, 211, 213, 214, 220, 222, 224, 229, 236, 247–249, 247n8, 251, 253, 256, 257, 260–267, 271, 272, 275, 276, 278, 281, 281–282n6, 282n7, 283–285, 294, 307–311, 323, 324
Womanist, 192

Printed in the United States
by Baker & Taylor Publisher Services